The Other Side of the Sixties

A volume in the series *Perspectives on the Sixties*
Edited by *Barbara L. Tischler*

SERIES EDITORIAL BOARD

The Other Side of the Sixties

Young Americans for Freedom and the Rise of Conservative Politics

JOHN A. ANDREW III

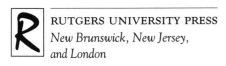

RUTGERS UNIVERSITY PRESS
New Brunswick, New Jersey,
and London

Library of Congress Cataloging-in-Publication Data

Andrew, John A.
   The other side of the sixties : young Americans for freedom and
the rise of conservative politics / John A. Andrew III.
      p.   cm. — (Perspectives on the sixties)
   Includes bibliographical references and index.
   ISBN 0-8135-2400-8 (cloth : alk. paper). — ISBN 0-8135-2401-6
(pbk. : alk. paper)
      1. Conservatism—United States 2. Young Americans for Freedom.
   3. United States—Politics and government—1945–1989.   I. Title.
   II. Series.
   JC573.2.U6A53   1997
   320.52′0973—dc21   96-48088
                                                              Cip

British Cataloging-in-Publication data for this book is available from the British
Library

Composition by Colophon Typesetting

Manufactured in the United States of America

*To political activists of all persuasions;
may they keep life interesting*

Contents

Acknowledgments

As HISTORIANS work on projects they incur many debts, and I would like to thank an array of institutions and individuals who made this research possible. For funding several research trips I would like to thank the Grants Committee of Franklin and Marshall College, which provided travel monies to use materials at the Rockefeller Archives Center, the Hoover Institution, the Dwight D. Eisenhower Presidential Library, and the Richard Nixon Pre-Presidential Papers at the Pacific Southwest division of the National Archives. I was also fortunate to receive a Moody grant from the LBJ Foundation, which enabled me to spend a week at the Lyndon B. Johnson Presidential Library.

Because there is no single collection of manuscript materials on conservatism or the right wing, my debts to archives, archivists, and private individuals are numerous. At the LBJ Library, Mary Knill and Linda Hanson provided guidance, as did Maura Porter and her staff at the John F. Kennedy Library. Dwight Strandberg suggested numerous leads in papers at the Eisenhower Library. At the Library of Congress, John Haynes and Kathleen Dondanville provided essential assistance, and Fred Bauman should be recognized not only for his help in accessing the Rusher Papers, but for providing wrenches and screwdrivers to open old microfilm cartridges so that they could be viewed on new machines. The staff at the National Archives, Pacific Southwest Region was unfailingly helpful, as were Susan Naulty at the Richard Nixon Library and Darwin Stapleton and his staff at the Rockefeller Archives Center.

I would like to thank the Republican National Committee for granting permission to examine its records at Cornell University, and the staffs at the Yale University Library, the Hoover Institution, and the Center for American History at the University of Texas at Austin for their assistance in accessing manuscript materials in their possession. Shelley Davis, who was IRS historian before her resignation, provided help with what limited information the IRS allowed to escape its walls. Congressman Robert Walker's office kept tabs on my Freedom of Information Act requests for IRS materials in an effort to curtail stonewalling. Don Joldersma of the Hillsdale College Library facilitated access to the Manion Forum tapes. A portion of chapter 2 appeared as "The Struggle for the Republican Party in 1960," *The Historian* 59 (spring 1997), and I would like to thank the editors for permission to use some of that material here.

Perhaps most essential for this study were the efforts of several key conservative activists and former YAFers. William Rusher and William F. Buckley, Jr. kindly granted me access to their papers, as well as permission to quote from them. Marvin Liebman and F. Clifton White did likewise. Former YAFers Robert Croll, Diarmuid O'Scannlain, George McDonnell, John Kolbe, and Douglas Caddy kindly allowed me to see materials they had retained. Carol Dawson gave me access to her rolodex, but more importantly she convinced me how important documentary written materials would be in this study.

Three individuals provided help in accessing materials from afar. Mary Shelly and the interlibrary loan staff at Franklin and Marshall College tirelessly pursued my requests for ephemeral materials. Kathryn Stallard, Senior Archivist at Southwestern University, kept me abreast of materials in the John Tower Papers as they were being processed. Raymond Boryczka of the Walter Reuther Library at Wayne State University tracked down a couple of key documents.

Finally, I would like to thank Michael Birkner for reading the entire manuscript and providing both helpful and encouraging remarks. Martha Heller at Rutgers University Press kept faith in the project's value and guided the manuscript through the internal bureaucracy. Several anonymous readers for the Press provided useful feedback on an earlier draft. Mistakes surely remain, but they are mine.

Lancaster, Pennsylvania
August 1996

The Other Side of the Sixties

Introduction

THE 1960s HAVE become an almost mythic decade, attracting the attention of historians, politicians, and sociologists. Some have come to document, some to celebrate, and others to condemn. But most chroniclers of the sixties, regardless of their politics, share two characteristics: they focus on the latter years of the decade and they emphasize the importance of movements and causes on the Left to the exclusion of almost everything else. This study is an effort to shift that focus, to examine the first half of the sixties and to emphasize developments on the Right, developments that outlasted the decade.

Although the sixties ended almost three decades ago, they remain an integral part of American politics and culture. The struggle to define the sixties has become a contest not only to write the "proper" history of that decade, but to control the public's memory of it. Publication of memoirs by various sixties activists have helped a Left perspective endure, but the most active propagators of sixties "leftism" have been conservatives, from Ronald Reagan to Newt Gingrich. They have repeatedly used the decade as a whipping post for liberals and liberal programs, blaming everything they do not like about contemporary American society and culture on what they charge were radical changes promulgated in the sixties. Teenage pregnancies, welfare costs, government social programs, urban disorder, educational problems, declining high school test scores—the list is virtually endless. They attempt to trace the roots of almost all current problems to the Great Society of Lyndon Johnson or to the social movements of the sixties. The opening lecture of Republican Speaker of the

House Newt Gingrich's course on "Renewing American Civilization" typifies their approach. Gingrich argues that "from 1965 to 1994 . . . America went off on the wrong track." Radicals in the sixties, he complains, criticized the United States as a "sexist, racist, repressive, vicious society" and urged that big government was needed to cure bad habits, thus reversing three hundred years of American history. Before then, he implies, a blissful consensus embraced a set of shared values whose historical roots could be traced to the Founding Fathers.[1]

Former sixties radicals and subsequent sixties critics Peter Collier and David Horowitz have labeled what they call "the Sixties generation" the "destructive generation." Through generational segregation they have tried to isolate people of the sixties as a peculiar breed that (hopefully) comes along rarely in our history. Lamenting that the "System" was "assaulted and mauled," Collier and Horowitz decry the sixties as "the decade that would not die, the decade whose long half-life continues to contaminate our own."[2] And in a recent essay, Cal Thomas, syndicated columnist for the *Los Angeles Times*, argues that if "you slept through the sixties, you woke to a different America. It was the pivotal point of the recent past—an authentic decade of decision."[3] Thomas goes on to paint a portrait of the American people as deeply wounded by the sixties experience, "left to walk carefully among the jagged shards" of a decade in which the Left monopolized the politics. The social crises of the nineties, he concluded, stemmed directly from the breakdown of cultural authority in the sixties.[4] In many respects, pejoratives aside, Collier, Horowitz, and Thomas are correct. The sixties did have a transformative influence on many aspects of American life. But the portraits of the decade presented by its critics are one-sided. It was not so much a radical decade as a polarized one.[5]

We need to try to recapture the spirit of that decade from the vantage point of the early 1960s, not the late 1990s, and regain a sense of historical perspective. In the early 1960s, Americans of all ideological and political persuasions, not only the Left, perceived the United States as the land of opportunity and possibility, of change and renewal. They believed, for various reasons, that they sat on the cutting edge of history. Although even conservative critics of sixties culture and history seem to have forgotten, it was a vibrant decade that witnessed challenges to the status quo from the Right as well as from the Left.[6] Making sense of the sixties is not possible without considering the impact of both movements together. If the Left attempted to subvert the prevailing politics and culture, so did the Right. What was deviant to one was not necessarily legitimate to the other, as both sought to undo much of Eisenhower's America. In the course of these efforts, the Right as well as the Left contributed to a significant change in American political habits.

Both the Right and the Left moved political discourse from an arena dominated and largely controlled by elites to one that sought to take its cue from the popular imagination. Although new elites soon emerged to retake control of popular politics, the genie never quite went back into the bottle. In the short term, at least for the duration of the 1960s, a cacophony of voices replaced the chorus of elites that had dominated American politics since the end of World War II. Because critics have lent ears only to the most liberal of these voices, we need to restore a sense of balance and recapture the vitality of conservatism in the first half of that decade. Cries for change sounded from both sides of the political spectrum.

At the outset of the sixties, the liberal consensus appeared to reign supreme. Aside from the question of civil rights, little public social dislocation was evident. Poverty remained to be "discovered." The central question for political elites appeared to be how to fine-tune liberalism within the context of an expanding economy. Most agreed with the words of Kennedy's 1960 campaign theme song and had "high hopes" for the future, believing that economic growth would resolve lingering economic and social inequalities. Since the public seemed convinced that economic growth was limitless, there was little fear that social change or the amelioration of economic inequality might threaten the existing structure of society. As a consequence, liberals saw no reason to offer a structural critique of the political or economic system, or of the tenets of their creed. The individuals who came to Washington in 1961 to join the new Kennedy administration were confident in their abilities and sure that they could manage the forces of change with a few well-placed reforms.

Senator John F. Kennedy had directed the public's attention toward the possibilities of a reformist paradigm as early as January 1960, when he urged Americans to confront their problems or else "trend in the direction of a slide downhill into dust, dullness, languor, and decay." Kennedy called on Americans to embrace change energetically, "for we seem to have lost both the sense of the promise of America and the will to fulfill it."[7] His challenge reflected the analysis of an advisor, Arthur Schlesinger Jr., who saw the country "paused on the threshold of a new epoch in our national life." The passive mood of the 1950s was changing; new energies were "straining for expression and for release." Even before Bob Dylan warned listeners that the answer was "blowin' in the wind," Schlesinger predicted that "Somehow the wind is beginning to change. People—not everyone by a long way, but enough to disturb the prevailing mood—seem to seek a renewal of conviction, a new sense of national purpose." The politics of the fifties, Schlesinger insisted, were the "politics of fatigue," a logical aftermath to the tensions of the thirties and forties. Although change was in the air, its direction was uncertain. "The beginning of a new political epoch is like the breaking of a dam. . . . The chaos of the breakthrough offends those who like everything neatly ordered and controlled; but it is likely to be a creative confusion, bringing a ferment of ideas and innovation into the national life. Thus the '60's will probably be spirited, articulate, inventive, incoherent, turbulent, with energy shooting off wildly in all directions. Above all, there will be a sense of motion, of leadership, and of hope."[8]

Schlesinger argued for a *"qualitative liberalism"* that improved people's lives. Government was to be an activist friend rather than the enemy. "The crust is breaking up," Schlesinger wrote, and he believed that the sixties promised "to be one of the great decades in our history."[9] While Schlesinger's arguments were designed to foster support for the nomination and election of a liberal Democratic presidential candidate, and were themes Kennedy later articulated during the campaign, they were perceptions shared by individuals with different political ideologies. Even Richard Nixon, although circumscribed by his incumbency and his need for Eisenhower's support, argued that change was a positive value and that the times called for action to advance the national purpose. But throughout the year it was Kennedy, campaigning to challenge and overturn Republican rule, who most clearly articulated the need for change. Although his rhetoric at times bordered on the apocalyptic, often to dramatize the dangers that would (presumably) attend a failure to embrace change (and elect him!), he repeatedly urged Americans to "climb to the hilltop" and commit themselves to a better world. There was, in the words of Democrat Chester Bowles, a "moral gap" between Americans' actions and their ideals. For Bowles as for Schlesinger, the 1960s were a watershed. The country sat poised between "the end of the postwar period" and the "opening of a new era in the history of man."[10] Liberal reform, in his view, held the key to that new era.

But in 1960 three insurgent organizations emerged to reject the reformist paradigm of liberalism and offer structural critiques of the status quo. In civil rights, the Student Non-Violent Coordinating Committee (SNCC) formed to challenge the leadership of both the National Association for the Advancement of Colored People (NAACP) and the Southern Christian Leadership Conference (SCLC). SNCC emphasized the importance of grass-roots organization, its existence an implicit (later explicit) critique of the predominant civil rights organizations. In Left politics, the Student League for Industrial Democracy (SLID) became the Students for a Democratic Society (SDS). Although their landmark Port Huron Statement was still two years away, SDS under the leadership of Al Haber sought to move the politics of the liberal consensus to the Left.

Despite historians' focus on these groups, there was another side to the sixties. That side was not a mere reaction to the supposed excesses of the decade, as Ronald Reagan, Newt Gingrich, and other politicians of the eighties and nineties would have us believe, but a set of concrete conservative ideas and programs that excited millions of Americans even before those supposed "excesses" occurred. The third group, Young Americans for Freedom (YAF), became a leading force in developing and promoting these ideas after 1960. Lee Edwards, a founding member of YAF, remembered that other side very clearly:

> For me, as for most young conservatives, the '60s were the decade not of John F. Kennedy but Barry M. Goldwater, not Students for a Democratic Society but Young Americans for Freedom, not *The New Republic* but *National Review*, not Herbert Marcuse but Russell Kirk, not Norman Mailer but Ayn Rand, not Lyndon Johnson's Great Society but Ronald Reagan's Creative Society, not a "meaningless" civil war in Vietnam but an important battle in the protracted conflict against Communism.[11]

Leading the revival of conservative politics in the early sixties, Young Americans for Freedom formed in 1960 as an outgrowth of efforts to develop a new conservative leadership cadre, capture control of the Republican Party, and ultimately shift that party to the Right. It was, in the view of one historian, "the most important organizational initiative undertaken by conservatives in the last thirty years."[12] Although never able to transform electoral politics or enact dramatic reforms during the period, YAF infiltrated the Republican Party at the grass roots and served as a breeding ground for future generations of conservative leaders. The Goldwater defeat in 1964, often considered a lethal blow to conservatism, stilled neither the excitement nor the commitment of Lee Edwards and his colleagues.

At first blush, YAF seems to have little in common with SNCC or SDS. The latter two viewed politics from the Left, YAF from the Right. SNCC and SDS were organizations whose ideas became influential during the decade, whereas YAF struggled to attract publicity and never generated the public response (either pro or con) that SNCC or SDS did. Yet there are critical links among the three organizations, aside from their founding in 1960. All three were youth movements that challenged the status quo, and all believed that the path of change lay through grass-roots organization and activism. Finally, all three criticized ruling elites, and combined ideology with activism, principles with politics.

Young Americans for Freedom emerged to offer an ideological and structural critique of the reigning liberalism. They sought to reject, not reform, the consensus liberalism. They hoped, as columnist Dan Wakefield reported from New York, to make "the vest the youth symbol of the sixties." A *New Yorker* cartoon in the early sixties caught their mood, with one father telling another:

"And then we have another son—a radical—who's joined Barry Goldwater's conservatives."[13] Although nominally nonpartisan, wedded to conservative principles rather than partisan concerns, YAF recognized from the outset that its path to power lay through the Republican Party. Consequently, the story of Young Americans for Freedom is intertwined with the history of the Young Republican National Federation and Republican Party politics during the first half of the decade.

YAF sought to place conservatives in control of the Republican Party, and to inject conservative politics into the mainstream of American political life. That struggle for power was significant, both then and now, for the history of American conservatism and of the Republican Party. By pursuing change in this manner, YAFers defined themselves as somewhat less radical in a structural sense than their rhetoric suggested. Theirs was an ideological and philosophical radicalism. Whatever their opposition to the prevailing political system, they retained a firm conviction that the system would respond to them if only they could seize power. They believed, in other words, that the system was still responsible and that they could initiate constructive changes through it. In the short term, therefore, YAFers did not turn to the nihilism or anarchism that came to characterize many in SDS, who saw the system as unresponsive and moved from frustration to anger to despair, and finally to hostility. Their goal was to bring together ideological fellow travelers rather than to marshall an immediate electoral majority.

Despite Goldwater's electoral defeat in November 1964, they largely succeeded. Along the way, however, they encountered a hostile press and challenges from other conservatives as well as from the Republican moderates they hoped to supplant. For much of the media, the dominant conservative image in the early 1960s was the John Birch Society, and the Birch Society's views cast a long shadow over conservative politics for most of the decade. Young Americans for Freedom, like other mainstream conservative groups, struggled to establish an identity independent of the Birch Society and other radical groups. The media, by and large, equated conservatism with extremism, and often ignored the existence of a broad grass-roots movement beyond the extremists in the headlines. When conservatives finally swept into power in the 1980s, therefore, they seemed to emerge solely as a reaction to contemporary political currents. But theirs was as much a triumph of organization as of opportunity, and the roots of that organization first flourished in the early sixties. The "revolution" did not begin with Ronald Reagan or Newt Gingrich.

This book explores the rise of conservative politics between 1960 and 1964 through a study of Young Americans for Freedom and its efforts to realize at least five objectives simultaneously. More often than not these goals fed on one another and were intimately interconnected. First there was the determination to form a viable organization by and for young conservatives. A second focus was the effort by these young conservatives to find and articulate their own voice in the Sharon Statement, to define a new conservative mainstream and project it to the broader public. Third, they launched a strident attack on the liberal establishment, from liberal student groups like the National Student Association to the policies of the Kennedy administration. To promote these efforts YAFers trained a new conservative leadership cadre, creating webs of ideological, political, and personal relationships that advanced each others' careers in moments of opportunity. And finally came the effort to seize control of the Republican Party as an electoral machine and promote a conservative presidential candidate, Barry Goldwater, in 1964. As YAFers struggled to realize these objectives, they had to contend not only with liberal critics, political attacks from the Kennedy administration, and visible voter hostility, but also internal ideological and political factionalism.

The early and mid-1960s were formative years for a budding conservative movement. Never a majority, its objectives focused on short-term gains within the Republican Party and the advancement of a conservative ideology, rather than on the election cycle. YAFers therefore did their best to shun compromise, for they were convinced that the politics of compromise had led to the "modern Republicanism" of Dwight Eisenhower, whose moderation they so detested. Barry Goldwater's 1964 campaign slogan, "a choice not an echo," best captured their purpose and illustrated why Goldwater became the chosen vehicle for their ambitions. He was, said YAFer James Roberts, "the knight on the white horse, the Lochinvar riding out of the west to do battle with evil, a rugged individualist evoking the great West's heroes who eschewed cant and guile and spoke their minds simply and to the point, a man who rose above the phoniness of the unprincipled politico and the fraud of the backroom bosses, a diamond in the rough who exhibited character (if not always tact). . . . A hero."[14]

During these years, however, the mood of the country's majority clearly reflected a conviction that the promised land lay in the future, not in the past. Young Americans for Freedom, accordingly, was out of touch with mainstream politics during the decade, and as a consequence was largely marginalized. That so many members went on to acquire influence in the 1980s and 1990s is therefore significant. Where did they come from? Are they idiosyncratic individuals or products of a broader movement? There is a lineage to their conservative discontent that is important. Although the path of their progress was not always direct, as the following chapters demonstrate, their gaze was steady. Their goal remained unchanged, their resolve steadfast. YAF was determined to change the political climate in the United States.

The roots of YAF and this conservative revival reached back into the late 1940s and early 1950s, and produced two great conservative crusades:

anticommunism and antistatism. Chapter 1 explores the origins of the "New Right" and its calls for change. William F. Buckley Jr., who became both a god-father to YAF and a midwife to the new conservatism, gave the new conserv-ative ideas able expression in the pages of his *National Review*, founded in 1955. Conservative intellectuals sought to develop and then proselytize a conserva-tive cosmology to provide a coherent conceptual basis for thought and action. By the late 1950s there were signs that the new conservative ideology was bear-ing fruit, and formation of the National Student Committee for the Loyalty Oath represented the first formal stirrings of conservative political activism.

That activism became public with the struggle over "modern Republican-ism" at the 1960 Republican National Convention. Determined to reject the Eisenhower legacy of moderation, conservatives tried to shape the platform and influence Richard Nixon, whose nomination was a foregone conclusion. In the end they not only failed, but saw Nixon cater to the liberalism of New York Governor Nelson Rockefeller by rejecting conservatives Walter Judd and Barry Goldwater as vice presidential nominees. As chapter 2 details, Nixon's selec-tion of moderate Republican Henry Cabot Lodge as his running mate not only confirmed that the Republican Party had sold out to the liberal consensus; it also convinced young conservatives that they had to look elsewhere if they were to advance conservative principles. The G.O.P. was apparently not hospitable to them, and they would have to form their own organization if they were se-rious about fomenting change.

In September 1960, young conservative activists met to define their prin-ciples at Great Elm, the Buckley family estate in Sharon, Connecticut. With a spirited optimism, they produced the Sharon Statement, a short but defini-tive exposition of conservative principles that became their ideological com-pass. Chapter 3 documents their efforts to organize for change, traces the in-fluence of conservative elder statesmen, and examines their philosophy as expressed in the Sharon Statement. This was the founding of Young Ameri-cans for Freedom, and after Sharon YAFers moved from principles to activism as they experienced the "thrill of treason" in challenging the liberal hegemony. From here the narrative focuses on the organization's struggles to develop a pha-lanx of young conservative leaders, create a base for conservative activism, and at the same time keep their ideological house in order. Chapter 4 chronicles their initial forays into partisan politics. Richard Nixon's defeat in November 1960 raised the prospect of sudden access to the levers of power in the Repub-lican Party. YAF was quick to move—perhaps too quick. Attacks on Republi-can moderates and later on Kennedy administration policies attracted public-ity but also fanned the fires of opportunism within the organization. Encounters with the John Birch Society led to further divisions in conservative ranks. As chapter 5 recounts, by the summer of 1961 Young Americans for Freedom was struggling to retain its organizational coherence. Even as it launched a broad and frequently bitter attack on the United States National Student Association, YAF fell victim to brutal infighting that threatened to fragment conservative politics even before they solidified. Only careful planning by William Rusher and other adult conservatives, together with their youthful allies, brought YAF back together in the fall of 1961.

Young Americans for Freedom then launched a series of attacks on the Kennnedy administration and the domestic and foreign policies of the New Frontier. Chapter 6 details these attacks, which concealed from the public continuing contentiousness within the organization. Opposition to New Frontier policies united young conservatives, but when they moved beyond opposition to advance positive programs for change the nightmare of factionalism persisted.

The public and the Kennedy administration, however, seemingly lumped all voices from the Right together. While this failure to distinguish themselves from more extremist elements plagued Young Americans for Freedom throughout these years, never was it more problematic than when the Kennedy administration launched a counterattack against the right wing. Chapter 7 details an unprecedented effort by the administration to silence right-wing critics, chiefly by using the Internal Revenue Service to conduct politically motivated financial audits. Dubbed the Ideological Organizations Project, this illegal endeavor targeted right-wing organizations and stemmed from a lengthy memo prepared by Walter Reuther of the AFL-CIO suggesting a series of steps to quell right-wing criticism of the administration and its policies. While some of this material remains in the confidential files of the I.R.S. even today, its outlines are clear and its implications alarming.

Whether or not Young Americans for Freedom or its supporters ever knew the extent of the administration's concern remains unclear, but YAF moved ahead undeterred. Pointing toward 1964, they battled to control the Young Republicans and jockeyed for position and influence within the Republican Party. Their purpose was not only to nominate a true conservative in 1964 and launch an ideological crusade to take the message of conservatism to the public, but to capture the Republican Party and transform it into a vehicle for conservative politics. Barry Goldwater was their hero, and YAFers had steadily pushed for his nomination ever since the 1960 G.O.P. convention. Although ultimately successful, the Goldwater candidacy not only failed to bind all the ideological wounds—it opened up new ones in a struggle for power. YAF was largely pushed aside, although YAFers' commitment to the conservative cause never faltered. Chapters 8 and 9 focus on this crusade as well as its candidate. Barry Goldwater lost the 1964 election, of course, but YAFers rejoiced at

Goldwater's vote even while they insisted that the problem had been the candidate rather than the cause.

Formation of the American Conservative Union (ACU) in December 1964 reflected the intention of leading conservatives (including many YAFers) to capture that momentum and give it permanence. In some respects, the conservatism of the early YAFers had matured, evolving from youthful activism to party building. Formation of the ACU also revealed the limits of YAF's efforts, for Young Americans for Freedom was chiefly interested in organizational politics rather than popular majorities. What YAFers seemed to want most was to place their own hands on the levers of power, and they believed that with solid organization they could induce a majority of voters to give them that opportunity. As such, YAF differed somewhat from other, more radical groups on the Right who sought to provoke grass-roots rebellions through populist rhetoric. The final chapter looks briefly at their plans for the future, draws some connections between YAFers' efforts in the early 1960s and the subsequent dominance of conservatives within the Republican Party, and highlights the careers of leading YAFers. I have focused on this leadership cadre because they led the fight and articulated the new conservative agenda. They could not, of course, constitute a conservative majority. But they could forge one, and that is what they set out to do in 1960.

From 1960 through 1964 the Right battled the Left on more than equal terms. Young Americans for Freedom demonstrated that ideas were important, even though most voters clearly dismissed their ideas at the time. But they had staying power and a dogged commitment to those ideas. They not only attacked the liberal consensus, attracting in the process considerable attention from the press; they successfully captured one of the two major parties. After 1964, however, the Left unquestionably provided the dominant critique of the liberal consensus.[15] But the years of truly dominant Liberal Democratic political control, 1964–66, were more of an interlude than a continuing characteristic of the decade. If we are to understand the sixties, or American political culture since then, we must put the Right back into the picture.

Young Americans for Freedom provides an important focal point for that effort. It opens an early window to an examination of the new conservatism, at the moment when that conservatism was struggling to find its voice and deliver its message. By painting a more balanced portrait of political thinking in the sixties, it also offers a more compelling look at the vibrant political atmosphere of the decade. Finally, it provides one key element in the genealogical origins of the so-called Reagan revolution of the 1980s and the broader conservative revival of the 1990s. There was another side to the sixties, and its voice was Young Americans for Freedom.

The Origins of the
"New Right"

THE INTELLECTUAL and ideological impulses that led to the formation of Young Americans for Freedom had roots that reached back to the years immediately following World War II. They drew on a muscular and often strident anticommunism as well as a principled opposition to New Deal policies. In the late 1940s and early 1950s, postwar conservatism struggled to find a voice and an audience, but it remained chiefly an intellectual rather than a political movement. After the mid-1950s, with the founding of *National Review*, it discovered an intellectual guru with a taste for political action in the person of William F. Buckley Jr. By the end of the decade it had found its political action hero in Arizona Senator Barry Goldwater. Both were appealing because they eschewed the language of consensus. But what appealed to ideological conservatives in those years frightened others. Breaking out of the consensus mold was difficult. Then events of the late 1950s, from economic recession to Communist advances, the Cuban revolution, and the launch of *Sputnik*, produced a crisis of confidence in the United States that afflicted liberals and conservatives alike. With a presidential election in the offing, politicians in both political parties seized the moment to offer their assessment of the crisis. Demands for change echoed from across the political spectrum, and political activists stirred.

A Search for Conservative Principles

By the fall of 1945, with Franklin Delano Roosevelt dead and World War II over, conservatives in the United States hoped to regain political power and capture the White House in 1948. Once there, they planned to roll back New Deal measures and arrest the process of change underway since the Great Depression of the 1930s. They were to be disappointed, failing even to recapture the Republican Party. That failure revealed how discredited and out of touch conservatism had become. Not only did the majority of Americans clearly reject conservative ideas; encounters with fascism in the 1930s and 1940s had led most Americans to be wary of mass movements and ideological crusades. Voters instead sought consensus, and Democrats and Republicans alike moved to embrace what Arthur Schlesinger Jr. called the "vital center." Indeed, much of the problem faced by principled conservatives between 1945 and 1960 can be symbolized by two books published at either end of that era: Schlesinger's *The Vital Center* (1949) and Daniel Bell's *The End of Ideology* (1960). The dilemma for conservatives became that of extremism; whatever seemed to deviate from the "consensus" position on any issue became susceptible to charges that it represented an "extremist" view and should therefore be dismissed as dangerous and perhaps even un-American.

In a sense, therefore, conservatives had to start over after World War II. The country was not willing to return to the 1920s, nor could the ideas of a Herbert Hoover simply be resuscitated and made part of the contemporary political dialogue. Anticommunism was attractive, but since liberals as well as conservatives embraced it there was nothing particularly distinctive about being anticommunist in postwar America. Indeed, the only way to be truly distinctive as an anticommunist was to advocate something more radical than mere containment. The anticommunism of the postwar conservative movement, however, *was* different in one respect: its personnel. Attracting men like James Burnham, Frank Meyer, and Whittaker Chambers, postwar conservatives could point to these men as true witnesses. They were all former Communists who had seen the light and recanted their previous ideological convictions. Particularly influential was Whittaker Chambers, who outlined his story in *Witness*. This became almost an ideological Bible to William F. Buckley Jr. and his followers, with its apocalyptic warnings that humanity was engaged in a cataclysmic struggle between Communism and freedom. But the general public had little interest in sending their young men off to fight the Red Army in distant lands. Eventually conservatives embraced the exploits of Wisconsin Senator Joseph McCarthy and his crusade against Communism within the United

States, but this tended to move foreign policy to the right rather than repeal the social and economic reforms of the New Deal.

In short, conservatism lacked any intellectual relevance to the concerns of most Americans. In addition, the failure of conservative Senator Robert Taft to capture the G.O.P. presidential nomination in 1952, and then his death in 1953, robbed conservatives of political leadership. During the Eisenhower years, as both political parties struggled to claim the center, dissenters from their party lines faced the prospect of being classified as deviants outside the party structure and then marginalized as fringe extremists alienated from the mainstream of American political dialogue. Indeed, mainstream political choices varied only between an Adlai Stevenson (classified as liberal) and a Dwight Eisenhower (classified as conservative). Between 1945 and 1960 conservatives moved to rectify this problem, but only after 1955 did their progress become very visible.[1]

The revival of conservatism in the postwar years began as an intellectual movement that encompassed several divergent principles. In the decade following World War II American conservatives slowly collected their intellectual resources. Beginning in 1944 with *The Road to Serfdom* by Austrian economist Friedrich von Hayek, they argued against national economic planning as a threat to individual freedom. Promoted in this country by Frank Chodorov, who founded the Intercollegiate Society of Individualists as well as several small publications like *The Freeman*, this libertarian strain of conservatism tried to revive classical liberalism and attracted a small following. It attacked Franklin Roosevelt's New Deal, charging that it had imposed a welfare state on the American people which threatened to palsy individual initiative, the free market, and personal responsibility. After 1944 this viewpoint also found constant expression in the pages of *Human Events*.

A second group of conservatives, traditionalists, soon emerged to argue the importance of transcendent values. Led by Richard Weaver, a Southern Agrarian who forcefully articulated their position in his 1948 volume *Ideas Have Consequences*, traditionalists argued that the decline of "transcendental values" had promoted the deterioration of Western culture. An orgy of relativism had led Americans to forget the centrality of original sin and the value of private property. They argued, in essence, that a fascination with what Henry Luce called "The American Century" had seduced Americans to ignore or forget the great traditions, the moral and religious foundations, on which their success rested.[2]

By the mid-1950s other intellectuals had joined the effort. Classical political philosophers like Leo Strauss emphasized the importance of natural law, and philosopher/historian Russell Kirk published *The Conservative Mind*. In the short run Kirk's 1953 volume was perhaps the most essential development for the postwar conservative movement until William F. Buckley Jr. founded *National Review* two years later. For while von Hayek, Weaver, Strauss, and a coterie of other conservative intellectuals sought to define the fundamental principles of a postwar conservatism, Kirk gathered and codified them in such a way as to articulate a conservative tradition. Devoted chiefly to American thinkers, Kirk's study insisted that there was a conservative tradition sufficiently respectable to stand alongside the liberal tradition then dominant in American intellectual and political life. Budding conservatives could find in *The Conservative Mind* both reassurance and inspiration. But there remained a vacuum. The studies noted above were chiefly historical and frequently didactic. Conservatives still needed a contemporary voice, a vehicle not only to articulate conservative ideas but to promote conservative activism.

National Review, under the leadership of William F. Buckley Jr., tried to fill this vacuum. "If I had not been introduced to *National Review* as a college student," wrote one future member of Young Americans for Freedom, "I feel certain that I would be a typical ritualistic Liberal today. . . . Without the benefit of exposure to conservative criticism, reason and principles, [the average college freshman] will perhaps never have the opportunity and satisfaction of committing himself to a guiding philosophy through the process of rational, deliberate exclusion." Founded by Buckley in 1955, *National Review* became the leading public forum for the expression of conservative viewpoints. Although it struggled financially, its pages offered opportunities for conservative intellectuals to attack the prevailing intellectual order and to posit a variety of alternative paradigms. The arguments were often more intellectual than pragmatic, but they provided sustenance, and occasionally direction, for budding activists. Frank Meyer's argument in early 1958 typified the efforts of *National Review* to fuse together contending schools of conservative thought. "In a fundamental sense," Meyer insisted, "the dominant forces in American life today are revolutionary, that is, they are directed towards the destruction of the principles of Western civilization and the American tradition. The politics of New Dealism, Fair Dealism, and New Republicanism are directed towards the strengthening of the State and the diminution of the person." Internal debates among the staff in 1960 over the proper course of action—support for Nixon or a principled abstention—reflected that division between a pragmatic political activism or a principled conservatism. "It's too bad that there isn't a third and better way," James Burnham wrote Buckley, "but there isn't. . . . And if that's the way it is, then a conservative has to set his course within the frame of reality. It is the sectarian, the radical, the ideologue who leaves reality for his private dream."[3]

What Burnham and his colleagues at *National Review*, particularly William Rusher, were hoping for was the rise of a "New Right." This would be a revitalized and principled conservatism to repudiate not only liberalism but moderate Republicanism, and would transform the Republican Party. Between 1955 and 1960 the editors at *National Review* unleashed a steady attack against the political tendencies of the era. They focused on intellectual currents and party platforms, and many of their propositions were grounded in the experience (often very personal) of 1930s ideological convictions. Several, such as Burnham and Whittaker Chambers, were former Communists who had since swung to the right. Like their counterparts in the Old Left, however, they were unable to communicate the lessons of their ideological experiences to a new generation. Perhaps the most they could hope for was a rebirth of ideological conviction, whatever form it took.[4]

William F. Buckley Jr. had tried to spark that rebirth with a strident attack on liberalism in his 1959 book, *Up from Liberalism*. Deliberately paralleling Booker T. Washington's title, *Up from Slavery*, Buckley argued that the United States had sacrificed its principles in the name of flexibility. "I think the attenuation of the early principles of this country," he warned, "has made America vulnerable to the most opportunistic ideology of the day, the strange and complex ideology of modern liberalism."[5] The problem with liberals, he insisted, was their belief in human perfectability and their reliance on reason as the tool for social progress. Liberals, according to Buckley, believed in the use of state power to foster equality and eliminate social and individual differences. This social scientific paradigm left no room for a conservative opposition, and dissent from it was marginalized as irresponsible or even pathological.

Buckley lamented that modulation had replaced clarity and definition as the prevailing intellectual mode. "It has been the dominating ambition of Eisenhower's Modern Republicanism to govern in such fashion as to more or less please more or less everybody. Such governments must shrink from principle: because principles have edges, principles cut; and blood is drawn, and people get hurt. And who would hurt anyone in an age of modulation?" This blandness was reflected in liberals' lack of fervent anticommunism and had led to a lack of leadership. It also infected education, dulling students' sensibilities. "It seems to me," Buckley concluded, "that there will not again be a robust political life in the undergraduate world until the student becomes convinced that *it matters* what he thinks about public problems."[6]

Conservatives, on the other hand, believed in eternal truth and principles. They looked to the past for guidance in the future. Conservatism, according to Buckley, was the "tacit acknowledgement that all that is finally important in human experience is behind us . . . ." Conservatives, he insisted, grounded their convictions on substance, the substance of the past, whereas liberals substituted method for substance. That difference, and the liberals' reliance on statism to solve problems, was what should unite conservatives of all stripes. But it had not because conservatives had "failed to alert the community to the interconnection between economic freedom and freedom." Economic freedom, he insisted, was the foundation upon which all other freedoms rested.[7]

The underlying problem, in Buckley's view, was that conservatives remained disoriented. He asked: "Up where from Liberalism?" There was "no conservative political manifesto which, as we make our faltering way, we can consult, confident that it will point a sure finger in the direction of the good society."[8] What bound conservatives together at this juncture was a "negative response to Liberalism." A more positive affirmation was needed, one that rested on "right principles," and tried to restore those principles—abused or abandoned by liberals—to public affairs. What were they? Buckley outlined his vision:

> a determined resistance to the spread of world Communism—and a belief in political non-interventionism; a disgust with the results of modern education—and sympathy for the individual educational requirements of the individual child; a sympathetic understanding of the spiritual essence of human existence—and a desire to delimit religious influence in political affairs; a patriotic concern for the nation and its culture—and a genuine respect for the integrity and differences of other peoples' culture; a militant concern for the Negro—and a belief in decentralized political power even though, on account of it, the Negro is sometimes victimized; a respect for the omnicompetence of the free marketplace—and the knowledge of the necessity for occasional interposition. There is a position from which these views are "in range"; and that is the position, generally speaking, where conservatives now find themselves on the political chart.[9]

Buckley's central argument that "pragmatism had deteriorated into a wayward relativism" became a rallying cry for conservatives during the next few years. What was needed, in his view, were some tough-minded decisions and not more soft humanism. The latter only shielded people from reality, often using the power of the state to modulate the impact of change. But within Buckley's tough-minded antistatism lay a libertarian opposition to the cession of power and a latent fear of popular majorities. "I will hoard my power like a miser," he proclaimed. "I will then use *my* power as *I* see fit. I mean to live my life an obedient man, but obedient to God, subservient to the wisdom of my ancestors; never to the authority of political truths arrived at yesterday at the voting booth."[10]

Buckley's conservatism rested on faith, a faith that apparently conceded nothing to the stark and humble realities of life itself. His position in *Up from Liberalism* was similar to the one he had advanced in *God and Man at Yale* a decade earlier: that conservatives, true conservatives, stood outside the intellectual consensus in America. This enabled Buckley to argue ideology and ignore concrete problems. He presented, said one observer, "an ideological interpretation of reality."[11] Because of that, and because he presented his readers with stark contrasts and binary options—good or evil, conservatism or liberalism—he became the intellectual godfather to the new conservatism.

Barry Goldwater: Action Hero

What James Wechsler called the "sparks of earnestness" flared first among students on the Right rather than on the Left, and as the new breed of conservatives looked to William F. Buckley Jr. for intellectual guidance, so too they looked to Arizona Senator Barry Goldwater as the symbol of conservative activism. "For us," Lee Edwards remembered later, "the '60s began not with a bang but with a book, *The Conscience of a Conservative* by Barry Goldwater." At the urging of Dean Clarence Manion of Notre Dame, and with the assistance of L. Brent Bozell, Goldwater issued what he called a "straightforward delineation of conservative principles."[12] Goldwater's message was stridently anti-New Deal in its conceptual paradigm as well as in its ideological and programmatic imperatives. Although not a new message for conservatives, it fell on receptive ears. It was a rousing call to reject the passive 1950s, repudiate the Eisenhower legacy of coexistence and compromise, and embrace an emotional and ideological crusade to chart a new course for the country. As such, it tapped the cynicism and malaise on the Right to mobilize for political activism and long-term change.

Goldwater insisted that liberals, or what he often termed radicals, had shaped American policy for a generation, and that young people yearned "for a return to Conservative principles." More important, he blamed conservatives themselves for failing to demonstrate the relevance of their principles to the "needs of the day." Foremost among those needs, Goldwater argued, were the spiritual wants of the American people. Liberalism spoke to man's material side; conservatism needed to enhance individuals' spiritual nature. "Only a philosophy that takes into account the essential differences between men, and, accordingly, makes provision for developing the different potentialities of each man, can claim to be in accord with Nature."[13] For Goldwater, spiritual and economic concerns were intertwined. Political freedom was an illusion if people were dependent on the state, for state power threatened individual autonomy.

In a similar vein, to regard individuals merely as part of an undifferentiated mass was to consign them "to ultimate slavery." Politics, he argued, was the "art of achieving the maximum amount of freedom for individuals that is consistent with the maintenance of the social order." The preservation and extension of freedom, therefore, was the primary task of government.[14]

Statism was the "first principle of totalitarianism," and only limited governments fostered freedom. In Goldwater's conservative philosophy, the state had few legitimate functions: "maintaining internal order, keeping foreign foes at bay, administering justice, removing obstacles to the free interchange of goods." The Constitution, moreover, was a series of restraints, a protection against tyranny. That protection, Goldwater believed, had largely disappeared as the state steadily expanded its reach. Unlimited federal power, he insisted, was just as dangerous as subversion or invasion, as deadly as Moscow's communist designs. America must change, and change fast. Goldwater urged readers to "entrust the conduct of our affairs to men who understand that their first duty as public officials is to divest themselves of the power they have been given."[15]

States' rights was his answer, and in 1960 it was a potentially explosive answer. In the aftermath of the 1954 *Brown* decision "states' rights" increasingly seemed antithetical to democracy. Although Goldwater insisted that states' rights and civil rights did not conflict, his definition of civil rights as those rights protected by some law, such as voting rights, failed to resolve the dilemma because he insisted that the federal government could not enforce its will against that of a state. He called the *Brown* decision in 1954 wrong, and professed to be unimpressed "by the claim that the Supreme Court's decision on school integration is the law of the land." His disclaimer that he personally thought it healthy for black and white children to attend school together did not diminish the force of his argument, which essentially insisted that "social and cultural change, however desirable, should not be effected by the engines of national power." It was just one more example of concentrated power that endangered freedom. "The enemy of freedom is unrestrained power," he concluded, "and the champions of freedom will fight against the concentration of power wherever they find it."[16] Goldwater in effect argued that the Constitution was what its founders said it was or intended it to be—nothing more. That alone represented "Constitutional Government."

Although the conservative philosopher Russell Kirk had said much the same thing some years earlier, Goldwater's arguments found a broader and more receptive audience. Not only did they come at what conservatives saw as a critical juncture in American history and politics; their author was a prominent politician. While the Goldwater book led to the Goldwater candidacy at the 1960 Republican convention, for younger conservatives its importance lay in the articulation of conservative principles. Goldwater attacked not only liberals and Democrats, but Republicans as well. This gave his message an aura of principled purity that sharply contrasted with other rhetoric of that political year. He attacked not only Democratic spending, but Republican spending, for accelerating the trend toward statism. Goldwater articulated a systemic attack, one that could only lead to fundamental structural reform. And, almost by definition, the proponents of that change would have to be ideologues. Much of his attack centered on "welfarism," that apparently humanitarian effort that bestowed responsibility for individual welfare on the state rather than on the individual. This subordinated the individual even while it was "compatible with the political processes of a democratic society."[17] In addition, his attack focused on a range of statist developments: federal aid to education, the progressive educational philosophies of John Dewey, the social homogenization of the individual.

Goldwater's second theme was the communist menace. The United States, he insisted, was in "clear and imminent danger of being overwhelmed by alien forces." He worried that the threat of war and a "craven fear of death" might overcome a fear of communism and lead to compromise with the Soviet Union. Faith needed to replace fear—faith in traditional values and in the American system. "Young men who are inexperienced but have faith," Goldwater thundered in a strident speech before the National Inter-Fraternity Conference in November 1960, "are more useful than older, experienced men without faith." He believed that fear had already led to a significant deterioration of American national security, and Americans needed to understand better the nature of the conflict if they were to reverse their course. The communists were in earnest and we were not. His solution was simple and direct: victory. Peace could only come after victory over communism, and victory, not peace or coexistence, should be our objective. This was a fundamental intellectual and ideological conflict, Goldwater argued, and material wealth did not change political goals. The struggle, therefore, was for men's minds rather than their stomachs. American ideology, not economic aid, should be our primary export.[18]

The United States needed to go on the offensive, to win the cold war. It should encourage "captive peoples" to overthrow their communist masters, for they were our strongest weapon against communism. Military superiority was essential, as was a commitment to the use of nuclear weapons. Goldwater believed, moreover, that the Kremlin would retreat before any serious American threat or ultimatum. The choice was a binary one.

> The future, as I see it, will unfold along one of two paths. Either the
> Communists will retain the offensive; will lay down one challenge

after another; will invite us in local crisis after local crisis to choose
between all-out war and limited retreat; and will force us, ultimately,
to surrender or accept war under the most disadvantageous circumstances. Or *we* will summon the will and the means for taking the initiative, and wage a war of attrition against them—and hope, thereby,
to bring about the internal disintegration of the Communist empire.

Either option might lead to war; but one led to war and probable defeat, the other
to war and possible victory. Goldwater's message was a passionate plea for a new
crusade based on conservative principles, and contrasted sharply with John F.
Kennedy's insistence that cool pragmatism would lead to orderly change.[19]

Calls for Change

In 1960 there were other calls for change as well. Among liberals, Democratic
Senator John F. Kennedy urged Americans to face their problems and attacked
a static consensus. Kennedy's repeated insistence that the sixties would be
challenging and revolutionary led, as journalist Henry Fairlie observed, to the
"politics of expectation." More important, however, was his demand for commitment from the American public. Together with a broader, introspective public search for the national purpose and national goals, and political efforts to
link Richard Nixon to the "passive" 1950s, this demand for commitment served
as a call to action. But it was an undifferentiated call; what it sought to do above
all else was to argue the value of and necessity for change. A campaign tract by
Harvard historian Arthur Schlesinger Jr. perhaps best dramatized the choice.
As part of his argument that there were significant differences between the two
candidates, and that those differences were vital to the country's future,
Schlesinger cast Nixon as the apostle of the directionless past.

> Nixon is in many respects a good example of midcentury man,
> obsessed with appearances rather than with the reality of things, ob-
> sessed above all with his own appearance, his own image, seeking re-
> assurance through winning, but never knowing why he is so mad to
> win or what he will do with his victory. Issues for him are subordinate
> and secondary, to be maneuvered and manipulated. What matters is
> stance, not substance: what matters is a felt righteousness of motive, a
> sentence of humility on the lips, a look of dedication on the face.

Yet, during the 1960 presidential campaign, even Richard Nixon called for the
emergence of a "flaming idealism" in the United States.[20]

The argument that the sixties would be an exciting and challenging decade
was not confined to political rhetoric, however. National polls and symposia

came to the same conclusion, although most found few Americans wanting anything more than economic growth and continued prosperity. "The highest excitement," concluded a *Fortune* magazine editorial, "will lie in Americans' decisions about the uses of abundance." Teenagers and technology would drive that abundance, and "true poverty will be hard to find." But aside from a neo-Malthusian fear about population growth in an industrial society, the editors of *Fortune* could find little to cloud the future. Indeed, they predicted that the sixties would be the "decade of the discretionary dollar." What was perhaps most significant about their analysis, however, was that it focused solely on domestic matters and expressed no concern about the issue of communism.[21] A Gallup poll commissioned by *Look* magazine revealed that Americans were concerned about Russian space exploits, but concluded they were "not in a worrying mood" and were "calmly fatalistic about world events." Indeed, the poll depicted Americans as "relaxed, unadventurous, comfortably satisfied with their way of life and blandly optimistic about the future." They wanted tranquility, not excitement, leisure time rather than new challenges, vacation trips rather than ideological crusades.[22]

Much of this fit comfortably with the arguments in sociologist Daniel Bell's *The End of Ideology*. Published in 1960, Bell's tome adopted an anti-ideological but not necessarily conservative viewpoint. He insisted that the prosperity of the 1950s demonstrated the exhaustion of nineteenth-century ideologies, particularly Marxism. This was to be celebrated, because ideologies carried with them a dangerous and compulsive commitment to "intellect and feeling" that could arouse the masses to utopian social action. Yet, while he rejected the theory of mass society, realism compelled Bell to admit that the United States stood vulnerable "to the politics of disaffection." He worried that this disaffection, along with the American propensity toward moralism, might recharge ideological conflicts and divide society. There was, he feared, a "restless search for a new intellectual radicalism," a radicalism that would simplify answers in its search for utopian solutions.[23]

Other intellectuals of the 1950s shared Bell's pragmatism. Reacting not only against a fear of the masses drawn from the 1930s, but against the ideological excesses of McCarthyism in the 1950s, they believed that perfectionist tendencies led to the curtailment of freedom. As such, they tried to divorce sociological issues from political issues. Reform was still needed, but it should be driven by empiricism rather than passion. Intellectuals like Bell, Daniel Boorstin, and Seymour Martin Lipset argued that the 1960s should embrace a moderate liberalism that pursued incremental reforms drawn from rational planning rather than ideological zeal.[24]

Not everyone agreed. Democratic presidential candidate John F. Kennedy gave scant evidence of launching an ideological crusade, but his rhetoric was apocalyptic and his call to action direct. Theologian Reinhold Niebuhr was concerned about ideology, warning that communism represented a threat and that "our moral and political complacency exposes us to the dangers which all soft nations of history have enountered in contests with tougher, sometimes more 'barbarous' foes." More searching was the commentary by Emanuel Geltman in the winter issue of *Dissent*. Geltman bemoaned the lack of ideological alternatives in the current political spectrum, insisting that there were real issues and considerable anxiety in the country. "But they do not intrude into consciousness to the point where there is articulate pressure or desire for action." Despite calls for change from various political candidates, those issues did not necessarily lend themselves "to solution by traditional political means." In effect, Geltman called for new modes of political action, outside the traditional political structure and driven by angry pressures for change.[25]

More ideological, and in hindsight more significant, were warnings from William F. Buckley Jr. on the Right and sociologist C. Wright Mills on the Left. In the pages of *National Review*, Buckley attacked the political dullness evident in students who evinced little interest in the political world. Seeking to revitalize conservatism, he urged students to become exercised over moral truths and public questions. His world was a binary one, divided between communists and conservatives. He lamented that conservatives were moribund, lulled into apathy by the absence of a liberal vision and the lack of any call for passionate commitment. From the Left, Mills agreed that contemporary political dialogue was dull, but attacked the end-of-ideology school for allowing their distaste for Stalinism to blind them to the "uselessness of the liberal rhetoric." A passionless politics had led to apathy and complacency. Whereas Buckley called for a revival of conservatism, Mills called for a New Left to promote structural change. Both, ironically, hoped that a new generation of intellectuals would be the agents for radical change.[26]

The Search for Meaning

But if intellectuals, and particularly students, were to be the new agents of radical change, were there any signs of ferment? In 1960 two leading students of youth culture found evidence of discontent, but not ferment. Paul Goodman, in *Growing Up Absurd*, argued that American society seemed irrelevant to the younger generation. It was a "closed room," a room dominated by the values of the rat race. "This does not give much motivation for a fundamental change, since there are no unambiguous motives to fight for and no uncontaminated means." Kenneth Keniston agreed, noting that the "age inspires scant enthusiasm." Individuals, especially youth, were uncommitted and alienated from their society. Keniston argued that efforts to rediscover or redefine the national purpose would not reverse this tendency, for youth lacked "any radical criticism of our society or any revolutionary alternative to the status quo." Affluence had produced apathy; larger social goals were needed.[27] Writing from a student's perspective, Richard Flacks (later influential in the New Left) agreed.

> As President of the campus Young Democrats, I circulated petitions supporting civil rights legislation, attended meetings, and passed out a lot of leaflets. Of some 10,000 students on my campus, perhaps 50 of us were politically active: that 50 included all the Young Democrats, Young Republicans, Young Socialists, Young ADAers, Student NAACPers, and student government politicians that there were. Usually, our efforts to persuade students to sign civil rights petitions were met with the response that signing or joining anything "might jeopardize the government job I'm planning to get." In short, it was a time of almost total political apathy, produced, at least in part, by a fear that taking any kind of stand on any issue might get you into trouble.[28]

But these studies of absurdity and alienation also depicted a society fraught with subsurface tensions. After a rather unsuccessful confrontation with the beat generation and writer Jack Kerouac, James Wechsler found the stirrings of a political revival amid the wreckage of an evening's debate. Wechsler not only failed to understand Kerouac; he was disturbed that the audience did not understand Kerouac's writings yet liked them. He dismissed the argument that the country lacked purpose because it was awash in abundance. There was something much more fundamentally wrong with that portrait of serenity, he insisted. Uneasiness, malaise, discontent—all bespoke the failure of existing institutions forthrightly to address the future.

> In recent years "compromise" has become almost an end in itself, and it is the liberal who is deemed extremist when he voices any strength of conviction; the result, in fact, is not "compromise," but stalemate, not the achievement of the possible but the enthronement of the status quo, not moderation but immobility, not the clear delineation of public issues but a spreading sense that there are no longer any important public questions on which men may reasonably be asked to give more than equivocal answers. There is no shortage of great themes for political combat, but rather a loss of nerve among most of our political warriors. It is time for a new beginning.[29]

For Wechsler, the new beginning began with a search for meaning.

Other observers from across the political spectrum agreed. While Dr. Edward D. Eddy, Provost of the University of New Hampshire, described the current generation as "neatniks"—a "creature who has sold his birthright for a mess of mortgage and traded in his masculinity for a tail fin"—he also admitted that beneath the apparent indifference lay "an unfashionable but searching desire for meaning in all that he does." Traditional politics appeared incapable of providing that meaning, so students sought fulfillment elsewhere. This is why the southern sit-ins, launched in the winter of 1960, seemed so promising. They provided a direct action alternative to a stagnant politics, and brought a whiff of meaning to a generation seemingly bereft of commitment. They also attacked the root causes of problems, representing a moral crusade that seemed immune from equivocating compromises. Later, demonstrations against the House Un-American Activities Committee fostered a similar spirit. Parallel movements erupted on the Right. Together they shared a belief that commitment to a cause was possible, as a new generation shed the McCarthyite fears that youthful commitments would come back to haunt your future.[30]

Concern about a flagging sense of national purpose also created a climate conducive to change, even though it failed to chart any particular direction for the country. At the outset of the decade the urge for change particularly energized conservatives. The retirement of Dwight D. Eisenhower freed them from any commitment to an incumbent Republican and offered an opportunity to reclaim the party, if not retain the presidency. What conservatives lacked was any cohesive movement or integrated ideology. McCarthyism loomed as a specter from the recent past, but while many on the Right defended him, Senator Joseph McCarthy's legacy was divisive and too negative to serve as a broader rallying point. In addition, even some conservatives found McCarthyism to be a repressive movement that conjured up images of antidemocratic mass movements from the 1930s. What was needed was a positive affirmation of conservative principles, not political opportunism.

Stirrings of Activism

The Conscience of a Conservative tapped a wellspring of conservative discontent and roused conservatives to action. It articulated and popularized a variety of themes that dated back at least to the 1930s and had found expression in National Review and other conservative writings during the 1950s. But the book and its author particularly influenced a new generation of conservatives, a generation more interested in activism than in intellectual debate over the fine points of conservative ideology. For them the 1960s beckoned as a decade of opportunity. They had voiced their discontent with Eisenhower Republicanism during Ike's second term, a discontent particularly visible in internecine battles within the Young Republican organization. These individuals had never given up on Taft Republicanism; indeed, they never really considered Eisenhower a Republican. Eisenhower's retirement and the approaching presidential election provided an opportunity for a renaissance of traditional Republicanism through "the elimination by operation of Eisenhowerism and of those who have fostered that infection."[31] Goldwater's *Conscience* touched and stirred their soul in ways that Buckley's writings did not, convincing them that the time was ripe for a conservative counterattack.

Buckley also focused on the twin evils of statism and "ideological plasticity," but his public complaints about the "sonorous vapidities of Mr. Eisenhower" during the 1950s had failed to dent the General's popularity among Republicans. Despite that, his often shrill crusade attracted other true believers and won some victories behind the scenes. Beginning with the Young Republican convention in 1957, when YRs adopted a platform unalterably opposed to federal aid to education, to all military assistance to communist nations, to UN membership for Communist China, and to union shops, Young Republicans turned decidedly conservative. By the 1959 YR convention in Denver, conservatives had taken over that element of the party. After a series of brutal floor fights, they openly repudiated Eisenhower Republicanism, booed the name of Chief Justice Earl Warren, censured Republican Senators Margaret Chase Smith and William Langer for opposing the appointment of Lewis L. Strauss, and mobilized against the Rockefeller forces in the party. A coalition of southern, midwestern, and western conservatives elected a conservative, Ned Cushing of Kansas, chairman.[32]

Certain that Richard Nixon would be the 1960 Republican presidential nominee, conservatives sought to force Nixon to the Right. Jane Buckley Smith, sister to the *National Review's* editor, noted that if "he is a so-called liberal Republican, far better to know it now, when there is still time to work for another candidate—one whom we can trust." Many young conservatives, however, determined to mobilize college support for Nixon, perhaps in the hope of ultimately gaining some influence. Frank Meyer of *National Review* cautioned them not to waste their energies on Richard Nixon and traditional politics, but instead to build a "serious conservative opposition."[33] As more and more young conservatives read Barry Goldwater's *Conscience of a Conservative*, this became an increasingly popular position.

During the winter and spring of 1960, quite apart from presidential politics or Goldwater's book, some of those men and women actively worked for various conservative causes. This conservative activism accentuated their distance from the Eisenhower-Nixon wing of the Republican Party, and led older conservatives like Russell Kirk to hope that college youth were stirring. Kirk particularly noted the activism of AWARE, a New York organization against communism in the theater and arts, where individuals such as Annette Yvonne Courtemanche, Douglas Caddy, and David Franke were active.[34]

But the central focus during the winter of 1960 was the National Student Committee for the Loyalty Oath. Eisenhower had urged repeal of this provision in the National Defense Education Act, on the grounds that it was unnecessary. In addition, several colleges and universities had objected to its inclusion, and twelve had withdrawn from participation in the program. The act had originally passed Congress on September 5, 1958. It required recipients of student loans and NDEA fellowships to file an affidavit stating that they were not members in nor supporters of any "organization that believes in or teaches the overthrow of the United States government by force or violence or by any illegal or unconstitutional methods," and to swear an oath of loyalty to the United States. Organized by David Franke and Douglas Caddy, the National Student Committee for the Loyalty Oath emerged in late 1959 to block Congressional repeal of those provisions. They also hoped to use the issue to mobilize conservative students nationwide.[35]

Seeking to offset what they charged was a "barrage of anti-oath propaganda" from liberals, Caddy and Franke established a national headquarters in Washington, D.C. and contacted students across the country. Franke wrote a ringing defense of the oath in December 1959 that served as the catalyst for that recruitment. Admitting that on the surface supporters of limited government might be inclined to endorse removal of the requirements, Franke argued that they were instead legitimate requirements for the government to impose and did not violate freedom of belief or conscience. Loyal students should not be ashamed of their allegiance, and disloyal students should not receive taxpayers' funds. More central to the emerging conservative ideology, however, was his insistence that the "freedom of belief" opposition rested on "a species of relativism which admits to no moral standards or absolutes outside the individual." Individuals who objected to all federal influence in education should argue for removal of the entire program rather than just the loyalty oath and affidavit.[36]

This attempt to define moral absolutes and emphasize the importance of anticommunism undergirded the new conservative attack against both liberals and the moderate middle. Perhaps because it reminded many of Joseph McCarthy, the attack drew immediate attention from liberals and moderates. A bill to repeal the oath had lost in the Senate by only two votes, and the matter obviously touched a sensitive issue. In a letter to the *New York Times*, Douglas Caddy rejected Senator John F. Kennedy's argument that the oath was discriminatory. He also agreed to debate opponents of the oath on the American Forum of the Air. In response, Americans for Democratic Action solicited speakers to oppose him, but ADA Director Sheldon Pollack warned that "I can't think of any of our students who would be able to hold his own against Caddy. He is a junior edition of Buckley and a rather vicious debater."[37] Liberals launched other attacks. *The New Republic* portrayed the entire matter as merely an "outburst of servility" among "ineducable" college students. The danger of such an oath, the author warned, had seemingly escaped its supporters. One could not swear what one would do in the future without either lying or resting content in intellectual bondage. The real problem, therefore, was that the oath's supporters simply did not understand "the nature of freedom," or that intellectual freedom undergirded all other freedoms. Since Caddy, Franke, and others would apparently never think about deviating from their current beliefs, they saw no difficulty with the oath. But for free-thinking individuals it was a different matter.[38]

In late February Caddy addressed the sixth annual AWARE conference on education in New York City. He insisted that repeal of the loyalty oath would endanger the internal security of the country, provide a great psychological victory "for the enemies of the American way of life," and advance the "Communist conspiracy." The issue was, in his view, the "most lively issue on college campuses today." Meanwhile, as Caddy and Franke recruited support for their position from college students, they created what became the base for Young Americans for Freedom and a future conservative leadership cadre.[39]

As conservative students made contact with one another, they also mobilized support to nominate Barry Goldwater for either president or vice president on the 1960 Republican ticket. An April meeting of the thirteen-state Midwest Federation of College Young Republicans attracted a record 435 delegates. The delegates not only endorsed the loyalty oath provisions; they opposed federal aid to education and federally financed medical care. Northwestern University delegate John Kolbe offered a resolution endorsing Goldwater as the G.O.P. vice-presidential nominee. Despite efforts by the Michigan delegation, which opposed any endorsement at that time, the resolution carried by a voice vote after only ten minutes of debate. By May students for Goldwater had focused their attention on the vice-presidential nomination, and Douglas Caddy—then a twenty-two-year old senior at Georgetown University—had become national secretary of the Youth for Goldwater for Vice President. Headquartered in Chicago, the fledgling organization quickly formed forty-five chapters. The national chairman was Robert Croll, a graduate student at Northwestern University, who told a gathering of high school and college newspaper editors that "American youth is swinging to the right—and swinging more rapidly all the time. . . . I think the next ten years will see a full-scale triumph for conservative ideas in the decisive center of campus opinion. For it is precisely the most active, the most interested, and the best informed students who are the conservatives."[40] This was just as well, because older conservatives like William Rusher of *National Review* were pessimistic: "I think we had better pull in our belts and buckle down to a long period of real impotence. Hell, the catacombs were good enough for the Christians!"[41]

The National Youth for Goldwater organization pursued two objectives. The first was to secure Goldwater a place on the G.O.P. ticket in 1960. The second was to build within the Young Republican National Federation (YRNF) "a permanent, nationwide unity of youthful supporters of the same Conservative political and economic philosophy embraced by Senator Goldwater as set forth in his recently-published book *The Conscience of a Conservative*." According to Croll, most Young Republican organizations already supported Goldwater. Polls by the YRNF of 40,000 Young Republicans across the country had shown that Goldwater was their first choice for Vice President. Indeed, Young Republicans controlled the Youth for Goldwater effort. Robert Harley, a twenty-year-old sophomore at Georgetown University and chairman of the District of Columbia YRNF, managed the national office. David Franke, editor of the national Young Republican college publication *College Republican* and organizer of the Loyalty Oath Committee, was Eastern Vice Chairman. Richard Noble of Stanford, treasurer of the California Young Republicans, was the Western Vice Chairman.[42]

As the Youth for Goldwater effort materialized, it frequently clashed with Youth for Nixon, which had also drawn a number of conservatives into its ranks. For individuals like Robert Bauman, a founder of Youth for Nixon in the fall of 1959, the greater danger was Nelson Rockefeller and the liberal Republicans. (Also, in 1959, Goldwater had not yet caught the eye of young conservatives.) But once Goldwater seemed a possible nominee, conservative midwestern supporters of Nixon raised questions about his position on several issues: the loyalty oath, federal aid to education, and federally financed medical care. Young Republicans at Earlham College, Butler University, and Indiana University all affirmed their opposition to New Dealism and endorsed Goldwater for a spot on the ticket. James Abstine, who had narrowly missed being elected chairman of the Midwest Federation and chaired the Indiana Collegiate Republicans, expressed students' concern about Nixon's weak positions on those issues. Abstine told Nixon that Goldwater had strong support for the vice-presidential nomination among this group, and warned that their "convictions are deeply held and will not be changed because you, President Eisenhower, or anyone else, as such, directs to the contrary." He even threatened to bolt rather than compromise his ideological positions. "We have worked, are now working, and will continue to work actively for your election as President," he said, "but if to so work for you requires the accommodation of our thinking so that we agree with you on all issues at all times just for the sake of agreeing with you, then, I suppose, that many of us would prefer the freedom to think our own thoughts than to be active politically in such a way that we could not do so."[43]

Their cause received further impetus in May 1960 with a series of "riots" against the House Un-American Activities Committee in San Francisco. The anti-HUAC protests, ironically, served as a lightning rod to mobilize both conservatives and liberals, but conservatives seized on them first. Noisy outbursts had characterized several HUAC hearings from 1957 to 1960, but the events of May 1960 far outstripped other protests. At the very moment when young conservatives were becoming politically active in Republican Party politics, Bay area youth were throwing off the mantle of cold-war conformity themselves. Demonstrations against the execution of Caryl Chessman and protests against McCarthyite tactics by local boards of education had drawn the attention of San Francisco and Berkeley students. The presence of three members of the House Un-American Activities Committee at hearings in San Francisco's City Hall touched off an explosive confrontation, a clear signal that the passivity of the fifties was fading. An editorial in *The Daily Californian* urged all students to oppose the hearings and recommended the "abolishment of the entire Un-American Committee as it is now constituted and as it now operates."[44]

For conservatives, such criticism of HUAC was evidence that a communist conspiracy still threatened the country, and was tantamount to treason. William F. Buckley Jr. defended the committee, warning that communism remained a threat and that there was no significant difference between external and internal threats. The United States was in far greater peril from communists in 1960 than it had been in the 1940s, Buckley insisted, and "as the power of the enemy abroad increases, so necessarily does his arm here, unless we chop it off." M. Stanton Evans attacked the "riots" as communist-inspired, and saw them as a "frightening example of how guileless students can be manipulated by Communist agents."[45]

Conservative students threw their support behind FBI Director J. Edgar Hoover, who blamed communists for the anti-HUAC protests, and cheered *Operation Abolition.* HUAC commissioned the film, which was made from subpoenaed news films, and distributed 250,000 copies of J. Edgar Hoover's report, *Communist Target—Youth.* The film's purpose, according to conservative activist and newspaperman Stanton Evans, was to "alert the viewer to the dangers of internal Communism . . . and to suggest sinister impulses behind much of the opposition to the Committee." Relying heavily on Hoover's report, Evans insisted that the protestors were either communists or their dupes and that they, not the police, were responsible for the violence.[46]

While liberal opponents of HUAC formed the National Committee to Abolish HUAC, the Young Republican Executive Committee, meeting in Reno, Nevada, passed a resolution praising HUAC. Meanwhile, conservatives took *Operation Abolition* on the road as a recruiting instrument for their cause. Fulton Lewis III, who narrated the film, spoke on its behalf at more than two hundred colleges. The John Birch Society became a principal distributor of the film at the community level. *Operation Abolition* also became a regular feature at American Legion post meetings. The film was propaganda; even Stanton Evans admitted its flaws, but conservatives insisted that its message was un-corrupted by "documentary" manipulations and ignored the opposition of com-munity organizations across the country. The value of the film to conservatives was its simplicity and its moral appeal. It gave voice to a cry to take back the country, to take it back from its downward slide under liberal Democrats and moderate Republicans. This paralleled the message in Goldwater's *The Con-science of a Conservative*. As Youth for Goldwater spokesman Robert Croll announced:

> Senator Goldwater carries the torch which fell from the hands of the
> late Senator Taft as the leading spokesman for American conser-
> vatism. His unrivalled popularity among college students and young
> persons in general should provide a clear warning to both political
> parties that American youth is turning away from the dogmas of the
> left and will not devote its loyalties to candidates who espouse the
> blatantly paternalistic policies of the New Deal or even the somewhat
> milder statism that Nelson Rockefeller would impose on us.[47]

These three stimuli—Goldwater's *The Conscience of a Conservative*, the Na-tional Student Committee for the Loyalty Oath, and the anti-HUAC riots and the film that followed—helped energize youthful conservative activists.

Youth for Goldwater for Vice President, along with other Goldwater sup-port in the spring of 1960, gave these activists a focal point for their activism and led them to battle Republican moderates at the G.O.P. national conven-tion in Chicago that July. With the aid of older conservatives like Marvin Lieb-man and Charles Edison, Youth for Goldwater for Vice President opened a head-quarters at the Pick Congress Hotel. Robert Croll organized hundreds of local conservatives, carrying signs and placards backing Goldwater, to greet Richard Nixon at his hotel. Even though some of these conservatives supported Nixon for the Presidential nomination, believing that he had earned it despite his convention-eve deal with Nelson Rockefeller, they stood firmly behind Goldwater for the vice-presidential nomination. That battle shaped the future of Republican Party politics for the next several decades. Although Goldwater fell short of the nomination, he encouraged his youthful supporters to continue their efforts. After delivering his plea for party unity to the convention, Goldwater met with the Youth for Goldwater activists and advised them to "turn your group into a permanent organization of young conservatives. The man is not important. The principles you espouse are. Do this and I shall support you in any way I can."[48] The Youth for Goldwater efforts at the 1960 Republican convention created the nucleus for Young Americans for Freedom. The subsequent defeat of Richard Nixon in the 1960 presidential election gave them an opportunity. Together these events accelerated the rise of a new conservative movement in the United States.

The Republican Party, 1960, and the Struggle over "Modern Republicanism"

Chapter 2

The story of the 1960 presidential election usually focuses on John F. Kennedy's campaign for the Democratic nomination, the controversy over the religion issue in American politics, the Kennedy-Nixon debates, and finally the emergence of the New Frontier following Kennedy's razor-thin victory in November. But before all that, another struggle erupted—a struggle for the soul of the Republican Party. It erupted with the certainty that Dwight D. Eisenhower would no longer be the party's presidential candidate, and with a determination by conservatives that the moment had arrived to define the future of the party through its platform in 1960 and perhaps its nominee in 1964. From this controversy emerged Young Americans for Freedom and the effort to reconfigure the Republican Party within the parameters of a new conservatism.

Debates over "Modern Republicanism"

The central issue in this struggle was whether the Republican Party should continue to embrace the Eisenhower program and philosophy or adopt a more conservative ideology. Conservatives had long argued that ideas had consequences, and they opposed the ideas embraced by "modern Republicanism." President Eisenhower implied that unless the Republican Party embraced "modern Republicanism," it would go the way of the dinosaurs. For Eisenhower, "modern Republicanism" was the type of political philosophy that recognizes clearly the responsibility of the Federal Government to take the lead in making certain that the productivity of our great economic machine is distributed so that no one will suffer disaster, privation, through no fault of his own. . . . We believe that it is free enterprise that has brought these blessings to America. Therefore, we are going to try our best to preserve that free enterprise, and put all of these problems in the hands of localities and the private enterprise of states wherever we can, because it happens that the great difference, as I see it, between myself and people of a philosophy that believes in centralized government, is that I believe to have this free enterprise healthy, you must have, first, integrity in your fiscal operations of the government; second, you must preserve a sound dollar or all of our plans for social security and pensions for the aged fall by the wayside, they are no good; and thirdly, in this dispersion of power. Now, that, at home, as I see it, represents modern Republicanism.[1]

This was, in Eisenhower's view, the future of the Republican Party.

More than anything else, this concept of Republican ideology sought a consensual middle that shunned more extreme ideologies of the Right and Left. In 1956, Under Secretary of Labor Arthur Larson proclaimed it to be the "New Republicanism." Larson argued that these views coincided with those of the great majority of Americans in their postwar acceptance of labor relations legislation, social security, and government intervention to alleviate suffering or correct substandard conditions. The middle-of-the-road position, he insisted, now called for the federal government to take firm responsibility for the general welfare. While it could delegate some of that to state or local governments, the choice of means was a federal responsibility. For Larson, the "New Republicanism" and the American consensus were coterminous. If Republicans lost sight of that truth and nominated a candidate "identified with an extreme conservative position," he warned, the Democrats would choose a candidate from that great middle and control the government. Thereafter, "it would be difficult indeed for the Republicans to get back in."[2]

Conservatives vehemently disagreed, and embraced ideology over political pragmatism. William F. Buckley Jr. led the assault, complaining that

What the New Republicans needed was a great political shapelessness, an infinite ideological plasticity which, on approaching the great unresolved political problems that have arisen out of the growth of Communism and the omnipotent State, could be relied upon to ooze its way over those problems, without grind, or tear, or rasp or friction. The Eisenhower approach was designed not to solve problems, but to refuse, essentially, to recognize that problems exist; and so, to ignore them.

Old Guard Republicans and a group of newer conservatives complained that all Eisenhower had done was to codify the New Deal. "Modern Republicanism" seemed like nothing more than moderate nonpartisanship. They were bitter about his refusal to defend Senator Joseph McCarthy, upset at his acceptance of most New Deal legislation, and outraged that he had continued Truman's policy of containment and apparently supported coexistence with the communist world. Their voices muted if not stilled by Eisenhower's defeat of Robert Taft for the 1952 nomination, conservative Republicans had found their access to power frustrated by Eisenhower's persistent popularity throughout the 1950s. But as 1960 approached, they saw an opportunity to shape party ideology for a new decade and with new candidates. They believed that the likely Republican nominee, Richard Nixon, might be one of their own. In any case they intended to shape the platform on which he would run.[3]

Liberal and moderate Republicans determined to oppose them. As they looked to 1960, they sought not only to consolidate "modern Republicanism" but to move beyond its fiscal contraints by increasing defense spending and being more aggressive in the area of civil rights. One group, Citizens for Modern Republicanism, opened a national office in New York City to promote the Eisenhower philosophy and find a successor for 1960.[4]

The 1958 elections had sharpened the conflict. Republicans lost forty-eight seats in the House, sinking to their lowest level of representation there since 1937. Those defeats dashed hopes that Eisenhower's victories had moved the party toward majority status. They also encouraged both liberals and conservatives to escalate their attacks on "modern Republicanism" and Eisenhower's programs. Led by Nelson Rockefeller, liberal and moderate Republicans promoted the conclusions of the Rockefeller Brothers Fund Special Studies Project that urged more aggressive federal action in foreign as well as domestic policy. Eisenhower's fiscal caution, they insisted, was a barrier to needed economic growth and provided an insufficient defense program for the country's national security needs in the 1960s. Conservatives, on the other hand, saw an opportunity to declare "modern Republicanism" bankrupt and insisted that only a truly conservative position could guarantee the future of the Republican Party. "The present administration," Frank Meyer wrote in *National Review*, "does not perhaps swim so enthusiastically with the tides as its predecessors; but this is a minor difference of mood; it is not a difference of principle."[5]

Party officials initially encouraged this debate. Republican National Chairman Meade Alcorn asked party leaders nationwide to assess the defeats and suggest remedies. Alcorn found a faction-ridden party with a big-business image and little support among working Americans, and a growing disenchantment with Republican programs among party regulars.[6] The depth of the problem was revealed in correspondence between Texas state Republican chairman Thad Hutcheson and Vice President Richard Nixon. Hutcheson urged Nixon to take a more active leadership role in the party to clarify its basic philosophy.

> Frankness compels me to report an overwhelming apathy and an almost sullen resistance toward the Republican cause, arising out of an apparent feeling that the Administration's program had veered far away from what was originally promised toward big Federal government and big Federal spending, and that there was really not much basic difference between the two parties. . . . A fight on such principles would spread great enthusiasm for the 1960 election among our workers and potential supporters, whereas any turn toward the principles which seem to be involved in the popular concept of "Modern Republicanism" would, in my opinion, be disastrous to the future of the Party.[7]

But while Hutcheson argued in essence for a philosophy in accord with that of Barry Goldwater, Nixon's former press secretary, James Bassett of the *Los Angeles Evening Mirror News*, urged a completely different approach, one that essentially embraced "modern Republicanism." Concluding that there really was not much difference between the two parties, Bassett urged Nixon to give the party some humanity to overcome its "soulless" image and to emphasize the danger of big government to individual freedoms. Bassett called his approach "progressive independence."[8]

Taken together, Hutcheson and Bassett reveal the problem facing the Republican Party as it looked toward 1960. For eight years the party had basked in the national popularity of Dwight Eisenhower, but the general's personal popularity failed to rub off on other Republican candidates. Control of the White House had masked problems at the party's foundations. Now, with Eisenhower about to retire, the 1958 election defeats demonstrated the stark realities facing Republicans in 1960. In the words of *National Review*'s Brent Bozell, "The Republican Party *made* Dwight Eisenhower its high priest, in exchange for its soul." There was no automatic conservative vote ready to back Republican candidates. The party had no national organizational power; it was "recognizably a corpse." Bozell, of course, knew what direction the party should take; it should move to the right. "A conservative electorate has to be created out of that vast uncommitted middle—the great majority of the American people who, though today they vote for Democratic or Modern Republican candidates, are not ideologically wedded to their programs or, for that matter, to any program. The problem is to reach them and to organize them."[9]

The Committee on Program and Progress

The post-mortems of November and December led liberal and conservative Republicans alike to call for a statement of policy around which the party could rally. G.O.P. national chairman Meade Alcorn had opposed this in the past, fearing that no statement could reconcile the opposing views of conservatives like Senator Barry Goldwater of Arizona and liberals such as Senator Jacob Javits of New York, and that any attempt would only increase factionalism. But devastating losses in the 1958 elections, coupled with the need to energize the party for the 1960 elections, led Alcorn to appoint a Committee on Program and Progress. Chaired by Charles Percy, president of Bell and Howell, the committee was charged to define "the challenges and responsibilities facing the Republican Party in all areas of political activity" and to suggest policies for the 1960s. Endorsed by President Eisenhower, and approved by the Republican National Committee at its January meeting in Des Moines, Iowa, the committee paralleled other efforts by Eisenhower to revitalize public policy debate in the country. In December 1958 the president had invited half a dozen leading Republicans, including Percy, to an early January White House discussion about the need to establish national goals. Asked to chair that committee, Percy refused. But he agreed to chair a more partisan effort, telling Eisenhower that "the two parties, in the best sense of competition, ought to say then, how we should achieve those goals, and we ought to have competition of ideas, and we haven't really had enough of that in the two party system. If you want a program laid out for the Republican Party as to how we should achieve those goals, that kind of a committee I'd be happy to set up, and chair."[10]

At the first meeting of the Committee on Program and Progress (which quickly became known as the Percy Committee), Meade Alcorn outlined their objectives. They were not to draft a legislative program, nor were they to formulate a platform for 1960. They were to produce a declaration of principles, but also to move beyond that declaration to something larger. Alcorn tried, without much success, to define that larger mission.

> I hope that this Committee will provide the Republican Party with a concise, understandable statement of our Party's long-range objectives in all of the areas of political responsibility and activity in the light of the social, technological and economic developments which you can reasonably anticipate during the years immediately ahead. You should establish guideposts which will aid Republican policymakers, office-

holders, workers, and voters to deal forthrightly and vigorously and effectively with the problems they must solve. You should clearly mark for us all the path we should follow toward a maximum of human freedom, dignity and opportunity through the application of sound and acceptable Republican principles.

The committee was to balance the "exciting, the fearless and the theoretical on the one hand and the acceptable and attainable on the other." And through it all they were to avoid factionalism. It was a daunting task.[11]

The committee quickly established four task forces: national security and peace, human rights and needs, the impact of science and technology, and economic opportunity and progress. The broad responsibilities of each task force were in part an effort to control the problem of special interest domination and resist the urge to draft specific legislation. The sweeping scope of each task force also reflected a determination that the Republican Party needed to be forward-looking, to avoid rehashing the arguments and issues of the past and shape an agenda for the sixties.[12]

Establishment of the Committee on Program and Progress brought a mixed reaction from Republicans. Richard Nixon, who expected to be the Republican presidential nominee in 1960, spoke at its opening meeting and kept in touch with Percy throughout the committee's deliberations. To the extent that Percy sought to liberalize the Republican agenda, Nixon supported him. Conservatives were wary at the outset, but soon became comfortable with the committee's work. Stephen Shadegg, campaign manager for Barry Goldwater in 1952 and 1958 and a member of the committee, wrote Goldwater that "you will recall I came away from the original meeting of the Republican Committee on Program and Progress with some reservations. I hasten to report the two day session of our task force in Chicago, concluded yesterday, was a thrilling and productive experience." He believed that the group would clearly enunciate conservative principles, and classified many of his colleagues as "Goldwater Republicans" who would avoid "any support of 'Me-tooism' or for the world of life adjustment." Shadegg was convinced that the task forces would bluntly outline future Republican policies and avoid temporizing, and that "there would be no consideration given at all to the possible present preferences of the mass voters." He kept Goldwater closely informed about the committee's thinking, although Goldwater himself was not above communicating his own thoughts directly to Percy. Less than a month after the organization of the task forces, Goldwater expressed his pleasure at being able to participate in their work, but warned that one of the parties "must be to the right, and that one must be ours." Three weeks later Shadegg told Goldwater that the committee recognized that "there is one great over-riding issue confronting the American public and indeed the world today. This is the total war being waged between those who believe in individual responsibility and freedom, and those who believe in a totalitarian materialistic philosophy."[13] His optimism about the committee's work seemed boundless.

By June the four task force reports were ready in draft form, and committee members met on July 16 in Denver to settle any differences so as to complete the final report by the committee's September 1 deadline. Before that meeting, Richard Nixon and his staff also examined the drafts carefully, with an eye toward 1960. Nixon particularly liked the draft on human rights and needs. "On the one hand," he observed, "it is consistent with conservative Republican philosophy on the role of government and on spending programs of the federal government. On the other hand, it has a broadly liberal tone and is not merely negative (another lock on the safe)." Nixon offered several suggestions for improvement, but they were general rather than specific in nature. He also noted that "someone ought to read it just for political impact, and the presence of programs that would really strike the public." He was particularly concerned that the report present the Republican Party as the party of the future, and sent Percy a memo from Karl Harr, Special Assistant to the President, that outlined "The Operational Importance of Goals that Promise Hope."[14]

By September the final report was ready, and Percy reported that reaction to the drafts from Thruston Morton (the new Republican National Chairman), administration officials, and the Republican Congressional leadership was one of "enthusiastic approval." Percy concluded that "this report can demonstrate that the Republican Party is not charting a course for the future by looking into a rear view mirror; that we will look like a party that enjoys solving problems, making decisions, and that regards the future with hope and confidence. . . . We have taken pessimism out of the report and yet tried to be factual and honest in pointing out the challenge of our times and the obligations and responsibility we have as a people." Among conservatives, however, Stephen Shadegg was now less enthusiastic. While he agreed that the report contained some good suggestions, he complained that it was too scholarly for the public to read and lacked a preamble that clarified basic philosophical concepts of the individual and government. "I feel that if we fail to present in singing language our determination to keep men free and to preserve the traditional values of our Judio-Christian [sic] society, we will be losing by default what otherwise might have been a great opportunity."[15]

Published in paperback as *Decisions for a Better America*, the report of the Republican Committee on Program and Progress sought to achieve consensus between the liberal and conservative wings of the party. That effort produced a rather vague and somewhat bifurcated document. On the one hand, the committee insisted that Republican doctrine rested on faith in the individual and an aversion to "government's intrusion into the affairs of men in every walk of life." Government should only aid those who cannot help themselves—for instance, by responding to the problems wrought by technological change with retraining programs. Government restraint would best stimulate economic growth. The committee argued, at the same time, that economic growth would lead to social progress, and would provide social programs, medical security, and investment in the arts and education. The incremental growth of resources, an assumption that underlay most of the committee's projections, would provide Americans the ability to initiate new programs.[16] In one instance the committee proclaimed that the "federal government has a role to play only when individuals, communities or states cannnot by themselves do the things that must be done." At the next instance, it argued that the "Republican Party stands for a strong, responsive federal government, opening and advancing economic opportunities for the American people . . . using its strength to ward off inflation and depression . . . restraining and disciplining any who use their power against the common welfare . . . regulating wisely where the national interest demands it."[17] This balancing act between conservatives' insistence that Republican ideology should promote individual freedom by embracing limited government and liberals' conviction that the public expected government to protect civil rights, promote economic growth, and sustain basic social programs provided something for everyone but did not create a party doctrine to unify the divergent factions.

The committee's recommendations focused on incremental rather than structural changes in American life and public policy. They pushed for expanded health care, for instance, with the "wise support of government" but "without bureaucratic restrictions or interference . . . ."[18] Rather than recommending any sweeping changes, the report concentrated on tinkering with the system. It seemed to imply that the real question was how best to manage the country's resources to solve problems, and did not see existing problems as challenging anything essential in the structure of American society. By accepting New Deal reforms on the one hand, and asserting the desirability of limited government on the other, it essentially endorsed "modern Republicanism" without speaking directly to that issue. Occasional rhetorical attacks on "governmental paternalism" and expressions of faith in private enterprise passed for attacks on their Democratic opponents, and a few brief passages opposed Democratic proposals for "massive government intervention" as an effort to "meet the needs of the American economy of the sixties by refurbishing depression-born ideas of the thirties." But these efforts articulated few essential differences between the parties. As such, the report could at best only temporarily mollify party conservatives.[19]

That the committee tried to accommodate all points of view was particularly evident in its discussion of national security and peace. Freedom was the key to American foreign policy, it maintained, and the greatest threat was communism. This was the touchstone of conservative ideology, and the committee regarded "as a paramount goal of foreign policy the peaceful but unremitting support of the restoration of freedom to those who have been deprived of it by communism." At the same time, however, the committee recommended that the United States "insist on trade conditions that will help thaw the cold war." It supported the Eisenhower Administration's policy of a strong nuclear retaliatory force to prevent communist aggression, but warned against the "temptation to put too many eggs in one basket," embracing the arguments of administration critics by urging a "balanced" military force and the provision of "whatever is necessary to insure our security as a nation."[20]

The Republican Committee on Program and Progress undertook a difficult task, and in the short term it at least partially succeeded. Its report cast the Republican Party in a positive light, looking ahead to the sixties rather than backward to the twenties. The report fed the hopes of both liberal and conservative Republicans that Richard Nixon, virtually assured the nomination in 1960, might tilt his policies in their direction. But it failed to project a strong vision that differed markedly from that of the Democrats. It touted freedom, but failed to indicate what this meant other than anticommunism coupled with the relatively unfettered individual pursuit of wealth. And its frequently conflicted rhetoric revealed a persistent and perhaps unbridgeable difference between what liberals and conservatives wanted from the party. Liberals emphasized a desire to embrace particular programs to secure or advance social welfare and civil rights that would garner votes throughout northern states in the fall elections. In the words of Senator Jacob Javits, it "demonstrates again when a composite of our Party is taken, the thinking is Eisenhower (modern) thinking." Conservatives, on the other hand, seemed much more concerned about general statements of principle and resisted Eisenhower's moderate pragmatism. In the words of one conservative: "I hope that none of those connected with the present regime will get the idea that people are not waking up to the probably National objectives of our present leadership—namely, World Government (a Communist-Socialist World Government). May the devil take you, Eisenhower, and all the rest of the gang that are involved in this criminal operation."[21] A more balanced assessment from a conservative viewpoint came from future Goldwater supporter Karl Hess, who complained that the report was "the ultimate, it may be hoped, in the lemming-like Republican urge to accept

Democratic programs, tacitly approve Democratic principles, but to propose implementing them in a more businesslike manner. Yet . . . it was done so well and so conscientiously that most Republicans could find some rationalization for not opposing it."[22]

Percy admitted that the committee's report was, "of course, a *political* document. That is what we intended it to be." The Republican purpose, he wrote Eisenhower, was to "lift the ceiling over personal opportunity and strengthen the floor over the pit of personal disaster." Eisenhower gladly accepted the report, hoping that it would be the basis for the 1960 platform and increase public support for Republican candidates. He did not publicly acknowledge the undercurrent of discontent that coursed through Republican ranks.[23] In that sense the report was a failure. It was too much a public document. The question remained as to how ideologically inclusive the Republican tent might be.

House Republicans Respond

Soon after Meade Alcorn had announced the membership of the Committee on Program and Progress, *Human Events* reported Republican lawmakers' complaints that it was "just loaded with docile White House followers." Upset that Senator Everett Dirksen and Representative Charles Halleck were the only two members of Congress on the committee, conservative Republicans were miffed that the White House had engineered the committee appointments. To forestall any party revolt, and to communicate their own message of party unity, in mid-January 1960 House Republicans began a series of speeches on "Meeting the Challenges of the Sixties," inserting them into the *Congressional Record* and distributing them to the press. Wisconsin Republican John Byrnes, chairman of the House Republican Policy Committee, inaugurated the series by arguing that the Republican purpose should be to "clarify the differences in party responses to the challenges of the 1960's." Skirting particulars, but quoting from *Decisions for a Better America*, Byrnes asserted that the party was united in a sense of purpose that rejected excessive spending or "statism" at home.[24]

The remaining speakers focused on the Sino-Soviet peril and the need to encourage economic freedom. Congressman Bob Wilson of California warned that any change in national leadership or foreign policy would tempt the Russians to launch "Korean-type wars or nuclear blackmail." Recent surges in Russian economic growth, moreover, should not induce the United States to abandon its free society for greater centralization in an effort to match the Soviets. Representative Gerald Ford of Michigan echoed these themes, warning against "appearances of softness and domestic divisions which might spark the Communists into a miscalculation that could fuse a war." Quoting repeatedly from the Percy Report, and attacking Democratic spending plans, Ford concluded that our "ideas and faith can never be victorious over Communistic ideas through a greater application of materialism, statism, and socialism." Ford's Michigan colleague, Congressman Robert Griffin, lashed out at labor unions. While he grudgingly recognized their legality, Griffin argued that their power should be curbed because responsible labor-management relations were essential for victory over communism.[25]

Economic freedom and economic growth were the twin themes of Representatives John Rhodes of Arizona and Thomas Curtis of Missouri. In their eyes the battle was joined between irresponsible advocates of increased federal spending and the "octopuslike growth" of statism on the one hand, and the sober guardians of fiscal responsibility on the other. Statism, they argued, begun with the economic tyranny of the New Deal, encouraged federal subsidization, which in turn led to totalitarianism. The ideas of the Democrats, Rhodes cautioned, "can steal from our grasp the opportunities of the age ahead." Curtis joined the arguments of Griffin and Rhodes, positing that the "robber barons" in labor and Democratic programs threatened the free enterprise system. Those programs contained built-in spending spirals that promised massive fiscal deficits. In a peacetime economy, which he attributed to Republican leadership, such policies would be folly. In his concluding remarks, Representative Charles Halleck of Indiana returned to the theme that the Republican Party was best suited to meet the challenges of the sixties. It was, he insisted, united in a basic philosophy, whereas the Democrats were the party of expediency, of "gliberalities" without principles. At the same time, however, he urged Republicans to "disenthrall ourselves with attitudes that old ways of expressing ourselves are good enough."[26]

Another attempt to foster party unity and undercut criticism of Republican stewardship over the previous eight years came in June, with release of a task force report on "American Strategy and Strength" sponsored by the House Republican Policy Committee. Its membership drawn largely from Republican moderates and conservatives, the Policy Committee sought to discredit claims of a missile gap and correct perceptions outlined in the Gaither Report that the United States had slipped badly in its race with the Soviet Union. Although Congressman John Rhodes of Arizona claimed that the document was "nonpolitical," the report attacked Truman's policy of containment while praising Eisenhower's determination to tie American strategy to nuclear power. It also endorsed Eisenhower's policy of cutting back nondefense programs. Many of the research papers that accompanied the document encouraged contemporary efforts to define American goals and national purpose, arguing that mere opposition to communism was insufficient to sustain sound policy. They also lamented that postwar abundance had led the "great moderate masses of our society" to withdraw from politics, while "highly militant and well-organized minority groups control the body-politic." For too many Americans, a longing for security had replaced the quest for opportunity. Looking to the 1960 campaign, the report warned that the "great moral issue" of the year was "whether we will continue to hold a pessimistic view of the national self while ignoring our true faults or taking them much too lightly. Are we going to continue to display a naive confidence in Americanism and to deprecate constantly our illusions and complacency, and materialism? Or will we realistically defend the national interest of the United States and love what we truly are?"[27]

The report went to great lengths to discredit critics of Eisenhower's policies. Debate about the credibility of the nation's military deterrent was a luxury that should be eliminated before it led to national disaster. Without mentioning any names, the document particularly singled out Democrats campaigning for political office, whose criticisms forced the administration either to remain silent or to release classified information. These critics inadvertently aided the communists; American pessimism gave communism the initiative and stilled any offensive for freedom. Essayist Ralph de Toledano went even further in his research paper. He blasted the administration for being too moderate in its anticommunism and complained stridently that during the last four years militant anticommunists in the United States had been "systematically discredited and destroyed." Former communists who had turned anticommunist with a vengeance had found their "specialized knowledge" discredited in the "marketplace of ideas" and had been driven out of the respectable intellectual community, according to de Toledano. The real issue, the report concluded, was a need to recognize that the fundamental struggle was not one of greater defense spending or more missiles, but a question of national will and the clear formulation of national purpose that forged a consensus that everyone in public life endorsed.[28]

As this debate unfolded, Republican National Committee staffer Robert Humphreys prepared a confidential analysis and a set of policy recommendations for the White House that concluded: "*We must realize we are talking about a whole new world!*" Whichever party and candidate best understood the mood of the country would win the 1960 election, he warned, for voters were more consumed by fears than by specific policy concerns. Humphreys outlined seven basic fears: space, missiles, automation, cold war, integration, inflation, and bigness. They encompassed, he concluded, "what might be called a 'Mr. Cypher' complex in the average person. He feels lost and without guideposts; he suffers from a 'please go-away' psychosis; he over-indulges in the 'escapism' of religious revival, do-it-yourself, painting and photography, model making, etc., etc."[29] In the absence of any sharply defined national issues, this sense of unease or malaise *was* the central issue. Eisenhower, among others, had also detected this; his formation of a commission on national goals represented an attempt to defuse it. But Humphreys warned that merely trying to redefine or reformulate a consensus on traditional issues was insufficient. The successful party or candidate in 1960 would be the one that provided "hope and confidence" by advocating new and bold ideas. At a time when fear had replaced hope, Republicans needed to rekindle hope rather than exploit lingering fears if they were to retain power in the 1960s.[30]

Conservatives and the Republicans' Dilemma

Just how to do that was the problem Republicans confronted as they moved to develop a platform for the 1960 campaign. De Toledano's essay revealed their dilemma. Eisenhower's critics included not only Democrats, but conservative Republicans. Defending the administration's record to ward off Democratic attacks in 1960 would not mollify ideological conservatives, who saw little difference between "modern Republicanism" and Democratic alternatives. Yet Republican moderates feared that should conservatives' ideas become dominant the party would wither beyond recognition. Press Secretary James Hagerty warned the president that the public image of the G.O.P. was distorted, and urged Eisenhower to clarify what the party stood for and to fight for legislation that would return a Republican to the White House.

As the heir apparent, Richard Nixon labored to heal the widening breach. Nixon repeatedly characterized the chief issue for 1960 as the question of survival against the communist menace. In his eye, the issues of economic growth, civil rights, inflation, or urban redevelopment paled in contrast. But he spent much of his time and energy in the spring of 1960 on organizational tactics and strategy: organizing Nixon clubs to supersede or take over state organizations, exploring ways to attract independents and Democrats, and trying to develop a basic philosophy to undergird his campaign. Although party conservatives rejected not only liberalism but Eisenhower's "modern Republicanism," Nixon's dilemma was that he needed to embrace these ideas to reach successfully beyond the party. Without those votes, he stood little chance of victory in November. Nixon acknowledged his problem: "The critics have done such an effective job of creating the impression that I take positions solely for expediency that I think some drastic counter-offensive must be launched," he wrote in early April. "Of course," he admitted, "the very conservative Republicans are not going to be satisfied with the position that I take until they see what the choice is. . . . They are against any change whatsoever, including good change. Whenever we talk about good ends, they charge us with being 'me too.'"[31]

That was a dilemma not easily resolved, and G.O.P. conservatives brooded about their course of action in 1960. For one thing, conservative southern voters were beginning to take a close look at the Republican Party in the aftermath of the Little Rock crisis and continued civil rights activity. But to woo those Democrats, conservative positions were essential, and not just on civil rights. A related problem was the continuing discontent among conservatives with "modern Republicanism" and anyone who smacked of it.[32]

In December 1959 William F. Buckley Jr.'s *National Review* sponsored a debate over the question "Nixon or Not?" Although he believed 1960 to be a transition election, and feared that Nixon was too liberal, conservative author Ralph de Toledano nonetheless took the affirmative and argued that rejection of Nixon would only give comfort to the liberals. Nixon was, at least, strongly anticommunist. Robert Wood, president of Sears Roebuck, had warned two years earlier that the Republican Party was not the Eisenhower party. Insisting that the mood of the people had shifted, he urged the party to tap into a popular outcry against the rising federal presence in American life. Another correspondent complained that Eisenhower was "trying to cram 'Modern Republicanism' down our throats but you have nothing to sell us; no cause is identified with the term." Unrest was particularly rampant in the West and South. Reporting on the mood in the West, Nixon friend Loyd Wright pleaded that "I do hope that when it comes time for the Platform we can have representation from the vast hordes of Republicans who have supported the Party for years, and who have well nigh abandoned hope because of modern Republicanism and the crucifying of our real Republicans such as Joe McCarthy . . . ."[33]

Conservatives close to *National Review* argued that 1960 was the time for a clean break with "practical politics" and that loyalty to a truly conservative ideology should supersede all other considerations. "What use is it to spend energy to achieve political power," Frank Meyer asked, "if the positive result is going to be nothing better than a mild decrease in our rate of growth towards collectivism at home and our surrender to collectivism abroad?" Worse, those efforts drained off energies that would be better applied to "building a serious conservative opposition." A "principled boycott" of the 1960 presidential election would be preferable, in Meyer's opinion, to continued support of "modern Republicanism." That alone could assure that "1964 may promise a possibility of conservative victory, whether through recapture of the Republican Party or through creation of a new alignment of forces." Stanton Evans noted an even more sinister development when he observed that fear of hurting Richard Nixon's chances in 1960 had stilled conservative opposition to Nikita

Khrushchev's visit to the United States in 1959. This reflected, in Evans's view, "an alarming decline of will among conservatives—and considerable confusion among them as to immediate and final goals."[34]

Conservatives' efforts to influence Republican policy began in earnest as early as January 1960. The first salvo was the publication of Barry Goldwater's *The Conscience of A Conservative*. It quickly became a best seller. "Our objective," Goldwater wrote Stephen Shadegg, "is to take the onus from the word 'Conservative' and to make it acceptable to people who shy away from it today. . . . We can do this in a philosophical way, then we can attach the definitions and expositions to the concrete subjects of legislation." Within a year the paperback version had sold over 700,000 copies.[35]

The success of Goldwater's book emboldened ideological conservatives to carry their message directly to the Republican National Convention. Throughout the spring various Goldwater for President committees formed, flooding G.O.P. delegates with postcards and telegrams advocating his nomination. That most of these originated in the South created a difficult problem for the party. Goldwater advocates were committed and vocal, and they evoked a sympathetic response from many convention delegates, but most of them came from traditionally Democratic states—indeed, from states where the Republican Party was essentially nonexistent. They could cause turmoil at the convention, but did not have sufficient strength to carry their states for the Republican nominee. At least that was the prevailing political wisdom. The groundswell even surprised Goldwater, who fully expected to support Nixon for the nomination. Whether driven by ego or by conviction, or perhaps both, Goldwater began to waver. Complaining to fellow Arizonan (and future Supreme Court Justice) William Rehnquist that "in the last six weeks Dick has shown a decided tendency to drift far to the left . . . and this has caused such consternation among the party workers across the country that we must employ means to get him back on the right track," Goldwater hoped that the pressure would influence Nixon. If not, he concluded, "I would rather see the Republicans lose in 1960, fighting on principle, than I would care to see us win standing on grounds we know are wrong and on which we will ultimately destroy ourselves."[36]

By mid-April at least two states, South Carolina and Arizona, clearly intended to cast their convention votes for Goldwater. Richard Kleindienst, Arizona State Republican Chairman, warned Nixon aide Charlie McWhorter that the reason for this activity was a perception among "hard core" Republicans that Nixon was flirting with liberals. "According to Dick," McWhorter told Nixon, "these conservatives don't even want to accept a 'middle of the road' position, thinking that the voters are entitled to a clear choice between a pure liberal and a pure conservative." From California came a warning that these "are not crackpots. . . . They are people upon whom we must rely to punch door bells and to put up money." They wanted Nixon to articulate clearly conservative positions. "New Dealism, Fair Dealism and Modern Republicanism are nothing but socialism and fringes of communism." These groups could cause serious trouble for Nixon unless he seized their issues and expressed some "fundamental ideas." Without his leadership, either "Barry Goldwater will stampede the convention because, as you well know, thousands and thousands of people every day are singing his praises for furnishing Republican leadership, or, we will have another fiasco such as we had in 1948 and 1944, when Tom Dewey thought he could win by saying nothing."[37]

Nixon tried to mend fences behind the scenes, declaring that he would clarify his positions once the campaign began. More important was what he did not say. In his correspondence with Republicans around the country, Nixon never directly answered questions about his political philosophy, and evaded the conservatism issue completely. Instead, he focused on practical political questions—securing the nomination, suppressing open intraparty dissent, and essentially banking on the assumption that conservative Republicans would prefer him to any Democratic nominee. President Dwight D. Eisenhower expressed a similar conviction in a personal and confidential letter to his sister-in-law Lucy, who had warned that Nixon should pick Goldwater as his running mate if he wanted to capture conservative voters. In response, the president endorsed Nixon and expressed his lack of patience with political extremists. The United States, he observed, was "*not* going to the right." It was not going to return to a nineteenth-century view of political and economic affairs. Times had changed, and the vast majority of the American people, in Eisenhower's view, "are going to demand that the government do something to give them an opportunity to live out a satisfactory life."[38]

But Nixon could not quash conservatives' efforts. In April the midwestern Young Republicans endorsed Goldwater, and by May a Youth for Goldwater for Vice President group had formed. Organized by Douglas Caddy and Marvin Liebman, it was headquartered in Chicago (site of the Republican National Convention) and chaired by Robert Croll, a student at Northwestern University. By June "Americans for Goldwater" had formed, chaired by Clarence Manion. One of the members, Brent Bozell, outlined their objective: "Conservatives' most urgent task this election year—and there is no second job that remotely approaches it in importance—is to make sure their ideological position is preserved as a recognizable political alternative." In addition, South Carolina Republican chairman Aubrey Barker wrote convention delegates that "If there ever was a 'time for a change' it is now. It is high time for some plain 'cracker-barrel' decisions for a change, designed to protect the

American Individual, for a change. . . . All the candidates holding themselves out for presidential nomination, proffer us the same bowl of thin soup we have already endured so, so long . . . ." That change would come only if they supported Barry Goldwater for president. The John Birch Society also joined the effort, sending postcards endorsing Goldwater for President to Republican politicians around the country.[39]

The 1960 G.O.P. Convention

Even if they could not nominate Goldwater, these groups were determined to present their case against "modern Republicanism" to the convention. Goldwater himself appeared before the platform committee, urging it to adopt only a short statement of principles rather than lengthy positions on various issues. Goldwater released his "Suggested Declaration of Republican Principles" to the press, further publicizing the party's ideological fissures. His declaration was a ringing statement of broad conservative principles, perhaps epitomized by his insistence that "any government or political system which seeks to level all men to a common standard of achievement by penalizing ability, initiative, and thrift, is guilty of opposing God's will and our expressed recognition of the source of our freedoms." By now Goldwater seemed willing to believe that he could capture the vice-presidential nomination, remarking that he would have to have "marijuana in my veins" to pass up the opportunity.[40] Young G.O.P. conservatives, acknowledging that Nixon had earned the presidential nomination, were solidly behind Goldwater for vice president. Their position was important, for they provided evidence that support for Goldwater was not confined to fringe or extremist groups like the John Birch Society. Drawn from campuses around the country, they also formed a nexus for an organization that could reach beyond the South and West. As such, they represented a powerful force for change within the Republican Party. But despite their sudden emergence and evidence of grass-roots support, in 1960 they were still too new and their organization too skeletal to force significant concessions from Richard Nixon.[41]

A more immediate problem was Nelson Rockefeller. Although columnist Drew Pearson asserted that President Eisenhower had asked Rockefeller to withdraw from the presidential race, and despite Rockefeller's awareness that Richard Nixon would be the G.O.P. nominee, he remained active in presidential politics and sought to influence the platform adopted at the convention.[42]

Rockefeller, like his conservative counterparts, attacked Nixon where he was most vulnerable, on ideas and issues. On "Meet the Press" in June he challenged Nixon to define where he stood on the major issues of the day. Surely aware that a party debate on issues would be fractious, Rockefeller nonetheless called for just that as a final attempt either to derail Nixon's nomination or to shape the tenor of the campaign. In the April issue of *Foreign Affairs* Rockefeller outlined his ideas, essentially a condensation of the RBF Special Studies Project. "The central fact of our time," he warned, "is the disintegration of the nineteenth century political system, which for all its failings provided order, economic exchange and a means for settling disputes." In its place he advocated United States leadership, attention to the problems of Third World development, arms control, economic growth, civil defense, and the extension of freedom throughout the world. His ideas, in short, represented a progressive extension of "modern Republicanism."[43] Rockefeller's strategy was effective; Nixon worried about its impact.

In contrast to Rockefeller's positive vision of the future, Nixon's concentration on anticommunism seemed not only negative but dangerously narrow. Rockefeller's challenge also posed a strategic political dilemma for the vice president. While party conservatives fretted that Nixon was too liberal, he in turn worried that a careless response to Rockefeller would cast him as too conservative to attract the middle-of-the-road voters necessary for victory in the fall. Attorney General William Rogers, a Nixon friend and advisor, reviewed Rockefeller's June statements carefully, and concluded that there was little in them that Nixon could not endorse and that he should avoid any head-on disagreements. That was small consolation, however, and did not resolve the problem.[44]

In July Rockefeller advanced a series of proposals for an activist national government that embraced all sectors of the nation, "from depressed farm areas to disordered urban areas." In addition, the government should forge ahead in its protection of civil rights, guaranteeing every American the right to vote, equal educational and job opportunities, equal access to public facilities, and the right to live "where his heart desires and means permit." Seeking to paint Nixon as too passive for the 1960s, Rockefeller essentially urged the G.O.P. to adopt the conclusions of his Special Studies Project as its platform. The real danger from these proposals lay in their call for specific remedies for specific ills. The Percy Committee had managed to finesse or supersede party divisions by resorting to vague language about the value of individual freedom and the need for self-discipline. Now Rockefeller was calling for Republicans to be "as specific as we can be so that we don't back into what seems to be the trap of what the Democrats did of broad objectives promised to large groups of people and citizens but with no clear indication as to how they were going to carry them out."[45]

The struggle shifted to the 1960 platform committee. As Eisenhower's pick to chair that committee, Charles Percy was caught in the middle. Both Nixon and Rockefeller worked to shape the final document, but conservative delegates from the South and West dominated the committee and were determined not to perpetuate the Eisenhower philosophy. Percy's only solution was to avoid specifics and stick to vague generalities, but Rockefeller threatened a floor fight if his ideas were not incorporated into the platform. A floor fight, ironically, would offer conservatives a forum to advance their arguments for less government activism, a stronger policy of anti-communism, and opposition to civil rights activity in any form at the federal level. Such an event threatened to break open the party, and was something Nixon wanted to avoid if at all possible.[46]

That determination led to the controversial Nixon-Rockefeller meeting on Fifth Avenue in New York City on July 22, where the two men hammered out platform language that each could accept. While both later claimed victory, the result of that meeting was a more energetic G.O.P. platform that endorsed the need for change. Its emphasis on the 1960s as "an age of profoundest revolution" glossed over the scant praise for the achievements of the administration. Instead it heralded a series of transformations: "the birth of new nations, the impact of new machines, the threat of new weapons, the stirring of new ideas, the ascent into a new dimension of the universe—everywhere the accent falls on the new." A need for greater economic growth, development of new weapons technology, federal aid for public school construction, and active attention to human welfare issues formed the foundation of the G.O.P. platform. Even stronger measures for civil rights received approval, although not until conservatives led by John Tower of Texas inserted language acceptable to southerners, language that avoided any direct endorsement of the sit-ins. Despite a declaration that racial discrimination was immoral and unjust, the final platform advanced only a vague remedy: "As to those matters within reach of political action and leadership, we pledge ourselves unreservedly to its eradication."[47]

Acceptance of the platform by the convention led Vermont Royster to praise Nixon's political skills in using the platform to "cut the umbilical cord that bound him to the Eisenhower program." But while compromise had been reached, the realities of political power rather than ideological conviction kept conservatives within party ranks. The New York Times warned that Barry Goldwater's sentiments reached beyond fringe groups of the far right and were "privately expressed by many influential Republican conservatives supporting the Nixon candidacy."[48] Walter Judd's keynote speech on July 25 offered clear evidence of that.

A former missionary in China and a strident anticommunist, Judd was a hero to conservatives. His name had repeatedly surfaced as a vice-presidential possibility, a possibility kept alive by Nixon's failure to choose a candidate well before the convention. Insisting that the times were too perilous for the traditional attack blaming Democrats for everything wrong in the country, Judd presented a long and vigorous defense of freedom (in which he nonetheless bashed the Democrats). The country's very survival was at stake, he argued, and now was the time to build up the United States, not tear it down. There was, in his view, only one alternative to the communist conspiracy, and that was to "*win the cold war.*" To do that, "we must let loose in the world the dynamic forces of freedom in our day as our forefathers did in theirs, causing people everywhere to look toward the American dream." The United States must, in short, "develop a strategy for victory." Only a restrained government that promoted freedom, not centralization and statism, would succeed. Partisan and persistent, Judd provoked the assembled delegates to enthusiastic demonstrations. He also boosted his vice-presidential stock and emboldened conservatives to believe that Nixon now owed them that post.[49]

Although Nixon would disappoint them, conservatives found one more moment to demonstrate their convictions when another of their heroes, Barry Goldwater, was nominated for president. Goldwater commanded the hearts, if not the votes, of many delegates in the convention hall, and while his nomination was more symbolism than threat, it gave him a chance to seize the podium. Demonstrations, some barely contained, had erupted when Goldwater addressed the convention two days earlier "about the heart and soul of our great historic Party." Now, as he urged Republicans of all ideological persuasions to unite behind the candidacy of Richard Nixon, Goldwater warned conservatives to "show the strong sense of responsibility which is the central characteristic of the conservative temper." This election was not about getting even with other Republicans.

> We have lost election after election in this country in the last several years because conservative Republicans get mad and stay home. Now, I implore you, forget it. We have had our chance and I think the conservatives have made a splendid showing at this Convention. We have had our chance. We have fought our battle. Now, let's put our shoulders to the wheel of Dick Nixon and push him across the line.
>
> This country is too important for anyone's feelings. This country, in its majesty, is too great for any man, be he conservative or liberal, to stay home and not work just because he doesn't agree. Let's grow up, conservatives. If we want to take this Party back, and I think we can someday, let's get to work.[50]

Those efforts began even before the delegates went home.

In his speech accepting the Republican presidential nomination the next evening, Richard Nixon did not mention the struggle over "modern Republicanism" and the platform that had so consumed the party during the preceding months, but he did articulate a favorite theme of party conservatives (and one that Walter Judd had emphasized in his keynote address) when he argued that "It is time to speak up for America." Outlining the forces of aggression that would confront the next president, Nixon warned that a "race for survival" would characterize the 1960s and attacked the Democrats for their political cynicism—even as he admitted that the differences between the two parties involved means rather than goals. Seeking to undercut or discredit Democratic criticism of Republican policies by associating it with the "Communists running us down abroad," Nixon insisted that "while it is dangerous to see nothing wrong in America, it is just as wrong to refuse to recognize what is right about America."[51]

Nixon's anticommunist rhetoric did not really satisfy Republican conservatives, who were upset at his choice of Henry Cabot Lodge for vice president and were determined to oppose the forces of liberalism within the party that had shaped the 1960 platform. For the moment they appeared to heed Barry Goldwater's advice, knowing full well that Richard Nixon controlled the party apparatus and perhaps recognizing that the Democratic nominee and platform were a far more important concern in the short run. But as columnist Richard Rovere observed, conservatives seemed to respond more to the pleader (Goldwater) than to the plea. Many of the delegates remained determined to fasten a more conservative ideology on the G.O.P., and even Goldwater himself indirectly attacked the Republican plaform, arguing that Republicans could win in 1960 only by proclaiming "their devotion to a limited government which is the servant and not the master of the people." Indeed, supporters of Judd and Goldwater met in the Pick Congress Hotel before leaving Chicago to discuss a nationwide conservative movement and to formulate plans to take over the party by 1964. National Review even held out the possibility that conservatives might boycott the 1960 elections, warning that "conservatives now feel, and some will doubtless continue to feel through and beyond election day, that neither Kennedy-Nixon nor Democratic-Republican any longer offers conservatives a meaningful choice. If so, conservatives cannot in conscience support or vote for either one or the other, but must find other channels for giving expression to conservative principles."[52] Conservatives had tired of compromise and the politics of moderation.

The Sharon Conference
Chapter 3   and the Founding of YAF

As the fall campaign opened, and as young supporters of Goldwater sought direction, L. Brent Bozell warned the Arizona senator that he should not try to deliver the conservative vote to Nixon, come out against him, or urge conservatives to oppose the Republican presidential candidate. Bozell instead urged Goldwater to campaign around the country, to attack communism and the welfare state and remind voters that the Republican Party was hostile to conservative principles. "Slicing it this way," Bozell concluded, "Goldwater wins no matter what happens. If Nixon loses it will be because of *Nixon's* failure to create a conservative image—and not for any failure of yours or of the conservatives. Conversely, if he wins the claim can be cogently made that the conservatives elected him. Should Nixon later go off on a Liberal binge, conservatives can claim 'betrayal,' and make plans for next time." The key was to "create a political situation in which the opportunities for the victory of conservative principles are the greatest."[1] Aubrey Barker, chairman of the South Carolina Republican Party, was blunter: "One man alone has had the integrity and moral courage to break publicly with these fallacious, fruitless dogmas; Senator Barry Goldwater. Through his pronouncements he has exposed these new-deal creeds for the barren theories they are, and has shown us the course we can follow with national self-respect."[2]

    This prospect for change led Republican moderate Charles Percy of Illinois to address student leaders at the late August meeting of the National Student Congress in Minneapolis about "New Challenges and New Opportunities."

Percy urged young people to play a larger role in politics and to implement the principles of the Republican platform. The platform, Percy said, "tells something of the nature of our times and of the questions which puzzle all of us and with the problems which all of us face." He observed that there was a "swelling tide of revolution" across the globe, with the young frequently in the vanguard of change. They were "eager for action, crying for leadership, groping for answers." Protesters should be constructive, develop a sense of self-discipline, and encourage self-reliance. Individual action, not the statism of a Soviet Union, was the key to a bright future.[3] The convergence of a principled conservative opposition to "modern Republicanism" and youthful conservative activists at the 1960 G.O.P. convention in Chicago led directly to Sharon, Connecticut in September 1960 and the founding of Young Americans for Freedom.

Organizing for Change

Members of the Youth for Goldwater effort in Chicago, along with a few Nixon supporters and others who had pushed Walter Judd's name forward for vice president, moved quickly to maintain their momentum. The Judd for Vice President headquarters in the Pick Congress Hotel had adjoined that of Youth for Goldwater. Marvin Liebman, friend to William F. Buckley Jr. and public relations guru for many right-wing causes during the 1950s, had organized the Judd efforts. During the course of the convention both Liebman and Buckley (who was in Chicago to cover the convention for *National Review*) met Youth for Goldwater leaders. David Franke and Douglas Caddy particularly impressed them, and they took the two under their wing. Franke became an intern at *National Review*, while Caddy joined Liebman's public relations firm. As the convention ended, Liebman and former New Jersey governor Charles Edison met with the executive committee of Youth for Goldwater and a few other conservative activists in the Columbia Room of the Pick Congress Hotel. They urged Caddy and his colleagues to unite conservative students in a formal organization, and Edison contributed $500 to further the cause.[4]

Within days an Interim Comittee for a National Conservative Youth Organization sprang into existence. Members included James Abstine, Douglas Caddy, Robert Croll, David Franke, George Gaines, Robert Harley, James Kolbe, Richard Noble, Suzanne Regnery, Clendenin Ryan, Scott Stanley, John Weicher, and Brian Whelan. Although they met in Chicago, only Weicher, Whelan, and Regnery were from the immediate area. Caddy and Franke called New York City home; the rest of the Interim Committee came from Indiana, Illinois, Louisiana, the District of Columbia, Arizona, California, New Jersey, and Kansas. On August 16 they issued a call for a meeting to be held at Great

Elm, the Buckley family estate in Sharon, Connecticut, September 9–11. This invitation to an "initial organizing effort" went out to 120 "outstanding youth leaders across the Nation" who were known "to be active and influential Conservatives." Franke and Caddy had found many of them during their loyalty oath efforts earlier in the year. Others had written letters to *Human Events* or the Young Republican National Federation. They formed the nucleus of the Sharon delegates. The tone of the call was apocalyptic:

> America stands at the crossroads today. Will our Nation continue to follow the path towards socialism or will we turn towards Conservatism and freedom? The final answer to this question lies with America's youth. Will our youth be more conservative or more liberal in future years? You can help determine the answer to this question.
>
> Now is the time for Conservative youth to take action to make their full force and influence felt. By action we mean *political action!* An inter-collegiate society for Conservative youth has been in operation for several years and has been most successful in bringing about a Conservative intellectual revival on the campus. Many feel that now is the time to organize a complementary nationwide youth movement which would be designed almost solely for political action—implementing and coordinating the aspirations of Conservative youth into a dynamic and effective political force.[5]

"The Sharon Conference," announced its organizers, "can be of historic importance. The formation of a national Conservative youth organization—utilizing the ready-made enthusiasm of this National election year—will be a great step forward for Conservatism." Much of the planning was done by Douglas Caddy, with help from other members of the Interim Committee. Attendees paid their own travel and living expenses, although meals were provided at no cost.[6]

David Franke also called for business support. In an essay, "Revolt on the Campus: Why Businessmen Should Support Conservative Student Enterprises," he argued that businessmen who opposed the welfare state should support the formation of conservative youth groups. Issued on the letterhead of the McGraw-Edison Company Committee for Public Affairs, whose address was identical to that of the Interim Committee, Franke's essay insisted that organizations "such as the Intercollegiate Society of Individualists, the National Student Committee for the Loyalty Oath, and Youth for Goldwater" were "proof that conservatism has returned to the campus." Businessmen should volunteer their services as advisors and contribute financially, for businessmen and students were "fighting for the same ideals of individual liberty and economic freedom. . . . As the socialists proved, the campus is the key to the future."[7]

The invitation also outlined an agenda that included speeches from Brent

Bozell on "Why a Conservative Political Youth Organization Is Needed," along with panel discussions about projecting conservatism on campus and exploring what might be the most effective organizational structure for such a group. Delegates screened two films: the "Wisconsin Story," an antilabor film about the infamous Kohler strike; and "San Francisco Riots," on the experience of the House Un-American Activities Committee the previous May in San Francisco. Charles Edison, former governor of New Jersey, head of McGraw-Edison, and a leading financial contributor to the China Lobby and other conservative causes, addressed the delegates. In his presentation, Edison argued that the "American Eagle needs two strong wings to fly. The left one is too strong now. We need to strengthen the right wing so the Eagle can fly straight." The host, and hero to many delegates, William F. Buckley Jr., also spoke to the gathering at the conclusion of the conference.[8]

The Sharon Statement

The centerpiece of the delegates' agenda was the preparation and ratification of a statement of principles. Although the bright blue skies, the warm September sun, and the broad lawns of Great Elm hardly seemed the setting from which to launch an ideological crusade, the delegates who gathered there were firmly committed to the conservative cause and believed that ideas were critical to that cause. They debated questions of membership, dues, location of the national office, and the size of the national board all day Saturday. Their two central concerns, however, focused on the purpose and name of the organization. After dinner with some of their more senior hosts, including Buckley, Frank Meyer, Marvin Liebman, and Brent Bozell, they split into small groups to discuss parts of the constitution. According to Lee Edwards, who was at Sharon, Stanton Evans, Carol Dawson, and a few others went off to write the statement of principles, a first draft of which Evans had composed during his flight from Indianapolis. The group made few changes to Evans's draft, which the delegates approved Sunday morning after church services. The phrase "God-given free will" evoked much discussion, but it remained in the final document. Only the choice of a name remained. Militants argued for "Young Conservatives of America." Others, led by Franke and Edwards, feared it would scare off liberal anticommunists and libertarians. They pushed for Young Americans for Freedom. Franke in particular urged the group to "keep title to the word 'freedom' and not let the Left capture it as they had 'democracy' and other useful words." The other difficulty was defining "young." Initially the age cutoff was set at 27, then raised to 35, and later to 39. Although most of the delegates were under 30, they feared excluding numerous young people "on the way up," and

39 paralleled the age limit for membership in the Young Republicans. On a 44–40 vote, Young Americans for Freedom became the organization's official name.[9]

They met, Evans noted, in a "time of moral and political crisis." Because of that crisis conservatives needed to "affirm certain eternal truths." What followed was terse, but revealed an ideological perspective significantly at odds with mainstream political thought. Their arguments and, they insisted, life itself were grounded in the "individual's use of his God-given free will." Liberty was "indivisible," and political freedom could not "long exist without economic freedom." In this tradition, government had only three essential functions: the "preservation of internal order, the provision of national defense and the administration of justice." Whenever government strayed beyond those "rightful functions," its accumulation of power diminished order and liberty.[10]

These conservative students held to a very limited role for government, at least in certain areas. They believed that governmental powers rested on a narrow constitutional base, and that the Constitution was at heart a device to restrain government from the accumulation and exercise of power. Consequently, they embraced an expansive definition of states' rights. This, they insisted, was the "genius" of the Constitution. It delegated very little to the federal government, reserving the rest to the states or to the people. Joined to this limited view of governmental power was an undying faith in the market economy. The iron laws of supply and demand, they argued, represented the "single economic system compatible with the requirements of personal freedom and constitutional government." Whenever government interfered with that economy, it reduced the "moral and physical strength of the nation." This was a thinly disguised attack on the notion of a progressive income tax, a system YAFers believed diminished incentive and corrupted individual integrity and "moral autonomy."[11]

The Sharon Statement concluded with a warning that "the forces of international Communism are, at present, the greatest single threat to these liberties." Only by pursuing a policy of victory over communism, rather than coexistence, could the United States successfully defend its way of life. All foreign policy ventures should be judged by one criterion: did they advance the interests of the United States? A strong defense was all that stood between national sovereignty and slavery to communism, for freedom existed only when citizens militantly defended their rights.[12]

Ironically, the characterization of the United States in the Sharon Statement was similar to that adopted by Students for a Democratic Society in their Port Huron Statement two years later. Both groups saw the early sixties as a time of great crisis and choice for Americans. Both believed that an earnest ideological crusade was essential to change the country's course and deliver the promise inherent in its founding. A fundamental difference between the two groups, however, lay in their respective paradigms of power. Both attacked the prevailing liberal paradigm. SDSers postulated the need for structural change not only to alter the ruling elite, but to change the paradigm that underlay the exercise of power in the United States. YAFers sought primarily to substitute a conservative elite for a liberal one. Theirs was an ideological criticism, not a structural one. They valued power, not process. William F. Buckley Jr. alluded to this question of power when he hailed the emergence of Young Americans for Freedom in *National Review* with a mixture of puffery and perception. He not only endorsed the Sharon Statement as a credo for all members, but reveled at the arrival of a generation of conservative activists.

> But what is so striking in the students who met at Sharon is their appetite for power. Ten years ago the struggle seemed so long, so endless, even, that we did not even dream of victory. Even now the world continues to go left, but all over the land dumbfounded professors are remarking the extraordinary revival of hard conservative sentiment in the student bodies. It was Goldwater, not Nixon or Eisenhower, who was the hero of the bright and dominant youth forces at the Chicago Convention. It is quixotic to say that they or their elders have seized the reins of history. But the difference in psychological attitude is tremendous. They talk about *affecting* history; we have talked about *educating* people to want to affect history.[13]

Although the Sharon Statement outlined in stark language a conservative credo to which Young Americans for Freedom subscribed, drawing upon a set of draft bylaws for an organization of Conservative Youth of America, it was perhaps as significant for what it did not include as for what it did. It emphasized antistatism and anticommunism through a celebration of liberty and individual freedom, but insisted that both would be secured only if the right people exercised power. Nowhere did it address the principles of due process, equal protection under the law, or the general welfare. More than anything else, it was a statement of faith, of conviction. Its framers simply asserted that a withdrawal of the state from the affairs of individual citizens would promote freedom and advance the common good. Just how that might occur they never made clear.

In addition, the Sharon Statement addressed few specific issues or contemporary problems. Presumably its ideological tenets were universal, but this failure to grapple with specific cases obscured some serious divisions among the young conservatives who gathered at Great Elm. These later surfaced when moderate conservatives, objectivists, libertarians, and others divided over specific policies and processes. The gloss given conservative beliefs by the Sharon Statement could not persist once the realities of politics and power intruded. Unlike SDS's Port Huron Statement, which was an analytical critique of American society that evolved into an ideology, YAF's Sharon Statement sought to express an ideology that presumed an analytical critique. As Richard Cowan, a member of YAF's board of directors and a student at Yale, proclaimed, it was a "Declaration of war against the forces of campus collectivism who would impose upon us facism in the name of Liberalism, and a national purpose as a substitute for freedom."[14]

The one specific issue addressed by the Sharon Statement was anticommunism. Indeed, in many respects this was the core of the document. But here antistatism gave way to statism, and the document seemed to legitimate almost any action by the state to combat communism. Victory was their goal, and they believed that nothing should stand in its way. This apparent contradiction reflected the failure of the document to recognize the complexity of political life. Content to stand behind simplistic ideological barricades, the Sharon delegates refused to test their principles on complex issues. How, for instance, did one reconcile the centrality of individual freedom with a reliance on states' rights in the question of race relations? Were they willing to countenance federal intervention to secure justice for African American citizens? The document seemed to answer the question by focusing instead on the market economy. That is, segregation was a question of interpersonal relations; what was paramount were *economic* rights. Apparently unaware of, or at least unwilling to admit, the state's historic role in maintaining competition, the delegates at Sharon embraced the doctrine of *laissez faire* with a vengeance. Only the market economy, in their view, provided "the requirements of personal freedom and constitutional government." The question of means—of just how this would occur—went begging.

The Sharon Statement, in short, sought to provide an ideological umbrella for a new conservative activism. As such it was a fusion of competing conservative credos. Stanton Evans later remarked that the "idea was to get a declaration which was broadly representative but internally coherent."[15] Any document that seeks to define the true faith of a movement is exclusionary. It defines not only those within the cause, but also those unfit to march under its banner. The fusionist approach adopted by Evans and the other delegates at Sharon was an effort to draw conservatives of varying persuasions together in the belief that there existed an ideological core to which all could subscribe. So long as conservatives remained content to discuss broad philosophical questions it remained fairly effective. But when they turned to particular matters of policy, or sought to exercise power, the fusion frayed.

YAF's Ideological Heritage

The intellectual roots of the Sharon Statement, with its amalgam of traditionalism, libertarianism, and anticommunism, did not originate with the gathering at Great Elm that September. The document drew upon a conservative intellectual legacy that had been developing throughout the 1950s and which was familiar to many of the delegates. All of its permutations are not relevant here, but certain underlying (and often conflicting) themes shaped the intellectual horizons of the men and women who met at Sharon.

Historian George Nash delineated three key elements in postwar conservatism, all of which found their way into the Sharon Statement. First was the classical liberal or libertarian outlook. Opposed to any expansion of the state, which they equated with socialism, libertarians (or "libs") championed private enterprise and individual liberty. A second strain of conservative thought, commonly called traditionalism, grew out of the writings of men like Richard Weaver, Russell Kirk, and others. Traditionalists (or "trads") opposed what they saw as the ruthlessly secular society of the 1930s and 1940s and demanded a return to "traditional" religious, ethical, and moral values. Finally, there was an overriding commitment to anticommunism. Its most militant advocates were ex-radicals like James Burnham, Frank Meyer, and Whittaker Chambers. For these individuals, the threat of communism dwarfed all other considerations.[16]

Perhaps the underlying theme, not only for these conservative intellectuals but for the youthful activists as well, was best expressed in Richard Weaver's book *Ideas Have Consequences*. Published in 1948, it argued that decadence, not progress, best defined man's transition to the present. "In the final reach of analysis," Weaver wrote, "our problem is how to recover that intellectual integrity which enables men to perceive the order of goods." And the problem lay with the middle class. "Loving comfort, risking little, terrified by the thought of change," Weaver argued that "its aim is to establish a materialistic civilization which will banish threats to its complacency. It has conventions, not ideals; it is washed rather than clean."[17]

American society had become too centrifugal; modern man suffered "from a severe fragmentation of his world picture." As a consequence, individuals knew particulars rather than general principles, "techniques rather than . . . ends." Egotism and selfishness had eroded any sense of obligation to the larger society. The dogma of progress, "the Great Stereopticon," was the "great projection machine of the bourgeois mentality." The West had become spoiled, and as a consequence was not attuned to the dangers of communism. Unlike us, the "Bolsheviks . . . have never lost sight of the fact that life is a struggle." Weaver called for greater discipline in American society, as well as for an offensive against the barbarities of communism. "We live in an age," he lamented, "that is frightened by the very idea of certitude, and one of its really disturbing outgrowths is the easy divorce between words and the conceptual realities which our right minds know they must stand for."[18]

In 1959 Weaver updated his argument in an essay "Up from Liberalism." For Weaver, perhaps the greatest fallacy of liberalism was its belief in the perfectability of man. Evil was a palpable presence, he insisted, and an understanding of original sin was essential to an understanding of mankind. It was "a parabolical expression of the immemorial tendency of man to do the wrong thing when he knows the right thing." Peace and plenty may be the ideal for socialists, but more often than not men reject them for "crime and aggrandizement." Eternal and universal truths were vital if societies were to survive, and Weaver warned that an excessive reliance on majoritarian rule too often led to evil. "Democracy finds it difficult ever to say that man is wrong if he does things in large majorities. . . . this notion has to be rejected . . . ." Weaver counseled restraint.[19]

Young conservatives also drew upon the writings of Russell Kirk for intellectual sustenance. Kirk, whose *The Conservative Mind* had been at the forefront of conservative thought in the 1950s, argued for a Burkean traditionalism. Like Weaver, Kirk asserted the importance of universal truths that transcended time and place. He outlined a six-part philosophy that emphasized divine intent, the need for order and classes, a connection between property and freedom, the importance of restraint and control of the will, an assertion that "change and reform are not identical," and an opposition to "uniformity and equalitarianism."[20] Particularly galling to Kirk was the liberal embrace of levelling and its contempt for tradition. The underlying basis of conservatism, for Kirk, "had to be understood in terms of conformity to what was universal in Burke and not what was exceptional in America."[21] This attack on liberal exceptionalism ran counter to prevailing currents of political thought in the 1950s and provided both a spark and a grounding for the new generation of activists.

Another strain of conservatism found among the intellectual baggage of those at Sharon was the objectivism of Ayn Rand. Rand's philosophy, essentially a defense of anarchic individualism (and selfishness), emphasized the centrality of the marketplace. Unlike Weaver or Buckley, Rand exalted the dollar over the divine. Her followers were essentially libertarians, and they found nourishment in what they saw as a libertarian undercurrent in Goldwater's *The*

Conscience of a Conservative. Indeed, perhaps to dramatize their opposition to the statism of liberals and moderates, many conservatives in 1960 embraced elements of libertarianism. In the words of one former objectivist: "Objectivism and its ethic of self-sufficiency and achievement was intoxicating to the sons and daughters of the middle class, graduating from college at the end of the Eisenhower era. The watertight, compartmentalized structure of Randian logic was every bit as self-delineated as that of Karl Marx . . . ." Rand herself had argued that "a free mind and a free market are corollaries."[22]

Only after the conservative revival gathered steam did the divisions within conservative ranks become open and fractious. Then the underlying anarchism of objectivism led to disarray among young conservatives. But the difference between the conservatism of William F. Buckley Jr. and the *National Review* on the one hand and that of Ayn Rand and fans of *Atlas Shrugged* or *The Fountainhead* on the other had always been profound. Each had denounced the other during the fifties, and the followers of both were committed to a conservative revival on their own terms in the sixties. "Many Objectivist students joined YAF," admitted one Rand follower, "for the simple reason that they had no place else to go in order to engage in political activities, and there is no question that most of them joined with the explicit intention of transforming YAF into an Objectivist-oriented political institution."[23] For the short term, their common commitment to private property and free enterprise bound them together.

A third strain of conservative thought that influenced delegates to the Sharon Conference was the fusionism of Frank Meyer, a philosophy that sought to find common ground from among the conflicting camps for a synthesis of conservative principles. A former communist who had then turned more toward libertarianism, Meyer had attacked traditionalists like Kirk in the 1950s. Individual freedom remained the cornerstone of his political philosophy, and Meyer embraced an abhorrence of statism that reflected the views of Weaver and other traditionalists. Like them, he insisted that the state had only three legitimate objectives: national defense, domestic order, and the administration of justice. He called for a "*conscious* conservatism."[24]

> In a fundamental sense the dominant forces in American life today
> are revolutionary, that is, they are directed towards the destruction of
> the principles of Western civilization and the American tradition.
> The politics of New Dealism, Fair Dealism, and New Republicanism
> are directed towards the strengthening of the State and the diminu-
> tion of the person. The positivist and materialist philosophy of our ed-
> ucational theory and practice, of our radio and television and press, of
> our academic and intellectual circles, eats away at the fabric of princi-

ple and belief which is Western civilization. . . . For the conservative
to compromise with it is to give up his reason for being.[25]

While Meyer's efforts sounded more like a compromise than a system of belief,
they found an effective voice at Sharon in the person of Stanton Evans and
were reflected in the cryptic phraseology of the Sharon Statement.

The final piece of the ideological heritage the young conservative activists
brought to Sharon was a fanatical dedication to anticommunism. This was evident not only in the authors they had read, like Whittaker Chambers, but in
their prior activities, like the Loyalty Oath Committee. Perhaps more than anything else, except possibly a loathing for what they considered liberal fallacies,
their anticommunism bound them together and made possible agreement despite the conflicting strains of conservative thought. As historian John Diggins
has noted, theirs was primarily a cold war and anticommunist conservatism. Not
only were there many former CIA connections among their elders; men like
Buckley and William Rusher had strongly supported the internal security crusades of the 1950s.[26]

Conservative Elder Statesmen

A small coterie of conservative elder statesmen guided these events—some from
the shadows, others in the spotlight. The inspiration for all of this was William
F. Buckley Jr., who sought to exercise a guiding influence while remaining in
the shadows. It was no coincidence that the Sharon Conference met at his family's estate in September 1960. Ever since his bombastic *God and Man at Yale*
in 1951 Buckley had insisted that certain truths were self-evident, foremost
among them individual freedom. "Individualism is dying at Yale," he had written, "and without a fight." Patrick J. Buchanan, an influential conservative
voice in later decades but not an early YAFer, highlighted the importance of
Buckley for his generation.

> It is difficult to exaggerate the debt conservatives of my generation
> owe *National Review* and Bill Buckley. Before I read *NR*, there was vir-
> tually nothing I read that supported or reinforced what I was coming
> to believe. We young conservatives were truly wandering around in a
> political wilderness, wondering if there was anyone of intelligence and
> wit, any men of words, who thought and felt and believed as we did.
> Other than that one magazine, young conservatives had almost
> nowhere to turn for intellectual and political sustenance. For us, what
> *National Review* did was take the word *conservatism*, then a synonym
> for stuffy orthodoxy, Republican stand-pat-ism and economic self-
> interest, and convert it into the snapping pennant of a fighting faith.[27]

Where Buckley provided a messianic presence, his publisher provided a dose of practical politics. Long involved in Republican Party politics, a graduate of Princeton and Harvard Law School, William Rusher connected the conservative philosophers Buckley gathered at *National Review* with budding conservative activists among the Young Republicans. "I think I can assure you," he wrote Ned Cushing of the Young Republican National Federation (YRNF), "that there is no necessary conflict between the objectives of this bunch and the YRNF. It is a serious bunch, highly conservative and generally oriented along *National Review* lines." If Buckley was determined to effect an intellectual revolution, Rusher was committed to a political revolution. Rusher hailed from the Midwest, the descendant of a socialist grandfather. At Princeton he had supported Wendell Willkie and then Tom Dewey. After the Alger Hiss case he moved rightward, driven by a commitment to anticommunism. Looking back on the early sixties, Libertarian Murray Rothbard later wrote that the early conservative movement "combined a traditionalist and theocratic approach to 'Moral values,' occasional lip service to free-market economics, and an imperialist and global interventionist foreign policy dedicated to the glorification of the American state and the extirpation of world Communism. Classical liberalism remained only as rhetoric, useful in attracting business support, and most of all as a fig leaf for the grotesque realities of the New Right."[28] As the following section will illustrate, it was the twin sirens of Buckley's inspired philosophical example and Rusher's political connections that brought most of the future YAFers to Sharon in September 1960.[29]

Two other individuals were instrumental in laying the groundwork for Young Americans for Freedom. One was Marvin Liebman. A former member of the Young Communist League and the CPUSA from 1938–1945, Liebman left the Party to protest its expulsion of Earl Browder. He became an anti-Stalinist, but not yet an anticommunist. His search for purpose and a cause led him to the Irgun Zvai Leumi, the Israeli underground organization, then to the American League for a Free Palestine, and by 1948 to the United Jewish Appeal. Still a leftist, by the early 1950s he came to see the Soviet Union as a worldwide threat largely as a result of conversations with Eleanor Lipper, who had been in the Soviet gulags. Feeling betrayed, Liebman became a dedicated anticommunist and entered fund-raising with Harold Oram. Organization of the Aid to Refugee Chinese Intellectuals led him to Charles Edison, Walter Judd, and Mrs. Alfred (Ida) Kohlberg, stalwart anticommunists and political conservatives. Liebman then organized the Committee of One Million to Keep Red China out of the United Nations, perhaps the "most successful and long-lived, anti-communist conservative organizations in modern politics." Work on the Committee of One Million led him to William F. Buckley Jr. In short order Liebman became the wizard of direct-mail fund-raising. "By then," Liebman wrote later, "I had learned a political rule of thumb: perception is more important than reality."[30]

By 1957 Liebman had struck out on his own, forming Marvin Liebman Associates with initial funding from Charles Edison. He was now "ready to take over the American Right." Embracing the conservatism of Buckley and *National Review*, Liebman moved from a communist collectivism to a strident individualism. He also made contact with younger conservatives, particularly Douglas Caddy and David Franke. In July 1960 Liebman was in Chicago to boost Walter Judd's vice-presidential chances at the Republican national convention. There he encountered Robert Croll and other Youth for Goldwater activists. "Caddy and his young colleagues," Liebman reflected later, "were ambitious, sophisticated, smart, and, I was soon to learn, ruthless in pursuing their political agenda." Caddy soon went to work for Liebman, and from Liebman's offices in New York he organized the Sharon Conference. Liebman joined them at Sharon, and became a godfather to Young Americans for Freedom.[31]

The other "senior" individual instrumental in the formation of Young Americans for Freedom was M. Stanton Evans, principal author of the Sharon Statement. Although Evans was only twenty-six years old, he had considerable journalistic experience with an array of conservative publications prior to the conference at Sharon. A Yale graduate, he had served as assistant editor of *The Freeman*, as a member of the editorial staff of *National Review*, as managing editor of *Human Events*, and as publications director for the Intercollegiate Society of Individualists. In 1960 he was chief editorial writer for the *Indianapolis News*. Close to William F. Buckley Jr., Evans also had connections in Young Republican circles.[32]

By 1960 Evans had already spent several years attacking liberal positions and ideology. "The conservative," Evans argued, "believes ours is a God-centered, and therefore an ordered universe; that man's purpose is to shape his life to the patterns of order proceeding from the Divine center of life; and that, in seeking this objective, man is hampered by a fallible intellect and vagrant will."[33] He argued that Americans for Democratic Action (ADA), which he considered socialist, was taking over the Republican Party outside the South and had become a bulwark for statism. "Unless vigorous political action is taken to halt the ADA drive," Evans warned in 1958, "America may soon be plunged into the depths of a collectivism from which there is no return." He also bemoaned the "intellectual slither" and lack of "sanity" evident in the modern temper. "Metaphysical speculations" had replaced a concern for revealed truths. This had led to flabby thinking and a passive foreign policy, both of which endangered the nation. By early 1960 Evans believed that a conservative revival was imminent. "This disagreeable poltergeist," he observed, "long silent and docile . . . of late has even been making off with the young." In the summer Evans met with William Rusher to explore the possibility of organizing those young conservatives. Rusher insisted that "just possibly the time is here when something should be done to integrate some of the good things (and people!) that are now visible in various parts of the country."[34] This led them both to Sharon.

The Young Activists

The early YAF leadership reflected an ideological commitment, not an irrational dysfunctionalism as their liberal critics frequently claimed. More than ninety of them spent a weekend together in Sharon, Connecticut in September 1960, ultimately approving a statement of conservative principles—the Sharon Statement. They believed firmly in those principles, and took them to be working guidelines for a fruitful life. They represented an activist elite of young conservatives, albeit somewhat self-anointed. Several had already established small networks of interpersonal connections in various political circles, networks that grew in time to form a New Right. Many later carved out successful careers in politics. Few deviated from their conservative tenets. Who were their leaders? Where did they come from? How did they get to Sharon?[35]

The two men who initiated the call to meeting, Douglas Caddy and David Franke, had already attached themselves not only to conservative causes (such as the National Student Loyalty Oath Committee in 1959 and 1960) but to leading conservatives as well. Born March 23, 1938 in Long Beach, California, Caddy attended high school first in Houston, Texas and then in New Orleans, where he graduated in 1956. Caddy had admired Senator Joseph McCarthy, circulated petitions supporting McCarthy's efforts in New Orleans while a sophomore in high school, and was an inveterate writer of letters to the editor in support of such conservative causes as the Bricker Amendment. He later became a volunteer worker for Phoebe and Kent Courtney's early publication, *Free Men Speak*, which grew out of that petition drive. In 1956 he entered the School of Foreign Service at Georgetown University. Active in student affairs in Georgetown, he served as class treasurer (while a classmate, Tongsun Park, was president), was twice elected class president, lost a bid for student body president, and later became editor of a school publication, *The Foreign Service Courier*. As a sophomore he received a journalism scholarship from the Intercollegiate Society of Individualists, designed to "establish conservative press representation in the Nation's Capital." This led him to a part-time position at the very conservative *Human Events*, where he labored with later colleagues and fellow scholarship recipients David Franke and William Schulz. In these years the

managing editor of *Human Events* was M. Stanton Evans, a recent Yale graduate and primary author of the Sharon Statement.[36]

In December 1959, while a senior at Georgetown, Caddy published his first
article with Evans, then editorial writer for the *Indianapolis News*. The article,
"Hugo Black: A Study of Conflict," attacked Black and the Supreme Court for
"Constitution-changing jurisprudence." Subtitled "The Story of the Ku Klux
Klan's Favorite 'Liberal,'" the article highlighted Black's background with the
Klan before his appointment to the Court. None of this was new, but the authors argued that Black had frequently backflipped in his legal opinions—
opinions marked, they insisted, by "a consistent pattern of left-wing voting."
Caddy and Evans particularly attacked Black's record on internal security cases,
charging that he voted "in favor of Communist or pro-Communist defendants
in ten internal security rulings by the Court within a 19-month period." Black,
in their view, had become the "master of self-contradiction" and had ingrati-
ated himself "with the two outstanding subversive groups of 20th-century
America—the Ku Klux Klan and the Communist party."[37]

Caddy was also active in Republican Party politics while at Georgetown.
He became president of the Conservative Students Forum and he reactivated
the Young Republican club on campus, which later tried to wrest control of the
Young Republican National Federation from Eisenhower supporters. Caddy
eventually helped create the College Young Republican Federation of the District of Columbia, for whom he served as convention arrangements chair in
1959. In 1960 he was vice chair of the District of Columbia Youth for Nixon,
chaired by Robert Bauman. He also founded the National Student Committee
for the Loyalty Oath, and published an essay on its work in *The Congressional
Digest*. Before graduating in 1960, Caddy published his first article on national
politics in *National Review*. A broadside on Louisiana politics, particularly the
campaign of Governor Earl Long, the article caught the attention of Washington journalist Forrest Davis. Davis was then busy arguing against the admission of "Red China" to the United Nations, and the Committee of One Million Against the Admission of Communist China into the UN hired Caddy to
help Davis with his research. The Committee of One Million was run by Marvin Liebman, who in 1960 hired Caddy to a position in his public relations firm.
Caddy solicited recommendation letters from William Rusher, who called him
a "strong-minded and able young man, militantly and intelligently conservative." Under Liebman his formal title was Executive Director of the Committee on Public Affairs of the McGraw-Edison Company. Although he officially
worked for Charles Edison, his office, like that of Young Americans for Freedom, was inside Liebman's suite at 343 Lexington Avenue in New York.[38]

David Franke, who with Caddy was responsible both for the National

Student Loyalty Oath Committee and for the organization of the Sharon Conference, also had a rather extensive record of political involvement prior to the formation of Young Americans for Freedom. Born in 1938 in Houston, Texas, the oldest of three children, he came from an apolitical family. Franke graduated in June 1957 from Del Mar Junior College in Corpus Christi, Texas, where he edited the college newspaper and wrote a number of sharply worded editorials on such subjects as the Kohler strike and federal aid to education. Several of them were reprinted in *Human Events*, *The Houston Chronicle*, and *The Freeman*. He later spent two weeks as a scholarship student at the Freedom School in Colorado Springs. Franke also received a scholarship in political journalism from the Intercollegiate Society of Individualists, and enrolled in George Washington University. But after one semester he quit, "convinced . . . that college is a complete waste of time, effort, and money." He worked four days each week at *Human Events*, and often spent another day reading in the Library of Congress. He also served as treasurer for the District of Columbia Youth for Nixon. Franke soon returned to college, edited the *Campus Republican* (the national publication of College Young Republicans), and served as a staff writer for *Human Events*. By 1960 he was an editor of ISI's *The Individualist* and had also joined the staff of *National Review*. To celebrate his move to New York, Douglas Caddy threw a testimonial dinner for Franke at a Washington hotel. Speakers included William F. Buckley Jr., William Rusher, James L. Wick from *Human Events*, and Reed Larson of the National Right to Work Committee, for whom Franke had once worked. About twenty-five individuals attended to honor what had to be the youngest recipient of a testimonial dinner on record.[39]

Franke's thinking drew heavily from John Flynn's *The Road Ahead: America's Creeping Revolution*. Originally published in 1949, Flynn's book narrated the rise of socialism in Britain and its creeping influence in the United States. "My purpose," wrote Flynn, "is to attempt to describe the road along which this country is traveling to its own destruction." Communism was dangerous, but socialism "in our own institutions" at home was even more dangerous. By socialism, he did not mean any political party, but the growing state control of the economic system which was leading to a planned economy. Nonetheless, Flynn saw communists and communist-front organizations everywhere, and found little difference between communists and socialists. It began with the New Deal, he asserted, and spread to include even the Federal Council of Churches of Christ in America. "What the American must understand," he warned, "is that while each of these proposals—federal invasion of banking, federal invasion of power and socialized medicine—is promoted as if it were just a single reform unrelated to all the others, the simple fact is that *each is intended to liquidate some sector of the private enterprise system and expand the area of socialism."* Americans needed to restore human freedom and defend capitalism.[40]

Franke's essay, "Why Businessmen Should Support Conservative Student Enterprises," reflected Flynn's influence. Although originally a printed newsletter "Confidential to McGraw-Edison Executives," it received a much wider circulation. Franke argued that for "several decades the United States has developed steadily and continuously into a Welfare State." As Americans looked to the federal government to solve their problems, the function and power of government increased to the point where "the individual has found his liberty correspondingly reduced, and his property increasingly confiscated by taxation and inflation." Businessmen could help end this outrage, he argued, by supporting "the growing conservative movement on the campuses across this Nation." He noted that the Intercollegiate Society of Individualists and his own National Student Committee for the Loyalty Oath had become forces for conservatism, as had the Young Republican National Federation in its opposition to the Eisenhower administration during the preceding two years.[41]

Carol Dawson, secretary to the fledgling Young Americans for Freedom, hailed from a background more political than ideological. Born in Indianapolis September 8, 1937, but raised in the Washington, D.C. area, she had graduated from Dunbarton College in 1959 as an art and English major. Her father, Gene Dawson, was a newspaper reporter who became an administrative assistant to Indiana Congressman Homer Capehart. While at Dunbarton, a Catholic women's college, Dawson edited the campus newspaper, headed the Dunbarton Young Republican club, and worked part time for Vice President Nixon in 1959. Her political resume was impressive. She attended graduate school in politics at Catholic University, worked for Americans for Constitutional Action, and served as national college co-chair for the Young Republican Federation. She was at Sharon, and eventually served as a member of YAF's national board from 1960–62, as managing editor of YAF's publication *The New Guard*, and as a congressional aide: first to Senator Kenneth Keating of New York, and then to Representative Donald Bruce of Indiana. Dawson later claimed that she became an activist because she had to, "for my country, my son, my family and my conscience."[42]

Driven by conviction, Dawson moved into politics through the Young Republicans. Reading *National Review*, *Human Events*, and *The Individualist* helped shape her philosophy of "natural law, and traditional American conservatism." In a review of Joseph Wood Krutch's *Human Nature and the Human Condition*, she objected that the criterion for the "good life" seemed no longer to be "determined by the metaphysical nature of man, but by his current economic and social condition." Life was becoming "devoid of value judgments," she warned. There was too much emphasis on technology and physical comfort. "Not until man refuses to accept his status as determined by machines will he regain his true human nature."[43]

These convictions led her into electoral politics. Her work for Nixon in 1959 and 1960 brought her into contact with other conservative students like Douglas Caddy. At that time both Dawson and Caddy believed Nixon had "won the hearts and support of the younger generation." In the summer of 1959 she was elected co-chair of the College Service Committee of the Young Republican National Federation. From this position she not only advanced Nixon's cause but became acquainted with a wider circle of Republican conservatives (like William Rusher). During the winter Dawson helped form College Youth for Nixon, and by the spring of 1960 there were more than 200 such clubs. The group published newsletters and an organization manual, and generated publicity for Nixon's candidacy. "Students are a vital force in this nation," she wrote Peter Flanigan, National Director of Nixon volunteers, "and are genuinely enthused about the election." Although Dawson tried to work through state Young Republican groups and senior party officials wherever possible, Republican state chairmen feared that any independent student political organizations for Nixon would siphon off "young talent which might be used in the state campaign." They pressured the Nixon campaign to work through existing Young Republican clubs instead. But Dawson and her colleagues persisted. In her role as executive secretary of College Youth for Nixon, during the spring of 1960 she asked William Rusher to recommend individuals for the steering committee. While Rusher advised that he had few good contacts in college circles, he did recommend his good friend Diarmuid O'Scannlain, a Young Republican from New York City. O'Scannlain, who later joined Dawson and the others at Sharon, coordinated about twenty-five American youth groups as chairman of the Young Adult Council. He also served as chairman of the External Affairs Committee of the YRNF. This connection reflected the network that was developing among conservative activists within the party.[44]

Dawson continued in this position throughout the fall campaign, even as she was working with others to establish a conservative organization outside the formal party structure. She was joined in this effort by several other future YAFers, including Howard Phillips of Harvard and her future husband, Robert Bauman. She had met Bauman, who later became National Director of YAF, in 1959 when Douglas Caddy introduced them. Bauman had served as personal assistant to Representative Charles Halleck of Indiana, worked for the party on the floor of the House of Representatives, and was president of the Georgetown University Young Republican Club. They had, as Bauman later noted, a lot in common, including "our religious faith, our mutual passion for politics and conservatism. Our zeal for advancing the cause, our strong distaste for liberalism. We both came from modest, middle-class homes, both our fathers were alcoholics, both of us had to work to put ourselves through college." Bauman actually served as the first chairman of Youth for Nixon, but his "already well-known hard-line conservatism" led to his replacement by Dawson. They were married after the election, on November 19, 1960. Fellow YAFers Douglas Caddy, David Franke, and Lee Edwards (who was best man) attended. The conservative network grew tighter.[45]

Despite their efforts to find common cause, YAFers' differing political and philosophical backgrounds did not always jell right away. Many were busy in College Youth for Nixon. They included James Abstine, a state co-chair for Indiana; George Gaines, state chair for Louisiana; Howard Phillips, state chair for Massachusetts; William Madden of Holy Cross; William Schulz of Antioch College; and James Harff. Other future YAFers strongly favored Barry Goldwater. They advocated a principled conservatism and opposed Nixon's handling of the convention. One of them, John Kolbe, chairman of Arizona Youth for Goldwater, sharply attacked the behavior of Nixon supporters at the convention in a letter to conservative newspapers around the country. Kolbe, Goldwater's former Senate page, particularly protested the "cordon of armed guards" that had prevented many Goldwater supporters from reaching the floor of the convention. He noted that Nixon demonstrators, on the other hand, were allowed onto the floor even without passes. "This letter is to let your readers know," he wrote, "that had it not been for the actions of the convention authorities, what appeared on the nation's television screens would have been an even more stunning expression of loyalty to Goldwater and his principled conservatism." This put Kolbe on the Nixon campaign's "black list," and they asked Carol Dawson (who knew him) to contact Kolbe and "try to straighten him out."[46]

This was not the only split evident among Young Republicans. Robert Schuchman, the first national director of Young Americans for Freedom, typified the philosophical diversity of the young conservatives. Schuchman, then a student at Yale Law School, also had prior connections to William Rusher and the editors of *National Review* through his efforts to revive the Law School Conservative Society at Yale. Schuchman brought a libertarian influence to the cause. In an essay in a Yale undergraduate journal, he argued that the "keystone of a libertarian's vocabulary is, as the term implies, *liberty*. Only the free man is the creative, the active man. The ultimate entity in this world is the individual, not society, not the state, not the race, the nation, or the class." The purpose of society, he observed, was to "provide a framework for life under the division of labor wherein man can best attain fulfillment."[47]

Drawing on the language of Ayn Rand, Schuchman concluded that "the fountainhead of democracy is liberty." Civil liberty was essential to individual freedom, but economic liberty was a critical precursor to civil liberty. He compared the intervention of government in the economy to looting. "As long as we look to the coercive force of government as the guarantor of our livelihood, we will remain unable to actualize fulfillment and we will stifle the creative minds and forces which may still exist." Democracy too often denied freedom to the individual and restricted self-realization. "The libertarian goal is freedom of enterprise—but this means an unfettering of intellectual, artistic, and emotional enterprise, as well as the central economic doctrine of an unfettered industrial enterprise." Only then would "democracy become a desirable and an attainable goal." He warned that a Kennedy victory meant more socialism.[48]

Finally, continuing division among adult conservatives strained the effort to join the young conservatives in common cause. Symptomatic of this problem was a lengthy letter to conservative youth from Gerhart Niemeyer, a political scientist at the University of Notre Dame. Submitted to *National Review*, but rejected by Frank Meyer, it questioned the very need for the Sharon Statement. The attempt to define conservatism forced one to take a stand, and Niemeyer stood against it. It was divisive, and he questioned the assumption that the time was right for such a manifesto.

Niemeyer then spent six pages dissecting the Sharon Statement. It was, he lamented, a restatement of classical liberalism, which he abhorred. He objected to the idea that any use of man's free will had transcendent value, and opposed the notion that economic rights undergirded political rights. "The web of economic activities," he insisted, "is characterized not by freedom but by objective necessity inhering in the very nature of material production." Freedom belonged to the political sphere. "Be concerned with freedom in politics rather than economics," he concluded. Conservatives should try to develop a solid philosophy before declaring themselves in manifestos. He believed the Sharon Statement to be premature.[49]

One of the prime objectives of YAF's bylaws was to "maintain unity within the organization." But that would prove difficult. Despite their common attachment to the principles of the Sharon Statement, many leaders of Young Americans for Freedom held different and often conflicting ideological and political objectives. Many had expressed their views in print and had worked in political offices prior to the Sharon Conference. William Schulz, for example, had helped lead a public attack on New Jersey Governor Robert Meyner's welfare program and had published essays in *Human Events*. Schulz emphasized anticommunism and argued that the United States was weakening its defenses. He particularly supported the continuation of nuclear testing, insisting that test bans or disarmament were "militarily suicidal and politically indefensible" for the United States. "Future historians," he warned, "may well record a nation, at once the most powerful and the most gullible in the world, that committed neuclear [sic] suicide in the cause of 'peace.'"[50]

Lee Edwards, later founding editor of *The New Guard*, also had considerable political and journalistic experience and had served as secretary for the Committee of One Million under Marvin Liebman. Edwards was active in Young Republican politics in the District of Columbia, edited the YRNF newspaper, and had served as press secretary to Senator John Marshall Butler of Maryland. Butler had been so disgusted with "'modern' Republican control of the GOP convention" that he had left Chicago two days early. This was a commitment Edwards shared, and he relished the activism that led to YAF. He later warned that "if the day should ever come when Young Americans for Freedom becomes respectable, preoccupied with its image and overly sensitive to public and press opinion, that day will mark its decline and possible fall."[51]

Background information on the other founders of Young Americans for Freedom is rather sparse. Robert Croll had been active in the Indiana University Young Republican Club and at the 1960 G.O.P. convention. While a graduate student at Northwestern University he had chaired National Youth for Goldwater for Vice President. James Kolbe was, like Robert Bauman, a graduate of the U.S. Capitol Page School. Many others had been active in Young Republican circles or student politics. Comparative studies of early SDS and YAF activists indicate that involvement in campus politics was characteristic of both groups. For Croll and Kolbe, as for most other founders of YAF, political involvement preceded their commitment at Sharon. While Barry Goldwater became an attractive candidate for most of them, what really shaped their activism was a conservative ideology and a determination to create a conservative alternative in national politics.

Although YAF was nominally a nonpartisan organization, it drew primarily from Young Republicans and individuals usually attracted to Republican politics. Given the parameters of national party politics in 1960, with the South still solidly Democratic at least in name, YAFers' only functional option was to work within or try to take over the Republican Party. The defeat of Richard Nixon in November 1960 opened the doors of opportunity for them. Conservatives argued that the election represented a rejection of Eisenhower Republicanism, and Barry Goldwater emerged as the leader of Republican conservatism. Even as six men met with Senator Goldwater at the Jefferson Hotel in Washington within weeks of Nixon's defeat, attempting to convince the Arizona senator to run in 1964, YAFers were already committed to his cause.

With the Sharon Statement in place, Young Americans for Freedom now turned to organizational development in an attempt to make an impact on national politics. Robert Schuchman became YAF's first national chairman, apparently because he was an articulate spokesman and had Ivy League credentials. Douglas Caddy, who was chiefly responsible for organizing the Sharon conference, was chosen national director of the new organization. Carol Dawson was elected secretary, and David Franke became treasurer. The group named six regional directors: Walter McLaughlin Jr. of Harvard Law School (New England); Robert Harley of Georgetown University (Central Atlantic); George Gaines of Tulane (South); Richard Noble of Stanford (West); James Kolbe from Arizona, then at Northwestern University (Southwest); and Robert Croll of Northwestern University (Midwest). Named to the board of directors were David Franke (New School for Social Research), Richard Cowan (Yale), Tom Colvin (Davidson), Carol Dawson (Washington, D.C.), Carl McIntire (Shelton College), William Madden (Holy Cross), William Schulz (Antioch), James Abstine (Indiana), Howard Phillips (Harvard), Scott Stanley Jr. (University of Kansas Law School), Lee Edwards (press assistant to Senator John Marshall Butler), and Herbert Kohler (Knox). YAF established its headquarters in Marvin Liebman's offices in New York, and retained Marvin Liebman Associates to coordinate its affairs for a fee of $850 per month. Within six months YAF had received almost $45,000 in contributions. It spent almost half that sum on printing and mailing to broadcast the new conservative message, and anticipated raising more than $85,000 in the following year.[52]

Chapter 4   The Thrill of Treason

In an introduction he wrote in the late 1960s to a biography of Alfred Kohlberg, a leading conservative active in the China Lobby, William F. Buckley Jr. urged readers to "think back to some of the causes that bring us together. We are always being reminded that these are changing times, and that it is the duty of modern man, lest he sin against reality and consign himself to irrelevance, to accommodate these changes. What does it mean, 'the times are changing?' I am less and less certain."[1] Perhaps Buckley was less certain, but as the decade opened many young conservatives were not at all uncertain. Having banded together to form Young Americans for Freedom, they eagerly looked forward to solidifying their organization and working for conservative causes. Writing in the *New York Times Magazine*, Harold Taylor observed that "a new generation has appeared . . . and already begun to transform that part of our society which belongs to youth." Although Taylor focused on the student sit-ins at Southern lunch counters, he also recognized "stirrings of new interest in political dialogue" among conservatives as well. On campuses across the country, Taylor noted, students were responding to Senator Barry Goldwater. They had found in his "principles of conservatism" the first statement of conservative political belief around which they could rally.[2] In the words of Robert Claus, president of Wisconsin's Conservative Club, "You walk around with your Goldwater button, and you feel the thrill of treason."[3]

From Principles to Activism

As it entered its first year, Young Americans for Freedom faced the task of trans-forming the ideological principles enunciated in the Sharon Statement into an activist program. In a year characterized by what *The Nation* called "Rebels with a Hundred Causes," and at a time when the southern civil rights movement entered a new and exciting phase that pricked the country's moral conscience, Young Americans for Freedom enjoyed considerable success. Despite the prophecy of Clark Kerr of the University of California-Berkeley that "the em-ployers will love this generation . . . they are going to be easy to handle," stu-dents became increasingly indignant. Historians of the sixties have focused chiefly on the Left as an advocate for change, but in the early sixties the Right was actually more active in challenging the status quo.

Tom Hayden, later the chief author of SDS's Port Huron Statement, rec-ognized this reality. Writing in the summer of 1961, Hayden warned liberals that the "new conservatives are not disinterested kids who maintain the status quo by political immobility. . . . They form a bloc. They are unashamed, bold, and articulately enamored of certain doctrines: the sovereignty of individual self-interest; extremely limited government; a free-market economy; victory over, rather than coexistence with, the Communists. . . . What is new about the new conservatives is their militant mood, their appearance on picket lines." "When we observe an elderly gentleman approach a student in his area and offer to help him establish a YAF chapter," Hayden wrote, "we are not just watching a political maneuver, we are also watching the exposure of anxiety about status, a stubborn resentment of the social revolutions that are firing up the world, and a fear that all is not well with the West."[4] Howard Phillips, student council pres-ident at Harvard and a Sharon delegate, insisted that the "main thing we're concerned with is the responsibility of the individual." John Weicher, a grad-uate student at the University of Chicago, observed that "not all of the kids who were at Sharon want to go into business, or to professional schools nor do I think they were all very selfish, though many were. Most of them are driven by a desire to be free to see what they can do in life without interference." Robert Schuchman, a graduate of the Bronx High School of Science and a student at Yale Law School, added that "we do not want to be told what we must do . . . we want to be self-determined."[5]

After the Sharon Conference, YAFers began to develop an organizational presence on college campuses and to recruit conservative students. They cast themselves in the role of underdog, "bucking tremendous liberal opposition which is well financed and has the experience of almost thirty years of activity among the youth of our nation" in their effort to foment change and implement conservative principles. Recruiting brochures announced that their "resources, when pitted against this massive Liberal establishment, seem almost negligible in terms of finances and facilities." Their advantage, or so they hoped, lay in their "dynamic philosophy" and in a conviction that liberalism, "stemming from socialist theory and often serving as an unwitting handmaiden of Communist subversion—has lost its power to attract." Liberalism was, in their eyes, "old-fashioned and has ceased to be idealistic." They looked to youth to "shoulder the burdens imposed by the mistakes of the past, and . . . be responsible for the future. With the very survival of their nation and their freedom at stake, the youth of America must participate more than ever before in the political life of their nation."[6]

When YAF's board of directors met following the Sharon Conference, they focused on the connection between ideology and activism. To demonstrate this link, in October they organized the program for the *National Review* Forum, preparing a series of presentations on the history, principles, and future of the conservative student movement, and featuring a debate between YAFers Lee Edwards and Richard Cowan over the utility of conservative students withholding their votes from Richard Nixon in the fall election. YAF's board of directors voted not to endorse the Nixon-Lodge ticket for the 1960 election. Although many YAFers supported Nixon, Douglas Caddy explained the decision as a "tactical move to help promote long-range goals, namely the promotion of Goldwater conservatism." This decision—and the vote was close—reflected what became a persistent split among YAFers and their mentors as well as an effort by YAFers to establish their own conservative principles.

Perhaps the leading crusader for a politics of principle was William Rusher, publisher of *National Review*. In October 1960 Rusher attacked the Republican Party as merely another vote-getting machine remote from political principles, warning that to work within the party was to "forever be forced into enervating compromises." Conservatives, he insisted, should oppose Nixon "not simply as a means of recapturing the Republican Party, but as a first step in breaking away from the Republican Party altogether—toward a third party, to be formed when the moment is ripe." To vote for Nixon only strengthened the present Republican Party, a party that principled conservatives would have to oppose in the future. Rusher rejected the pleas of fellow conservatives who argued that a Kennedy victory was worse than a continuation of moderate Republicanism.[7]

Nixon's defeat in November freed Rusher and other principled conservatives. "For the first time in eight years," he wrote shortly after the election, "we are going to have a vocal conservative opposition to the leftward trend of American policy . . . ."

> As for the Republican Party, there are going to be some perfectly won-
> derful fights in it during the next few years. I will participate in them,
> merely because there is nothing much else to do at the moment,
> rather than because I seriously expect that it will ever turn truly con-
> servative again (e.g., by nominating Goldwater, or something like
> that). An authentically conservative mass movement in this country
> is still in the future; but meanwhile, the Liberals are a long, long way
> from their New Frontier.[8]

Rusher's conviction that the Republican Party had always seemed to choose power over principle tempered his euphoria. Nonetheless, he strenuously re-cruited support for Goldwater among members of the Young Republican Na-tional Federation as well as among Young Americans for Freedom.[9]

Others in the *National Review* camp sympathetic to YAF, like Frank Meyer, were equally determined to develop a new conservative force in American pol-itics. Meyer was more optimistic than Rusher about a possible takeover of the G.O.P. "If captured by conservatives," Meyer insisted, the party could "sweep into its support Southern conservatives and create a new majority of the South, the Midwest, the Mountain States, the Far West, and some smaller states of the East." A Goldwater candidacy in 1964 would advance those efforts, even if he failed to win the election. Like Rusher, Meyer very much wanted a "*con-scious* conservatism" fused from the various conservative ideologies. But he firmly believed that this could be accomplished by capturing rather than re-jecting the Republican Party.[10] Both Meyer and Rusher influenced YAFers, but the students were more interested in building their own organization and look-ing ahead to 1964.

The Tuller Foundation drew up a list of conservative professors across the country and made it available to YAF. Adult sympathizers helped raise funds. Al-though YAFers were enthusiastic, the organization was $350 in debt. Herbert Kohler, an ultraconservative Wisconsin businessman whose son had been at Sharon, agreed to solicit funds on his own stationery. Kohler lamented that "Americans of my generation do not have much to be proud of. Although many of us have fought the good fight, we have neither succeeded in stemming the en-croachments of socialism and federal control nor the creeping and concurrent cancer of national demoralization. . . . it is the young people of America" who had to save the nation. A similar letter went out over the signature of Charles Edison. The National Association of Manufacturers gave YAF a list of "3000 of its most Conservative businessmen." Until funds became available for YAF to publish a newsletter, the directors focused on inexpensive ways to attract publicity. Several members urged the group to "think about the areas in which we might set up 'front' groups." Particularly appealing were suggestions to form Medical Students against Socialized Medicine, a National Student Committee against Admission of Communist China to the UN, and the National Student Committee for the Loyalty Oath. Chairman Robert Schuchman warned that "the front groups be 'for something' rather than 'against something.'"[11]

Although Robert Schuchman was national director, much of the early organizational work seems to have fallen to Douglas Caddy and David Franke. Franke compiled a college organization manual, and Caddy ran the office as director. Franke's manual relied on standard templates of organization, providing a model constitution and bylaws. It also insisted that the first rule to building membership was to "*concentrate* on the incoming *freshman class*. . . . The watchwords are tact, discretion, thoughtfulness. You must always strive to maintain a mature image." Caddy organized the *National Review* Forum, attacked the Young Democratic Clubs for their voting record at a youth conference in Accra, Ghana, and worked with William F. Buckley Jr. to develop support for YAF among influential conservatives.[12]

Those efforts frequently met resistance, precisely because many authorities considered political activism to be inflammatory, and therefore undesirable. When George McDonnell, a junior at the University of Detroit and chairman of Detroit Republicans for Nixon, invited William F. Buckley Jr. to campus for a speech on "The Superstitions of Academic Freedom," the Dean of Men rejected the request as too controversial. YAF was also refused permission to circulate petitions protesting removal of a ban on Communist speakers. Yet Arthur Schlesinger Jr., a braintruster for Democratic presidential candidate John F. Kennedy, received permission to speak on that campus the same week.[13]

At their fall Board meetings, YAF directors tightened their organizational structure and established their positions on national issues. From that point on, they decided, no group could affiliate with YAF without the Board's permission, and each group's members must be in good standing with the parent organization. They also amended their fledgling bylaws, granting the national director power to revoke the membership of individuals or chapters who violated the principles of the Sharon Statement, which were incorporated within the bylaws. The bylaws reflected a decidedly top-down orientation. Regional chairs appointed the state chairs, and the state chairs could appoint local chairs. YAF charters gave new chapters full autonomy, but only in local matters. Even there they could not use the YAF name to issue local statements or raise local funds without prior approval. The board filled its own vacancies, and all officers and directors could serve a limitless number of terms. For an organization formed in opposition to centralized power, and one that had already placed extraordinary authority in the hands of a few directors, this was a bit paradoxical.[14]

Their issues focused more on anticommunism than on Republican politics. To generate publicity and give an impression of a vibrant conservative movement, they established front groups. One, led by Robert Croll and James Kolbe, pressed for stronger security legislation; another, led by Robert Harley, tried to arouse student sentiment against the admission of Red China to the United Nations. These were ad hoc committees run and staffed by YAFers, but without any overt connection to the national organization. This decision to create a network of seemingly independent political action groups reflected both the experience and the influence of Marvin Liebman, who had created dozens of anticommunist groups throughout the 1950s. The board also decided to continue membership in the National Student Association (NSA), but only for the purpose of "reformation from within," and agreed to reconsider that position after the summer 1961 NSA convention. In addition, the Board adopted "Operation Legislature," an effort to "stimulate YAF activity on the local level" and work for the election of conservative candidates in municipal and state elections. Finally, they decided to make "no attempt to push the nomination of Senator Barry Goldwater for the Presidency" at the "present time."[15]

Although only a small corps of activists by early 1961, YAF was determined to project the image of an energetic conservatism on the march. With the aid of their senior backers, they were at least modestly successful. William Rusher urged National Review to turn its annual fund-raising party into a publicity event for Young Americans for Freedom. In early 1961 John and James Kolbe formed the Student Committee for Congressional Autonomy, essentially to defend the House Un-American Activities Committee. David Franke organized a Committee for an Effective Peace Corps, advocating the use of Peace Corps volunteers to fight communism in other countries. And when the Eighty-seventh Congress convened on January 3, 1961, 400 people demonstrated both their support for HUAC and their opposition to the 200 demonstrators protesting HUAC. John Kolbe, who helped organize the demonstration, argued that the "past trend toward liberalism having reached its inevitable impasse, the pendulum is now making a broad, sweeping swing to the right." Kolbe insisted that college students wanted to shed the paternalistic legacy of the New Deal, which was ripe to be repealed. Offering both a history lesson and a rallying cry, Kolbe traced the roots of the new conservatism to "sound principles and great traditions," and charted its growth in intellectual circles since the mid-1950s. The youth movement, he noted, was "strictly political." Young Americans for Freedom was its "coordinating body."[16]

Signs of Progress

The progress of YAF could be measured in a series of small steps. A political action conference sponsored by the ultraconservative *Human Events* attracted more than 700 participants rather than the expected 500. Circulation figures for *National Review* improved steadily; more important, revenue losses declined substantially from previous years. In the spring, YAF issued a "Directory of College Conservative Clubs." *Time* magazine noted the rise of conservatism in a February issue, quoting YAF chairman Robert Schuchman's observation that "My parents thought Franklin D. Roosevelt was one of the greatest heroes who ever lived. I'm rebelling from that concept." In midwinter YAFers endorsed Barry Goldwater's "Statement of Republican Principles, Programs and Objectives," which emphasized law and order along with the need to control labor unions, curb the right to strike, and cut social welfare programs and taxes.[17]

Throughout the spring journals on the Right boosted the fortunes of Young Americans for Freedom. Stanton Evans, principal author of the Sharon Statement, argued that "student conservatism . . . has become the wave of the future." *Human Events* published an essay on the youthful revolt and traced its origins to a paternalistic economic system and the lack of choice in the 1960 election. Peter O'Donnell, a conservative Texas Republican, offered to fund training programs for young conservative writers at *National Review*. Even the liberal Americans for Democratic Action recognized the trend, warning that the "activities of the Young Americans for Freedom indicate that we need to do some serious thinking about our course of action in the next few months."[18]

Despite these efforts, YAF's treasury remained low. To correct that problem, and to attract greater publicity, YAF's directors recruited well-known conservatives to speak in support of their efforts, prepared to publish a monthly magazine, and planned a massive March rally for Madison Square Garden in New York. Anticommunism remained the focal point of their appeal, particularly the efforts of their various front groups. In a letter to Congressman Walter Judd, Douglas Caddy outlined the work of these committees and argued that the publicity they generated would "do much to further stimulate Conservative student political action" as well as give "needed moral and physical support to those adult groups working in the same areas." Although YAF officially continued to represent itself as nonpartisan, it was really an organization of conservative young professionals who were well to the right of the Republican Party.[19]

In March YAF launched their own monthly publication, *The New Guard*. Edited by Lee Edwards, the journal quickly announced its politics: "We are sick unto death of collectivism, socialism, statism and the other utopian isms which have poisoned the minds, weakened the wills, and smothered the spirits of Americans for three decades and more." Young Americans for Freedom, Edwards explained, was but another piece in a conservative revival that began in the 1950s. Its lineage included the Intercollegiate Society of Individualists, *National Review*, and *Modern Age*. Its ideology was one of "eternal truths," outlined in the Sharon Statement. Its key word was *"Action." The New Guard* proclaimed that YAF was riding a rising tide of conservatism, and it proposed to offer liberals "the pincers of liberty, individualism and initiative to free themselves of chains as rusty as the shibboleths which undoubtedly our opponents will attempt to wrap around us."[20]

The New Guard was designed not only to publicize YAF's activities around the country and communicate decisions of its board of directors, but to articulate the opposition of youthful conservatives to the liberal consensus. In an article on "Breaking the Liberal Barrier," David Franke revealed that YAF intended to form conservative clubs in places like Greenwich Village, to "let liberals know that no bastion is safe for them anymore." The journal also publicized the triumphs of conservatives at all levels of government. In 1961 this was a rather daunting task, for few conservatives whose philosophy aligned itself with that of Young Americans for Freedom yet held office.[21]

Without question, however, the most striking success of YAF in the spring of 1961 was its "Freedom Rally" at the Manhattan Center in New York. Held in early March, the affair drew more than 3,000 conservatives and featured Senator Barry Goldwater as the main speaker. In what became characteristic of future YAF rallies, it also featured a bevy of awards to professionals active in conservative causes. The awards in 1961 went to: William F. Buckley Jr.; author Taylor Caldwell; conservative intellectual Russell Kirk; Herbert Kohler, president of the Kohler Company; Eugene C. Pulliam, publisher of the Pulliam newspapers; columnist George E. Sokolsky; Lewis L. Strauss, former chairman of the Atomic Energy Commission; Francis E. Walter, chairman of the House Un-American Activities Committee; and the ambassador from the Republic of China. One young conservative, James Abstine, state chairman of the Indiana College Young Republicans, also received an award.[22]

Goldwater took as his topic "The Conservative Sweep on the American Campus," and described the movement as "an intelligent and responsible revolt from the pigeon-holing effects of regimentation and centralization of power in the United States." The vitality of the conservative revival, he claimed, was "directly related to the cause of individual freedom." It brought with it an exhilarating prospect for change, a conservative wave that "could easily become the political phenomena of our time." Goldwater told the audience that they all must realize that "something phony" was going on when the President said that millions of Americans went to bed hungry every night or lived in substandard housing. Attacking the New Deal and its legacy, Goldwater railed against a tax-and-spend philosophy of government and a planned economy. He urged his listeners to engage in political action and reverse those philosophies, "to become a part of that machinery which produces public officials and make sure that the right kind are turned out for the important jobs of running this country." But beyond political action and ballot victories lay the real task, a spiritual purpose and the "regeneration of the spirit of freedom in the hearts of our countrymen."[23]

Not only were 3,200 people present to hear Goldwater; another 6,000 were turned away. The next day the *New York Times* warned that "something is afoot which could drastically alter our course as a nation." Murray Kempton, writing in the *New York Post*, agreed, but doubted that it would be influential. "We must assume," he observed, "that the conservative revival is *the* youth movement of the 60s and may even be as important to its epoch as the Young Communist League was to the 30s, which was not very." Kempton tried to dismiss YAF as an "archeological society" out of touch with American values, attacked their leaders as arrogant "brats," and complained that their "posture was infuriating; their rhetoric deplorable."[24] But even as he attacked its politics, he admitted that YAF embodied a new activist spirit. "Its literature pulses with the drum beats of the counter-attack which means to become the offensive; its slogan is, 'The tide has turned.'"[25]

The rally energized Young Americans for Freedom. Marvin Liebman told the board of directors that of the many organizations he had assisted, YAF had "the greatest potential for influencing the course of events." Liebman not only praised YAF, but argued that the time was ripe to reconsider its relationship to Marvin Liebman Associates. YAF's national headquarters had remained in Liebman's New York offices, and he had bankrolled most of its early operations and salaries. YAF paid him for services rendered and for rent, but those payments did not cover the costs of Liebman's assistance. In addition, some YAFers believed that the relationship had adverse effects on the organization. Convinced that YAF was now on firm footing, Liebman presented it with two choices. It could organize a separate national office and raise funds to support its activities, thereby establishing a completely separate identity. This necessitated, in Liebman's opinion, a budget of about $7,000 per month. Or it could continue its relationship with Marvin Liebman Associates. If it chose this course, YAF had to "assume a greater share in the over-all financing of our entire operation." This entailed a signed contract and $2,000 per month for services.[26]

At their March 25 board meeting, YAF's directors discussed the options

with Liebman and their attorneys, agreed to sign a contract with Marvin Liebman Associates, and moved to incorporate Young Americans for Freedom.
The board commended the film *Operation Abolition*, officially condemned the
activities of the American Nazi Party, the Fighting American Nationalists, and
the National Student Association, and agreed to send a delegate to the Peace
Corps conference in Washington at the end of March. They also began a search
for an interim director to replace Douglas Caddy, who was about to enter military service.[27]

Finding a Voice

The question of continued affiliation with Marvin Liebman Associates revealed YAF's growing pains as it sought its own voice. That is why the close relationship with Liebman bothered some YAFers; it also explains their mount-
ing concern about being too closely identified with *National Review*. With their
own publication, *The New Guard*, they hoped to loosen that connection. But,
as the board's March decision revealed, YAF was apparently not yet ready to
step out entirely on its own. One antidote to any perception that Young Americans for Freedom was merely a front for other conservative groups was for individual YAFers to speak out. In the spring of 1961 they began to do just that.

The comments of Robert Schuchman, national chairman of YAF, were typical. He was one of a handful of YAF delegates to a spring national conference
on the Peace Corps. As part of YAF's formation of a Committee for an Effective Peace Corps, Schuchman issued a press release attacking the unrealistic
and naive thinking that underlay Peace Corps planning. "It should be obvious,"
he warned, "that any young people sent abroad by our government will be involved there in political debate and discussion, perhaps with trained and articulate agents from the Sino-Soviet bloc." All Peace Corps volunteers, therefore, needed "training in Communist propaganda, and in the methods of
combatting it . . . to prepare them for the political pitfalls which they may have
to face, abroad." In addition, all "Peace Corps training programs should include
extensive, rigorous training in political tactics, democratic theory and the
Communist menace."[28]

Other YAFers spoke out on an array of national issues, chiefly through essays in conservative publications like the *New Individualist Review*. In an appraisal of the new Kennedy administration, John Weicher argued that conservatives needed to take the offensive to block Kennedy's legislative proposals.
Insisting that the philosophy of individualism was on the rise, Weicher
lamented that conservative political activism had not kept pace with the new
intellectual current. As he looked ahead to 1964, Weicher insisted that "the

Republicans offer conservatives their only hope for recapturing political power." Conservative Democrats were not sufficiently strong to control the national party, and there was no time to build a third party based on individualism. It was simply "too dangerous for the individualists to put all their hopes in a long-run new party." Weicher saw some hope for a Republican/conservative comeback in 1964 with a Goldwater candidacy, but warned fellow libertarian conservatives that there were dangers there too.

> Goldwater may offer a great opportunity . . . should he win the Presidential nomination in 1964 *and go on to win the election*. At the same time, unfortunately, he would also present the last such opportunity, for the Republican left [Rockefeller] might be willing to concede him the nomination in 1964 on the certainty that he would lose. And if he should lose, no matter by what margin, political conservatism would take a very, very long time to recover from his defeat.[29]

Robert Schuettinger, like Weicher a Sharon Conference attendee, also attacked the Kennedy administration, thrusting the conservative lance into proposals for federal aid to education. Schuettinger blistered the education profession as a complete failure, a failure he blamed on the "Deweyites", who had failed to emphasize the virtues of competition. "There is no shortage of evidence," he claimed, "to substantiate the fact that most of our public school teachers denigrate competition and the pursuit of excellence in the classroom. Their own sense of mediocrity is so great, in fact, that the lengths to which they will go to avoid any comparison with their colleagues can only be described as desperate." Federal aid to education, he insisted, discriminated against students who sought their education in the private or parochial sectors. Its supporters, Schuettinger charged, would destroy equality of opportunity and were enemies of democracy.[30]

The New Guard articulated YAF's philosophy and tried to create an image of independent action. The new publication had two central purposes: to advance conservative positions on leading issues and to profile new conservative activists. It even drew praise from Republican moderates like Richard Nixon for its "lively writing" and "wide range of subjects covered." Its essays focused on the centrality of the cold war and the importance of a principled conservatism. Indeed, the two were joined from the outset. Lee Edwards warned, for instance, that the Peace Corps was solely an exercise in the cold war. A profile of Stanton Evans, as well as an article by Howard Phillips, attacked the National Student Association as a leftist group unfit to represent American students abroad. *The New Guard* also opposed Republican liberals, particularly those associated with a new Harvard publication, *Advance*. William Rusher had urged Douglas Caddy to make a public political attack on *Advance* and then insert it into the *Congressional Record*. In "To the Rear, March," Edward Talbot charged liberal Republicans with being leftist New Dealers, and claimed that such people as Henry Kissinger, John Lindsay, and Clifford Case were merely stalking horses for Nelson Rockefeller in 1964. The enemies of conservatism, it appeared, were just as likely to be Republicans as Democrats. Conservatives' efforts to take over the Republican Party were clearly underway.[31]

As they outlined a conservative ideology, articles in *The New Guard* drew heavily from Richard Weaver's 1948 book *Ideas Have Consequences*. They emphasized five basic principles, particularly the right to private property—"the last metaphysical right"—which provided a person with "privacy, responsibility, and a place in society." In addition, they stressed that people needed to understand how philosophies affected their lives, the "symbolic and logical powers of language," the need to "return to piety and justice," and the importance of avoiding a Whig theory of history that exalted recent developments at the expense of classical principles. In many respects, this added up to a rejection of the modern for the traditional. It certainly was an affirmation of rugged individualism and a bulwark against any humanistic communal ideal. As David Westby and Richard Braungart argued in their study of student activists, YAF embraced a hegemonic individualism muted only by a loose federalism. Like SDS on the Left, YAF hoped to awaken students to its own definition of the dangers facing the United States in the early 1960s. This awakening, which Westby and Braungart liken to a conversion experience, was in effect an effort at revolutionary change. By the spring of 1961 many conservative activists echoed the words of Stanton Evans:

> When I say the conservative movement is spreading, I don't mean to imply that the majority of students are conservative. They are not. Most students, I think, are still indifferent to political matters. But the conservative element on the campus is now on the offensive; it is articulate, resourceful, aggressive. It represents the group which, in 15 or 20 years, will be assuming the seats of power in the United States. That is why, in my estimation, it authentically represents the future of the country.[32]

During the spring and summer YAFers articulated their positions on these and other issues through columns in *The New Guard*. Local chapters organized anticommunist weeks, mourned May Day, and attacked Fidel Castro's rule in Cuba. College YAFers struggled to obtain formal institutional recognition as student groups, so they could sponsor showings of *Operation Abolition* and actively recruit students to the cause. They frequently encountered opposition

from deans, or ran afoul of speaker bans. Ironically, those bans had been insti-
tuted to prevent "communists" from speaking on campuses. In effect, this represented a peculiar twist on the legacy of McCarthyism, when colleges and universities shunned controversial speakers as a matter of policy in hopes of
remaining hotbeds of apathy. Now speakers like William F. Buckley Jr. encountered administration opposition, ostensibly because administrators feared
they might attack institutional decision-making.[33]

These and other controversies reflected the young conservative movement's success in finding its voice. As new chapters formed, YAFers explored
the meaning and nature of conservatism. Most echoed the words of Patrick Hill,
executive council member of Fordham University's Young Americans for Freedom, who explained that "We stand in opposition to the sociological concept
of man, which views man in the light of what he does rather than what he is."
But not everyone agreed on the policies that might follow from such a pro-
nouncement. Did it represent simply an expression of man's spirituality as the
essence of conservatism? Or did it reflect commitment to a libertarian outlook?
The central relationship, all agreed, was between freedom and responsibility.
But drawing the boundaries proved more difficult than the Sharon Statement's
skeletal framework implied.[34]

By early summer Lee Edwards warned that Kennedy was "veering dangerously toward the Eisenhower policies of sweet reasonableness and enlightening mediation" in its relations with the communist world. Edwards not only defended the presence and utility of loyalty oaths, but posited a "platform for
young Americans" that included support for the resumption of nuclear testing,
opposition to organized labor, an attack on summit diplomacy, and opposition
to all federal agricultural programs. Washington, he warned, was a "City of Delusions." John Weicher weighed in with a strident attack on federal aid to education. It stemmed, Weicher noted, from the Soviet's launch of Sputnik. But
this should lead the United States to promote higher educational standards and
tighter discipline, not federal controls.[35]

In May 1961 Young Americans for Freedom held a rally in Washington,
D.C. to address both issues. Featuring three conservatives—Congressman Donald Bruce of Indiana, Senator Strom Thurmond of South Carolina, and Congressman Bruce Alger of Texas—the rally attracted about 250 partisans. They
heard federal aid to education described as a dangerous welfare measure, and
listened to calls to ostracize the Soviet Union by ending any negotiations and
withdrawing recognition. Two weeks later, speaking to a radio audience on the
Manion Forum, Donald Bruce further explained his argument that principles
were possible in politics and attacked the statism of the Kennedy administration. Arguing that "the great danger in our society today is inherent within

government itself," Bruce insisted that only free societies were productive and complained that Americans had become increasingly dependent on the power of the federal government. The material benefits of freedom, he warned, were luring Americans into a dependency corrosive of individualism and destructive of liberty.[36]

Attacks on administration policy, liberalism, or support for a strident anticommunism were effective in appealing to YAFers and other young conservatives. But they also obscured a continuing division between conservatism and individualism within the movement. Most of the authors of the Sharon Statement were traditional conservatives, but there was a libertarian presence at Sharon. As conservatism had grown, the libertarian voice had deepened. Two veterans of the Sharon Conference highlighted this split as they joined battle in a summer issue of *New Individualist Review*. Edward Facey attacked the Sharon Statement as "heavily conservative." He believed it neglected the fact that "the individual man is the epistomelogical starting point in any social analysis. His nature and rights must be closely regarded before any consideration may be given to his place in society." Society was nothing more than a loose arrangement that enabled its individual members to achieve their goals more easily. Statism, indeed the use of the state in almost any form, denied them that right. Individualists, therefore, opposed granting powers to the state. But conservatives, Facey warned, supported the "establishment of an external nonsocial-market institution, government."[37]

Although Facey acknowledged that both conservatives and libertarians supported a strict interpretation of the Constitution, he attacked conservatives for going beyond that in a "Messianic pledge to defend what they call Western civilization." In this crusade they supported NATO and other foreign alliances as well as military intervention in remote lands to block the spread of communism. They would, in effect, embrace statism to defeat communism. But for Facey and the libertarians, the real threat was statism or socialism, not communism. Only the reduction of government intervention would promote freedom, he warned. "Yet, the Young Americans for Freedom are calling for the strengthening of the subpoena-empowered House *Un-American Activities* (whatever these two terms can or may mean) Committee." This was dangerous, he argued, for the "individualist cannot countenance the coercing of peaceful individuals to appear before a tribunal unless there is evidence that these persons have injured others who are willing to press charges."[38]

Facey launched a libertarian attack against YAF on other issues as well. Although YAF ostensibly opposed federal aid to education, he complained, they nonetheless supported it for those who took loyalty oaths. Rather than attack the Peace Corps, YAF wanted to make it "effective." Indeed, the entire domestic program of Young Americans for Freedom seemed to embrace federal power if exercised on grounds agreeable to them. He saw little principled difference between this position and the "Kennedy Welfare State." The state was the "real aggressor," Facey insisted, "and it cannot be too often repeated that it is folly to extend and deepen the hegemony of one state in order to diminish that of another."[39]

John Weicher attacked Facey as an anarchist or Constitutional Libertarian, and claimed that he was "manifestly unfair to Young Americans for Freedom." While Weicher admitted that conservatives "tended to be paternalistic and nationalistic," he insisted that "we must take into consideration the objectives conservatives have had in view in seeking political power." In other words, power in the right hands could not possibly be used for the wrong ends. Weicher's relativism defended YAF's simultaneous opposition to the principle of federal aid for education and support for it as a defense measure. More to the point, he reminded Facey that while Young Americans for Freedom stood strongly behind the principles of individual and economic liberty in the Sharon Statement, YAF was a political organization. That is, while "philosophically the hydra must be attacked *in toto*, politically it is necessary to cut off its heads, beginning with the most dangerous. To the conservative, the most dangerous is Communism."[40]

In testimony before the House Special Subcommittee on Education that June, YAF's national director, Douglas Caddy, defended the loyalty oath provisions of the National Defense Education Act, and by implication the act itself. The intervention of the state, he argued, was justified when exercised in the name of national security. Elimination of the loyalty oath provision of the NDEA would "be a serious blow to the internal security of the United States" and would provide a "psychological victory to the enemies of the American way of life." Indeed, colleges and universities that refused to participate in the NDEA discriminated against students by denying them opportunities to continue their education. Caddy insisted that most of the academic community did not favor repeal, but he could only cite six college presidents who favored retention of the loyalty oath provision.[41]

Caddy used his few moments before the Congressional subcommittee to tout YAF. Although unable to document his figures when pressed, Caddy testified that YAF had 27,000 members nationwide and that it was a "young professional and college organization." He admitted, however, that he really did not know how many college students favored the loyalty affidavit, despite his claims that the vast majority supported it. Representative Robert Giamo of Connecticut praised Caddy as a good advocate for YAF, but observed that Caddy lacked any substantive evidence to support his statements. Indeed,

Caddy's strongest testimony came when he quoted opponents of the affidavits to the effect that repeal would "encourage the pressure group of ritualistic liberals and the confusion of democracy with the insane mixture of anarchy and statism which it promotes."[42] Congressman John Brademas of Indiana, whose district included many of the colleges cited by Caddy as loyalty oath supporters, pressed Caddy to see if he believed that either President Eisenhower or President Kennedy would endanger national security. Caddy backpedaled quickly on the specifics, but asserted his conviction that Eisenhower and Kennedy were simply wrong. Brademas counseled that "this is so absurd a conclusion to be reached that you might be well advised to reevaluate your position on this matter."[43]

By the end of June 1961, ten months after its formation, Young Americans for Freedom had established itself as a leading voice for young conservatives. Still not much more than a small cadre of articulate and committed conservatives, it had artfully used public relations and political proselytizing to develop an organization and broadcast its views to the public. Although technically a nonpartisan, independent voice for conservatives, it remained closely tied to *National Review*. YAF was a tightly structured organization, a far cry from the participatory democracy advocated by Students for a Democratic Society. A committee of four individuals decided policy and carefully selected the issues on which YAF took public positions. Even YAF's national director, Douglas Caddy, admitted that the policy committee tried to choose "positive and winning issues . . . because we realize that we are still a weak and not too well organized association." Association with the wrong groups could retard YAF's growth. In this respect, Caddy warned William F. Buckley Jr.: "Our only fear is that the public image which we have worked so diligently to create may be destroyed unless all moves are carefully weighed. We both know that *National Review* and YAF are almost inseparable entities today (see enclosed article from the *National Guardian*). Thus, anything that appears in *National Review* might readily and justly so be taken as the gospel of YAF."[44]

In a memorandum to members and friends that June, Caddy highlighted the achievements of Young Americans for Freedom during its first ten months. Carefully casting YAF as an underdog, Caddy insisted that the "dynamic Conservatism" of YAF had "captured the imagination of American youth." Liberalism was socialist in theory and often the "handmaiden of communist political action," and that, in Caddy's view, accounted for its declining power to attract devotees. It was "old-fashioned" and had "ceased to be idealistic." In contrast, what Young Americans for Freedom offered was "youth, enthusiasm, faith in the future of our nation and an understanding of the historic issues which face us." It still lacked adequate financing, however, and Caddy appealed to senior conservatives for financial support. Since September Young Americans for Freedom had received over $69,000 in contributions. It had spent almost half that sum on printing and mailing, and most of the rest on advertising, travel, meetings and rallies. Only $680 had gone toward research. Despite a current bank balance of about $2,100, YAF anticipated spending another $86,000 by the end of the calendar year. Almost forty per cent of that would be for administrative expenses, the bulk of the rest for printing and mailing expenses. YAF's finances faithfully reflected the top-down structure of the organization.[45]

What remained to be seen was whether or not Young Americans for Freedom had any depth of membership. By summer 1961, YAF had clearly met the objectives outlined by Stanton Evans at the fifth anniversary dinner of *National Review* the previous December. At that time Evans had pleaded as much for a conservative public relations crusade as for a principled conservative politics. "The wordspinners of the Left," he observed, "have so befogged our moral senses, and so clouded our intellects, that the natural piety of the people has been undone. It is no longer enough to depend on instinctive conservatism; we need word-spinners—grasshoppers—of our own." Despite the appearance of those wordspinners in *The New Guard* and elsewhere, doubts remained about the efficacy of this new conservative movement. Campus conservatism, complained one critic, was not only a small movement; it expressed an "underlying mood of selfishness, complacency, timidity and fear." Where was its social conscience? Writing in *The Nation*, Alan Elms, a graduate student at Yale's Institute of Human Relations, argued that the new conservatism had successfully created the illusion of a wave. But he insisted that its membership was inflated and its action limited to a few instances of picketing. Publicity had supplanted action as a measure of success, and Elms concluded that there had been "no mass conversion to conservatism on the campus."[46]

Fighting the NSA

In the summer of 1961 YAF met that issue head-on when it challenged the National Student Association at its annual meeting in Madison, Wisconsin. The NSA was the most important student organization of the period, essentially an assembly of student governments from several hundred college campuses where delegates debated and passed resolutions on national and international issues in the name of American college students. Unaware that the NSA was secretly funded by the CIA, conservative youth under YAF's banner charged that it was nothing more than a liberal front group and tried to organize an effective opposition. "We will attend in force," Douglas Caddy warned. "NSA has never before been challenged. They have a bureaucracy committed to an extremist liberal viewpoint. They are completely out of line with what the average American student thinks."[47]

A year earlier Carol Dawson had prepared a confidential report on the Thirteenth Annual Congress of the National Student Association, held at the University of Minnesota in August 1960. Dawson, then working for Richard Nixon, released that report to YAF. Together with Howard Phillips, chairman of Massachusetts Students for Nixon and president of the Harvard University student council, she had debated Chuck Manatt, chairman of the College Young Democrats, along with a representative of the Young Socialist Alliance. Dawson noted that the "whole auditorium had been stacked against us" and that a chorus of boos had greeted any mention of their principles or their candidate.[48] Dawson and other Young Republicans nonetheless believed they had made some inroads. Initially "the speakers scheduled to deliver the key addresses at the NSA Congress were heavily loaded with left-wing Democrats." But they were "successful in convincing the leaders of NSA that they should at least try to create a more balanced program. . . . We feel that this is a breakthrough in the NSA situation."[49]

Dawson reported that the working papers and the resolutions were "completely slanted to the 'liberal' viewpoint." Opposing arguments received short shrift, and the available literature reinforced liberal positions on such issues as federal aid to education, disarmament, pacifism, and international relations. It was "obvious to me," she concluded, "as it was to many people there—that the congress certainly does not represent American student opinion." SLATE, the University of California-Berkeley student organization, along with Students for a Democratic Society, Americans for Democratic Action, the Progressive Student League, and the Young Socialist Alliance, dominated NSA. Despite this preponderance of liberal-left representation, Dawson believed that the constant turnover of students through graduation left an opening for YAF. "I do think," she concluded, "that we cannot ignore the potentialities in NSA, and we should always try to make our viewpoint well represented there."[50]

YAFers demanded that NSA confine itself to "matters of generic concern to the college campus," and questioned "whether it in fact speaks for anyone at all beyond a coterie of liberal NSA officers."[51] Robert Walters, NSA administrative assistant, warned Americans for Democratic Action in early July that YAF had targeted NSA for a takeover. Citing both YAF and its front group, the Committee for an Effective National Student Organization (CENSO), chaired by Howard Phillips, Walters noted that YAF "has published a vitriolic attack on us in their magazine, has announced that the Congress will be their 'showdown' with the liberals, and is currently making extensive plans for a well-financed, well-organized conservative machine at the Congress." He also pointed to the existence of another conservative opponent, Students Committed to Accurate National Representation, headed by "a Northwestern sorority girl named Kay Wonderlic," that emphasized organizational rather than political reform for NSA. Walters asked ADA for whatever help they could provide. "It will be a blow to the entire liberal community," he warned, "if the conservatives can claim a victory at this meeting."[52]

Led by Howard Phillips, and creating an impression of strength well beyond their numbers (perhaps 30,000 strong by now), YAF attacked the NSA as an elitist organization, isolated from mainstream student political opinion, that used "abusive procedures" to eliminate conservatives. Al Haber of SDS counterattacked with charges that YAF was associated with "racist, militarist, imperialist butchers."[53] At the same time, ironically, leftist students led by Rennie Davis and Paul Potter complained that on "most campuses, student representatives are selected because they are unusually glib, attractive, athletic, or 'Greek.' Their philosophy of a student's role in his university, their concern for Southern Sit-Ins, their interest in the NDEA disclaimer affidavit—in short, their involvement with those issues which entangle every NSA Congress, have little importance to their campaign, their election, or their work in student government."[54] Both Left and Right moved simultaneously along parallel tracks, each seeking greater influence in the National Student Association and each focusing on similar issues from opposing ideological perspectives. "If there is to be student political consciousness," wrote one liberal, "it can only come through organizations like SDA [Students for Democratic Action], Young Dems, Young Republicans doing a good job of interesting the students in political issues. It will take every politically active student to accomplish that much, and if it could be done it would be a real advance."[55]

Faced with a conservative challenge, NSA liberals attacked YAF as an autocratic organization that posed "grave threats to a democratic student government." In their analysis of YAF's bylaws, the Liberal Study Group of SDS concluded that YAF's hierarchical power structure reflected a decided lack of commitment to internal democracy. Only four individuals legally exercised all powers, and members lacked the right to recall officers or to petition for meetings. "Adhering to a tight structure of direction-from-above," the report concluded, "YAF's organization closely parallels the authoritarian pattern of the Soviet Union and its satellites." The report implied that should conservatives gain influence they would impose the same ideological structure on the NSA.[56]

Usher Ward produced a document on "The Young Americans for Freedom and the New Conservatives" for the Liberal Study Group of SDS. Designed to disseminate information about YAF as well as to "reveal more generally, some of the assumptions, premises and fallacies in extreme conservative thinking," the document was distributed in preparation for the NSA Congress. Although it used the terms "right wing," "rightist," and "conservative" interchangeably, it outlined conservative principles rather evenhandedly. The report concluded, however, that "conservatives mask[ed] *all* opposition to progressive economic, political and social change behind anti-Communist sentiment," embraced economic rights above human rights, and believed that Americans should be "concerned only with their own well-being . . . ." Ward warned that "YAF takes the conservative line on almost every issue that's current. It is against the Peace Corps except as a tool of the Cold War, against foreign aid except on a very limited basis, against anything but a negative foreign policy that is based on the silliest criterion, suspicious of further U.S. participation in the UN, and against civil rights and the National Student Association."[57]

YAFers also embraced a conspiracy theory of history.

> Since YAF has stated its belief in a menacing, conspiratorial apparatus grinding its way deeper into the fabric of American life, it supports any attempt by any person or group to limit, expose and destroy the alleged conspiracy. HUAC and the Senate Internal Security Subcommittee, YAF feels, help expose and destroy the alleged conspiracy where it is; security regulations such as loyalty oaths and anti-Communist affidavits are supposed to keep it from going any further.[58]

Further evidence of this conspiratorial bent could be found in Carol Dawson's "inaccurate report" on the 1960 NSA Congress. Ward's document attacked her charges that liberals rammed proposals through the Congress, and countered that her report "[depicts] herself and Howard Phillips as a gallant conservative minority fighting overwhelming liberal odds and generously covers both with a halo of valor."[59] Ward linked radical conservative groups like YAF to more extreme right-wing organizations such as the John Birch Society to place them outside the acceptable mainstream of American politics and consign them to fringe status as conspiratorial kooks.

As if to emphasize this point, the study cautioned that, quite aside from the question of personalities, the real danger from YAF lay in its methods. Warning that YAF's behavior at the NSA-sponsored Peace Corps conference that spring in Washington would be replicated at the NSA meetings, the document cited an account by Walter N. South II, a member of the American Friends Service Committee who had infiltrated YAF at that conference. Because it provides an insider's view, South's report is worth quoting at length.

> The dynamics of the meeting were interesting. It was authoritarian. First an "educational" discussion was conducted. Each of the various workshops of the Conference held that day were reported on by the

individuals in the YAF grouping who attended. Each in turn was asked: what happened, who controlled . . . who were the resource personnel for the workshops, and what the "party line" was in each workshop. . . . Then . . . they proceeded to lay out their own political position and program for the convention, the direction being given by the core group. This was presented without discussion, evaluation, or any manifestation of delegation of responsibility or democratic process. . . . Next the procedure and tactical program for the Conference was announced. It was in its sloganistic form, "Impede, modify, whitewash." This meant that in the workshops and on the floor of the general assembly, they were to obstruct the orderly progress of business wherever, whenever, and however possible; to make proposals far to the left of their privately avowed political positions, in the hope of modifying and weakening the liberal proposals; and in the end to "whitewash" the whole Conference, which they interpreted to mean launching the most violent attack of which they are capable upon the Conference, the NSA, and liberalism in general.[60]

NSA officials did not relish the prospect of an ideological collision in Madison. Warning that the 1961 Congress "could be a real wild one," John Feldkamp, chair of the national executive committee, hoped that "outside groups such as the Students for Democratic Society and the Young Americans for Freedom would not place such heavy stakes on the outcome of the Congress." But to no avail. As the congress drew near, ADA developed several detailed strategies. First, warning that YAF was a monolithic organization, they insisted that liberal unity on all issues was essential. Second, liberals were to work with friendly newspapers to give YAF bad publicity and "run them into the ground." In addition, they were urged to associate YAF with the John Birch Society to discredit it as nothing more than another extremist group. Finally, ADA warned liberals that YAF would try to infiltrate their caucuses and study groups, and perhaps launch some surprise moves to catch liberal leaders outside their caucuses and without communications. In short, YAF would be disruptive and use whatever means seemed at hand to generate publicity and win some rhetorical victories. David Allen of Campus ADA reminded liberals that "Y.A.F. offers a fresh new approach to college students who are seeking answers to the pressing political problems of the day," and articulated "the point of view of a substantial portion of the college campuses of our country."[61]

"The biggest ideological battle," Betty Binder, mid-Atlantic coordinator for the Democratic National Student Federation, warned ADA officials, "will be over resolutions of national policy. The conservatives will not only fight the liberal on the context of resolutions, but on the very right or need to pass resolutions on certain issues." At stake was whether a national student organization should concern itself with pressing national issues or only provide services for students on the campus. Fearing that YAF would reverse recent liberal support for sit-ins or opposition to the House Un-American Activities Committee, liberals opposed any dilution of the NSA's positions and cautioned that YAF would use "reform" as a vehicle to elect YAF supporters to national staff positions. "YAF will not try to sell conservatism on its own merits," one ADA document noted, "but will carry it into the Congress on the crest of a reform movement. Through a back door technique, YAF will probably try to persuade delegates to accept the recommendations of 'non-political' reform groups whose programs will pave the way to electing officers who appear to be non-political but who are in reality sympathetic to YAF." National ADA voted to cooperate with its campus division to combat YAF's efforts.[62]

YAF's proposals for reform focused on the NSA's million-dollar budget, the independence of the national executive committee, and the so-called "professional students" who actually ran the organization. Reform appealed to moderates as well as conservatives, and therefore represented a much more dangerous challenge than did a frontal conservative assault. Delegates might find voting against "reform" proposals difficult, for they appeared democratic. Moreover, while this reform agenda moved behind the scenes through an unofficial YAF delegation that focused on the theme of "fairness", the YAF delegation would sponsor specific conservative programs in caucus and on the floor. In its formal presentations, YAF would defend HUAC, support the NDEA loyalty oaths, and oppose federal aid to education.[63]

What made the prospect of ideological collision more traumatic for NSA officials was that, perhaps indicative of an eroding consensus, the action-oriented critiques of both Left and Right focused on many of the same issues. Through its Liberal Study Group, SDS prepared to use the NSA Congress to "involve relatively uncommitted students in a forum dedicated to a dynamic conception of the 'student in the total community,'" to advance the liberal agenda, to "clarify the 'dialogue' with the 'new student conservatism', and to serve as an agency of response to its thinking, propagandizing, and other activities."[64]

A discussion paper prepared by Al Haber and Sandra Cason for SDS's Liberal Study Group, titled "Civil Rights in the South," argued that students "have a mystique about action, without a solid appreciation for the social dynamic that radical direct action mobilizes." Students believed that action itself was sufficient, and seemed unaware of the complex community relations needed to make that action effective. "This means," the authors concluded, "that students employ very little shrewdness in developing strategy; there is not a rational analysis of institutions, the kinds of pressures that will influence them, when and how to act, how to develop community support, and so forth." The document sought to prepare students for effective and concerted action on behalf of structural change—anathema for conservatives, but a developing theme for the Left. It tried to reach beyond the facts of segregation or the morality of protest to foster broader social perspectives and a more complex political education. As such, it intended to shape the future student agenda, and dramatized the methodological as well as substantive distance between Left and Right.[65]

In his report to the executive committee, NSA president Richard Rettig noted that 1960 "marked a turning point for student activity in this country." Citing the sit-ins, picketing and boycotts, protests against compulsory ROTC, demonstrations against the House Un-American Activities Committee, and the campaigns for and against the loyalty oath provisions of the National Defense Education Act, he concluded that

> the emergence of the new "student politics" has undoubtedly been one of the most newsworthy features of the last two years. The initial thrust of this movement was moral in tone, as any number of observers have pointed out. A plateau has been reached, at least among liberal students, where the initial moral impetus is giving way to a more sophisticated approach to social-political issues involving a thorough analysis of the problem and the power structure that has to be changed. The conservative student movement has not yet lost its initial sense of moral imperatives guiding its action. If it assumes an increasing role of importance, it will be interesting to see what the strength of its appeal is based upon.[66]

The confrontation in Madison put some of that in perspective. For the first time, the NSA prepared to take stands on major issues such as the House Un-American Activities Committee, the Peace Corps, Cuba, and nuclear testing. Representatives of Young Americans for Freedom set up headquarters in a motel close to campus. According to liberals, their numbers were small. "In fact, they could fit quite easily in a Cadillac, with enough room in the trunk for a mimeograph machine, several prints of *Operation Abolition* and a complete file of back issues of the *National Review*." Apparently willing to spend upwards of $10,000, conservatives equipped their delegates with two-way walkie-talkie radios (using the secret code "Big Brother"), brought tape recorders to sessions, and duplicated prepared texts in advance for press releases.[67]

The major address of the Congress, by Wisconsin Governor Gaylord Nelson, ridiculed the notion that young people were turning conservative. "I find this hard to believe," Nelson told the delegates, "although conservative youth today may be better organized and financed by their elders." He attacked the "sheer lunacy" of Goldwater supporters who advocated repeal of the income tax, the dismantling of TVA, or an end to foreign aid. "It is clear from the avowed commitments of such groups as the John Birch Society," Nelson warned his audience, "that the real goal is far less to combat the pathetic remnants of the Communist Party in this country than it is to emasculate progressive legislation that has developed directly out of American experience and American needs."[68]

Despite efforts to organize a "middle-of-the-road caucus" and divide the Congress, YAF failed to make any significant dent in the liberal dominance of NSA. Its only real challenge came with an effort to marshall support for a minority resolution supporting HUAC. Led by Fulton "Buddy" Lewis III (whose father, radio commentator Fulton Lewis Jr., was a leading national spokesman for the right wing), and with sympathizers placed strategically throughout the hall, YAFers defended the House Committee and the basic validity of *Operation Abolition*. After five hours of bitter debate, the resolution lost, 236 to 212. Later that evening, a resolution urging the abolition of HUAC passed 269 to 156. Although upset at the defeat, Robert Schuchman later insisted that a "beachhead has been established."[69]

Young Americans for Freedom fared better in other efforts, even though they failed to win any electoral victories. Robert Schuchman pleaded at the outset of the Congress that the NSA support Albert Muler, a Cuban student about to be tried (along with forty other Cuban students) for leading a demonstration in Havana protesting the visit of a Russian delegation. Schuchman asked the NSA to send a delegation to Cuba on their behalf. A popular move, because even the liberals supported the accused students, it nonetheless failed to pass for fear that it would hurt the Cuban students' cause. The delegates did urge other Latin American student groups to intervene, but did not support the NSA's intervention.[70]

This effort galvanized YAF's determination to make its voice heard. Tom Charles Huston, a YAFer from Indiana University, charged that the entire Congress was rigged and blasted the NSA for discriminating against conservatives. Insisting that the delegates should hear all voices, Huston attacked his critics: "During the course of this Congress, my fellow conservatives and I have been referred to by Al Haber, of the Students for a Democratic Society, as consorting with 'RACIST, MILITARIST, IMPERIALIST BUTCHERS,' a vicious and slanderous innuendo. You have refused to hear our speakers." The NSA executive committee had turned down requests that Congressmen Donald Bruce of Indiana and John Rousselot of California, or Senator John Tower of Texas, be allowed to address the delegates. The delegates' refusal to suspend the rules and place William F. Buckley Jr. on the agenda infuriated YAF, and it attacked the Congress for refusing to hear conservatives as well as liberals. Buckley later delivered an inflammatory speech on civil rights and colonialism to about 400 persons in the parking lot of YAF's motel headquarters, after which, in answer to a question, he "referred to the leaders of the Congo as semi-savages." In a press release, Tom Charles Huston lashed out at liberals who had attacked Buckley's remarks, complaining that they had charged him with "possessing the 'BASE AND THE DEBASED COLONIAL REPRESSIVE, SLAVE-OWNING KIND OF MENTALITY THAT CAN EXIST IN A HARD FASCIST-TYPE OF REGIME.'"[71]

After the Congress, the conclusions of each side were mixed. Some liberals admitted that many campuses felt "alienated and distant and unrelated to the activity of the Association." But they also remained optimistic that the Congress had charted a new course for the NSA, insisting that it had "finally emerged as a voice, if not of the American student, then of the American student leader. The question is now," according to outgoing president Richard Rettig, "whether it can translate the enthusiasm of a few into a device for awakening the still 'silent' American college community." Other liberals recognized that YAF's attacks would continue, but observed that "YAF retreats from its position if confronted orally with its charges."[72]

Others were not so sure. Writing in the liberal *New University Thought*, three delegates admitted that while they found YAF's activities at times amusing and annoying, and while many liberal delegates believed that YAF would now fade away, that was not likely to be the case. "YAF has found," they observed, "that charges repeated often enough will soon come to carry weight, regardless of how thoroughly they are refuted." Like Senator Joseph McCarthy's tactics a decade earlier, these methods would create an aura of conspiracy as well as attract youth disenchanted with current affairs. With continued financing from sympathetic adults, Young Americans for Freedom would remain "a force to be contended with in any student community."

> YAF is a group with ancient ideas using modern political tactics to great advantage. Its essential appeal to young people is that it attacks in simplistic terms the attempts of the Establishment to solve the highly complex problems of modern American life; it does so primarily by attributing the problems, the solutions, or both to "creeping socialism" and the welfare state, which in turn it attributes to the "pernicious influence of the international communist conspiracy." It declaims that the liberals have "taken over" all the institutions of the society (education, religion, government, the press), while at the same time crying that the mass of the people are basically conservative and that the liberal institutions mold, rather than reflect, American opinion.[73]

A subsequent national tour by Fulton Lewis III condemning the National Student Association confirmed YAF's determination to persist in the face of liberal opposition. Richard Lambert, ADA field representative, warned that there "will be a lot more challenges from this particular portion of the lunatic fringe."[74]

YAFers could point to two victories that summer in their efforts to advance a conservative agenda. First, a Goldwater conservative named John Tower won a special election to fill the Texas Senate seat vacated by Vice President Lyndon Johnson. Tower attacked liberals for trying to reduce the American people to "a state of dependency on the national government." Although he embraced an essentially libertarian philosophy, insisting that "the government gives us nothing that it does not first take away from us," Tower's assertion that liberals were taking the country down the road to socialism, which was the prelude to communism, aroused conservatives of all stripes. *The New Guard* announced that "it would seem that the time has now come for conservatives to recognize that they can no longer afford to split their forces between two political parties." Conservative Democrats should realize that "times have changed, and if ever conservatives are going to make the switch, the time is now."[75]

The second victory came in a struggle to control the Young Republican National Federation. This group was a breeding ground for future Republican leadership, and Richard Nixon's supporters feared that Rockefeller Republicans might dominate the organization and use it to advance Rockefeller's influence in the party. But Goldwater conservatives made their own move first, seizing the chair of the Young Republican National Federation College Services Committee that summer with the election of YAFer James Harff of Northwestern University. In addition, the convention warmly applauded the arrival of John Tower, as Harff announced that the "conscience of the conservative has spoken at this convention." Although the convention eventually selected a Nixon candidate (Leonard Nadasdy) over a Goldwater supporter (Robert Hughes) to chair the YR Federation, conservatives' ardor cooled a bit when Richard Nixon arrived. Despite this setback, the Federation adopted a platform opposing any federal aid to education and supporting the immediate resumption of nuclear testing as well as a total trade embargo of the communist bloc.[76]

As Young Americans for Freedom concluded its first ten months in a flush of success, it also faced an array of perplexing problems. Not only did it need to raise considerable funds to support its activities; it needed to find some way to break free of its image as a group subservient to older conservatives. In addition, YAF needed to become a broader-based political action organization to mitigate its image as a rigidly hierarchical organizational structure. Finally, in mid-1961 YAF stood almost alone in its image of disruptive protest against the status quo. Granted, SNCC-led sit-ins and CORE's freedom rides had spread across the South, but those were protests based on moral conscience rather than ideological principles. YAF needed to find some way to demonstrate the need for political protest based on ideological principles to effect structural change.[77] All of these problems emerged with a vengeance in the next few months, as divisive factionalism over conservative principles threatened to destroy the organization.

Chapter 5

Divisions in
Conservative Ranks

As it struggled to find its voice and shape its activist agenda, Young Americans for Freedom became embroiled in a series of controversies that unleashed a frenzy of factionalism. Some originated outside YAF, but had ramifications for individual YAFers as well as for the organization itself. Others sprang from philosophical and political differences among its leaders. These divisions were not only the result of growing pains and the attempt to forge a New Right; they often represented conflicting ideologies and clashing ambitions.

Encounters with the John Birch Society

The John Birch Society embroiled the movement in controversy with its flamboyant rhetoric and charges that former President Dwight Eisenhower was soft on communism. The failure of other conservatives to denounce Birch Society rhetoric, along with the unfavorable publicity Birchers and their leader, Robert Welch, attracted, threatened to undermine conservative efforts to foment change. The *National Review* crowd, so instrumental in the formation of Young Americans for Freedom, was particularly concerned that the Birch Society might appear to be the mouthpiece for all conservatives. But Buckley, Rusher, and the other editors delayed entering the fray for fear that it was "fraught with great danger for *NR*." A flurry of memos in early April bared their concerns and attempted to chart a strategy.

William Rusher insisted that if they were to remain the leading conservative journal, then they had to say something. How much to say and when to say it were the critical questions. "What concerns me," Rusher confessed, "is what an injudicious editorial will do to *NR's* position *as a leader of conservative opinion* in this country."

> We naturally welcome—nay, rightly prize—the influence we exert on
> the borderline conservatives, on the unformed minds of students, etc.;
> and it is with these in mind that I would insist on publicly dissociating
> *NR* from Welch. But the great bulk of our readership, of our support,
> and of the warm bodies available to us to lead in any desired direction
> lies in the more or less organized Right, and large segments of that
> Right are more simplistic than we are, or than we can perhaps in time
> bring them to be, and also far more closely tied to the John Birch So-
> ciety than we are or, if the truth were known, than they would proba-
> bly at this moment themselves prefer to be.[1]

National Review gained certain advantages by remaining independent of the organized Right, but it could not afford the Right's enmity. "Let's face it," Rusher warned his fellow editors, "small as it is, the American conservative movement is crawling with rivalries and jealousies, and *NR* has its full share of Rightist critics and enemies." He hoped that Welch and the Birchers would qui- etly fade away so that conservatives could support more respectable organiza- tions and ideas. A precipitous attack might trap moderate conservatives be- tween a choice of "followerless eccentricity" or "bondage to the main line of the Republican Party."[2]

William Buckley argued that, because of Robert Welch's influence, the Birch Society was "incurable." Rusher disagreed vehemently, reminding him that it contained many good people and urging him not to be so impatient "with an organization of conservatives that is not obediently following *our* lead." Since the Birch Society was not likely to die soon, the options, according to Rusher, were to "stay in the ring" or "retire to our ivory tower to write books about how it is impossible for intellectuals to beat any sense into the skulls of the hard Right."[3]

The division was one of style as well as ideology. Buckley was a patrician and a conservative; the John Birchers were the advance guard of New Right pop- ulism. The *National Review* crowd, like their protégés in Young Americans for Freedom, sought to reform the American body politic by cutting away the can- cer of statism. But their emphasis was more on reform than on structural change. The Birchers, on the other hand, seemed to argue that the entire structure of the governing system was rotten to the core and needed a radical overhaul. This may well explain why the "establishment" saw the John Birch Society rather than

Buckley, Rusher, *National Review*, or YAF as a radical threat. The strength of the John Birch Society lay, as Rusher recognized, in its grassroots support among a portion of the populace hitherto somewhat estranged from the political process. On the other hand, Buckley's perspective, reflected in the structure of Young Americans for Freedom, was very much a top-down elitist vision of conservative activism. A small cadre of intellectuals and activists would frame the issues, and the mass of conservative voters would then follow their lead. The Birch Society controversy, therefore, raised questions about the very structure of the conservative movement.

In a subsequent memo to Buckley, Rusher recommended weaning away the "good conservatives" from the inflammatory and irresponsible rhetoric of the "hard Right." Any editorial denouncing the Birch Society, he warned, needed to address three key points. First, what would its effect be on "non-Birchites among our readers?" He particularly noted the role of *National Review* in mobilizing "the college students and the semi-committed conservatives," neither of whom was particularly enamored of the "hard Right." Second, what about readers who were members of the John Birch Society? Would they cancel their subscriptions and thereby jeopardize the journal's financial health? Finally, what would be the reaction of liberal critics? Any attack on the Birch Society by another conservative group would likely be big news, and the reasons for the split should be carefully and clearly explained.[4]

The dilemma here for YAF was that it sought to welcome virtually all conservatives, regardless of their other affiliations. Typical was their early support for Congressman John Rousselot of California. Rousselot stood strongly behind the principles of limited government, equated liberalism with socialism, and was militantly anticommunist. But he was also a member of the John Birch Society. The effort to distinguish between various approaches to conservatism soon led to further schisms within the organization.[5]

Beyond that, however, lay a much more serious problem: the effort by YAFers sympathetic to the John Birch ideology, as well as others close to Nelson Rockefeller, to wrest control of the group from those oriented more toward the *National Review* ideology. The latter, representing a centrist position within that ideological spectrum, faced daily rebellions from the extremes.[6] Since everyone concerned believed conservatism to be the wave of the future, the internal intrigue seemed significant. All parties believed they were battling for not only control of YAF, but also the ability to shape the future of the conservative movement and ultimately achieve political power. The Birch Society debate was symptomatic of serious philosophical differences among YAFers, as well as among conservatives in general.

Theology, Ideology, and Conservative Politics

The split between philosophers and politicos plagued Young Americans for Freedom. The problem was not so much the differing emphases of the two groups, but the conviction of the former that conservatives should share some common understanding about the nature of man and the danger that techni- cal philosophical disagreements could balloon into political divisions within YAF. The issue came to a head following the issuance of Pope John XXIII's en- cyclical *Mater et Magistra* in July 1961. It focused on the problems of the Third World, calling for an end to colonialism as the cornerstone for a renewed com- mitment to poor and oppressed peoples. William F. Buckley Jr. attacked the en- cyclical in *National Review*, charging that it bordered on socialism and was ir- relevant because it ignored the preeminent danger of communism throughout the world. Other Catholics opposed Buckley, and a lengthy article by Carol Bauman in the December 1961 *New Guard* brought Young Americans for Free- dom into the fray. Under the title "Mater Si, Magistra Si," the article criticized the encyclical for ignoring communism and argued that individual Catholics did not have to support the Pope. Bauman urged YAFers, many of whom were Catholics, to get involved in local affairs: "it is imperative that community re- sponsibility not be ignored while patriots apply themselves to the larger prob- lems of international communism and national political power."[7]

Young Americans for Freedom had always been particularly strong on Catholic college campuses such as St. John's, Fordham, and Notre Dame, as well as among Catholics generally. In their study of conservatism, Paul Got- tfried and Thomas Fleming found that 26 percent of YAFers were Catholic. Ed- ward Gargan observed that conservatism was rampant within the Catholic church, and had introduced a "bitterness and tension not normally called forth by differences of political affiliation." He found Catholics deeply divided about the "nature and necessity for a conservative approach to the needs of man and society." The dispute revolved around the role of the state versus the role of the individual in dealing with social issues and conditions. The Pope's encyclical intensified those tensions. The growing conservative movement in the United States further stirred the ideological waters, as American Catholics were in- creasingly attracted to an ultrapatriotism. Robert Welch estimated that 50 per- cent of John Birch Society members were Catholic. Gargan warned that "Catholics who subscribe to the John Birch Society share this tension, this ex- perience of being trapped in a society assaulted from every side. The view of the everyday world as a massive conspiracy makes impossible the use of any nor- mal criteria for judging the political and social action of man."[8]

As religious tension spilled over into political philosophy, some conservatives fused the two to form a coherent political ideology based on their understanding about the nature of humanity. Carol Nevin, who had attended the
Sharon Conference, wrote that "I believe that man's ultimate destiny of union
with God in the Beatific Vision is his most important consideration. Therefore
any philosophy, to be tenable and true, must take into consideration what man
is and what his destiny is." She concluded: "I find that politically, conservatism
with its emphasis on the individual exercising his freedom while respecting the
rights and freedom of his fellow men is the only position which I can hold and
still be faithful to my basic premises, philosophically and theologically." Speaking before the National Freedom Education Center at King's College, YAFer
John Kolbe linked theology with the politics of anticommunism.

> Implicit in this movement is the conviction that the heritage of the
> Christian West, and *not* some conglomeration of opinions and oppo-
> site moralities, offers the only hope for a world besieged by an ideol-
> ogy which teaches that there is no God and that wrong is right—if it's
> for the Party. . . . Note, for example, the Sharon Statement, YAF's
> statement of principles, which begins with the recognition that the
> crisis facing Western civilization is *moral*, as well as *political*, in
> nature.[9]

The conjunction of theology and politics was a fundamental precept for
many early YAFers. Paul Niemeyer of Kenyon College, also a Sharon delegate,
argued that his idea of conservatism arose from a "belief in an absolute moral
law which cannot be tested by scientific and epistemological questions." It was
a faith, given by God and recognized by humankind. Its foundation was freedom. Conservative Washington columnist Holmes Alexander went even further, exalting free enterprise as a "human institution" whose competitiveness
was the "Life Force in us all." Property distinguished human from beast. But
how far should one go? This debate over essentials divided YAFers as often as
it united them, particularly when the question of Ayn Rand and objectivism
surfaced. Since Rand was an atheist, could objectivists also be conservatives of
the YAF school?[10]

For William F. Buckley Jr. and many writers at *National Review*, this debate
was fundamental to the future of the conservative cause. It plagued Young Americans for Freedom, not only in 1962 but for the rest of the decade. Buckley and
his colleagues had always hoped that YAF would follow their lead and embrace
their version of traditional conservatism. In an effort to define that course, and
at the same time read Ayn Rand and objectivism out of the conservative movement, Buckley attempted to define conservatism empirically. He explored var-

ious ideas with which *National Review* had "had trouble making common cause," but the one that really seemed to trouble him was objectivism. He cited Whittaker Chambers's observation that Ayn Rand really advanced the "materialism of technology" in a godless world. Rand's philosophy was "dessicated," Buckley argued, and was incompatible with "the conservative's emphasis on transcendence, intellectual and moral." Buckley also repeated his earlier criticisms of the ideas of Robert Welch and the John Birch Society, and attacked radical antistatists like Murray Rothbard, whom he considered anarchists. Conservatism, Buckley concluded, "is planted in a religious view of man."[11]

Beyond these religious tensions within conservatism, YAFers also became embroiled in a related dispute, between the relative importance of freedom and virtue for conservatives. Its essential outlines emerged in the source of YAFers' sustenance, the pages of *National Review*, with a debate between L. Brent Bozell and Frank Meyer. Bozell urged conservatives to examine more closely the "presumptive correlation between freedom and virtue." Noting that Meyer and Stanton Evans had tried for years to promote a fusion of traditional and libertarian ideals, a fusion expressed in the Sharon Statement, Bozell raised doubts about its viability. He questioned whether it could hold the movement together and whether it could "succeed in midwifing the movement to power." Bozell's chief target was libertarianism and its emphasis on freedom, and he argued that the idea of freedom was not responsive to the "root causes of Western disintegration." Virtue, in his view, was far more essential. Only virtue could restrain the latitudinarian exercise of man's free will. Libertarians would eliminate structure, thereby undermining order and destroying society.[12]

Bozell drew upon his strict Catholicism to argue that a "Christian metaphysic" formed human nature and gave humans the capacity to deviate from "patterns of order." Freedom, together with "the ravages of original sin," led to disorder. God's purpose, to Bozell, was to "establish temporal conditions conducive to virtue" and to "build a Christian *civilization*." Western civilization, consequently, emphasized the relationship "between the good commonwealth and the virtuous man." Bozell thus moved away from a strict antistatism, arguing that the exercise of power by the state was acceptable if it advanced the good of its individual members. The purpose of traditional conservatism, according to Bozell, was to "aid the quest for virtue." But, he lamented, the "story of how the free society has come to take priority over the good society is the story of the decline of the West."[13]

Frank Meyer responded with an argument that freedom, unrestricted liberty, was the central value of conservatism. Meyer argued that his position constituted a conservative consensus that embraced "the existence of an objective moral and spiritual order . . . *and* the freedom of the individual person as a decisive necessity for a good political order." A combination of the two was essential, because each gave content and purpose to the other. Pure libertarianism and pure traditionalism were, for Meyer, mere ideological abstractions and distortions. Warning that Bozell's ideas would lead to a theocracy, Meyer insisted that freedom was essential to a virtuous society. "What is meant by political freedom," Meyer concluded, "is the limitation of the power of the state to the function of preserving a free order. It demands that the state be prohibited from positive actions affecting the lives of individual persons, except insofar as such action is necessary to prevent the freedom of some from being exercised to limit the freedom of others." True conservatism therefore joined the traditionalists' emphasis on virtue with the libertarians' emphasis on freedom.[14]

The debate did not end here; indeed, there was really no final resolution of the issue. That same year Meyer published *In Defense of Freedom: A Conservative Credo*, which further elaborated the fusionist position. In her review of the book in *The New Guard*, YAFer Carol Bauman observed that 1960s conservatism was a "savory blend of traditionalist, Federalist, libertarian, and the so-called Randian philosophies."[15] Bauman praised the book, but generally avoided taking sides—perhaps because there was another issue behind this debate, the issue of whether conservatives should mute their differences in the pursuit of political power or engage in heated debates over the fine points of conservative philosophy in an effort to "purify" the blend.

This ideological focus also caused problems among young and old within Republican ranks. Dean Edstrom, president of the Macalester College Republican Club, summarized them in a letter to Walter Judd. Noting that he had always considered Judd a moderate, Edstrom expressed his dismay at finding the congressman's name on the YAF national advisory board. Young Americans for Freedom, he warned Judd, was reactionary. Edstrom, who admitted that he was a "liberal" Republican, built a case against YAF. It was a striking expression of Republican divisions.

> Hidden behind the generalities of the "Sharon Statement" of the YAF
> is a group dedicated to ideals which 1) appear to me to be completely
> contrary to some of our most fundamental ideas of equality in America and 2) will effectively kill the Republican Party if adopted in large
> measure, especially if in conjunction with a re-alignment of the
> Southern political spectrum. Among these ideals represented by many
> members of the organization are: 1) Racial inequality and segregation
> hidden by a mask of state's rights; 2) The halt and repeal of generally
> accepted (even by the great majority of Republicans) economic and
> social legislation (Social Security is frequently mentioned); 3) Complete isolation in international affairs coupled with the withdrawal of

the United States from participation in the United Nations. I would suggest that you look at the personalities involved in the movement. You will find that several are dedicated union-haters;—surely both of us see faults in the unions of our country, but these people are often against the very principle of unionization and collective bargaining. You will find some (especially those with whom I am acquainted) are members of and tools for political machines for which I would have no respect regardless of party affiliation. I cite the machine in the state of Indiana as a prime case.[16]

There is no evidence that Judd ever replied, but in a later letter of inquiry about Young Americans for Freedom, he praised the organization. Acknowledging that many feared YAF to be too far to the right, Judd found this a normal reaction to the "predominant leftism" of the past. "Their final position," he concluded, "is likely to be a sensible and sound conservatism, as opposed to radicalism on one hand and reactionaryism on the other."[17]

Internal Divisions

For the moment, however, the greatest threat to Young Americans for Freedom was not their theoretical differences, but internal schisms. Factional divisions among the YAF leadership surfaced in the spring of 1961 when National Director Douglas Caddy left to enter military service. His departure led to a power struggle that involved, in Caddy's words, "those who wanted to make YAF part and parcel of the Young Republican National Federation and move it to Washington and others, such as myself, who wanted it distinct from the GOP to appeal to conservative Democrats and Independents and kept in New York City." Caddy later admitted that "my side lost and the organization moved to Washington, where it quickly got caught up in endless power struggles and, in my opinion, never fulfilled its potential."[18]

Divisions within YAF, however, were as much a matter of maturity and ideology as they were questions of political allegiance. William Rusher, close to both YAF and the YRNF, has argued that much of the problem was that YAF ran its operations out of Marvin Liebman's offices in New York, and Liebman, "who had innocently fallen into the role of a sort of rich and adoring uncle who could deny these youngsters nothing, unwittingly spoiled a number of them badly." YAF directors ran up large travel bills, and spent money "lavishly."

Ideology also begot political intrigue. William Rusher believed that Douglas Caddy was trying to draw YAF close to the Rockefeller forces, while his fellow board member, Scott Stanley, inclined toward the John Birch Society. Rusher feared they would form an alliance against his *National Review* faction.

Both Lee Edwards and Marvin Liebman also suspected Stanley's intentions. The growing estrangement of *National Review* from the John Birch Society exacerbated tensions. In addition, David Franke split with Caddy, forming a Greater New York Council of Young Americans for Freedom. YAF's attorneys informed Franke that only YAF could grant affiliated status, and threatened to sue if he persisted in using the name. All of this was too much for Buckley, Evans, Liebman, and Rusher, who had tried not to meddle in YAF's internal affairs. They fired off a telegram to Caddy and Franke (along with Carol Bauman and Robert Schuchman).

> We have in the past, and will in the future, refrain from intruding in any way into the administrative affairs of Young Americans for Freedom. But our investment in the organization, emotional and political, is too great to permit us to stand apart at this moment of high and dangerous tension. We therefore offer to act as an independent committee to crystallize, consider and evaluate outstanding disagreements and make recommendations to the Policy Committee, upon the completion of our survey, within ten days. Pending that report, which the Policy Committee will accept or reject, it is understood that Caddy would withdraw his instructions to the attorneys and that Franke would endeavor to get all New York chapters to file their charter applications, and that no public allusions will be made to the dissension.[19]

Throughout the remainder of the summer Marvin Liebman worked with YAF's executive committee to try to resolve these problems. Many stemmed from the internal structure of the organization. Since YAF was so hierarchically structured, any individual or group that captured a couple of key offices could effectively speak for the entire organization. Buckley and YAF's other founding fathers sought to safeguard their influence, and at the end of May they presented a series of recommendations to the policy committee. Insisting that YAF still had "tremendous potential," they warned against "inter-organizational conflict or the creation of various cliques and/or power blocs." Their recommendations endorsed the organization's current structure and made any deviation from its decisions more difficult. Local chapters and community councils could not invoke the name of Young Americans for Freedom without explicit authorization from the national organization. In addition, community councils existed only "at the pleasure of the local chapters," and at least three-quarters of their directors must be chapter-approved. No local chapters or community councils could open bank accounts without authorization from the national director and treasurer, nor collect dues until they had satisfied all their national obligations.[20] A subsequent meeting between Liebman, Buckley,

Caddy, and Franke led to a few changes in the recommendations. Although the changes appeared to grant greater local autonomy to YAF councils, in many respects they further centralized authority by requiring local chapters and councils to seek permission for their mandates and secure approval of their bylaws from YAF's national policy committee.[21]

They also insisted that YAF needed an executive director. Caddy's absence had forced William Cotter, YAF's organizational director, to abandon his own work to carry out administrative responsibilities. This jeopardized "our organizational drive." In a confidential memorandum to the Board of Directors, Liebman, Buckley, Evans, and Rusher noted that Liebman had found a person for the job after interviewing several candidates. He was Richard Viguerie, who would officially be employed by Marvin Liebman Associates rather than Young Americans for Freedom. They requested that YAF's board meet him in advance of his appointment, even though he would not hold a policy-making position within the organization, and the group gathered in Liebman's New York offices on August 12, 1961 to discuss with Viguerie his responsibilities toward YAF.[22]

Viguerie would administer the programs for which YAF had contracted with Marvin Liebman Associates, as well as supervise the operation of YAF's national office, improve its efficiency, raise funds, and promote YAF and its magazine, *The New Guard*. He held the title of "Executive Secretary," even though he was not an official in YAF itself. Born in Houston, Texas in 1933, Viguerie had lived in Houston almost all his life and was a graduate of the University of Houston. He had served a brief hitch in the United States Army, was a Catholic, and was currently employed in the land department of the Western Natural Gas Company in Houston. He brought to his new position considerable political experience as a former chairman of the Harris County Young Republicans as well as in various political campaigns, and had served as Harris County campaign manager for John Tower in 1960. "It is easy to see that my main interest lies along the organizational phase of politics," he wrote on his resume. "I am very interested in a career in politics. My political philosophy is that of a conservative. I am a great admirer of Barry Goldwater and naturally Texas' own John Tower."[23]

In their confidential memorandum to the board of directors, Carol Bauman, Robert Croll, Lee Edwards, David Franke, James Kolbe, William Madden, and William Schulz expressed concern that there were too few individual chapters and a "relatively small number of members" after almost a year of activity. All hoped that Viguerie would launch an intensive membership drive and spend most of his time in the field organizing. They also insisted that YAF expand its board of directors and policy committee to create a more equitable geographic representation. Both the Midwest and the Far West were underrepresented. Too many members believed that a small clique on the east coast ran the organization, and felt left out. They sought to refocus the organization on its original objectives.

> We reaffirm our faith and confidence in our officers, and we wish to commend them for what has been an outstanding job. . . . We present our recommendations with the sincere desire to further the goals of the Sharon Statement. We are positive that YAF can be a genuine national conservative youth organization; but we as its officers have the solemn obligation to see that it attains the goals of its founders. We hope the Board will accept our recommendations in that spirit.[24]

The question now remained: what would the board do at its September meeting?

The Role of William Rusher

William Rusher, acting as point man for the *National Review* godfathers of Young Americans for Freedom, drew up balance sheets of "solid" and "hostile" board members as he prepared for the September meeting. He feared that YAF would fall prey to libertarians, Birchers, or the naked opportunism of some youthful directors. His memoranda make clear the naive belief of the *National Review* editors that YAFers would compliantly do their bidding. They forgot, he observed, "that the creation of any such organization gives rise to politicians the way warm weather gives rise to dandelions." At present the "weeds" were few, but they threatened to spread.

> It seems perfectly clear that, as early as March, Caddy had already invented the concept of his own personal master of YAF, and had divorced it in his own mind from his relationship and obligations to the Marvin Liebman office. He subsequently brought in Cotter, infected him with the same virus, and left him in control of their mutual enterprise while he went off to the Army. The two of them won Phillips to their side by backing him for YR College chairman in Minneapolis, and made a firm alliance with Schuchman in July, when Marvin blocked their attempt to oust that friendless young opportunist and he decided that at last he could no longer afford to play on all sides simultaneously. These four—plus that incredible cornball from Kansas, Scott Stanley—were the bloc that opposed us on Saturday; no one else.[25]

Rusher's careful planning paid off. At a heated meeting of YAF's national board on a sultry Saturday in Marvin Liebman's office, after "elaborate parliamentary arabesques" and threats to withdraw the support of Marvin Liebman and *National Review*, the insurgents were defeated. But despite defeat, the Caddy bloc did not resign. Working control of YAF was guaranteed only until its next national convention, in the summer or fall of 1962. Rusher warned that "We have scotched the snakes, not killed them. We must find friendly forces in YAF as strong and resourceful and determined as Caddy and Cotter and Phillips—or almost as strong (for we can always add our own majestic baritone to their tenor)." From now on YAF would have to be handled as a political issue. They had been too trusting, and had overlooked the importance of the board of directors and the damage its members could do to their dreams for a conservative movement wedded to the *National Review* philosophy. YAF was a dynamic organization, not merely a front group. The central question now was: "upon whom can we build our church?"[26]

The central problem was how to pull the discordant threads of YAF together, and Rusher bent to the task, hoping in hindsight that the problem was one of growing pains. Thanking George McDonnell (midwest regional chair) for his support, Rusher observed that it "could not possibly have been healthy for YAF to cut itself wholly adrift from the main body of American conservatism merely in order to please or propitiate a faction. And yet that is exactly what was at stake Saturday afternoon." To soothe wounds, the board offered to employ John Birch sympathizer Scott Stanley to raise funds and organize chapters, but the John Birch question continued to vex Young Americans for Freedom and the conservative movement in general.[27]

Rusher and Liebman argued that factional fights were endemic to organizations such as YAF, and insisted that they were actually signs of "health and vigor." YAF director Jack Molesworth agreed, writing Rusher that he was pleased at the outcome and believed that the dissidents remained "in the family" and would continue to work together. He hoped critics appreciated the efforts of Caddy, Cotter, and Phillips to build YAF as an organization, even if they questioned their judgment at times. Personal differences, he believed, should not intrude on political decisions. Rusher agreed, and hoped future internal disagreements (such as YAF's $20,000 in unpaid bills) could be kept confidential: "the stream of mutual recriminations has to stop somewhere, and as far as I am concerned it can stop here."[28]

In a long letter to Brent Bozell that September, Rusher assessed the progress of conservatism and detailed the YAF imbroglio. He reported that Goldwater was getting a "very big press," and that Nixon seemed to be going nowhere. More fascinating to Rusher, however, was the case of Nelson Rockefeller. Rockefeller had begun to court conservatives, and had hired Martin McKneally, the immediate past national chairman of the American Legion, as his "Vice President in Charge of Capturing Conservatives." McKneally had struck up personal friendships with YAFers Douglas Caddy and William Cotter. In early August a delegation of YAF board members visited Governor Rockefeller and he pitched his conservative credentials to them. Rusher worried that they might succumb to this courtship and thereby blunt the "remarkable upsurge of conservative interest and activity around the country." As he reminded Bozell, that growth remained fragile.

> It would be easy to overrate what these and similar groups have already done; I know the YAF story from the inside, and it is considerably less impressive than the public facade Marvin has so ably created. I suspect the same may be true of the John Birch Society—though, of course, the tremendous publicity they have received this year has made them a Mecca for every crackpot in America. But, when all appropriate discounts have been made for exaggeration, it seems quite clear that these organizations are the beneficiaries of a growing urge on the part of conservatives to Do Something . . . .[29]

A Goldwater candidacy in 1964 was the best vehicle to advance conservative objectives, and even if he failed to win or even be nominated the effort might be sufficient to capture control of the Republican Party.

The central question, as in the YAF dispute, was that of leadership. Who would lead, and in what direction? Those leaders, he warned, "are not necessarily going to save a place for *National Review* at, or even necessarily near, the head of the parade." Partly as a result of the YAF dissension, Rusher now concluded that active involvement rather than pious editorializing was needed to lead the conservative movement in the "proper" direction. To abstain from the fray was to concede leadership to others. That had led to the difficulties with Young Americans for Freedom, and it lay behind the controversy with the John Birch Society as well as with conservative groups led by Clarence Manion, Billy James Hargis, and "a score of lesser lights."

> As nearly as I can tell, the sentiment in the higher reaches of *National Review* seems to be that, when we want the conservatives of America to organize, we will tell them about it; and that meanwhile they can darned well wait. My objection to this viewpoint is that, in all likelihood, they *won't* wait; that, instead, increasingly frustrated by their country's desperate situation and justifiably contemptuous of both major parties, they will fall into the hands of men and organizations woefully unsuited to the responsibility—and, with just a little further bad luck, into the hands of the first really slick demagogue that comes along.[30]

Rusher monitored the actions and activities of YAF and its leadership closely, and encouraged conservative groups at the local, state, and national levels. He quietly urged friends to steer Howard Phillips (who had participated in the effort to seize control of YAF in September) back into the mainstream. "This young man is worth saving," Rusher wrote, "but he is going to have to do most of the work himself."[31]

The November board meeting in Washington would be the real test of the September agreements, and since Rusher was going to be in California, he carefully planned strategy. Particularly crucial was a "bloc of more or less non-aligned members who can't stand the sight of blood." He warned Robert Croll that his supporters needed to avoid alienating this group, lest they join the opposition. Rusher suggested turning YAF's barren treasury to their advantage. End YAF's employment of Stanley (a Bircher) and Cotter (a Rockefeller supporter), to prevent Cotter's salary from passing to Caddy when he returned from the Army in December. "Why can't we just wipe a tear from our eye and announce that, much as we love them, there is no money with which to employ them?" Avoid personalities, he counseled Croll, because Molesworth, McIntyre, McDonnell, and Madden found them offensive. "I am far less concerned about having vengeance upon Stanley than I am about looking reasonable in the eyes of the neutralist bloc." This might sound "namby-pamby," Rusher admitted, but he believed the "neutralists" were "good people, who simply have not become involved in our factional brawls." Every effort ought to be made "to avoid alienating them permanently."[32]

The other part of Rusher's strategy was to eliminate the position of national organization director. He asked George McDonnell to propose the appointment of regional and state organization directors, to serve without pay much as Young Republican organizers had always done. The main point, however, was to avoid alienating the neutral bloc while ending Cotter's salary and connection to Rockefeller. Finally, he asked Croll to scout around for a new national chairman, and to look particularly at Robert Harley. "We have some good politicians on our side," Rusher admitted, "but most of them are either geographically too inaccessible or politically too committed to a career in Young Republicanism or something like that; and this has bothered me badly, because whatever we may think of Caddy, Cotter and their allies, YAF will be electing new national officers in less than a year and 'you can't beat somebody with nobody.'"[33]

Rusher's strategy worked. At its November meeting the YAF board took note of the fund-raising failures of Bill Cotter, Scott Stanley, and Lynn Bouchey, and decided to retain their services but eliminate their salaries. It also abolished the national organization director's position, although Cotter retained his board membership. "In political terms," Rusher observed, "all this suggests a continuation of the trend that dominated the meeting on September 2nd." Richard Viguerie was doing a good job in Marvin Liebman's office handling YAF's business affairs, and new members of the board seemed promising. Particularly appealing to Rusher was the work of Robert Bauman. "It may be that he is the man that we have all been looking for to unite YAF in the days ahead. However, it may be a little early to be thinking such thoughts just yet; it will be enough to get through the next few months."[34]

Rusher's caution proved well-founded, as YAF experienced almost unremitting internal warfare throughout the next year. Citing an "ugly and increasingly serious situation involving the national Board of Directors of YAF," Rusher continued to urge his fellow editors to become involved and straighten out YAF's problems. They were problems, he insisted, that "will arise in any mass political action organization we form," and his colleagues could not avoid them if they wanted such an organization to do what *National Review* itself lacked the means to do. The fact that the backbiting was usually personal and conducted behind the scenes, however, kept the public largely unaware of YAF's problems and did not seriously erode its public image.[35]

In September 1960 they had "presided over the birth of a social organism," and then turned it over to a public relations firm to run on their behalf and walked away, believing that everything would turn out all right. Marvin Liebman, whose public relations firm had guided YAF's day-to-day activities, had done a superb job, but he was not a politician. Either his associates supported Young Americans for Freedom, Rusher warned, or they risked seeing a massbased conservative organization develop without their "guidance or blessing."

Despite the expansion of YAF's board and reorganization of the policy committee to solidify the pro-*National Review* majority, Douglas Caddy and his cohorts continued their efforts to seize control. Caddy obtained a position with the United States Chamber of Commerce after his discharge from the Army, and cultivated friendly contacts with Texas Republican leader Peter O'Donnell Jr. Cotter found a job with the National Association of Manufacturers, and maintained his ties with Martin McKneally. Scott Stanley eventually resigned from the board and went to work for Robert Welch and the John Birch Society. Schuchman and Phillips remained in school. Marvin Liebman became the lightning rod for persistent dissidence.

The Issue of Marvin Liebman

Rusher noted that Caddy and Cotter had tried to smear Marvin Liebman as a way of getting at YAF itself. Cotter attacked YAF at the December meeting of the National Association of Manufacturers, raising questions about its finances and its relationship with Liebman. Scott Stanley also attacked both YAF and Liebman at the December meeting of the National Council of the John Birch Society. These and other attacks led Liebman to ask that the board sever his firm's relationship with YAF. Rusher reluctantly agreed. Although he believed that Caddy and the other dissidents were trying to destroy YAF rather than capture it, separating it from Liebman's firm might undercut many of the attacks.

The Liebman issue had actually been festering since summer 1961, when some YAF board members suggested ending the formal relationship with Marvin Liebman Associates. After a small adjustment, YAF's board voted to continue the relationship. Later, at its November 19, 1961 meeting, YAF's directors had suspended the agenda to discuss proposals from Liebman for increased staff and salaries for YAF's New York office. Liebman argued that he was spending $2,780 per month on behalf of YAF, most of it for five full-time staff members, and he was losing money. The board unanimously accepted his proposals to provide fewer services for the same fee, and to give YAF the option of increasing those services for additional fees. Attacks on the YAF-Liebman connection escalated with the new year, however, and in January Liebman offered to resign by April 1, 1962. He argued that YAF was in sound financial health and had a solid national membership base, and that there was little else his firm could contribute. He also recommended that YAF move its national office to Washington, D.C., and continue to employ Richard Viguerie as its executive secretary.[36]

Liebman's letter hinted at the underlying problems when he urged YAF's directors to remove Scott Stanley and William Cotter from the board. A month later he elaborated some of the difficulties in a confidential memo to the board. For two months, Liebman said, he had heard rumors that he considered YAF to be his "personal fief" and that he had been "looting" the treasury to line his pockets. Letters to Fulton Lewis Jr. and others had claimed that he was sabotaging the anticommunist campaign, and was some sort of "com-symp" himself. The American Nazi Party had circulated a pamphlet attacking YAF and its supporters as "Jew-Led Kosher Conservatives," labeling Liebman a "fanatical Zionist' who exerted "dictatorial control" over YAF.[37]

Liebman not only found these matters personally distasteful and professionally damaging, but feared they would discredit the entire organization and the broader conservative cause. He blamed Douglas Caddy, William Cotter, and Scott Stanley for the rumors, and admitted that they were the chief reason he had submitted his resignation. "If YAF is to survive and flourish," he warned, "some stringent house-cleaning must be undertaken with all possible dispatch." As for himself, he would sue any individual who persisted in such damaging attacks on his personal, professional or political integrity. Rusher wrote Buckley that Liebman's "impulsive action" was understandable, would not likely hurt YAF, and might energize efforts to oust Cotter and Stanley at the March board meeting.[38]

In a letter to Charles Edison, Douglas Caddy claimed that it was "irrational" for Liebman to blame them for his sagging reputation, and that some YAF board members believed the award to be presented to Liebman at a March rally should be "rescinded." In addition, T. Coleman Andrews apparently wrote to Edison about Liebman being a leftist plant to take over YAF. Edison talked with Liebman about the matter, and the award was not rescinded. But photostats of the various letters flew fast and furious, leading Rusher to ask that *National Review* profile Liebman and his "really tremendous services to the cause of conservatism."[39]

A Struggle for Control

But the prey was bigger than Marvin Liebman, and the dissenters changed their tactics, "quite as if they had all suddenly had prefrontal lobotomies." Whether Liebman's resignation or something else had changed their minds, they now tried again to capture control of YAF rather than destroy it. They cried "peace," and urged the board not to oust Cotter and Stanley at its March 8 meeting. They won over three neutralists, and the board failed to muster the required two-thirds majority for ouster despite the pleas of Rusher, Liebman, and Stanton Evans. Rusher warned Buckley after the meeting that they needed a "strenuous exercise of the force of your hitherto unexpended personality" at YAF's biennial convention in September if the *National Review* forces were to prevail. "I know of no other way," he concluded, "to keep YAF, after September, out of the hands of their designees—and hence of their elders." Defeat would mean replacement of *National Review* by a "rather gamay [*sic*] combination of Welch, McKneally, Sligh and (perhaps) O'Donnell."[40]

Much of the maneuvering by Caddy and his fellow dissenters stemmed from political ambition rather than ideology. Although the stakes seemed small at the time, at issue, at least from their perspective, was the future leadership and control of the conservative movement. Caddy had argued that, with the *National Review* attack on Robert Welch and the John Birch Society, YAF should move to a more independent stance so as not to isolate itself from potential conservative supporters. At the same time, however, he had endorsed Nelson Rockefeller for reelection as governor of New York, despite Rockefeller's increasingly strident attacks on the Birch Society. He also continued to call himself a supporter of Senator Barry Goldwater! Caddy, said Rusher, was being "swivel-hipped." With all the YAF board seats up for election at the September convention, YAF was in danger of a takeover. "If we are not careful," Rusher warned, "there will be a '*National Review* slate' of Franke types versus an 'anti-*National Review* slate' backed by everybody from Welch to the NAM, the

Chamber of Commerce and Rockefeller." He hoped for a behind-the-scenes so-lution—seeking the help of O'Donnell and others to end the "weird Welch-Rockefeller alliance." The choice was whether to wade in or stand aside.[41]

During the next several months Rusher, Buckley, and others associated with *National Review* carried on an extensive correspondence about YAF's affairs and future. Critics called Rusher "imperious," and the various factions caucused fu-riously. Robert Croll warned Rusher that while both he and James Abstine sup-ported Rusher's position, they worried about the "unconscionable East coast domination" of YAF. The issue, at least for midwesterners Croll and Abstine, was the political apportionment of power within the organization, and they threatened to withhold their votes on critical matters until midwestern and western YAFers received greater recognition. Croll warned Rusher that "I doubt if YAF can stand another national chairman and national director who are both from the East coast." In the face of these problems, Rusher wondered if the "whole conservative renaissance" was not "premature as a political movement." Perhaps, he concluded, "we must reconcile ourselves to being tablet-keepers, and let it go at that for the moment."[42]

This represented despair more than conviction, however, and Rusher waged a determined battle to chart YAF's direction. During the next few months he corresponded furiously with various members of the YAF board, hoping to maintain or recruit allies for the September convention. YAF's internal bick-ering, however, stemmed not only from factional efforts to control the organi-zation, but from tangible differences among conservatives. Douglas Caddy wrote a letter, published in the *Wall Street Journal*, that typified the quandary for Young Americans for Freedom and conservatives generally. Joining an on-going debate about how best to advance the conservative cause, Caddy attacked those who advocated formation of a third party. The two-party system was the only viable political structure, he insisted, and the Republican Party was the conservatives' route to power. Noting that he supported Senator Barry Gold-water, Caddy nonetheless attacked the plan for a newly organized Conserva-tive party in New York to oppose Governor Nelson Rockefeller. That might defeat Rockefeller, he admitted, but it would elect a liberal Democrat in his place. What would that gain for conservatives? "Why should conservatives fur-ther drain the waning power of the GOP by starting a third party?"

Caddy's letter set off another firestorm within YAF. Frank Meyer of *Na-tional Review*, a supporter of YAF and an organizer of the Conservative party of New York, blasted Caddy for opposing YAF's national policy committee, which had "dissociated themselves from his position." The *Wall Street Journal* rejected efforts by the policy committee to insert a reply to Caddy. Caddy later attacked Rusher's influence in the organization, and argued that YAF suffered from "internal impotence" because of the infighting. The timing of Caddy's letter, coming only two days after the March board meeting, added further fuel to the open warfare within the YAF board. Marvin Liebman wrote William F. Buckley Jr. that Caddy "seems to be afflicted by paranoia. He has an extremely vicious streak in him and, I believe, the less to do with him, the better."[43]

From the fragmentary information available, the bickering also seems to have infected the chapters. The Boston College chapter passed a resolution of censure against Howard Phillips, charging that at the 1962 annual meeting of the Massachusetts Council of Young Republican Clubs he had supported non-YAF candidates against YAF members on five occasions, and petitioning for his removal as New England director for YAF. Critics also attacked Richard Viguerie for his earlier involvement in factional struggles within the Texas Republican Party. Rusher acknowledged that he knew of these charges (Viguerie had told him), but defended Viguerie and observed that he had done an outstanding job as YAF's executive secretary. Although these were controversies confined to particular locales, they reflected the general organizational instability that had begun to plague Young Americans for Freedom by the summer of 1962. Rusher admitted that the "YAF feud is still boiling and belching along," but hoped for the best. "The feud may not precisely die out," he wrote Peter O'Donnell, "but I have high hopes that most of the participants will simply graduate from their present positions and pass on to other things."[44]

The Douglas Caddy Affair

Rusher's hopes were in vain. In early July Caddy, Cotter, and another individual ("a big guy") barged into the YAF offices, overpowered the two YAFers on duty, and made off with the general membership list, the general ledger, and a list of four or five thousand financial contributors to YAF. Caddy apparently photocopied them at his Chamber of Commerce offices, returning the originals to YAF a few days later. Robert Bauman threatened Caddy with a felony prosecution, and Caddy turned over the copies to YAF. He was then fired by the Chamber of Commerce. These events triggered yet another crisis for YAF. Caddy had apparently intended to document rumors that YAF had severe financial irregularities, which would likely dry up the organization's financial support from prominent backers such as the Pew family and conservative politicians. William F. Buckley Jr., in a calming letter to an alarmed Barry Goldwater, labeled Caddy a "troublemaker" and assured him that there were no financial irregularities within Young Americans for Freedom. Factionalism was the problem, Buckley noted, and he hoped that Stanton Evans would come in and run the organization to "cut out this nonsense." He also told Goldwater that certain conservatives, like Pew, really wanted to take over YAF and run it themselves. "YAF is not available for him to run," Buckley advised.[45]

The so-called Caddy affair, and what to do about it, further divided YAF. Because the relationship between Caddy and several YAF board members had been turbulent prior to this affair, a majority of the board was ready to expel him immediately. But Caddy charged that the version of events relayed by Rusher and Bauman was distorted, and threatened to sue for slander. Board member William Madden complained that Bauman had contradicted his earlier story somewhat, worried that the immaturity of some board members would exacerbate the affair, and urged YAF to sit tight and take no further action. "Expulsion would only add to the wrath of Mr. Caddy," Madden insisted, "and harden his determination to go to court, and in this case directly against YAF." The result would be further mudslinging by both sides.[46]

The real problem, Madden warned, was not just the dissatisfaction of Doug Caddy and some other dissenters. It was the attempt by William Rusher and others to merge YAF with the Young Republicans and take over the Young Republican National Federation. Madden urged Rusher to "leave the YRs alone!" Most of the troubles afflicting YAF stemmed, in his view, from "young Republican alliances." "Now either the best road to conservatism lies through the YRs or through YAF," Madden concluded. He noted that in his experience the Young Republicans became engulfed in annual election frenzies. As a result, "so much organizational energy, so much time of the leaders and so many friendships are wasted and lost as to make the YRs little more than a training ground whereby young people can develop the skill of surviving in the senior party." YAF, in his view, should be more than that. It should promote conservatism rather than merely train people how to wield power. "It is quite an art to ride two horses at once and keep them going in the same direction," he observed. "But what good does it do?"[47]

Rusher noted that a two-thirds majority of the board was ready to oust Caddy, and he thought with good reason. Not only had Caddy conspired with William Cotter and Scott Stanley to attack YAF the previous fall; he had been making charges about YAF's financial affairs for more than a year. Despite an audit of YAF's books, as well as an invitation to Caddy to designate his own accountant to examine the books, the insinuations continued and had led to the forced removal of records from YAF's offices. Regardless of whatever physical force had been used (and this seemed to be the only fact in doubt about the affair), it was illegal. "I care about YAF," Rusher concluded, "and I think— indeed, I *know*—that it has been terribly hurt, financially and otherwise, by the smears that Caddy, Cotter and Stanley have directed against it, and which Caddy, under the umbrella of your inadvertent but *de facto* protection, is continuing to broadcast from a privileged position on its Board."[48]

Rusher clearly was determined to back the board in its efforts to oust Caddy. He shared his Madden correspondence with Richard Viguerie, observing that he believed it summed up their case against Caddy "reasonably well." But Rusher's fears that Caddy had seriously damaged the organization seem to have been somewhat inflated and confined chiefly to easterners and a few insiders. Indeed, Madden responded by asking how YAFers in the East expected midwesterners to have known all those details, and worried that expulsion would trigger lawsuits and further damage YAF. Could not the board wait until the fall elections and remove Caddy that way? Claiming to speak for George McDonnell as well, he noted that "we would both put a great more faith and trust in the future of YAF if some of our close advisors such as you and Stan [Evans] would do your best to steer YAF clear from the mainstream of YR politics and would see to it that the evil effects of annual elections were eliminated. . . . Until our board decides to adopt a program with short range goals and to put aside the convention toys of the YRs, YAF will continue to flounder and breed 'Doug Caddys.'"[49]

Rusher and Buckley finally turned to the YAF bylaws in an effort to resolve the tensions. Buckley, who had tried to remain aloof from YAF's internal battles, argued that "during the next two years, most of the energies that have gone into political in-fighting should find expression, instead, in right-wing political action and thought." He suggested several changes in the bylaws to "remove existing temptations and distractions." Buckley identified three sources of persistent tension: endorsement of political candidates, attendance and voting at board meetings, and the power of the national chair. In each case his solutions sought to prevent small factions from disrupting the larger organization. Local chapters should seek permission from the national chair before endorsing local or state candidates. Should they be denied, they could appeal and try to secure a two-thirds majority of the board. In addition, endorsement of any third-party candidates needed not only the chair's approval, but the approval of two-thirds of the board as well. Board voting privileges would be restricted to board members or any proxies received within ten days of a board meeting for any matter of substance. Not only would last-minute proxies not be honored; the possibility of voting by mail would relieve some financial burdens on directors from distant points (such as the midwest). No longer would only those board members who could afford to attend meetings absolutely control the organization. Finally, Buckley recommended that "on such occasions when he feels that the life or good health of the organization" was "endangered as the result of factional or ideological divisions," the national chair (supported by at least five board members) could appeal to the executive committee of the advisory board. That committee, in turn, had the power to expel or suspend the YAF membership of any person or chapter after a hearing. Rusher joined Buckley in urging YAF to adopt the changes.[50]

In the meantime, Rusher recruited candidates for the YAF board and other offices. He was delighted to hear that Lynn Bouchey was running for Western Regional Chairman. "Naturally I am on your side all the way," he told Bouchey, "but I think that you and I had both better consider a little further whether it would be wise to endorse you publicly." Rusher also recruited Robert Bauman to run for the national chair, even sending along a financial contribution from both himself and William F. Buckley Jr. Admonishing Bauman to "treat this confidentially," he confided that "I also know that you are going to make a personally wonderful National Chairman of Young Americans for Freedom." Rusher had Viguerie write Bauman about plans for the convention, and Viguerie relayed Rusher's advice that YAF should do its "laundry in the back room" and try to minimize any efforts to "make a 'Coliseum-performance' out of the convention."[51]

Robert Bauman Takes the Reins

The first annual Young Americans for Freedom convention met at the Commodore Hotel in New York City, September 27–29. It provided a large dose of political analysis and activism in addition to internal administrative activities. The nearly 500 YAFers in attendance could choose from four policy seminars. William Rusher, James Burnham, and Ernest van den Haag presented an analysis of "American Strategy in the Cold War." Other seminars included one on the "Common Market and the Free Market," and another on the "Domestic Program of the New Frontier." Finally, William Casey, Clifton White, and two other presenters offered a session on the "Methodology of Political Action." Florida Congressman William Cramer spoke at the opening session and called for a strong effort to drive the Castro regime from Cuba. Delegates passed resolutions advocating a blockade of Cuba, opposing the recent Supreme Court decision outlawing school prayer, and upholding the "rights of voluntary association for fraternal organizations." At the conclusion of the three-day meeting, William F. Buckley Jr., still the patron saint of YAFers, attacked the Kennedy administration for its "diplomatic nothingness" in handling the Cuban situation, and insisted that the right wing did not advocate war. The surest way to avoid war, Buckley argued, was "to assert our willingness to fight it."[52]

Probably the most important action taken at the convention was the election of a new board of directors and a new national chair. Rusher and his allies had left little to chance. On the eve of the convention, Richard Viguerie provided Rusher with a detailed breakdown of potential candidates. Perhaps the greatest problem, he noted, was Robert Schuchman, who was running "for the Board so hard that he is falling all over himself . . . ." Schuchman's allegiances were not clear, and Viguerie warned that he would do business with any potential winner. Viguerie also pointed to David Franke's candidacy for the middle-Atlantic regional chair as a potential problem, given Franke's attempt to control New York YAFers. His survey of other potential candidates turned up only one other trouble spot. Rosemary McGrath (whom Dan Wakefield called "La Passionaria of the Right") was "on the war-path" with a major campaign for the board and was insisting that the convention remain open. Unless "someone greatly convinces her to hold her tongue," she "could make the difference in this thing."[53]

These fears turned out to be groundless, however, as Robert Bauman, the new national chair, and all the regional chairs were elected by acclamation. The fourteen candidates (out of twenty-four) elected to the national board included Lammot Copeland Jr., Robert Croll, Donald Devine, Antoni Gollan, Craig Ihde, James Kolbe, Fulton (Buddy) Lewis III, Marilyn Manion, Diarmuid O'Scannlain, Robert Schuchman, William Schulz, Don Shafto, John Weicher, and Ed Zanini. Most of these individuals supported Bauman as well the as yet unannounced presidential candidacy of Arizona Senator Barry Goldwater. The clique of dissidents failed to run for reelection. Urging Goldwater to meet Bauman, Rusher rejoiced at the results: "In a nutshell, therefore, I think it is fair to say that the long nightmare of internal factionalism in YAF is over. Of course, that doesn't mean that the millennium has arrived; there will still be disagreements, and a normal amount of politics. But I really do think that the situation is going to improve markedly; and, God willing, we will be able to restore YAF to the health and momentum it once had."[54]

Robert Bauman, the new national chair, was twenty-five years old, a graduate of Georgetown University's School of Foreign Service, and a student at Georgetown Law School. He was a native Marylander, had served as a congressional page as well as an aide to minority leader Charles Halleck. He had also participated in both the 1960 Chicago planning meeting and the subsequent Sharon Conference. Bauman was married to the former Carol Dawson, who had also been at Chicago and Sharon and was a conservative activist in her own right. Elected to the board of directors in 1961, he had served as YAF's liaison with Congress. He had also been organizing chairman for National Youth for Nixon in 1960. Bauman attacked President John F. Kennedy's lack of "guts to take care of Cuba," and argued that YAF "must go into politics with a determination to win for conservatism." He outlined an ambitious program for YAF. It included a national legislative service to alert YAFers to the substance and status of major bills pending before Congress, a national speakers' bureau, a YAF news service for college and local newspapers, an expanded series of rallies in major cities with closed-circuit television hookups, participation at the 1964 New York World's Fair, and a radio and TV program that could be used locally by chapters.[55] Bauman's election and the results of the September convention brought internal peace to Young Americans for Freedom. The national office moved to Washington, D.C.

What Young Americans for Freedom had gone through had been traumatic. Ostensibly committed to the Sharon Statement, YAFers' ideological commitments to conservatism were unquestioned but not very cohesive. The internal brawls, and even the assault on the National Student Association, revealed three major flaws. First, one could swear allegiance to the principles in the Sharon Statement without either revealing or compromising one's personal convictions. The Statement was far too general to be an exacting analysis of conservative programs or even to shape a coherent ideology. It lacked any specific analysis, and thereby allowed YAFers to embrace its generalities without debating details. Second, the Sharon Statement, and in many respects YAF itself, embodied an oppositional movement. The NSA struggle reflected this, in that YAFers with a wide range of conservative convictions united to oppose what they proclaimed to be a Left-liberal demonology. Their alternative was not a comprehensive conservative program, but the overthrow of those currently in power.

The final flaw lay in the inability of many YAFers to subordinate personal agendas and goals to a broader conservative agenda. Perhaps they were too young; perhaps they were too power-hungry; perhaps they confused the two. Whatever the cause, individuals' quest for leadership and power subordinated organizational and ideological imperatives. By the fall of 1961, only one year after its formation, Young Americans for Freedom had devolved into warring factions. William Rusher, together with the *National Review* faction and dedicated moderates, had patched together the organization. What remained to be seen was whether the stitches would hold. Would Young Americans for Freedom become the vehicle for a conservative advance by 1964, or would other more radical right-wing organizations claim the field and undercut the moderates?[56] Despite internecine quarrels between right-wing organizations, and despite the internal factionalism that had characterized Young Americans for Freedom, by the early 1960s this movement worried Democrats and liberals.

Chapter 6

Attacking the New Frontier

Even as Young Americans for Freedom battled internal factionalism, the organization moved forward in 1961 and 1962 to attack the New Frontier of President John F. Kennedy. In doing so, they focused on several objectives: broadening the conservative political base around the country by depicting the New Frontier as evidence of the dangerous statism inherent in a liberal establishment; marshalling support for a Goldwater presidential candidacy in 1964, chiefly by waging internal political battles within the Republican Party; and forging links to other right-wing groups active in political circles. YAF hoped to operate, in the words of Douglas Caddy, as an "umbrella organization."[1] Their ideological and political opposition to the New Frontier was the linchpin for all these efforts.

One phase of this effort was a broad critique of liberalism as a political system. Insisting that men should remain free to pursue "individual conceptions of the good," Stanton Evans argued that the chief problem with liberalism was that it sought to impose a single ethic. Abolition of plural sources of loyalty, according to Evans, was the first step in the destruction of freedom. It curbed individuals' freedom of intellect and action, and led to a totalitarian state under the guise of orthodoxy. Noting the growing criticism of American society, Evans found it ironic that much of the criticism came from liberals who claimed to be dissenters. But from what were they dissenting? He insisted that they were only dissenting from liberalism. The conformity they attacked, he observed, "by the tests of ideological congruity and regnant power is Liberalism itself." Liberals pictured themselves as outsiders and attacked their own orthodoxy. But they were wrong. "True rebellion must proceed, not from the obscure frenzies of 'activism,' but from the sustained clarity of ideation. In this time of Liberal orthodoxy," he concluded, "the authentic force of revolution reposes not in a more excited leftism but in conservatism, the vital traditions of the West reborn."[2]

In a November 1961 Manion Forum interview, William F. Buckley Jr. called the conservative movement the most vital political movement of the day. Exalting a wide array of conservative writers and spokesmen, and playing down the persona of Barry Goldwater, Buckley told listeners that the United States had to embrace conservatism if it was to survive the Soviet threat or domestic economic crises. Monopolistic labor unions, oppressive taxation, outdated depreciation laws, and excessive spending all threatened from within. To highlight the underlying differences between liberals and conservatives, Buckley defined a liberal as one who embraced a coherent ideology of governmental activism that translated into policy. Liberals, he said,

> tend to believe that the human being is perfectable, and social progress predictable, and that the instrument for effecting the two is reason, that truths are transitory and empirically determined, that equality is desirable and attainable through the action of state power, that social and individual differences, if they are not rational or objectionable, should be scientifically eliminated, that all peoples and societies should strive to organize themselves upon a rationalist and scientific paradigm.[3]

The conservative believed exactly the opposite. Later, a new publication aimed at young conservatives said much the same thing more directly: "that there is no governmental method of obtaining a free society."[4]

Domestic Programs

To help mobilize this invisible conservative majority, YAFers and their allies focused on the domestic and foreign policies of the Kennedy administration. Their tactic of opposing specific legislation on the grounds that it violated fundamental principles of conservatism masked to some extent their inability or unwillingness to advance alternative conservative policy solutions. This may have stemmed in part from their realization that President Kennedy was popular with the electorate. It also reflected their own admission that some of what he was doing was smart politics. Complaining that the "press is bewitched, the Left is bothered, and the GOP is bewildered," YAFer Lee Edwards admitted that JFK was the "most determined and calculating politician to reside in the White

House for 20 years and perhaps longer." Edwards, ironically, focused much of his criticism on Kennedy's failure to redeem campaign promises and actually move the country ahead. He was hypnotizing the press, Edwards argued, and wooing Nixon voters; both would help reelect him in four years, but would also spark liberal dissent. Yet, where could the liberals go? For Edwards the answer was clear—they had nowhere to go. Kennedy's moderate policy recommendations might not please the liberals, but Edwards worried that the slow pace of change would stifle any conservative opposition.[5]

YAF's attack in the early months of the Kennedy administration focused on the privileged position held by organized labor. Organized labor was an "overwhelming force" in American politics, Carol Bauman argued, and JFK had been labor's candidate. He was indebted, therefore, to Walter Reuther and other labor leaders. Bauman cited recent legislation raising the minimum wage and extending unemployment compensation as evidence of labor's influence within the administration, and warned that worse legislation lay ahead. Young Americans for Freedom particularly opposed efforts by labor to circumvent state right-to-work laws. Touting these laws as saviors of individual freedom, Bauman and her colleagues argued that labor opposed individual choice and sought to legislate a "collectivist and welfare state program." Right-to-work laws, for Bauman and YAF, protected the "constitutional right of freedom of association." But labor favored compulsory unionism even though "honest unions" had nothing to fear from that freedom. Freedom of association, Bauman concluded, was a "natural moral right" and a sound economic measure. It was, in short, a necessary protection to "balance the power of Big Labor and Big Business in the interest of the consumer, and the workingman . . . ." The statist approach to the issues of unemployment and economic growth only led to increased costs, higher prices, inflation, more taxes, deficit spending, and ultimately, national decay. She warned that free enterprise needed to be unleashed, not restrained.[6]

By summer, Young Americans for Freedom concluded that there was a clear trend. Not only did the administration support big labor with welfare legislation that fostered higher prices and greater unemployment; it also provided farm subsidies in an effort to regulate agricultural prices. What appalled YAFers almost as much as the programs themselves was the lack of public outcry against them. As Lee Edwards reluctantly admitted, because "there has been no outcry from the public—which has been conditioned to believe that the money for government programs comes from 'somewhere' but not from their pockets—and because there has been no effective organized opposition either in the Congress or in the Press, the trend toward Federalization will continue." The best Edwards could say was that Kennedy had failed to secure passage of two crucial elements of his New Frontier: medical care for the aged and federal aid to education. That was, of course, a peculiar criticism, since conservatives strongly opposed both measures. *The New Guard* editors fervently hoped that "conservatives in Congress can rally the votes to substitute a major portion of the President's program with a more realistic one of their own."[7]

YAFers' comprehensive attacks on the New Frontier emphasized the distinct ideological differences between Kennedy's proposals and programs on the one hand and pronouncements in the Sharon Statement on the other. They focused on the statist activism of the Kennedy administration. The New Frontier sought to provide, in the words of Edwards, "bread and circuses." "They pay lip service to the importance of local government, personal initiative and competitive enterprise," Edwards wrote in *The New Guard*, "but they insist upon providing Federal subsidies which will debilitate local effort, individual initiative and economic competition." Although mayors and other interest groups advocated new federal programs, Edwards attacked this dependency. The United States, he concluded, must rely on individuals and not the government to solve its problems. Recalling the Sharon Statement, he insisted that the federal government only "preserves internal order, provides for national defense and administers justice."[8]

YAF board member Howard Phillips sounded a similar message in testimony against approval of a medical care program before the House Ways and Means Committee. Accompanied by some fellow YAFers, Phillips told the congressmen: "It is our conviction, that the United States in the 1960's is at a crossroads between freedom and Federal domination." Americans faced a choice, he argued: either individual responsibility and a "belief in certain absolute moral principles," or the weakness and false security of federal dependence. Free enterprise, not federal legislation, was the answer to the country's ills. Phillips outlined eleven reasons why YAF opposed medical care for the aged. All embraced a definition of freedom that exalted individualism and private enterprise and assumed that all government programs violated those ideals and thereby threatened Americans' freedoms. Stanton Evans echoed these sentiments in his examination of political trends under the Kennedy administration, noting that the "ominous" growth of the executive branch had made it "all but omnipotent."[9]

A final theme in YAF's criticism of Kennedy's domestic legislation emerged in the strident attacks on welfare by Joseph Mitchell, city manager of Newburgh, New York. Speaking before the Bergen County, New Jersey chapter of YAF, Mitchell attacked the cost of welfare and produced a thirteen-point reform program that included work incentives, no payments to people who quit work, and no payments to mothers for illegitimate children born after adoption of the reforms. Mitchell titled his speech "What More Could a Communist Ask?" This linkage of domestic issues to anticommunism became a popular theme for YAFers and conservatives generally, and Mitchell's speech encapsulated its essential arguments. The United States was Russia's primary target, he warned listeners. Communists sought world domination by capitalizing on American weaknesses and turning the country from "rugged individualism into submissive leaderlessness." Central to America's strength was its moral fiber, and the enlargement of federal powers at the expense of local governments represented the beginning of decay. Mitchell urged listeners to "study the changes that have taken place" in the past decade, insisting that rising crime rates, increased unemployment, changing social habits, urban decay, and growing relief rolls all pointed to moral decline. Continually repeating his refrain, "What more could a Communist ask?", Mitchell argued that "the unbridled growth of welfare may well unwittingly destroy our society morally, economically and socially. . . . It is like a green mold which could rot the fabric of society."

In a review of Mitchell's speech, YAFer David Franke characterized the proposals as neither inhumane nor discriminatory. He also raised the issue of race, arguing that blacks were more likely to be on welfare than were whites, and cited statistics to demonstrate a correlation between the changing racial composition of Newburgh's population and rising welfare rates. "Newburgh has stirred the nation's interest," Franke wrote, "because its problem is not unique but is shared by hundreds of other northern cities that have played host to Negroes migrating from the South. Many have come in an honest effort to find work and a better life, but many others have come in response to their relatives' and friends' reports about the easy living on welfare payments."[10]

Older conservatives joined in these attacks, supporting YAF's criticisms and helping define Young Americans for Freedom as part of a broader conservative movement. In a radio appearance on the Manion Forum, Senator Barry Goldwater urged the country to focus on the old goals of life, liberty, and the pursuit of happiness instead of searching for new ones. His host, Dean Clarence Manion, labeled President Kennedy's leadership "socialist," and Goldwater did not disagree. Goldwater blasted Kennedy's domestic and foreign policies, complaining that he seemed to govern primarily by creating a sense of crisis around whatever legislation he wanted Congress to pass. Goldwater, Manion, William Rusher, Daniel Buckley, and other conservatives particularly lamented what they saw as the decline of a militant anticommunism, citing as evidence a directive from the Defense Department restraining military officers from advocating "Right-Wing political theories in official public appearances."[11]

In Congress, a so-called "Conservative Club" formed. Comprising freshman Republicans, the group delivered a series of speeches in the fall of 1961 under the rubric "Operation Survival." Congressman Donald Bruce of Indiana, who had links to both Young Americans for Freedom and the Young Republicans, reported that the group intended to focus on "issues that are vital regarding the survival of our constitutional form of government." They rejected the Marxist theory of the class struggle and the idea that government was the "provider of all good things," attacked expansion of the federal bureaucracy as excessive statism, and argued that the very idea of social planning threatened liberty. Bruce concluded: "We have dedicated ourselves in an attempt to restore a balance in government, a withdrawal of Federal control from the multiple intrusions into the lives of the people, a pledge to fiscal integrity, moral responsibility, and sound progress based upon constitutional liberty."[12]

The speakers who followed Bruce articulated similar themes. They railed, in turn, against the decline of the spiritual basis of freedom, federal aid to education, and federal activism in general. Tracing much of the problem to the New Deal in the 1930s, they bemoaned the linkages forged between government institutions and economic or social needs. This had contributed to, and was in turn driven by, the growth of executive power. They blasted the Kennedy administration for encouraging this concentration of power, and attacked its programs for medical care, housing, transportation, agriculture, and foreign policy. "Our government structure is weaving dangerously in the breeze of deficit financing, confiscatory taxation, and bureaucratic arrogance," warned Bruce in his concluding remarks. The battle outlined by the fourteen congressmen, he argued, was critical for the United States.

> Let there be no question but what we are involved in a battle for survival. It is a dual battle—a battle against a dedicated, worldwide Communist movement, which has as its goal our complete destruction, and, simultaneously, within our own country, an attempt by sincere but misguided arrogants, who assume unto themselves superior wisdom for handling the affairs of men and would usurp the rights of the people with a centralized, collectivist form of Government.[13]

The real problem for conservatives was what to do. The arguments of Edwards, Phillips, Mitchell, and Bruce rejected prevailing social and political trends, but Young Americans for Freedom risked being marginalized by their failure to stand for anything more than philosophical principles. In addition, they flirted with racism and the danger that critics might lump them with the array of extreme right-wing organizations then active across the country. William Rusher summed up the difficulty. Admitting that "the conservative case on the Freedom Riders is one of the most difficult to get across to a Northern audience," Rusher argued that communist despotism abroad was surely far more brutal than the denial of human freedom in the United States. "There has never been a time when this country was perfect," Rusher observed, "and undoubtedly there never will be. But I suggest to you that it takes a special kind of blindness for Americans to concentrate so furiously and so emotionally on the delicate social problem which is gradually working itself out in the southern United States, while tolerating amiably the infinitely more brutal despotism that is the daily bread of people behind the Iron Curtain." Rusher's argument for patience and gradualism ignored completely the transformation of civil rights into a compelling moral issue. But his position was also revealing. It made clear the conservative conviction that anticommunism took precedence over all else, and reflected a determination that the federal government not become involved in social issues or social change. Finally, it was a bit paradoxical. Young Americans for Freedom, after all, advocated anticommunism as a pressing moral crusade, and were willing to grant greater powers to the federal government and spend additional tax monies for national defense.[14]

Convinced that ideological arguments were insufficient, conservatives continued to organize. In the summer of 1961 Rusher, William F. Buckley Jr., and Marvin Liebman, together with several of their protégés in Young Americans for Freedom and Young Republicans, issued a call for the formation of a New York Conservative Political Association. At about the same time, New York City YAFers formed The Freedom Party, Inc. David Franke became chairman of its board of directors, and William Cotter was named executive secretary. Both were active YAFers. Like YAF, this new group stood for limited government and opposed governmental interference in private enterprise. In November Marvin Liebman, William Rusher, and Richard Viguerie joined an effort spearheaded by Americans for Constitutional Action to foster cooperation among a variety of conservative groups. At a luncheon meeting they enlisted the support of Young Americans for Freedom, the Political Action Committee of the American Medical Association, the National Right to Work Committee, the Manion Forum, the United States Chamber of Commerce, the National Association of Manufacturers, We the People, F. Clifton White, and the Tuller Foundation of New Jersey. Although conspicuous by its absence from that list, the John Birch Society apparently had been providing some covert financial support for Young Americans for Freedom. Birch Director Robert Welch had informed Marvin Liebman in October 1961 that the Society would "be pleased to supply all the funds and backing required to get Young Americans for Freedom off to a good start. Our only stipulation," Welch wrote, "is that our name does not appear on any list of contributors or that any of our Council be given any publicity what-so-ever . . . ." Conservatives also accelerated efforts to take over the Republican Party and nominate Barry Goldwater in 1964. YAF's Massachusetts chair, Jack Molesworth, in fact wrote Richard

Nixon to warn him that he needed to choose between moderate and conservative Republicans "I have no respect," Molesworth wrote, "for chameleons who take on the political color of the organization or the publication which they happen to be addressing."[15]

In August, Dean Clarence Manion used his radio forum to support YAF and to call for the formation of conservative clubs across the country to "save this nation from slavery." The United States, according to Manion, was being readied for a quick communist takeover because the Kennedy administration misunderstood the nature and danger of communism. He also attacked the "socialist centralists" that ran the government and called for a return to states' rights. John Ashbrook, a militant young Ohio conservative elected to Congress in 1960, made much the same appeal. Appearing on the Manion Forum in December 1961, Ashbrook argued that the formation of conservative clubs was essential to prevent "national suicide." Insisting that liberalism was bankrupt, Ashbrook praised Young Americans for Freedom as well as the Intercollegiate Society of Individualists for their pioneering efforts to advance the conservative cause. What was essential, he told listeners, was the preservation of America's spiritual and constitutional resources in the face of "Keynesian Socialist principles." The "radicals" on the Left had been successful chiefly because conservatives had remained quiet. There really was a conservative majority in the country, Ashbrook concluded, and conservative clubs could serve as a catalyst for mobilizing that majority.[16]

These steps formed the core of the conservative response to the New Frontier. During the next several months Young Americans for Freedom relentlessly attacked the policies of the Kennedy administration. Little escaped their notice, or their condemnation. At its September 2 board meeting, YAF endorsed the controversial Newburgh Plan and arranged to have a representative at the December meeting of the National Association of Manufacturers. Determined to promote YAF as a political action group, James Kolbe, Diarmuid O'Scannlain, William Schulz, and John Weicher joined YAF's policy board and the organization hired Richard Viguerie as its administrative secretary, although they were more than $13,000 in debt.[17]

This determination to become an influential political action group was important, because it entailed commitment to a long-term effort to effect change rather than the expenditure of short-term energies to win particular elections, in the style of a political party. It also had two other repercussions. First, it offered a way for Young Americans for Freedom to mute its continuing internal philosophical divisions amid debates over political strategy. Three approaches to activism contended for supremacy within the organization. The "antis," or the more traditional conservatives, opposed whatever the liberals, the Democrats, or the liberal Republicans advocated. While they held specific objections to the progressive income tax, welfare, foreign aid, federal subsidies, or deficit spending, their broader characteristic was a religious conviction that they were right and their opponents wrong. Compromise was heresy. The second faction was the "doctrinaires." Similar to the "antis" in the nature of their convictions, this group embraced a literal interpretation of the Sharon Statement and Barry Goldwater's *The Conscience of a Conservative*. They believed in God-given free will, individual responsibility, and local autonomy. They also saw themselves not as defenders of the true faith, but as rebels who opposed the liberal consensus. Like the "antis," however, they intended to convert nonbelievers until they forged a majority. The final element within YAF comprised the "problem solvers." More rational than religious in their adherence to conservative beliefs, they argued that the problem with liberal or Marxist approaches to domestic and foreign policy was that they had not worked. Their appeal was to reason rather than to faith, but they held firmly to the basic conservative tenets of individual freedom and private property. The other impact of YAF's commitment to long-term change was that it enabled the organization to remain essentially oppositional. While the various factions within YAF agreed generally on a set of beliefs, they did not agree at all in their analyses, priorities, or programs. Embracing an oppositional position, however, enabled the three groups to forge a unity, albeit a superficial one, as they attacked the policies of the Kennedy administration.[18]

Aside from attacking specific legislation throughout 1961 and 1962, YAF also opposed the principle of federal intervention and the growth of bureaucracy. Kennedy's proposal for a Department of Housing and Urban Affairs drew their fire on both these counts. That proposal, Lee Edwards warned, "is basic to the kind of government we are to enjoy (or suffer) in the United States. Shall it be a Federal government, that is, a division of power between Washington and the 50 states, or a welfare-socialist government with the great majority of decisions made at the center?" Legislation advancing medical care for the aged under Social Security evoked similar criticism. YAF's board of directors adopted a lengthy resolution opposing the proposal, claiming that it would inflate costs, discriminate against citizens not receiving Social Security, increase taxes, and bankrupt the Social Security system. The grounds for their opposition in this case, however, were revealing. Nowhere was there any general statement against statism and the principle of federal intervention. In short, YAF seemed ready to abandon ideology and principle should overtly political arguments seem more useful.[19]

A debate between William F. Buckley Jr. and Ronald Hamowy, associate editor of *New Individualist Review*, highlighted the dangers of this approach.

While Buckley defended a broad array of conservative principles, Hamowy issued a withering blast at Buckley, Young Americans for Freedom, *National Review*, and traditional conservatism. "One searches in vain," Hamowy complained with respect to YAF, "for any clear statement on the reduction of the economic intervention of the State. . . . The only real goal of the *National Review* Right is to keep the Federal government from advancing much further down the socialist road—a goal in itself contradicted by the war economy that it desires." Hamowy advocated rolling back the New Deal, and charged that Young Americans for Freedom and *National Review* wanted, "in gist, to substitute one group of masters (themselves) for another. They do not desire so much to limit the State as to control it."[20]

Foreign Policy

A more promising target for its conservative opponents was the administration's record on foreign policy. Here YAF believed the issues to be clear and simple. Anticommunism should be the linchpin of United States foreign policy; the more militant the stand, the better. This became clear in YAFers' reaction to the Peace Corps. Intrigued by the idea, they nonetheless worried that it was naive, unrealistic, and insufficiently anticommunist. In addition, they feared that it signaled a commitment to peaceful coexistence rather than victory in the cold war. Regardless of the intent, Lee Edwards warned, every Peace Corps volunteer would be part of the cold war struggle with communism. High political standards were essential to keep out the ideologically weak, for sending "hundreds and thousands of college graduates into the underdeveloped nations to do battle with trained, experienced communist agents would produce a political debacle almost beyond comprehension." YAF did not believe that words alone advanced peace and freedom, and Edwards worried that the administration was "veering dangerously toward the Eisenhower policies of sweet reasonableness and enlightening mediation," which, he insisted, had allowed the communists to advance their global objectives in the 1950s.[21]

YAF's central critiques, however, focused on administration policy toward the United Nations, Red China, the Congo, and Cuba. These were not unrelated for YAFers, since they opposed United States support of the United Nations on the grounds that third-world and communist nations dominated the U.N. and used it to frustrate U.S. policies. The possible United Nations admission of Red China typified their concern. With strong ties to the China Lobby, YAFers worried that divisions in the Kennedy administration over this question would weaken U.S. resolve and allow U.N. recognition of the "gangster government of Mao." They joined this fear with opposition to a U.N. bond issue. The United States, in their view, should simply not support an organization that was soft on communism and did not rigorously support anticommunist regimes around the world.[22]

Fidel Castro and Cuba also attracted considerable attention from YAFers. Castro's revolution symbolized for YAF the dangerous and relentless pace of communist subversion. YAF's position was clear and simple: invade Cuba and unseat Castro. To publicize their views, YAFers demonstrated in front of the White House and proselytized in numerous conservative publications. The "ultimate cause of failure" in Cuba, Stanton Evans asserted, "has been Liberalism's inability to grasp the true nature of the enemy." This intellectual failure represented an "internal danger" to the United States, and President Kennedy's attacks on anticommunist militancy highlighted it. Decrying "Liberalism's fatal misconduct of American policy abroad," Evans charged that President Kennedy ignored "the witness of history."[23]

Lee Edwards challenged JFK to stand up against the communists. Noting that the Bay of Pigs was Kennedy's first total defeat, Edwards argued that style rather than substance was the key to the New Frontier. This was dangerous in foreign policy, he asserted, and he blasted Kennedy for using tough words about Cuba during the presidential campaign and then timidly retreating behind a halfhearted invasion and a ludicrous Tractors for Prisoners deal after moving into the White House. Edwards proffered some advice to the president: "Let him ask himself not what he can do for his country, but what his country can do for him." The voice of America, Edwards insisted, wanted Kennedy to "remove the communist puppet" in Cuba and stand firm against communism around the world.[24]

For Edwards and other YAFers, that also meant a sturdy defense of West Berlin, an end to trade with communist nations, and a recognition that neutralism was all too often a cover for either communism or anti-Americanism and led to American inaction. To demonstrate its resolve, the United States should immediately resume nuclear testing. Arguing that the fallout issue was phony, YAF complained that the "agents of international Communism in the United States and in other countries of the Western world . . . have been active in organizing and participating in 'peace marches' and 'peace demonstrations.'" Although many participants were loyal if misguided Americans, the government should ignore their pleas and resume testing to keep pace with the Russians. "As young Americans," wrote one YAFer, "we are dedicated to the preservation of our society and the security of our nation. We are thus fearful of the voices of appeasement . . . ." Communists were dedicated to world conquest, including the destruction of the United States, and only military power could keep them at bay. "We must seek victory over Communism, not coexistence with it." "We call upon all Americans—young and old—to reject the counsels of cowardice and unreason and to revive the courage of free men. This is our nation's heritage and our responsibility to the past, the present and the future. We will have peace only if we are strong!"[25]

Young Americans for Freedom, in essence, embraced a foreign policy position most publicly articulated by Arizona Senator Barry Goldwater. In his book, *Why Not Victory?*, Goldwater argued that for conservatives the question of freedom was *the* overriding political question of the day. "A sound conservative philosophy can and must be extended into the area of foreign affairs just as it must be applied at home," Goldwater insisted. Victory had been the traditional American goal in past wars, and should remain the goal in the cold war against communism. "The disease is communism," he said, "a cancer that is world-wide and that shows symptoms within our own boundaries." Despite international tensions, the United States must not back down in the face of the communist challenge. Indeed, it should go on the offensive. "It is time," Goldwater argued, "that we ceased fearing to give offense to so-called neutralists, and unpredictable friends, and even the enemies who are resolved upon our destruction." Kennedy's Cuban policy was a particularly sore point, and Goldwater urged the United States to repeat its exploits of the Spanish-American War. Start with an economic embargo, he urged Kennedy, and then "take whatever action is needed to dislodge communism from the front yard of the Western Hemisphere." Goldwater also railed against the deceptive beauty of disarmament, excessive reliance on the United Nations, and the idea that Red China should be admitted into the U.N. "This is not time," he concluded, "for an American foreign-policy objective designed to erect an impractical international dream city of the future. Our objective must be the practical means of dousing the fire and smothering the flames of international communism."[26]

YAFers became particularly agitated over the question of the Congo, which seemed to them a prime example of the dangers Goldwater outlined. Belgium had suddenly granted independence to the Congo in 1960. The mineral-rich Katanga province had seceded; civil war had erupted. Young Americans for Freedom supported the Katanga government of Moise Tshombe because it was militantly anticommunist and pro-Western. The United Nations, and United States policy, opposed the Katanga secession. For YAF the problem was simple. The Katanga province, formerly the site of Belgium's prosperous mining industry, was susceptible to a communist takeover. Belgium had tried to maintain economic control of the area even after granting independence to the Congo, and the provincial president, Moise Tshombe, was pro-Belgian. Congolese President Joseph Kasavubu and Premier Patrice Lumumba, on the other hand, were hostile to any continued colonial presence. They asked the United

Nations to force Belgium to withdraw her troops and tried to coerce Katanga back into the nation. Conservatives signed a full-page advertisement in the *New York Times* that described Katanga as "the Hungary of 1961." Led by Senators Barry Goldwater (R-Arizona) and Thomas Dodd (D-Connecticut), conservatives evinced a romantic attachment to Katangan independence and considered the province a "paragon of African capitalism and anticommunism."[27]

The New Guard attacked Kennedy's support for the U.N.'s "war of aggression against Katanga in the Congo." YAFers picketed the White House to support Katanga, and members of YAF's Yale University chapter offered to go to Katanga to fight against United Nations mercenaries. Insisting that the Congo government was communist-infiltrated, student spokesman Ross Mackenzie warned that the "UN and the Kennedy Administration are embarked on a course that could be as tragically wrong as was the State Department support of Castro when he was seeking control of Cuba." Supporting their offer, one Republican congressman dubbed them the "Patriotic Corps," arguing that they would be far more useful than "the spineless Peace Corps which is only getting the U.S. into trouble."[28]

Conservative opposition to Kennedy's Katanga policy sparked some concern within the administration. The administration had been monitoring the activities of what it considered right-wing organizations for some time, and it categorized the pro-Katanga efforts in this vein. A confidential memo in December 1961 noted the formation of an "American Committee for Aid to Katanga Freedom Fighters," and detailed the background of those who signed the advertisement. They were, Kennedy aide Lee White observed, chiefly connected with *National Review* and other conservative publications or organizations.

White concluded that there were several dangers evident in the formation of this committee. Most of its leaders were men of influence—editors, publishers, public relations specialists. In addition, their presence indicated a "close coordination between the various right-wing groups." As for their motives, two possibilities emerged. First, they were perhaps concerned about protecting the significant Western financial interests in Katanga. A more likely explanation was their desire to use the Katanga issue "to discredit and mobilize public opinion against the United Nations in this country." This was particularly apparent because both *National Review* and the John Birch Society had previously opposed African independence and had supported continued Portuguese control of Angola. Indeed, *The New Guard* editorialized against continued United States support for the United Nations. The United States, it warned, cannot "concern itself with the vacuous vagaries of the United Nations when it is the U.S., not the U.N., which is the arch of the free world."

Finally, White concluded that the Aid to Katanga Committee would probably be a vehicle to spark rallies, meetings, and picketing across the United States. "If this prediction proves correct," White warned, "it will show an impressive and frightening ability on the part of the various right wing groups not only to agree on a common goal but to work toward it effectively on a nation-wide basis." Promising that a more detailed report would follow, White raised several questions about the financial connections between the various groups and individuals on the one hand and the Aid to Katanga Committee or the Katanga government on the other.[29]

A month later White again reported on the Aid to Katanga Committee. It had inserted another advertisement in the *New York Times*, but White noted that this time it had changed the list of sponsors. Eight identifiable members of the John Birch Society had been dropped, perhaps to defuse charges that this was only a radical right wing front organization. But he also noted that the names of other right-wingers had been added, and that some were Birch sympathizers.[30] This attempt to avoid a radical right image symbolized one of the major difficulties not only for Young Americans for Freedom, but for conservatives opposed to the policies of the Kennedy administration. They felt so much in the minority that they welcomed support from any and every ideological or political quarter. While YAF, *National Review*, and some of the other more moderate conservative groups wanted to distance themselves from less responsible critics, they were reluctant to dismiss potential allies in the conservative cause. This, in part, reflected an uncertain definition of conservatism. It also represented the fruits of an oppositional stance. That is, association in opposition led to association in cause.

Defining the New Conservatism

Underlying these attacks on the New Frontier was a persistent and difficult theme: defining the new conservatism of the 1960s. YAFers and Young Republicans alike opposed President Kennedy's foreign policy. But their articulation of that opposition often rested on a simplistic anticommunism not unlike that of other, more extreme groups. Efforts by Young Republicans at the University of Detroit typified these difficulties. Backed by local Young Americans for Freedom, Detroit YRs attempted to formulate "A Conservative Program for the 60's." Their program sprang from the views of Senator Barry Goldwater, and charged that President Kennedy had failed to protect the U.S. constitution, following a "feigned policy" rather than a foreign policy. They not only argued that Kennedy's foreign policy was contrary to American interests, but implied that it threatened to betray American freedom by supporting foreign aid for such "spineless scavengers" as Nehru, Sukarno, Nasser, Tito, and Nkrumah. Echoing Goldwater's call for victory over communism rather than coexistence, the group claimed that the disasters of Kennedy's foreign policy were "planned and premeditated."[31] This line of attack resembled oppositional charges advanced by extremist groups like the John Birch Society.

The difficulty, as YAF leader Robert Schuchman admitted, was one of definition. Just what was the conservative revival? Was it grounded in anything more than opposition to liberal Democrats and moderate Republicans? Schuchman believed that it was, that Young Americans for Freedom had been founded "on the idea that a constructive, responsible, and complete application of the conservative philosophy to the issues of our age could be of enormous value to an America adrift on a sea of moral and political neutralism." Conservatives, he argued, could "ill afford to substitute frivolous sloganeering or vulgar theatrics for the difficult task of successfully presenting a total new approach to world problems to the American people." Schuchman warned:

> One of the dangers facing the New Conservatism is an unfortunate tendency to splinter off into narrower and narrower factions and groups. One-issue organizations, dreamers who call for a third political party, those who confuse their ideas with their egos—these aberrations normally perform only injurious service to the political success and intellectual acceptance of conservatism. The New Conservatism is deeply committed to the entirety of our Western civilization. Unlike the liberals, we do not believe that any single-issue cause (like "peace" or "civil rights" with the liberals) can present these essential qualities of our American way of life which are worth fighting for.[32]

Joined to this problem of definition and application was the split between ideologues and politicos within Young Americans for Freedom. Robert Novak surveyed the new campus conservatives for the *Wall Street Journal* and concluded that they were essentially idealists and theorists. This had the virtue of simplicity, he noted, for the students never found themselves "in the position of the industrialist who opposes Federal regulations but welcomes Federal subsidies." Nonetheless, "this search for ideological consistency often leads to radicalism—a term the campus conservative does not necessarily find offensive."[33] Students' interest in ideological questions as a way to "flex their intellectual muscles," according to Novak, led them to be somewhat uninterested in the practical issues of the day. It also led them to "rejoice in doctrinal clashes," and he claimed that campus conservatives seemed most interested in disputing "an esoteric point with all the relish of a medieval scholastic." "They're generally seeking the right goals," admitted Richard

Cowan of Yale, "but they are naive and limited in taking such an inward view of things."[34]

Given their intellectual proclivities, the ideologues' hero was plainly William F. Buckley Jr. of *National Review*. But Novak's characterization of campus conservatives fell a bit short of being complete. In addition to the ideologues there were the politicos. The two groups weren't completely separate; many politicos also revered Buckley and grounded their political positions in ideological commitment. The pages of YAF's journal, *The New Guard*, were a battleground for political activists in the early sixties. The articles were openly political and policy-oriented. A few philosophical or ideological pieces appeared, often prompted by a particular policy debate, but even the book reviews usually focused on political subjects. Editorials and columns dealt with specific legislation before the Congress, or attacked domestic and foreign policy positions advanced by liberals.

The differences were significant because they reflected the lack of unity among the new conservatives. "Put 100 young conservatives in a room," Robert Schuchman admitted, "and you'll get 100 opinions." But where was the leadership? In what direction was the movement going? Douglas Caddy outlined the problem succinctly in a spring 1962 essay. Observing that conservatives faced a dilemma at the polls come November, Caddy lamented the "political immaturity" of conservative voters across the country and warned that a Democratic victory in the fall would doom conservatives' chances to capture the White House in 1964. Caddy's agenda was admittedly mixed; he not only wanted a conservative victory, but believed conservatives had to work within the system. "The single most important fact of reality which conservatives in America must accept today if they are to exert any influence at all on the Nation's future course is that they must work through the Republican Party." Nonetheless, his analysis was fundamentally correct. Despite a few halting efforts, there was little coordinated leadership. Contending groups and factions sought to capture the attention of the press and increase their membership, usually in isolation and often at odds with one another. Each advanced its own agenda, frequently focused on a particular issue or two; none sought to build winning coalitions. "Conservative societies, clubs, associations and the like—including Young Americans for Freedom," Caddy warned, "have their particular role to perform in the political process. But political victories can never be obtained by solely working through these groups."[35] Yet, ironically, their opponents had largely succeeded in lumping them together in the public's mind as extremist elements outside the "normal" American political spectrum.

A March 7, 1962 rally at Madison Square Garden highlighted both the strengths and the weaknesses of YAF and the new conservatism. Billed as a

"Conservative Rally for World Liberation from Communism," it drew an over-flow crowd to the Garden and grossed $80,000. As usual, Marvin Liebman was responsible for much of the organizational genius behind the endeavor, but the public response reflected the growing strength of the conservative movement.

Although designed to demonstrate YAF's independence from more extreme groups like the John Birch Society, the rally was not without problems. Clearly its greatest success was that it filled the Garden for no reason other than to cel-ebrate the ideology of conservatism. Its weakness was demonstrated in the range of individuals honored there. YAF celebrated the conservative upsurge by presenting awards to former president Herbert Hoover, Senator Thomas Dodd of Connecticut, Major General Edwin Walker, Katanga President Moise Tshombe, writer John Dos Passos, textile magnate Roger Milliken, former New Jersey Governor Charles Edison, Professors Ludwig von Mises and Richard Weaver, Marvin Liebman, M. Stanton Evans, columnist David Lawrence, and actor John Wayne. This was a list that included conservative philosophers, mod-erate conservatives, radical conservatives, and John Birch Society members and sympathizers. Partially because of this, Senator Thomas Dodd withdrew, call-ing it a "partisan gathering with extremist coloration." At the urging of Mar-vin Liebman, and after consultation with Senators Barry Goldwater and John Tower, YAF canceled General Edwin Walker's appearance because of his ex-tremist activities and John Birch Society membership. They replaced him with South Carolina Senator Strom Thurmond. This slightly toned down the list, but the original invitation list remained important because it reflected the in-discriminate nature of the new conservatism. As James Burnham of *National Review* (which had publicly condemned Robert Welch and the John Birch So-ciety) later observed, the "Rally wholly confirmed the necessity of the anti-Welch move. . . . [Walker's] absence meant hardly a ripple to the negative: the hall was full without him; a feeble attempt by a handful at 'We Want Walker' faded in moments."[36]

While anticonservative pickets demonstrated outside, the atmosphere in-side Madison Square Garden vibrated with chants and raucous enthusiasm. Dan Wakefield later provided a firsthand recollection:

> American flags, an explosion of confetti, then red white and blue bal-loons and a brass band filled the air as more than eighteen thousand young conservatives packed Madison Square Garden to overflowing on a spring night in 1962, where the Young Americans for Freedom showed their strength and support for Senator Barry Goldwater and his right-wing principles. Fresh-faced usherettes with good teeth and clean hair (what a refreshing respite for the press after the beatniks!)

cradled copies of Goldwater's *The Conscience of a Conservative* the way my friends and I used to hold *Franny and Zooey*, and welcomed the faithful who carried signs that said "Better Dead Than Red," "Let's Bury Khrushchev," and "Stamp Out ADA."[37]

The conservative faithful also booed the name of President John F. Kennedy and, in response to comments about Cuba, roared "Fight! Fight! Fight!"[38]

Senator Barry Goldwater was the honored guest, but awards, announcements, and other speeches took so long that by the time Goldwater appeared (after angrily pacing backstage during the delays), the night was almost gone and the crowd tired and thinning. The most dramatic remarks at the rally belonged to L. Brent Bozell, who launched a stirring attack on liberalism and delivered a series of challenges to the Kennedy administration. Bozell, brother-in-law of William F. Buckley Jr. and ghostwriter of *The Conscience of a Conservative*, linked culture, politics, and foreign policy in an effort to define a conservative credo and spur his listeners to new efforts. "We gather here tonight," he observed at the outset, "to celebrate recent advances, and to plot new victories. . . . we have come far, and we are going strong." Bozell attacked liberals for labelling conservatives "extremists," and argued that conservatism had grown strong because its ideas were right. The United States should eliminate Castro, resume nuclear testing, and take the offensive against communism. He insisted that conservatives were now on "the threshold of leadership: we now face the task of transforming an unarticulated popular majority into a working political majority, and of giving it responsible direction."[39]

Bozell grounded both his philosophy and his optimism in a belief that conservatives were on a divine mission, a mission not only to repel communism but to reject the gnosticism of liberals. The liberals were wrong, Bozell insisted, in believing that they could perfect man through the "agency of man." Their underlying failure, he told the audience, was not only a failure of policy but of philosophy: "Liberalism has not provided us with a mission comparable to the one that drives Communism forward . . . ." Conservatism stood for the "Christian West." Its purpose was to maximize human potential, not perfect the human race. The United States was a "God-centered civilization;" what it needed was "faith in itself." Bozell versed his prescription for instilling that faith in terms of an aggressive mission to reverse current policy.

To the Joint Chiefs of Staff: Make the necessary preparations for landing in Havana.
To our commander in Berlin: *Tear Down the Wall.*
To our chief of mission in the Congo: *Change sides.*

To the Chairman of the Atomic Energy Commission: Schedule testing of every nuclear weapon that could conceivably serve the military purpose of the West.

To the Chief of the CIA: You are to encourage liberation movements in every nation of the world under Communist domination, including the Soviet Union itself. And you may let it be known that when, in the future, men offer their lives for the ideals of the West, the West will not stand idly by.[40]

Looking back on the events of March 7, James Burnham agreed with Bozell's analysis if not with his conclusions. "The basic question," concluded Burnham, "thrusts out more and more insistently: where is 'the conservative movement' going? Pretty soon, it is going to have to have a strategy."[41]

By strategy, Burnham clearly meant something more than a reactive opposition to administration proposals or liberal legislation. Demonstrations at presidential speeches, attacks on the power of labor unions, an insistence that the United States pursue a policy of victory in the cold war with communism, even a generalized opposition to statism, were all activist measures that lacked any strategic dimension. Intellectual or philosophical discussions in conservative publications, furthermore, were no substitute for a strategy to enhance conservatism by using the political process to seize control of political institutions. Eugene Lyons, senior editor of *Reader's Digest*, warned YAFers that anticommunism and conservatism were not the same thing. Responsible conservatives, he cautioned readers of *The New Guard*, needed to understand that desegregation, NATO, fluoridation, social security, the income tax, or foreign aid were not manifestations of communism. Anticommunism, in short, was not an irreducible essence for conservatism and was a seductive but insufficient platform for conservatives.[42]

Lee Edwards tried to address the question in a 1962 essay on "The New Right: Its Face and Future." Concluding that the New Right had arrived only because the *New York Times* had taken notice of it, Edwards focused on the achievements and successes of Young Americans for Freedom, which he characterized as the political arm of the New Right. But he said little about the beliefs that had attracted supporters, aside from a brief acknowledgment that the Intercollegiate Society of Individualists was the philosophical arm of the New Right. Indeed, most of his article simply listed the various planks that YAF supported. Subsequent articles in *The New Guard* by Edwards and other writers had a similar focus, from opposition to the Supreme Court's outlawing of prayer in the public schools to a vigorous defense of fraternities as bastions of free choice and anticommunism.[43]

Robert Schuchman presented the other side of the YAF attack with a lengthy exposition of principles that should undergird a conservative philosophy. Schuchman, who harbored strong libertarian sympathies, argued that the fundamental issue facing Americans was that of civil liberties in a welfare state. Only a limited government protected individual freedom and sovereignty, and Schuchman's central thesis was that "the adoption and extension of what is called 'the welfare state,' together with current Liberal responses to national economic and diplomatic inadequacies, constitute a serious threat to the maintenance of civil liberties in America today." By the welfare state, he meant not just any particular set of economic policies, but the "patch-work of interferences in the private life of the citizen" undertaken by the federal government. These "interferences" included intrusions into private race relations, control of communications, granting of visas (in this case, the refusal to grant one to Moise Tshombe), federal sponsorship of research, efforts to define what was "obscene," control of the mails, and a host of other interventions. The choice, he warned, was between liberty and equality. The rise of statism, marked by these extensions of government, threatened to cost Americans their liberty "in the search for a chimera of equality."[44]

By the spring of 1962 it seemed Young Americans for Freedom had arrived as a political force of some (as yet undetermined) dimensions. YAF had emerged during the preceding two years in part as a response to conservatives' alienation from mainstream politics as represented by the two political parties. The centrality of this alienation was evident in YAF's oppositional approach to politics and ideology. They knew very well what they were against, but were a bit more uncertain regarding the specifics of what they were for. YAF had also emerged because there was no other conservative student activist group in the United States. The Young Republican organization, although a battleground between conservatives and liberals, was nonetheless firmly tied to the Republican Party and thereby susceptible to adult influences and the lure of electoral politics. In addition, YAF had carried out a series of projects and rallies, some of them sensational in their stylistic and political orientation. Amid a culture of consensus and moderation, YAF often rejected both, and had emerged as a strident voice for change. Under the tutelage of Marvin Liebman, it had skillfully generated publicity about its endeavors and constructed an impressive public façade.[45] Its appeal, according to Robert Schuchman, was a belief that "a constructive, responsible, and complete application of the conservative philosophy to the issues of our age could be of enormous value to an America adrift on a sea of moral and political neutralism."[46]

YAF's Appeal

The appeal of the new conservatism also attracted increasing attention from the media. The *New York Times* ran a series of articles in the spring of 1962 on the growing student interest in "causes," noting that the two most popular campus speakers were Barry Goldwater and William F. Buckley Jr. Student conservatives, the writer observed, were "for the first time, vocal, coalesced, active, financed by wealthy adults, with many new student publications. They have achieved respectability on campus. But they are not as numerous as the public believes them to be." Writing in the *Wall Street Journal*, Robert Novak found the new conservatives "deadly serious and virtually humorless, their faith in the individual and suspicion of Government . . . unbounded." From the Left, Michael Harrington argued that the idea of a campus conservative revolt was overblown, but admitted that a conservative movement was stirring. Calling its members "pro-vest and anti-guitar," he warned that student radicals critical of the status quo (which was liberalism) were moving Right as well as Left. The strength of the Right, such as it was, rested in his view on the financial resources of older conservatives. Kenneth Keniston largely agreed with Harrington. He found students politically apathetic, but among those beginning to stir YAF was making inroads. Keniston believed YAF's ideology gave students upset with the status quo a "voice for repudiating the soft-minded liberals, college professors, bureaucrats and others who epitomize the newer America . . . ." He concluded, however, that he saw "little likelihood of American students ever playing a radical role, much less a revolutionary one, in our society."[47]

A confidential report for American industry issued in 1962 noted a marked increase in campus political activity during the preceding two years, especially on the Right. Campus political debates, demonstrations, and picketing had become more common as conservative students rebelled against a liberal orthodoxy, although many of those students seemed more interested in "ideological disputation" than in activism. Still a distinct minority on campus, their strength lay in the intensity, energy, and devotion their members brought to the cause. More than 60 percent had read Barry Goldwater's *The Conscience of a Conservative*, and by and large they viewed their political activity as training for future leadership.[48]

Michael Harrington concluded that it was "useless to propose some general theory of the campus. The generations succeed one another with a rapidity almost like that of the tsetse fly." Most striking to Harrington was not conservatism or liberalism, but the rise of idealism. A survey by Robert Martinson reached much the same conclusion, and singled out Young Americans for Freedom. Calling it a "substantial nation-wide organization" dedicated to antistatism, he snidely concluded that its strength came from reality shock:

> The young American is uprooted from his small-town conservative family complex and transformed into a "junior organization man" capable of taking his place in the world of C. Wright Mills. This shock to his accepted theologies is perpetrated by the great impersonal university through the agency of its graduate-student teaching assistants who—adding insult to injury—taunt him with strange socialistic doctrines, invite Gus Hall to speak and, even more unspeakable, make ribald and contemptuous references to his fraternities. Who wouldn't join the YAF?[49]

Much less condescending was the analysis of Allan Brownfield. Conservative students, he warned, were "America's Angry Young Men." They were disillusioned with the answers they received in classrooms from liberal professors, and found Barry Goldwater attractive because of his honesty rather than because they always agreed with him. Conservative students feared continued government control because they believed it sapped individual responsibility, and Brownfield argued that their hero was as much J. D. Salinger as William F. Buckley Jr. What they sought was the revival of ideology. Conservatives—or "the right," as Irving Howe and other critics called them—had seized the initiative. Despite their tendency toward elitism and contempt for the masses, even a socialist like Howe professed to like them. "They speak as men of principle," he observed, "doomed to be a minority for a long time, but unwilling to go along with the expediency and eclecticism of the liberal establishment."[50]

Who were they? Historians and sociologists who examined the new conservatives in the early 1960s, interpreting their views and action through the medium of social psychology, concluded that they represented a paranoid, extremist element outside the American mainstream. These attacks frequently mirrored the arguments against "extremism" advanced by Arthur Schlesinger Jr. immediately after World War II in *The Vital Center*. As such, they more frequently reflected the political views of their writers than those of their subjects.[51]

The scholar who has most closely scrutinized Young Americans for Freedom at the individual level is sociologist Richard Braungart. Drawing on the limited studies of conservative youth, Braungart (along with David Westby) supplemented them with a careful analysis of conservatives attending a YAF convention in the mid-1960s at Franklin & Marshall College. Earlier studies, especially one by Lawrence Schiff of forty-seven New England YAFers in 1962, had concluded that the membership ranged from lower-middle to upper-middle class, from college dropouts to Rhodes scholars, and from moderate Republicans to John Birchers. Most were from lower-middle and "respectable working-class" families, whose parents possessed "low status relative to their occupation and education rankings." They tended to major in business, law, pre-med, and the physical sciences, and were very career-oriented. YAFers were also "more submissive to legal and institutional authority and tend to exert greater self-control over expressions of impulse and anxiety." They were not terribly altruistic nor humanistic, and seemed "highly susceptible toward charismatic authority."[52]

With the support and cooperation of the national office of Young Americans for Freedom, Braungart and Westby arrived at Franklin & Marshall College in the summer of 1966 to find 120 YAFers patiently waiting in a large lecture room to be tested and surveyed. The two sociologists discovered that YAFers were more likely to come from authoritarian homes than were either SDSers or Young Republicans, and corroborated Schiff's findings that they came predominantly from working-class backgrounds. Perhaps more significant was the fact that only 6.3 percent of YAFers' parents identified with the radical right; most considered themselves Republicans (50 percent) or independents (27.7 percent). The other significant finding, which reflects issues and positions discussed in YAF's publication *The New Guard*, was that 32.2 percent of those surveyed were Catholics, a much higher percentage than for SDSers (9.6 percent), Young Democrats (20.2 percent), or Young Republicans (19.3 percent). Most of the rest were Protestant. The demographic profile Braungart developed was also distinct from that of competing political groups. Young Americans for Freedom was male-dominated, with very few women as members, and lacked any meaningful minority presence.[53]

Additional studies by Richard and Margaret Braungart have examined life-course development of both SDSers and YAFers. A compelling and important feature in the early lives of many YAFers was a Catholic education and upbringing that "emphasized the importance of ideas and principles." In the words of David Franke: "I became interested in politics overnight. My parents were watching a friend's house and . . . I picked up books there—like *The Road Ahead* by John T. Flynn. . . . A lot of things had been milling around in my head and it brought things together." The key to their public political activism after 1959 was Barry Goldwater. "Both parties were of the same drift," Franke argued, "and *we* needed a party."[54] From that sprang a new conservatism organized around the ideological principles of the Sharon Statement.

Braungart and Westby provided a much more compelling microanalysis of Young Americans for Freedom than most analysts of the right wing, perhaps because they wrote within a historical framework and were not themselves part of the fray. Avoiding the polemics that portrayed conservatives as psychological misfits drawn by anticommunism and fear of moral decay to fashion a conspiratorial view of government, Braungart and Westby characterized Young Americans for Freedom as sincere. They quoted with approval the definition of social movements advanced by Gary Rush and R. Serge Denisoff: "social movements are emergent ideological realities given social significance during periods of a consciousness of dysfunction, which provide referents for mobilization to bring about desired change within and/or of the social system." YAFers, in short, were true believers. The "New Right," a phrase coined by YAFer Lee Edwards in 1962, sought to advance its own agenda. It had, as Richard Viguerie noted later, four defining characteristics: a "developing technical ability" (direct mail, for example); a "willingness to work together for the common good;" a "commitment to put philosophy before political party;" and an "optimism and a conviction that we had the ability to win and to lead America."[55]

In his *Revolt on the Campus*, M. Stanton Evans sought to both chronicle and celebrate this upsurge in conservative activism. Evans, a founder of Young Americans for Freedom, boldly trumpeted the future of the conservative cause. "Historians may well record the decade of the 1960's," he wrote, "as the era in which conservatism, as a viable political force, finally came into its own." The new conservatism had emerged, in his view, because it grasped the fact that American society had become permissive in its ethics and values and statist in its public policy. Those evils fed upon one another in a "baleful symbiosis" on which he blamed the nation's problems.[56]

Perhaps unconsciously, Evans had very aptly chronicled the weaknesses as well as the strengths of the new conservatism. He captured not only its opposition to liberal policies, but its growing conviction that immutable moral truths should guide political behavior. In the words of YAFer Carol Bauman, young conservatives not only feared the trend toward socialism advanced by the liberal establishment, but "longed for a philosophy, and a unifying belief for which to fight during this protracted conflict with Communism."[57] The values youthful conservatives embraced, according to Evans, were the traditional values of their parents. In the words of David Franke:

> I consider myself a conservative; one who accepts natural law and the lessons of history as the guides to judgment in matters political, social, philosophical, and religious. To me, history and the natural law reveal that the family must be the cornerstone of society, and that the protection of the individual and family rights is the principal duty of the state. Applying this philosophy to our modern age, I resist the intrusion of the state into areas which properly are the concern of the individual, alone or in voluntary cooperation with other persons; and I affirm that the government of the United States should apply itself

instead to its legitimate concern—the protection of the just interests of our country and its citizens, and defense against all enemies, foreign and domestic.[58]

Given this outlook, Evans argued, 1960s conservatives saw the New Frontier as nothing more than a continuation of the New Deal. Apprehensive about the failures of liberalism at home and abroad, they believed it had lost any sense of mission or purpose. "The ultimate object," he concluded, "is to see men in office congenial to the aspirations of the Sharon Statement."[59] William Rusher was more direct: "A serious interest in conservatism," he wrote Evans, "is simply incompatible with success in the Republican Party today."[60] In the meantime, while they had not yet coalesced into a cohesive opposition, the attacks of YAF and other right-wing groups worried Democrats and liberals.

Chapter 7   JFK and the Right Wing

STUDIES OF THE Kennedy administration have usually focused on the character of John F. Kennedy, his failure to get much domestic legislation through the Congress prior to his assassination, or foreign policy issues. With the Bay of Pigs, the Cuban Missile Crisis, and the country's growing commitment in Vietnam, foreign policy has particularly attracted historians. Missing from most of the studies is any attention to the growing presence of the right wing in American domestic politics.[1]

The failure to integrate the right wing into studies of the Kennedy administration and the history of the early 1960s has distorted our portrait of the decade. As Robert Ellwood argued in a recent book on the sixties, it "is important to recover the atmosphere of these stormy years." Even a cursory survey of the *New York Times* and the periodical press for these years reveals a wealth of material about the radical Right and the dangers of extremism. Although Barry Goldwater is undoubtedly the most identifiable political figure in these stories, the John Birch Society, Young Americans for Freedom, and an array of other organizations on the Right also draw considerable attention, and for good reason.

Throughout 1961 Robert Welch and the John Birch Society alarmed the moderate and liberal press. Welch's charges that former President Dwight D. Eisenhower was a communist, together with the expanding membership of the Birch Society, drew fire from Republicans and Democrats alike. In March 1961 even Richard Nixon criticized the tactics of the Birch Society. Its growing strength, particularly in the South and West, combined with what appeared to be a broader resurgence of conservatism, led to an increasingly bitter debate between those who found it repulsive and those who defended it as a patriotic organization formed to fight communism.[2]

The inauguration of a massive letter-writing campaign by the Birch Society to impeach Chief Justice Earl Warren provoked Attorney General Robert Kennedy to voice his "concern" about the Society and the growth of the right wing in general. Although he argued publicly that the John Birch Society was "ridiculous" and urged Americans to pay little attention to it, the press paid little heed to his pleas.[3] *Newsweek* and *The Christian Century* both ran several stories on the Birch Society. By May 1961 *The Nation* had also singled out Young Americans for Freedom as a particularly activist group on the Right. It warned that while liberals tended to focus on issues, conservatives were trying to build a "movement." For the moment, however, the strength of the conservative movement probably lay as much in "press-agentry" as it did in actual numbers. The flamboyant activities of Army Major General Edwin A. Walker, together with efforts by other military officers to indoctrinate their troops with radical Right views, excited interest on their own. When Secretary of Defense Robert McNamara disciplined Walker for violating an assortment of federal laws, the right wing rose to Walker's defense. Within months Attorney General Robert Kennedy assailed the Right as a "tremendous danger" to the United States.[4]

In the fall of 1961 President Kennedy also spoke out against the dangers of the right wing, particularly the John Birch Society and the Minutemen (who believed that guerrilla warfare was needed to save the country from its internal communist enemies). At a program to celebrate the 100th anniversary of the University of Washington, the president publicly lashed out at the Right. Noting that the United States was neither omnipotent nor omniscient, he warned that "there are others who cannot bear the burden of a long twilight struggle. They lack confidence in our long-run capacity to survive and succeed. Hating communism, yet they see communism in the long run, perhaps, as the wave of the future. And they want some quick and easy and final and cheap solution—now." Although the president also attacked the Left for advocating what he called the "pathway of surrender," his remarks were chiefly directed against the radical Right.[5] Two days later he renewed the attack in a speech before the California Democratic Party. Speaking about the "American spirit in this time of trial," he attacked fringe groups in American society as driven by frustration and tension and urged his listeners not to heed their "counsels of fear and suspicion."

They look suspiciously at their neighbors and their leaders. They call for "a man on horseback" because they do not trust the people. They find treason in our churches, in our highest court, in our treatment of water. They equate the Democratic Party with the welfare state, the welfare state with socialism, socialism with communism. They object quite rightly to politics intruding on the military—but they are very anxious for the military to engage in their kind of politics.[6]

By the fall of 1961 there had been many threats on the president's life—thirty-four from the state of Texas alone. After some conversations with his brother about how to cope with rising right-wing sentiment, Robert Kennedy turned to Walter Reuther of the United Auto Workers and liberal attorney Joseph Rauh Jr. for some concrete suggestions. Americans for Democratic Action urged formation of a new organization to fight extremism from both Left and Right, and union officials explored cooperation with the New Left. The administration, however, turned to something much more dramatic and far-reaching, something that was both secret and illegal. A memorandum prepared by Walter and Victor Reuther, together with Joseph L. Rauh Jr., formed the basis for a broad attack on the right wing by the Kennedy administration. It was the first step in what became a covert effort to discredit the right wing and undercut its sources of financial support.[7]

The Reuther Memorandum, as well as other efforts undertaken by the Kennedy administration to combat growing right-wing influence, had the effect of lumping together anyone on the Right who challenged mainstream thinking. Reuther had long been anathema to the right wing and to conservatives in general. During the 1950s he had been a major protagonist in the infamous and bitter Kohler strike. This strike (there had been an earlier one, from 1934 to 1941) lasted from 1954 to 1960. Herbert Kohler, president of the company, steadfastly stood his ground against labor and the NLRB. Kohler was a frequent contributor to right-wing causes, and served on the advisory board of Young Americans for Freedom. His son, Herbert Kohler Jr., was an active member of Young Americans for Freedom's board of directors in the early 1960s. The end of the strike had not ended the bitterness between Kohler and Walter Reuther's United Auto Workers, and Reuther's authorship of the memorandum on the right wing was a red flag to extreme conservatives like Kohler.[8]

Although Young Americans for Freedom seemingly escaped the most pernicious manifestation of the Kennedy effort, the IRS tax audit program, it did not escape the administration's scrutiny since it failed to distinguish itself from the more extreme and provocative groups on the Right. It got caught in a web of administration activities designed to counteract and erode the growing power of the right wing, a web that had at least four components: the Reuther Memorandum, IRS tax audits, White House monitoring of right-wing organizations, and a detailed effort to document those groups and their fund-raising sources undertaken at the request of the president. The administration and the public perceived YAF to be part of a tempestuous and unsavory mix of right-wing kooks. Its liberal opponents were more than happy to perpetuate that image.

The Reuther Memorandum

Delivered on December 19, 1961 to Attorney General Robert Kennedy, the so-called Reuther Memorandum ("The Radical Right in America Today") was a 24-page outline of "possible Administration policies and programs to combat the radical right." Noting that public discussion had produced few programmatic suggestions to deal with the problem, it warned that *speeches without action may well only mobilize the radical right instead of mobilizing the democratic forces within our nation.* Untold millions of Americans subscribed to the doctrines of the radical Right, it asserted, ranging from Senator Barry Goldwater on the "left" to Robert Welch on the right. Admittedly the activists were much fewer in number, but the "groups are probably stronger and are almost certainly better organized than at any time in recent history." Their growth would likely continue as cold war tensions persisted. The activists were well financed, and the memorandum briefly outlined the financial resources available to various right-wing organizations. "They traffic in fear. Treason in high place is their slogan and slander is their weapon." There is "no question that anybody even slightly to the left of Senator Goldwater is suspect."[9] What was needed was a sweeping attack on these groups.

The memorandum rejected as too superficial the notion that the radical Right was essentially a problem for the Republican Party. It might be an "inconvenience" for the Republicans, but

> it is far worse than that for the Nation and the Democratic Party—for it threatens the President's program at home and abroad. By the use of the twin propaganda weapons of fear and slander, the radical right moves the national political spectrum away from the Administration's proposed liberal programs at home and abroad. By vicious local pressure campaigns against teachers or preachers or any one else who supports anything from negotiation in foreign affairs, to governmental programs in domestic affairs, they frighten off support for much-needed Administration programs. Pressure tactics on already-timid Congressmen are reinforced with fanaticism and funds.[10]

The real question was: what could be done?

Insisting that the struggle against the Right was a long-term affair (and by Right it meant an array of groups to the right of center), the Reuther Memorandum advocated "deliberate Administration policies and programs to contain the radical right from further expansion" and "to reduce it to its historic role of the impotent lunatic fringe." It also urged private groups and agencies—churches, labor, the press, television, civic and political organizations—to mobilize their resources in this battle. The memorandum then outlined five steps the administration should consider. First, it needed to curb right-wing activities inside the armed services. This was an immediate problem, and threatened the "basic American concept of separating military personnel from partisan politics." The case of General Edwin Walker was only the most visible manifestation of right-wing influence in the military; too many officers belonged to these radical Right groups. Second, it claimed that the attorney general's subversive list aided the radical Right because it focused on the Left and omitted the Right. "The list today is almost like a Good Housekeeping seal for the radical right." The memorandum urged the attorney general to place several right-wing groups on the subversive list, insisting that many of them clearly met the criteria by which liberal and communist groups had been judged "subversive." In addition, the authors advised "the Attorney General to announce at this time that he is going to investigate one or more of these organizations with a view to determining whether charges will be filed and hearings held on the question of listing one or more of these organizations." The "mere act" of investigation would "certainly bring home to many people something they have never considered—the subversive character of these organizations . . . ." Finally, if it had not already done so, the FBI should plant informers inside the Right as it had inside the Left.[11]

The memorandum's third recommendation, and the one that particularly caught the Kennedys' attention, was that the flow of money to the radical Right be choked off. Arguing that "funds are a source of power to the radical right," Reuther noted that several radical Right groups—Dr. George Benson's National Education Program, Dr. Fred Schwarz's Christian Anti-Communist Crusade, Billy James Hargis's Christian Crusade, and the William Volker Fund, Inc.—all had federal tax exemptions. "Prompt revocation in a few cases might scare off a substantial part of the big money now flowing into these tax exempt organizations." Other individuals, such as H. L. Hunt, openly encouraged corporations to use their advertising funds to help the Right. The government should step in and ban "certain propaganda ads." Concurrently, the administration should use the Federal Communications Commission to crack down on radio and television programs that masqueraded as public service programs, which gave them free or reduced rates. Finally, the memorandum raised doubts about whether the various right-wing organizations were correctly and legally reporting all their income. Could the Internal Revenue Service be used to determine if they were complying with the tax laws? Could the Treasury Department, together with the FBI, utilize undercover agents to probe possible tax violations?[12]

A fourth suggestion advocated immediate measures against the Minutemen. Paramilitary guerrilla organizations went far beyond any constitutional mandates for free speech, and the Minutemen represented "a dangerous precedent in our democracy." State and federal laws should be used to curtail or end their activities. Finally, the memorandum urged the administration to put the current domestic Communist problem in its proper perspective. The radical Right based its appeal largely on its assertion that communism was gaining strength and represented a serious threat of internal subversion. This was fallacious, the memorandum concluded, and exposing this fallacy would undercut much of the Right's appeal. That would be difficult, however, for politicians had focused on the threat of communism since the end of World War II, and FBI director J. Edgar Hoover constantly exaggerated the domestic communist menace. Although the Communist Party might have been strong in the 1930s or 1940s, in the 1960s it had no capacity to threaten the country's internal security. Indeed, the memorandum concluded, the right wing was more of a threat. "It would be the easier course to look the other way and say that the radical right will disappear when we solve our problems at home and abroad. But the radical right may, if it is not contained, make it more difficult, if not impossible, to solve our problems at home and abroad."[13]

This fear that the right wing might become powerful enough to shape the country's political agenda had compelled the president and attorney general to invite Reuther to prepare his memorandum. Although the document's existence remained secret for much of the next two years, the administration quickly began to implement many of its recommendations. Despite denials from Robert Kennedy's office that he had even read the Reuther Memorandum, and despite Robert Kennedy's assertion in 1964 that neither he nor the president considered the right wing anything more than humorous "pains in the butt," their actions argue otherwise. Indeed, even before Reuther gave the memorandum to the attorney general the administration had begun to monitor the activities of right-wing organizations.

White House staff member Lee White prepared a series of monthly confidential reports on the activities of these groups. His first report, dated November 28, 1961, surveyed the periodical and newspaper press to abstract trends and targets of the Right. The purpose of the reports seems to have been to try to anticipate right-wing attacks and concerns. In his November report, White warned that the Right would likely focus on the sale of obsolete Sabre jet fighters to Yugoslavia, Moise Tshombe and Katanga, the Edwin Walker affair, some recent resignations from the National Security Agency, and the upcoming Reciprocal Trade Agreements Act to launch broadsides accusing the administration of advancing the communist cause. At the same time, FBI director J. Edgar Hoover responded to White House concerns by intensifying FBI surveillance of right-wing organizations (although he focused more on the Ku Klux Klan than on these political groups), and the Army Intelligence Command at Fort Holabird, Maryland listed right-wing groups (including Young Americans for Freedom) in its biographic data file. Later investigations revealed that this interest predated the onset of the civil disturbances that led to the computerization of the Holabird system. Shortly afterward the CONARC (Continental Army Command) computer system also listed groups on the "political right," including Young Americans for Freedom.[14]

The Ideological Organizations Project

The most far-reaching effort undertaken by the Kennedy administration, however, involved the Internal Revenue Service and became known as the Ideological Organizations Project. In late 1961 the IRS launched a program to audit twenty-two right-wing organizations. Its purpose was that outlined in the Reuther Memorandum: to investigate whether particular right-wing groups were illegally claiming tax-exempt status or otherwise violating the tax laws. Although the courts had generally permitted some political activity by tax-exempt organizations, that activity was not supposed to be significant with respect to the organizations' purposes. The administration clearly believed that these right-wing groups were essentially political in nature; therefore, virtually any evidence of political activity could be used to strip away their tax-exempt status. The public remained unaware of this attack until well after the assassinations of both John and Robert Kennedy—in fact until the hearings of the so-called Church Committee (officially the Senate Select Committee on Intelligence Activities) in the mid-1970s revealed the existence of the program and the outlines of its operation.[15]

In its public discussion of the tax exemption issue during the early 1960s, the IRS concealed this right-wing audit program behind a broader, less political examination of tax-exempt organizations and foundations. That larger effort stemmed from Texas Congressman Wright Patman's insistence that tax-exempt foundations gained an unfair competitive advantage in the marketplace. The IRS was in the process of examining more than 530 foundations named by Patman, but staffing shortages slowed its work. The agency also fought Patman's demand that it release to him the names of specific individuals involved in some of their rulings. "Not only would this affect the quality and correctness of our rulings and possibly bring about criticism of the Service," the Exempt Organizations Branch argued, "it would in effect deny taxpayers and organizations their right to a free and impartial judgment of their cases." The White House endorsed this interpretation.[16]

The Ideological Organizations Project actually began before formal delivery of the Reuther Memorandum to the attorney general. It began with the Justice Department. On November 16, 1961, the same date as the president's first West coast speech about the dangers of the right wing, Mitchell Rogovin, assistant to IRS commissioner Mortimer M. Caplin, received a telephone call from John Seigenthaler, special assistant to the attorney general, inquiring into the tax-exempt status of several right-wing groups. Although Seigenthaler later disputed the exact date, he admitted that he had several telephone conversations with Rogovin between November 13 and December 1, 1961. The initial IRS investigation focused solely on right-wing groups, although by the spring of 1962 a couple of left-wing groups were added for balance. In addition, Caplin himself received a call from the White House right after the president's speech, and he assigned Rogovin to run the project.[17]

On November 29, 1961, President Kennedy held a press conference. Responding to questions about his speeches during the previous week against the right wing, Kennedy stated that he believed the federal government could not interfere in the activities of such groups so "long as they meet the requirements of the tax laws." He further observed that "I'm sure the Internal Revenue System examines that." If it didn't yet, it soon would. The next day William Loeb, Assistant Commissioner for Compliance, sent a memorandum to Dean J. Barron, Director of the Audit Division, attaching a press clipping of the president's remarks and directing that the Audit Division secure from Rogovin a list of groups whose tax liability should be examined. "I think it behooves us," he told Barron, "to be certain that we know whether the organizations are complying with the tax law as a matter of fact." On December 20, 1961, Rogovin forwarded to Barron a list of eighteen organizations to be checked.[18]

At this time there were few meaningful statutes that limited the authority of the Internal Revenue Service to gather this sort of intelligence. Later, in the Nixon administration, this led to the creation of the Special Service Staff (SSS) and many well-publicized abuses of IRS authority. But in the early 1960s Americans still retained a basic confidence and trust in their government. Most people did not suspect the existence of an effort like the Ideological Organizations Project, even though the IRS later planned to expand the list of 18 organizations to a broad review of perhaps 10,000 tax-exempt organizations, and also to examine nonexempt right-wing groups (which would then include Young Americans for Freedom) by reviewing their contributors' tax returns for improper deductions. In fact, there is evidence that the Kennedy administration's interest in using the IRS for political purposes not only predates the Ideological Organizations Project, but was more than idle curiosity. In early 1961, under pressure from either the president or the attorney general, the IRS Office of Chief Counsel granted Carmine Bellino, a special consultant to the president (and the Kennedy family's accountant), access to tax returns. Subsequent discussions about this within the IRS concluded that the president was "entitled to all information relative to his control over the executive branch," and that this included any official acting on behalf of the president. This was, however, a closely guarded project. Even presidential advisor Arthur Schlesinger Jr. apparently remained unaware of its existence as late as June 1963.[19]

Once the Ideological Organizations Project was underway, it quickly became part of the normal bureaucratic procedures of the IRS. By January 1962 the audits had begun. The IRS requested tax audits of six large corporate taxpayers who had supposedly made financial contributions to "extremist groups" in New York and San Francisco, and of three right-wing groups in the San Francisco area. This effort soon spread to other regions. Despite the cover of tax audits, the IRS had clearly targeted these groups because of their political activities. In a summary memorandum for presidential aide Myer Feldman, Mitchell Rogovin observed that the study defined "ideological organization" as an organization "seeking to 'educate' the public in currently controversial fields. More specifically," he noted, "in addition to gathering and disseminating information they appear to direct their efforts toward influencing the beliefs or actions of others with reference to certain predetermined governmental, social or economic ends." Furthermore, Rogovin admitted that the IRS worked under the "assumption that the ideological activities of many of the organizations under study were not appropriate for exempt organizations . . . ." A March 9, 1962 memorandum admitted to "[using] the term 'political action organizations' rather than 'right-wing organizations' throughout this discussion. This has been done to avoid giving the impression that the Service is giving special attention to returns filed by taxpayers or organizations with a particular political ideology."[20]

A subsequent memorandum from Mitchell Rogovin added nineteen "left of center" organizations to the tax audit list, although not all were accepted. By May 1962 the project included 12 right-wing organizations and 10 left-wing groups. That the list included both exempt and nonexempt organizations revealed its bias against "political action organizations." The nonexempt groups on the Right included the National Indignation Convention, the Conservative Society of America, Americans for Constitutional Government, the John Birch Society, Robert Welch Inc., the All American Society, and The Conservatives. The exempt right-wing groups to be examined were the Christian Crusade–Christian Crusaders Inc., Christian Anti-Communist Crusade, Life-Line Foundation, National Education Program of Harding College, and the Christian Echoes Ministry Inc. of Sapulpa, Oklahoma. To "avoid any possible charges that the Service is giving special attention to a group with a particular ideology," the IRS added three nonexempt left-wing organizations: Fair Play for Cuba, Common Council for American Unity Inc., and the Kenderland Colony Association. It also included seven exempt groups: American Veterans Committee Inc., League for Labor Palestine Inc., Anti-Defamation League of B'nai B'rith, Bressler Foundation, Zionist Organization of America, League for Industrial Democracy Inc., and the Freeman Charitable Foundation, Gilbert.[21]

But IRS efforts remained focused on the right-wing organizations. A letter from IRS Commissioner Mortimer Caplin to Under Secretary of the Treasury Henry Fowler, while acknowledging that the IRS would examine the returns of left-wing groups, revealed this bias.

> The activities of so-called extremist right-wing political action organizations have recently been given a great amount of publicity by magazines, newspapers and television programs. This publicity, however, has made little mention of the tax status of these organizations or their supporters. Nevertheless, the alleged activities of these groups are such that we plan to determine the extent of their compliance with Federal tax laws. In addition, we propose to ascertain whether contributors to these organizations are deducting their contributions from taxable income.

The next day Commissioner Caplin sent a similar report to Attorney General Robert F. Kennedy about the Ideological Organizations Project. A subsequent letter from Acting Commissioner Bertrand Harding to Congressman Wright Patman admitted that most of these organizations had been selected because they used "mass media" to "'educate the public' with reference to certain governmental, social or economic concepts, activities, or ideologies." Indeed, White House aide Myer Feldman has since admitted that Young Americans for Freedom was the subject of an exchange of correspondence between his office and the IRS Commissioner because of questions raised "by the media" about YAF's eligibility for tax exemption.[22]

The first phase of the Ideological Organizations Project ran from the fall of 1961 until 1963. On February 8, 1963 the Assistant IRS Commissioner for Compliance, William Loeb, sent a status report on the project to Commissioner Caplin. Calling the program a "Test Audit Program of Political Action Organizations," Loeb noted that IRS efforts had been directed at 12 right-wing and 11 left-wing organizations. Nine of the right-wing groups had already been audited, including four that were tax exempt. "Revocation of exempt status was recommended in two of these cases. . . . No changes in tax liabilities were recommended upon examination of the five taxable organizations." This was an important admission. Not only was the IRS targeting tax-exempt organizations, as it had outlined at the start of the project; it was examining nonexempt organizations as well. The scope of the investigation had apparently expanded, following political and ideological fault lines. Indeed, a March 1962 internal memorandum indicated that, beginning in January of that year, the IRS had requested "that examinations be made of six large corporate taxpayers who are alleged financial backers of extremist groups." Finally, Loeb revealed that the IRS found no evidence that individual taxpayers were claiming tax deductions for their contributions to non-tax-exempt "political action organizations." In the future, he concluded, the IRS would concentrate on tax-exempt organizations. In July 1963 the White House was brought up to date, and "expressed renewed interest in the project."[23]

On July 5, 1963 Deputy Special Counsel to the President Myer Feldman requested that IRS commissioner Mortimer Caplin provide a report on the Ideological Organizations Project. Six days later Caplin complied, with a memorandum that outlined the history of the program's first phase, including a summary of the field audits. The tax-exempt status of two right-wing organizations had already been recommended for removal, and a third group had been notified that the IRS intended to revoke its exemption as well. In addition, the IRS denied at least one corporate taxpayer's deductions for contributions to a right-wing publication. The memorandum also discussed the difficulties of auditing so-called "educational" organizations, and noted that some legislative changes might be suggested to clarify and limit the political actions of exempt organizations as well as eliminate some deductions to extremist causes. It further noted the intention of the IRS to expand the project to include 10,000 organizations of all types in a second phase to begin in 1964. An August memorandum from Mitchell Rogovin to the regional IRS commissioners further highlighted the difficulties and time-consuming nature of the Ideological Organizations Project. The examinations, Rogovin noted, "require reorientation of the agent's thinking and place him into areas fraught with interpretative difficulties." They had to collect and analyze books, pamphlets, telecasts, broadcasts, and speeches distributed by the organizations and their members. Rogovin noted that hereafter field agents were to gather facts and materials, and then submit them to the national office. There a small group of individuals would evaluate that evidence, make recommendations concerning the group's tax status, and submit a "technical advice memorandum" to agents in the field.[24]

The White House was delighted with the IRS efforts, but demanded more aggressive action. On July 20 Commissioner Caplin met with Robert Kennedy to discuss the investigation, and the next day he met with Myer Feldman at the White House. Three days later President Kennedy called the commissioner about the memorandum of July 11, and urged the IRS to "go ahead with [an] aggressive program—on both sides of center." Three days later, on July 26, 1963, an IRS task force met to discuss the project. Chaired by Mitchell Rogovin, the meeting produced a memorandum that outlined the next phase of the project. It was to be considered an "extension of the technical advice procedure," and the national office would advise its field offices of particular organizations and their activities. It was to "first deal with right-wing groups," although the list of groups sent to the field offices also included organizations on the Left, probably as a cover for the real focus of the investigations.[25]

By early August the Internal Revenue Service had drawn up a list of ideological organizations whose tax status there was "probable cause" to examine. Compiled by IRS employees on the task force, the list relied on IRS files, material from various books and periodicals, and information from Group Research, a watchdog group that tracked right-wing individuals and organizations. According to Frank Chapper, technical advisor to the Division Director of the Tax Rulings Division, the criteria for selecting particular organizations included "whether the organization was trying to influence the legislative process, and also the publicity the organization was getting." Twenty-four ideological organizations (from a list of 109) were selected by August 21, 1963 for the second phase of the Ideological Organizations Project. Seven of them had also been selected in the first phase of the project. Of the 24 groups, the IRS characterized 19 as right-wing.[26]

During the selection process Mitchell Rogovin, assistant attorney to the commissioner, kept the White House informed through meetings with Myer Feldman and also acted as liaison with the Justice Department. Rogovin and Feldman met on July 29 and August 21 to review the second phase of the program, and at the latter meeting Rogovin reviewed the 24 organizations finally selected. After the meeting, two of the groups (the D.A.R. and the Zionist Organization of America) were deleted at the suggestion of Feldman. (Five more organizations were subsequently added to the list.) In addition, on August 20 Rogovin met with Attorney General Robert Kennedy and briefed him on the project's second phase. Kennedy urged Rogovin to accelerate the investigation of one right-wing organization in particular, and the IRS subsequently revoked the tax-exempt status of this organization.[27] Both Feldman and Kennedy pushed Rogovin to complete the project by October 1. During the fall the IRS moved ahead rapidly with its investigations, and by late November it had received reports on 19 of the 24 organizations. By February 1964 the national office had analyzed 18 of the 24 cases and concluded that there were grounds for revocation of tax-exempt status in at least 6 of them. In addition to investigating the tax-exempt status of these organizations, the Internal Revenue Service also launched a full-scale investigation of the ideological organizations in question, including their organization, use of media, publications, and finances. More than technical tax questions seemed at issue here, and the Internal Revenue Service felt enormous pressure from the White House to "'do something' about ideological organizations."[28]

Despite that pressure, the IRS plan to audit 10,000 tax-exempt organizations never became operational. Instead the agency concentrated on the 24 groups already under review. On March 23, 1964 Rogovin sent Myer Feldman a status report on the second phase of the project. The report described the activities and actions of the IRS up to that point. By the end of 1964 the Ideological Organizations Project had led to recommendations for the revocation of exempt status for 15 groups (14 of them right-wing). The IRS eventually approved four of the recommendations for continued action (3 right-wing groups), rejecting the rest or sending them back for further study. During the next year the IRS reported regularly to the Treasury Department on the status of the project, but the Johnson administration seemed little interested in continuing the investigations. The new IRS commissioner, Sheldon Cohen, presented subsequent status reports in 1966 and 1967, but by then a decision had been made to wind down the project on the grounds that it had fulfilled its major purposes. These later reports revealed that 3 groups lost their exempt status in 1966 (all right-wing) and 4 others lost their exemptions in 1967 (3 of them right-wing).[29]

Although the Internal Revenue Service justified the Ideological Organizations Project as an effort to strengthen its exempt organization laws, it initiated the project in direct response to White House and Justice Department pressure. Revocation of tax-exempt status had the potential to yield more tax revenue, but the IRS knew from previous experience that the potential was slight. Indeed, in his July 11, 1963 memorandum Commissioner Caplin admitted that previous examinations of exempt organizations had been time-consuming and costly, with "a potential loss of approximately $175,000 otherwise produced from income tax audits."[30] And still the IRS contemplated expanding the list of 24 organizations to a catalogue of 10,000.

The Ideological Organizations Project was not the only effort undertaken by the Kennedy administration to attack the right wing. While Young Americans for Freedom apparently escaped the scrutiny of the project (probably because it was not tax-exempt, primarily sought to change the direction of the Republican Party, focused on more mainstream conservative issues, and lacked the resources for national propaganda used by other, more extreme groups), it did not escape the attention of other investigators. Lee White of the White House staff continued to monitor the activities of various right-wing groups, from the John Birch Society to the National Indignation Convention to Young Americans for Freedom, preparing a series of confidential reports throughout 1962. White seemed to agree with YAF founder Stanton Evans, who argued that the flowering of right-wing organizations reflected "two decades of frustration" at the failure of the United States to be more aggressive against communism. Evans attacked the Kennedy administration, and liberals in general, for their efforts to discredit the right wing. They were, he concluded, scared of the right wing's popular appeal. Unaware of the administration's secret efforts to combat the Right, liberal publications condemned it for ignoring the "conservative conspiracy" that sought to take over the government.[31]

Many conservatives feared that actions of the extremist Right threatened to discredit more moderate conservative activity and opposition to Kennedy administration programs. Although this distinction was not always apparent in the administration's support for the Ideological Organizations Project, it reflected a critical dilemma for many individuals and groups on the Right. The concern of William F. Buckley Jr., National Review, and divisions within Young Americans for Freedom had illustrated the problem. In a confidential January 16, 1962 memorandum, Marvin Liebman outlined the problems inherent in the relationship between the John Birch Society and the larger conservative anticommunist movement in the United States. Liebman argued that the statements of Robert Welch and the Birch Society did not represent his views, and warned that their recklessness would injure political conservatism. At the same time, however, one could not simply "banish" Welch and the Birch Society, for neither National Review nor Young Americans for Freedom possessed that power. "It would be futile," he concluded, "because we do not control the right-wing movement in the United States."[32]

The basic problem, according to Liebman, was that the "Conservative-anti-Communist apparat that we all have hoped for" now existed throughout the country. But Robert Welch controlled it. "It seems to me," he concluded, "that our objectives should be to try to take over this apparat and not to destroy it." The way to do that was not to attack the John Birch Society, but to keep YAF's publications free from their excesses and develop a "responsible Right." Senator Barry Goldwater articulated a similar strategy when he argued before a joint

Washington meeting of the Harvard, Yale, and Princeton clubs that conservatives "must beat off the idiots that are always attracted to a movement at its beginnings." Although Goldwater defended the Birch Society, he tried to divorce himself from the views of Robert Welch. Later, in *National Review*, Goldwater insisted that Welch's views did not represent the thinking of most John Birch Society members. For some conservatives, however, this seemed to be a distinction without a difference. Walter Judd, in response to an inquiry about YAF, praised the Sharon Statement but warned that the Birch Society was "so violent that they defeat themselves."[33]

The growing strength of the right wing also sparked concern among liberal organizations such as Americans for Democratic Action. A confidential memorandum from the ADA Campus Division in January 1962 warned about the strength of Young Americans for Freedom as well as the "unholy alliance between the right-wing Irish Catholics and the 'grass-roots' fundamentalistic Protestants . . . ." Through YAF the right wing was penetrating college campuses, and this worried ADA, particularly in light of YAF's attacks on the National Student Association. Milton Shapp, chairman of the board of Jerrold Electronics Corporation of Philadelphia, was concerned enough to send YAF pamphlets on to the White House. Shapp, who later became Democratic Governor of Pennsylvania, warned that with "1964 creeping ever closer, I think it is imperative that we start assisting N.S.A.—or some other organization on the college campuses—in an effort to win greater support among the college students for the principles espoused by the president." The appeals of ADA and other liberal groups for a united front against the right wing, however, met with opposition from student groups on the Left. Jim Monsonis of Students for a Democratic Society rejected ADA's appeal, arguing that the right wing was not holding the Kennedy administration back from some ideal position on the issues of the day. Monsonis noted that both SDS and SNCC considered the administration far too conservative and wedded to the "military industrial complex which makes the basic decisions on the American economy." Both organizations were committed to "more radical change than the government is prepared to accept," Monsonis insisted. They would work with the administration when their objectives were parallel, but they believed that the government sought to consolidate the center and control the Right at the expense of meaningful change.[34]

In his series of confidential reports to the White House, Lee White noted the tension among conservatives that worried Liebman and other traditional conservatives. In its second *New York Times* ad, he observed, the American Committee for Aid to Katanga Freedom Fighters had dropped the names of eight identifiable members of the John Birch Society, apparently in an effort to counter charges that it was a radical right front and to advance a more moderate image. He also noted that at a recent *Human Events* Political Action Conference conservative speakers had urged moderation even while they launched partisan attacks against administration policies. White cautioned, however, that the audience did not seem to heed those warnings and was much more bellicose. In particular he pointed to a cluster of organizations allied with *National Review*—groups like Young Americans for Freedom, The Committee of One Million, The Aid to Katanga Committee, and the New York Conservative Party. These groups were more interested in "the winning of a national election, the re-education of the governing class" than in wild radical right charges. The danger, White noted, was clear.

> The real goal may be to replace the erratic [Robert] Welch with a man whose thinking parallels that of *National Review*, and who can guide the JBS [John Birch Society] back to the realities of everyday politics and can channel the frenzied emotional energy presently expended on futile projects to impeach Warren and repeal the Income Tax into effective political action. In this connection, it should be noted that the attacks on Welch have come from friends or members of the "National Review" group and that they have been directed specifically at the leadership, *not* at the membership.[35]

In late January White also received a memorandum from Sanford Gottlieb, lobbyist for SANE, urging that groups should be formed around the country to counter the growing right-wing activity. Titled "A Program to Counter Right-Wing Influence on U.S. Foreign Policy," the memorandum argued that Americans were "confused and frustrated" in a "world of rapid change and recurring crises." This led them to see conspiracies everywhere, and fueled right-wing attacks on the administration. It had allowed them to exert a "negative pull on the Administration's desire to create a more flexible foreign policy," and fostered an emotional climate of suspicion. Gottlieb urged the administration to support his project.

> A broad group of non-governmental organizations could be enlisted to undertake this kind of project. Among them are the American Association for the United Nations, American Veterans Committee, Americans for Democratic Action, Division of Peace of the Methodist Church, International Union of Electrical Workers, National Committee for a Sane Nuclear Policy, Oil, Chemical and Atomic Workers, and the United Auto Workers. Most of them are already cooperating in a recently-launched joint effort known as Turn Toward Peace.[36]

Like other Americans, of course, Gottlieb knew nothing about the Ideological Organizations Project already underway.

The Scope of Administration Concern

The series of confidential memoranda from Lee White, together with the Ideological Organizations Project, indicated the Kennedy administration's concern about the political threat of the radical right. By the summer of 1963, the FBI had also begun to investigate "rightist or extremist" groups on a "general intelligence premise" as well as under criminal or security programs.[37] In addition, Myer Feldman, deputy special counsel to the president, prepared a lengthy analysis of all these groups. Completed in August 1963 and forwarded to President Kennedy, the study provided synoptic overviews for twenty-six "major right-wing organizations" as well as an overall picture of financial support for the right wing. Feldman tried to distinguish between what he called the "conservative right" and the "radical right," and focused his attention on the latter. They spent, he warned, $15–$25 million annually and broadcast programs on at least a thousand radio stations around the country. Using material likely gleaned from IRS documents, Feldman found that funding for these groups came from "approximately 70 foundations, 113 business firms and corporations, 25 electric light, gas and power companies, and 250 identifiable individuals." There was considerable overlap in the contributions; individuals and companies that gave to one group often gave to several.[38]

But even as he drew distinctions between different elements on the Right, Feldman also blurred them. He warned that the outlook of "conservatives" and "radicals" differed "in degree and intensity, but not in kind." Organizations in both categories viewed "American domestic policy since the New Deal as Socialistic and dangerous, and foreign policy of the last 30 years as prone to 'softness' and appeasement in dealing with the Communist threat." As such, he drew little distinction between organizations such as Young Americans for Freedom and the John Birch Society. The tendency of both groups to endorse each other's candidates manifested an affinity of "leadership and sponsorship." They were, Feldman concluded, "an ideological blur." Together they made up a "band of conservative fellow-travellers."[39]

Of particular concern, Feldman concluded, was that the "right-wing seems to have been more successful, politically, than is generally realized." More than half of the candidates supported by Americans for Constitutional Action had been successful in the 1962 elections. Even though four avowed Birchers lost congressional races, each one polled about 45 percent of the vote and raised significant funds. Feldman outlined a series of steps that might blunt this right-wing assault. They included investigations of the groups' financial resources, their methods of operation (recruitment, propaganda, fund-raising, tax exempt status), possible violations of the Federal Communications Act in their radio programs, the "extent of the political contributions to right-wing candidates," the irresponsibility of much of their literature, and their use of favorable postal rates to distribute their material. In addition, Feldman warned that the radical Right had penetrated politics at the local level. He concluded that even though "little is known of the membership and finances of local right-wing organizations scattered around the country that harass local school boards, local librarians, and local government bodies," there was no doubt that the "radical right-wing constitutes a formidable force in American life today. It exerts an impact on the political scene from Washington all the way down to the various state capitals, to county seats, and to local communities at the grass-roots."[40]

Coming as it did in the summer of 1963, Feldman's memo was clearly designed for the 1964 presidential campaign. It was also, in some respects, the frosting on the cake. Should anyone question the president about his sources for information about the right wing, he could point to the Feldman memo and thereby continue to conceal the existence of the Ideological Organizations Project. The August 1963 study also documented both a fundamental problem for conservatives and a promising avenue of attack for the administration. Without question more moderate conservative groups had either refused or failed to distinguish themselves from their extremist counterparts. While conservative attacks on Robert Welch revealed the moderates' desire for such a separation, in the 1962 elections groups like Young Americans for Freedom and Americans for Constitutional Action had endorsed all the Birch candidates and, according to Feldman, "apparently made no effort to distinguish between conservative candidates and candidates of a Radical Rightist ideology." In key states such as California the right wing had taken over the Young Republicans and were close to controlling the statewide Republican organization. It was apparent that they would continue to join forces in support for Senator Barry Goldwater in 1964.[41]

Chapter 8   Taking On the G.O.P.

Dᴇsᴘɪᴛᴇ ᴇғғᴏʀᴛs by the Kennedy administration to undercut and neutralize the right wing, Young Americans for Freedom moved to capture the Republican Party, consolidate the conservative cause, and nominate a truly conservative candidate in 1964. This, after all, had been a central objective since their inception. Although they touted themselves as a nonpartisan conservative organization, YAFers had long since concluded that their path to power ran through the Republican Party. Their problem was to avoid the snare of extremist politics advocated by many of their conservative allies who were also excited about Barry Goldwater, even while they battled Young Republicans and party regulars for political influence.

Avoiding Extremism

The 1962 elections demonstrated clearly the difficulty of maintaining a separate identity for the "respectable" Right. Richard Nixon's campaign in the California gubernatorial primary was but one of many races where delineating the "respectable" Right from the "extremist" Right became an issue. Although Nixon denounced the John Birch Society, which supported his primary opponent Joseph Shell (who had said that the "middle of the road is 75 percent socialism"), the real goal of California right-wingers was to capture that state's Republican convention delegation should Nixon lose the fall election (which, of course, he did). In addition, the November defeats of Bircher John Rousselot

and three other candidates backed by the Birch Society proved a mixed blessing for YAF, since the organization had supported all four of them on the basis
that YAF should support *all* conservative candidates regardless of their other
affiliations. This support for *any* so-called conservative reflected divisions
within Young Americans for Freedom at both the national and the local level.
Clearly the efforts of William F. Buckley Jr. and others to separate Young Americans for Freedom and "respectable" conservatism from the Birch Society had
not completely succeeded.[1]

    Although reports from Kennedy staffers Lee White and Myer Feldman la-
beled YAF a "major" right-wing organization, their analyses recognized that the
organization focused largely on mainstream issues rather than quixotic crusades.
YAF was more interested in right-to-work laws, welfare reform, free market economics, student loyalty oaths, the reduction of federal spending, the continuation of nuclear testing, and a muscular anticommunism than in vague conspiracies and a devil theory of social change. Unlike the John Birch Society,
YAFers embraced ideology, not conspiracy, as the agent of change. When they
did see conspiracies, as noted earlier, they found them within the Republican
Party or even within YAF itself, not in broader historical processes. Many
YAFers were proud of the label "right-wing" because it distinguished them
from "moderate" conservatives (and "modern" Republicans), and they remained conservatives first and Republicans second. Their goal was to transform
the Republican Party into a vehicle for conservatism. Richard Allen, YAF's Indiana leader, typified their commitment. Only twenty-four years old, and with
a wife and three children, Allen quit his job as an insurance adjuster to become
a full-time crusader for YAF, forming eighteen new chapters in a year. This sort
of political passion often gave rise to extremist remarks. Passion and extremism were different, but both the media and YAF's opponents frequently failed
to distinguish between the two.[2]

    This increased polarization was reflected not only within the Republican
Party, but within the United States National Student Association. During the
preceding two years YAF had attacked the NSA as too liberal and unrepre-
sentative of students nationwide. By the summer 1963 NSA convention the
contentions of SDS and YAF severely strained the organization. SDS's Liberal
Study Group, which itself had tried to set the agenda for the NSA, observed
that "it is again possible to say that some of America's crucial political battles
are now being fought on the nation's campuses . . . ." Paradoxically, YAF argued against campus politics. It insisted that college life was a "transitional phase
in which the child becomes an adult, and concentrates on *learning*—not total
involvement in the weighty issues of national and international political life."[3]
YAF nonetheless enthusiastically engaged in campus politics and repeatedly

passed resolutions on national issues. Indeed, political action was its very purpose. W. Dennis Shaul, president of the NSA, acknowledged this in a letter to Richard Lambert, Director of Organization for ADA, reporting that "we have had a great deal of trouble with attacks from the right wing during the last few months. In fact vicious attacks have cost us affiliations at Indiana and Texas. Some of these were directed by YAF."[4]

Looking to 1964

These conflicts, however, were mere warm-ups for the big event, the 1964 presidential election. Executive Secretary Richard Viguerie announced that political action goals for 1963 included the organization of YAF chapters at every college and university in the fifty states. Although this was unlikely, the drive's fervor and purpose were clear in Viguerie's admonition that the "leaders of *tomorrow* will be conservative if organizations such as YAF can reach them *today*." A subsequent fund-raising appeal was even more dramatic: "Without the benefit of a YAF Chapter to supply them with the necessary facts concerning Constitutional government and Communist strategy and tactics for world domination, many young people attending school today will become liberals, socialists and, perhaps, even Communists tomorrow."[5]

YAF still seethed with internal schisms and backbiting about bureaucratic and administrative matters, while its members struggled to mobilize behind a common cause. Internal conflicts, which reflected ideological divisions within the new conservatism, dominated its spring board meeting. In addition, a ruling elite tried to run the organization by fiat, and tinkered with the bylaws at the expense of substantive matters. Fortunately these proved to be somewhat transient concerns. Throughout 1963 YAF channeled its energies much more vigorously toward two short-run objectives: the future of the conservative cause and the delineation of public policy issues. In most respects, the two were intertwined. Continued efforts to read Ayn Rand's objectivists out of the conservative movement, for example, stemmed from a conviction that her adherents were too self-centered and "material-worshipping" to embrace YAF's conservative tenets of community spirit and social responsibility. Although *The New Guard* continued to explore Rand's ideas, to which many YAFers subscribed, it insisted that the basic ideas of the Sharon Statement must be the foundation for the new conservatism.

In January 1963 *The New Guard* endorsed Goldwater for the Republican presidential nomination, arguing that he best represented those ideas. Youth for Goldwater formed later in the year, headed by James Harff, a YAFer and former national chair of college Young Republicans. Carol Bauman of YAF became its executive secretary. Despite its shaky financial foundation, Young Americans for Freedom escalated its political action crusade to capture control of the Republican Party and put Goldwater in the White House. National chair Robert Bauman issued the call to action and sounded the central themes of this crusade.

> Countless Americans have gone before us in the unceasing battle to preserve freedom in a chaotic world. To be true to our cause, we, too, must be willing to act. We are young people, inclined to be optimistic and idealistic, but old enough to realize the nature of the world our elders have left us.
>
> We conservatives are the ones who must express the vibrant sentiments of American patriotism during an era all too sophisticated and nonchalant about freedom. We cannot expect patrtiotism from the appeasers who deserted the valiant men dying before Castro's firing squads—while millions of Cubans remained imprisoned in a Communist satellite.
>
> The love of freedom will not be kept alive by self-styled economists who tell us we owe the national debt to ourselves; it will not come from socialist theorists, who are of one mind in imposing their alien ideas upon the American public. When even the pious civil libertarians condone, by their silence, government censorship of the news; when the Supreme Court can evidence maximum concern for the welfare of Communists and minimum concern for the encroachments of big government on the individual's freedom; then there is a need for all young Americans to redouble their efforts to continue the job we started in September, 1960.[6]

As part of this new action format, YAF launched a series of national political activities, including a monthly Washington report, a Young Conservative employment service, a campaign materials service, a book service, a speakers bureau, a film service, a special hot line to coordinate political action, a "how-to" service for organizing and fund-raising, and a series of audio tapes in conjunction with Clarence Manion of the Manion Forum. YAF also proposed a national youth conference, agreed to co-sponsor a political action conference ("Operation Young America") with *Human Events*, and voted to cooperate with the Committee for the Monroe Doctrine, organized by Captain Eddie Rickenbacker, long a participant in right-wing causes.[7]

From its new Washington, D.C. headquarters, YAF promoted its own leadership and attacked Kennedy administration policies. Each issue of *The New Guard* provided brief biographies of YAF state and national leaders to demonstrate the organization's breadth and commitment to conservatism. The journal also indicted President Kennedy and his administration for failing to drive communism from the Western Hemisphere. Together with *National Review* and the Committee for the Destruction of Communism, YAF sponsored a demonstration to counter 5,000 pickets at the United Nations who supported a nuclear test ban. Although only eight students showed up to oppose the ban (carrying signs such as "100 Megatons Makes a Hell of a Hole, But is Life Under Communism Better?"), they made the *New York Times* and got their message across. This reflected a return on the part of YAF to earlier tactics, when it concentrated on getting publicity in the belief that good publicity could create an illusion of strength and outweigh numbers in the long run.[8]

The central message propagated by YAF throughout the year was that Barry Goldwater could do more for conservatism than any other potential Republican candidate, and that political change was essential to curb the Kennedy administration's softness on communism and tendencies toward intrusive, big government. At their April meeting, YAF's board of directors passed a special resolution calling for an aggressive program to end communism in Cuba. It demanded that the United States implement a tight economic blockade, close the Panama Canal to trade heading for Cuba, sever diplomatic relations with the Soviet Union if it failed to withdraw its troops and missiles from Cuba, and recognize a Cuban government in exile. In July, Barry Goldwater was the keynote speaker at the *Human Events* political action conference. The 500 conservatives in attendance included about 200 YAFers. YAF also planned a panel on "Mobilizing Youth for the '64 Campaign" for its national convention in Fort Lauderdale that fall.[9]

The dominant ideological themes YAF advanced throughout 1963 found perhaps their clearest expression in its opposition to the proposed National Service Corps. To lead the fight, YAF formed a National Student Committee for Effective Social Welfare. National chair Robert Bauman testified against the proposed domestic peace corps before a congressional committee. One of only two organizations that opposed the National Service Corps, YAF based its opposition on several ideological and political principles, focusing on the means proposed to meet social work needs throughout the country. They emphasized private enterprise and initiative and, while Bauman admitted the need to serve the disadvantaged, he noted in his testimony that 22,000,000 volunteers currently did this through private and government programs. In this context, he insisted, not only would a National Service Corps needlessly compete with already established programs and endanger private welfare programs; its mobilization of 5,000 additional federal workers would be insignificant. In addition, if it cooperated with private groups, many of which were religious, would it not then compromise the separation of church and state?

Bauman also warned that the program bestowed enormous powers on the president. He counted thirty-five instances where the president could appoint, control, remove, act, or determine qualifications, and argued that this represented a dangerous centralization of power. The proposal threatened the rights of the states and localities in which individual projects would be located; federal power seemed limitless. Finally, Bauman argued that such a program would "be used to promote the political ends of the party in power." Since the program would be under the control of the president, it would be "impossible to ignore the political implications of the Corps of 5,000 roving welfare corpsmen who owe their jobs to the President and who can be sent by him to almost any part of the United States." The National Service Corps, he warned, was "a threat to our democratic way of life."[10] The alternative was to offer enticements to young people for private social welfare service, such as draft deferments or forgiveness for college loans incurred under the National Defense Education Act. "In short," Bauman concluded, "we have been taught that the answer to every problem is more power to a Government bureau and unlimited funds to make that power effective. All progress from the State. With that philosophy Young Americans for Freedom as a group, and I as an individual, violently disagree . . . ." The committee received Bauman's testimony rather coolly, except for two of its most conservative members—John Ashbrook of Ohio and Donald Bruce of Indiana, both of whom had ties to YAF.[11]

As YAF became more aggressive politically, it attracted the attention of Group Research, Inc. (GRI), an organization headed by Wesley McCune that tracked right-wing organizations and made monthly reports to subscribers. The AFL-CIO's COPE used Group Research extensively, and its documentation of right-wing activities appeared in numerous articles in moderate and liberal publications. GRI reported on the personnel, organizing, fund-raising, and political activities of right-wing groups, and in 1963 it began to include YAF in its reports. Noting that YAF started as a Goldwater-for-President group in 1960, GRI reported that it had "taken on more extreme right-wing roles" and "stepped up activity in the Nation's Capital." GRI analyzed reports, speakers, and films sponsored by YAF. In the July issue of *The New Guard*, YAFer Antoni Gollan blasted GRI as a "semi-secret organization" with leftist connections to labor and the American Civil Liberties Union. It was dangerous, Gollan argued, because its purpose was to discredit YAF. Gollan was essentially correct, but in ways he did not explore. GRI's threat to YAF was not its reporting, for it secured most of its information from public sources. The danger stemmed from the fact that its reports indiscriminately lumped YAF with more extreme right-wing groups. In short, by linking moderate conservatives with demagogic right-wing extremists, GRI undercut YAF's effort to develop public confidence in a responsible conservatism that opposed the consensus and argued for substantive change.[12]

Battling the Young Republicans

In June 1963 YAFers engaged in a bruising battle with Young Republicans for control of the Young Republican National Federation at the YRNF convention in San Francisco. They saw this as an essential prelude to the nomination of Barry Goldwater in 1964 and the transformation of the Republican Party into a vehicle for conservative ideas. The underlying issue was similar to that of 1960, when party moderates had tried to use the report of Charles Percy's Republican Committee on Program and Policy to blunt conservative arguments and perpetuate "modern Republicanism." That spawned a mini-revolt at the 1960 G.O.P. national convention, which led to the formation of Young Americans for Freedom. Then, in 1962, Melvin Laird had chaired a Joint Committee on Republican Principles. This time the committee included conservatives like John Tower of Texas in an effort at Republican unity, and its final report endorsed five general principles in words chosen to attract conservatives: "individual liberty," "limited government," "diffusion of power," "government with a heart," and "government with a head." Although it also endorsed individual freedom and a strong anticommunism, this constituted no assurance that Republicans would actually nominate a conservative as their 1964 presidential candidate.[13]

Conservatives were determined not to be cast aside again. Stanton Evans noted the significance of the YRNF convention when he observed that it had "become something of an axiom among G.O.P. professionals that the YR convention immediately prior to a Presidential showdown" was a "good indicator of party sentiment." If this was true, then the Republican Party was deeply divided, and aggressive conservative efforts to seize control were succeeding. John Birch Society members had already gained control of the California Young Republican Federation and, together with other right-wingers, dominated the San Francisco meeting. The National Draft Goldwater Committee secretly "activated a caucus" among Young Republicans to "try to insure control of that organization in 1963," and established other liaisons with Young Americans for Freedom. Although Oregon Governor Mark Hatfield warned YRNF delegates that Republicans could not "align ourselves with those who would turn their backs on brotherhood, or equality, or opportunity," they seemed more interested in party factionalism than in civil rights. Despite Hatfield's admonition that they "could not afford to adopt as a party a kind of social isolationism that might give us a few seats in Congress in the sixties but plague us forever in the seventies and eighties," delegates rejected calls for unity. Their focal point was the battle between Donald "Buz" Lukens of Indiana, a Goldwater supporter backed by YAF, and Charles McDevitt of Idaho, backed by moderates and Eastern liberals, for chair of the Young Republicans. Lukens's two-vote victory on the second ballot set the stage for another conflict, this time for national college chair. A moderate, Ward White of Kansas, was the apparent winner. But Lukens appealed the election to William Miller, chairman of the Republican National Committee. Miller intervened and ruled against White, warning delegates that Senator Goldwater was "going to the convention with enough votes to win, and if he doesn't his supporters are going to want to know why. We have to placate these people."[14]

Subsequent reports from the convention highlighted the internecine battles fought there. One report to William Rusher emphasized that "sentiment ran deep and vociferous for the Arizona Senator" at the convention. Goldwater Republicanism set the tone, and as conservatives reveled in victory they called for party unity. But events on the floor made that unlikely. The report blasted the outgoing national chair, Leonard Nadasky, for violating all rules of parliamentary procedure, refusing recognition of unfriendly speakers, attempting to rule by force, and openly comparing conservatives and their tactics to the communists. In addition, "a roving band of 'toughs' paraded up and down the convention floor harassing delegates, grabbing microphones from them while they were speaking and attempting to silence anyone disagreeing with the chair." Other reports indicated that name-calling, fist fights, cut telephone lines, and charges of fraud characterized the affair. Maryland Young Republicans later charged that "to a large extent, the disturbances were created by ultra-right wing elements in the party who seemed determined to take over the Republican Party and the YRs for their own selfish ends, hiding behind the mask of honest conservatives in the process. Actually, of course, they are not conservatives at all but extreme radicals of the right."

Stan Adelstein, Young Republican national committeeman from South Dakota, said simply: "We thought we knew exactly what it meant to be conservative until we saw these people." He complained that "suddenly we found ourselves—mostly pro-Goldwater—becoming 'middle-of-the-roaders' in comparison with extremists." Also significant was the absence of the host, California State Republican Chairman Caspar Weinberger, as well as national party chair William Miller. Other Republican leaders notable by their absence included George Romney and Nelson Rockefeller.[15]

Conservatives quickly counterattacked. Stanton Evans asserted that Rockefeller supporters, not conservatives, had used dictatorial tactics. Congressman John Ashbrook of Ohio, a member of YAF's national advisory board, argued that "harbingers of change are evident everywhere and the liberals just cannot get used to it . . . ." In a lengthy speech inserted into the *Congressional Record*, Ashbrook set the record "straight" by denying allegations that radicals had taken over the Young Republican movement. He was at the convention, Ashbrook reported, and the actions of the chair were reprehensible. The tone of the meeting was admittedly conservative, but he insisted that the John Birch Society was no more a threat to the United States than Americans for Democratic Action or other "leftwing organizations." Congressman William Brock of Tennessee agreed with Ashbrook's report of convention activities, and painted a positive picture of youthful enthusiasm. "True, emotions ran high. Pressures and counterpressures were delivered with gusto. One could sense the excitement and enthusiasm of the event just by entering the convention hall and viewing the banners, badges, and balloons. The battle was hardfought, but men with wounded pride, muckrakers and ambitious politicians do the country a disservice, I believe, by trying to dampen the interest of young people in politics."[16] A letter from Jack Quilico, chair of the Montana Young Republicans, was more succinct in its criticism of Nadasky and his followers: "To falsely label the great conservative element which exists in the Republican Party as extremists is to merely be a dupe of the opposition and sow the seeds for a Republican defeat in the polls come next November."[17]

The Young Republican convention anticipated the relationship between party moderates and conservatives in the year ahead. In his report on the convention, Stanton Evans noted how strong the young conservatives were and how hard they had worked during the preceding two years to reach positions of power and influence within the organization. They represented, he insisted, a "very real 'wave of conservatism'" and not some "sinister design." Their views were responsible, and they were not extremists. "They are sick of the present liberal administration in Washington," Evans concluded, "and just as sick of some 'Republicans' who are no better than a diluted version of the New Frontiersman."[18] They were, other observers agreed, ready to take over the Republican Party. California Republican Senator Thomas Kuchel warned Leonard Finder, publisher of the *Sacramento Union* and a staunch opponent of the John Birch Society, that the right wing was using the California Young Republican organization for its own purposes. "Is it not logical," Kuchel asked, "to assume that he [John Rousselot, a Birch Society member] and his kind have been pushing these resolutions in one more attempt to subjugate our party?"[19]

This was the dilemma for the party: was it to follow the path of conservatism or of moderation? The overpowering persona of Dwight D. Eisenhower had obscured this division for almost a decade. Now it erupted, as conservative bitterness, which had welled up almost to the boiling point during the 1960 elections, burst forth to reclaim what it believed to be its rightful place in the party.[20]

But Republican moderates and progressives were not willing to surrender quietly. Shortly after the Young Republican convention, New York Governor Nelson Rockefeller blasted Young Americans for Freedom and other conservatives, calling for party unity in 1964. Rockefeller insisted that he had been working for party unity all along, but had believed that "the activities of the radical right, while deeply disturbing in many ways, would represent an inconsequential influence on the Republican Party." The recent battles in San Francisco, he warned, should awaken the party to the dangers of "subversion from the radical right." If it failed to react quickly, "a radical, well-financed and highly disciplined minority" would capture the party. This minority, as evidenced by the Young Republican proceedings, used the "tactics of totalitarianism" and were nothing more than "purveyors of hate." Rockefeller also rejected the call by some conservatives to build a winning coalition by concentrating almost exclusively on the South and West in 1964. Calling the purpose of that plan "transparent," he warned that it would pander to segregationists and "transform the Republican Party from a national party of all the people to a sectional party for some of the people." It would destroy the Republican Party. The right wing, Rockefeller charged, was "boring from within." They were, he warned,

> embarked on a determined and ruthless effort to take over the party, its platform and its candidates on their own terms—terms that are wholly alien to the sound and honest conservatism that has firmly based the Republican party in the best of a century's traditions, wholly alien to the sound and honest Republican liberalism that has kept the party abreast of human needs in a changing world, wholly alien to the broad middle course that accommodates the mainstream of Republican principle.[21]

Party unity was an elusive quest.

Drafting Goldwater

The growing likelihood that Barry Goldwater would win the Republican nomination for president in 1964 further sharpened party divisions. Young Americans for Freedom and the John Birch Society jockeyed for influence and position. Although both groups supported a Goldwater candidacy, the issue was one of power and access to power. The dispute flared most openly in California—a key state, and one where the Birch Society had flourished. From the outset of the Draft Goldwater movement men like William Rusher had looked to California YAFers to influence the California delegation to embrace conservative candidates and prevent any pledge of support to Senator Thomas Kuchel as a favorite son at the 1964 convention. But they discovered that an even stronger threat lurked on their right. Led by regional director John Rousselot, the Birch Society had launched a membership drive and opened a six-state headquarters in San Marino. It had also succeeded in capturing several offices in the California Young Republican organization.

While this induced a group of San Francisco Republicans, led by the chair of Senator Kuchel's northern California reelection campaign, to petition state chair Caspar Weinberger to dismiss them from the party, it created a direct threat to Young Americans for Freedom in California. Under the guise of preparing for conservative action in 1964, Craig Ihde, a Bircher and State President of California YAF, warned Richard Noble, chairman of the board of California YAF, that the time had come to coordinate the political efforts of Young Americans for Freedom and Young Republicans. Arguing that YAF had "failed to justify its existence as an independent conservative group," Ihde demanded copies of YAF's constitution and bylaws. Too often, Ihde complained, YAF had "acted as a competitor" to California Young Republicans, which the Birchers now controlled. He also demanded that Noble appoint particular individuals (Birchers) to key YAF posts within the state. But Noble, a law student at Stanford, had long been the chief California operative for William Rusher and the *National Review* element in the party. At the same time, new YRNF chair Buz Lukens insisted that the Young Republicans could operate more efficiently if they were independent of the Republican National Committee. Obviously designed to enhance efforts for Goldwater, Lukens's position quickly came under attack from other Young Republican officers as well as from some Goldwater supporters at the national level. The conservative path to power clearly faced obstacles of its own making as well as from opposition elements.[22]

To further fuel the conflict, the Ripon Society issued a call to moderate Republicans for "excellence in leadership." Headquartered in Cambridge, Massachusetts, the Ripon Society was founded by a small group of liberal Republicans strongly opposed to any conservative takeover of the party. The Society's "open letter to the new generation of Republicans" argued that the 1960 and 1962 elections had revealed the absence of any political consensus in the country, and concluded that "a new majority" was "about to emerge." The issue for Republicans was clear, and the party needed to make a decision in 1964. "Shall it become an effective instrument to lead this nation in the remainder of the twentieth century" and emerge as the majority party? Or "shall it leave the government of the nation to a party born in the 1930's and without a leader capable of transforming its disparate elements to meet the challenge of a radically new environment?"[23]

The Ripon Society focused on three points it considered critical: a strategy for achieving a new Republican consensus, an appropriate Republican philosophy, and the qualities of excellent leadership. The letter argued that the choice was binary: "the strategy of the right" or "the strategy of the center." The Society clearly favored the latter, insisting that the strategy of the Right would only consolidate the party's minority position by constructing a coalition of "antis" devoid of positive political programs. "The size and enthusiasm of the conservative movement should not be discounted," it admitted. "It represents a major discontent with the current state of our politics, and, properly channeled, it could serve as a powerful constructive force." But since the strategy of the Right was based on "a platform of negativism," it "can provide neither the Republican party an effective majority nor the American people responsible leadership." It was also "potentially divisive," and the Society warned that we "must purge our politics of that rancor, violence, and extremism that would divide us."[24]

The assassination of President John F. Kennedy and the transfer of power to Lyndon B. Johnson, the document argued, meant that the center was now "contestable." Republicans must build a moderate, problem-oriented, pragmatic philosophy to succeed. Warning that extremists substituted simplicity for complexity in a belief that simple solutions existed for current problems, the Society insisted that moderation was far more realistic and effective. "The moderate realizes that ends not only compete with one another, but that they are inextricably related to the means adopted for their pursuit. Thus he will most likely set a proximate goal." That was the strength of John F. Kennedy, and the Ripon Society made clear its admiration for Kennedy's vision even while it opposed many of his programs. He had effected a revolution in American politics. "We have witnessed a change in the mood of American politics. After Kennedy there can be no turning back to the old conceptions of America."[25]

The Ripon Society document was important, not because it heralded the arrival of a new force in Republican politics, but because it offered a glimpse at the opposition facing YAF and its conservative allies in their quest to nominate Barry Goldwater. Throughout the spring of 1963 former President Eisenhower diligently encouraged other, moderate Republicans, to enter the fray against Goldwater. Although he always stopped short of endorsing any one of them, he clearly implied that their efforts were essential to prevent extremists from capturing the party. On occasion Ike conceded that he would back Goldwater if he were the nominee, but complained that "I believe that his depth of understanding of most of the national and international problems is not all that I could wish it to be." What really drove Eisenhower, however, was ego. He particularly disliked Goldwater's criticism of his own presidential actions and policies. As Ike admitted to one friend: "As a matter of fact, if the Senator should come out in earnest support of the ideals, principles, and policies of my Administration between 1953 and 1961, I think I would be inclined to do whatever I could to further his election."[26]

Meanwhile, for months Goldwater supporters had been meeting secretly to advance the Senator's candidacy. Led by Clif White, they organized a National Draft Goldwater Committee to lay the groundwork for a Goldwater nomination and labored to gauge Rockefeller's strength. They kept careful tabs on attempts by Eisenhower and Nixon to thwart their efforts, and especially opposed formation of a Republican Citizens' Committee, seeing it as merely a scheme to perpetuate the hold of modern Republicanism on the party. It was, said a Republican national committeewoman from Ohio who supported Goldwater, "another attempt to a take over by the left-wingers."[27]

YAFer Lee Edwards insisted that something beyond the nomination of Barry Goldwater was needed. Lamenting that even Goldwater's election in November 1964 would not cement conservative power in the country, Edwards urged the creation of a "Conservative Establishment" to offset the influential Liberal Establishment. Conservatives, Edwards warned, must gird themselves "for a long-range program and plot, not a Five Year Plan, but a Twenty-Five Year Plan." They must begin to "place themselves not only in the U.S. House of Representatives, but in the television networks, in the universities, in corporations and companies and, perhaps most important of all, in the Federal government."[28]

While some conservatives backed Goldwater because they were true believers, many YAF supporters joined Lee Edwards to pursue a larger objective. In the words of *National Review's* William Rusher: "I think it is extremely important that the Republican Party make a strong bid for southern support *in 1964*. This Rockefeller simply cannot do. The net effect [if Goldwater decides not to run] will very likely be to delay the reorientation of the Republican Party . . . along more conservative lines for four crucial years." Later, to Goldwater himself, Rusher admitted that "our project was designed from the outset to build up conservative strength at the 1964 convention, and was not centered on a particular candidacy." Rusher developed this theme at greater length in an essay, "Crossroads for the G.O.P.," where he argued that the only way for Republicans to beat Kennedy was to take the South away from him and then use it as a base to build a national party. Even if 1964 proved to be a Democratic year, as most pundits predicted, Republicans still needed to nominate a conservative candidate to "galvanize the party in a vast new area, carry fresh scores and perhaps hundreds of Southern Republicans to unprecedented local victories, and lay the foundation for a truly national Republican Party, ready to fight and win in 1968 and all the years beyond." In a note to Brent Bozell, he wrote that if "the analysis is right . . . the policy proposed far transcends, in its potential impact, any particular candidate or even any particular year; it might very well shape the broad outlines of American politics for a quarter of a century to come."[29]

Rusher's hopes seemed likely to be fulfilled as conservatives, led by Young Americans for Freedom, won local elections and began to control local and state organizations. The 1963 YRNF convention was only one instance of this. In February 1963, for example, Allan Howell, a YAFer and a Goldwater conservative, was elected to chair the Michigan Federation of College Republicans, despite "active opposition by the Michigan Young Republican Chairman and the Michigan State Central Committee of the G.O.P . . . ." The victory, according to YAF's state director, George McDonnell, followed "two years of extensive organization, planning and determination and proves that the upsurge in Conservatism is a reality." To advance their cause nationally, YAF planned a Goldwater rally for Washington, D.C. that summer. In support, *The New Guard* embraced Rusher's earlier political analysis and argued that Goldwater was the *only* candidate that could possibly defeat John F. Kennedy. During college spring break, YAFers set up tables on the beach in Fort Lauderdale, Florida to distribute literature. To fund these and other efforts, William F. Buckley Jr. wrote H. L. Hunt for money to support YAFers at the 1964 Republican National Convention so that they could take it "by storm."[30]

Meanwhile YAF focused on the Goldwater effort. Donald Shafto, who had founded the Bergen County, New Jersey YAF chapter in 1961 and subsequently held various positions in the national organization, coordinated arrangements for the July Goldwater rally. A part-time consultant for *National Review*, Shafto had previously worked for Marvin Liebman in direct mail promotion. "My work," he noted in his application for a position on the National Draft Goldwater Committee, "consisted largely of planning and managing programs of political and social action designed to arouse American opinion on important public questions." Meanwhile, Roger Steggerda, Executive Secretary of Michigan YAF, organized a Youth for Goldwater committee. Together with George McDonnell, he met with officials from Dow Chemical Corporation to discuss ways to control the organization so as to prevent "some of the 'nut' groups from becoming too involved in the picture." William Cotter, one of YAF's prominent "dissenters" during the previous two years, was also approached to work for Goldwater. This provoked considerable alarm within the YAF leadership, and William Rusher investigated the matter. Rusher later reported to Clif White that he did not believe that Cotter was still close to Martin McKneally or Douglas Caddy (both working for Rockefeller), and that he would be a useful addition to the cause if kept at arm's length. By July and the *Human Events* political action conference, YAFers seemed to be everywhere. The conference program highlighted at least a dozen YAFers in prominent positions, including Carol and Robert Bauman, Robert Croll, George McDonnell, Lee Edwards, William Boerum, Fred Coldren, Lammot Copeland Jr., Alan Wandling, Daniel Carmen, Tom Charles Huston, and Kay Kolbe.[31]

Conservative efforts to draft Goldwater maintained Democrats' attention on right-wing movements. "The right-wing problem," Senator Gale McGee wrote Myer Feldman that summer, "may well turn out to be a/or the winning issue for 1964." McGee then summarized what he had learned about the secret spread of the right wing into the Midwest and South, warning Feldman that its greatest progress had been made without publicity and that there was no apparent relationship between "the numbers of John Birchers and the impact of the extreme right." Radio coverage had effectively recruited members, and in Wyoming the Society had joined forces with more traditional Republican conservatives. This was now a nationwide crusade, and McGee urged Feldman to publicize its spread and its message in the belief that there would be a "popular revulsion" against it by the time of the 1964 presidential election.[32]

Perhaps to forestall such an attack, YAF once again tried to distance itself from irresponsible elements on the Right. But its only real weapon was persuasion, and that was rarely effective. A case in point was *The Westchester Conservative*, a publication of the Westchester County (N.Y.) Young Americans for Freedom that insisted fluoridated water was a communist plot. Speaking for the national organization, Robert Bauman cautioned that "there are some subjects about which Young Americans for Freedom can best express their opinions by word of mouth." Local YAF publications, he said, should devote their space to promoting YAF activities and not those of other conservative groups. But since so many pro-Goldwater groups had sprung into existence, the problem was difficult to resolve. William Best III, active in California YAF, noted that more than a hundred youth-oriented organizations were then functioning in the state. "This is great from the standpoint of drive and energy," he said, "but somewhat of a mess otherwise." YAF would focus on Youth for Goldwater, but he could not guarantee what the other groups would do.[33]

In a special fund-raising letter that fall, Bauman warned that the "next 15 months are crucial." Because of the anticipated Goldwater candidacy, he wrote, "now is the logical time to capitalize on this increased interest in Conservatism." In November YAF held its third annual convention in Fort Lauderdale, Florida, where they reaffirmed their support for Goldwater, expressed opposition to pending civil rights legislation, and heard a pep talk from Clif White, head of the National Draft Goldwater Committee. The convention focused almost entirely on the upcoming 1964 campaign. Marilyn Manion (daughter of Dean Clarence Manion) chaired a panel on "Mobilizing Youth," and other panels discussed the issues of the 1964 campaign. Although William F. Buckley Jr. had pleaded with Goldwater to address the convention, Goldwater apparently was on vacation and did not appear. Texas Senator John Tower replaced him.[34]

Internal Splits Resurface

Unfortunately, personal ambition once again vied with conservative politics, and Young Americans for Freedom found itself embroiled in internal controversies that drew attention away from its national objectives. Agreements concluded during the preceding months to avoid an "internal rupture" fell apart when four members of the national board tried to oust Robert Croll as national vice chair and remove him from the board of directors. Croll was an original YAFer, dating back to the 1960 G.O.P. convention in Chicago when he was national chair of Youth for Goldwater. Few people, Stanton Evans noted, had "contributed more to the cause of conservatism." He had worked in the Young Republicans, and had helped clean up YAF's internal mess the previous year. Evans professed to be at a loss as to the motivation for the move, unless it was to advance individual agendas.

> I believe they must be similar to those which led some years ago to other unfortunate actions in YAF—a mixture of ambition (if Croll is ousted, someone else can have the vice chairmanship), the youthful thrill of bringing off a power play for its own sake (this was an unhappy aspect of YAF's problems a year and more ago), resentment of Croll's independent power position in the Midwest (antagonisms between the East Coast and the Midwest have been, I am sorry to say, a regular feature of YAF imbroglios), and a natural animus against Croll's outspokenness on YAF policies and other matters.

Evans hoped that "for the good of the movement" the infighting would not get out of hand. If YAF were divided once again into warring factions, it would be of little use in any Goldwater campaign.[35]

The depth of the split is difficult to reconstruct, but at least one board member believed that national chair Robert Bauman and executive secretary David Jones were involved. The charges against Croll seemed to focus on his alleged failure to organize sufficient numbers of YAF chapters in Indiana and his continuing work within Young Republicans to influence them toward conservatism. That, of course, is precisely what Bauman and others had done at the recent YRNF convention. What is clear is that throughout the convention members and prospective members of the board lobbied delegates, making and then breaking agreements to support particular candidates. Losing sight of their larger objectives, various YAF leaders tried to control the votes from their own regions, hoping to leverage themselves into greater prominence. David Jones controlled most southern delegate votes, and Jones apparently refused to have Croll continue as vice chair "under any circumstances." Midwest regional chair Tom Charles Huston professed to keep his hands off candidate selection at the regional caucus, although he was apparently in league with Jones, Bauman, and others. Backroom meetings continued all night, amid charges that some regional delegations (New England and New York) possessed delegate strength disproportionate to that of other regions. Antoni Gollan (editor of *The New Guard*), who backed Croll, also found his board position threatened by Jones if he persisted in that support. Finally, Croll, Gollan, and Richard Allen (executive vice secretary of Indiana YAF) decided to keep the Illinois and Indiana delegations off the floor rather than participate in the proceedings. Bauman eventually nominated Croll (against Croll's wishes), and Huston seconded the nomination, but it was a charade since Croll was no longer in the running. The result was far more serious than any previous YAF controversy. Following the convention Stanton Evans wrote Robert Bauman to announce that he was severing his ties to YAF: "Please remove my name from your Board of Advisors, and from any and all literature which might be construed as constituting my endorsement for YAF." Bill Buckley wired Evans that this made him "heartsick," and asked him to reconsider. "In return," Buckley promised to "withdraw myself if by its deeds the organization in the coming months betrays its purposes." Hopefully, he concluded, Evans and Rusher would work with him as a group in all future dealings with YAF.[36]

One more flap ensued, this time involving YAF's efforts to back Barry Goldwater for the Republican presidential nomination. In December Young Americans for Freedom, short of funds, convinced Senator Strom Thurmond to write a letter requesting financial support for the organization. Writing on the letterhead of the Senate Committee on Commerce, and calling YAF a "patriotic anti-communist youth group," Thurmond urged recipients of the letter to give whatever they could to enable YAF to open chapters on every college and university campus in the country and thereby strengthen the cause of freedom. But YAF supplemented the letter with additional materials endorsing Barry Goldwater for president. Thurmond was outraged. Insisting that YAF had abandoned its nonpartisan position, and that he had not yet endorsed any candidate for president, he resigned from YAF's board of directors and demanded that no funds received from the mailing be used for any partisan purposes. In addition, he asked YAF to send out a second letter explaining that the inserts were made without his knowledge or consent and that they violated YAF's nonpartisan policy. This was an embarrassing incident, triggered not so much by the implication that Thurmond was pro-Goldwater as by his fear that the inserts might undermine his efforts to secure appointments for vacant judgeships in South Carolina from the Johnson administration. It revealed that YAF was apparently willing to use whatever advantage it could to advance Goldwater's candidacy.[37]

By late 1963 Young Americans for Freedom as an organization, and YAFers as individuals, diligently supported a Goldwater candidacy, even though Goldwater himself had yet to announce his intentions formally. Then the assassination of President John F. Kennedy in November shocked conservatives and liberals alike. A few conservatives, like Thomas G. Aaron, chair of Kentucky YAF, became disillusioned and withdrew, convinced that the right wing had helped create a "climate of political degeneracy and moral hysteria" that had led to the assassination. Calling Young Americans for Freedom "more a vehicle of political impoverishment than one of loyal and legitimate opposition," Aaron resigned from the organization. But he seems to have been an exception. From the offices of Youth for Goldwater, Carol Bauman sent a series of letters to potential supporters, drawn chiefly from YAF mailing lists. The Young Republicans refused permission to use their lists, although Bauman hoped to acquire copies through another source. But the YAF mailings alone, she reported in early December, had enlisted almost 2,000 interested college students and "turned up potential organizations on about 50 campuses," along with several high school students. The public neutrality of former President Dwight D. Eisenhower, as well as that of the Republican National Committee, indirectly aided the Goldwater effort by leaving the field open to those who organized first and most efficiently.[38]

YAF was in the vanguard of this effort, doing what it was created to do back in 1960: engage in political action. In the words of New Guard editor Antoni Gollan: "YAF represents part of what every political movement of substance requires: an ideological vanguard. The Young Republican National Federation's reaffirmation of the principles of freedom is but one prominent example of what a favorable climate of opinion can produce." Almost one year earlier Allan Brownfield, describing right-wing organizations like YAF as "America's Angry Young Men," had observed: "It is up to this generation to restore greatness to America, and meaning to our purpose as a nation. If we do not succeed, then there will be no winners but only a great blandness which was once the hope of the world, which was once America. This will be the coming conservative revolution. It will be a revolution for values, and not against them. It can restore dignity to man, and liberty to his life."[39] Young Americans for Freedom eagerly looked forward to 1964 as they prepared to participate in their most important crusade for conservatism.

Chapter 9

YAF and the Crusade for Conservatism in 1964

THE 1964 PRESIDENTIAL campaign and election climaxed a four-year effort by conservatives to capture the Republican Party and imprint a conservative credo on American politics. The story of the Goldwater campaign has been told elsewhere many times; the story of grass-roots Goldwater supporters like Young Americans for Freedom in 1964 has not. From YAF's formation in 1960 members had looked to 1964 as the culmination of their efforts, and to Arizona Senator Barry Goldwater as the vehicle for their deliverance. Four years of labor, although peppered with internal factionalism and the seductions of personal ambition, now produced the first truly conservative candidate for a major party since the Great Depression. This was, said one YAFer, the "catalytic moment for the conservative movement."[1] Although just one of many groups working outside the traditional Republican Party organization for a Goldwater candidacy in 1964, YAF was unique in that it had been boosting Goldwater since the 1960 Republican convention in Chicago. Aside from Clif White's National Draft Goldwater Committee, it was also the only one whose efforts had been consistently national in scope.

As Goldwater's name repeatedly surfaced as a likely Republican nominee, the prospect of his candidacy alarmed moderates as much as it excited conservatives. "The very qualities which make Senator Goldwater a favorite of southern reactionaries," publisher Leonard Finder wrote Richard Nixon in late 1963, "cause him to be regarded with widespread distrust elsewhere. Even among Republicans, there is a feeling, nearly a fear, about what his election could mean."

Moderates feared the infiltration of "extremists" into the Republican Party, particularly in the West and South, and a conservative takeover. "This capture of the Republican Party—with the substitution of an antediluvian, authoritarian philosophy—is a very real and grave danger," Finder warned Dwight Eisenhower. "Republican moderation must win as against the arbitrary dictatorialness of these closed-minded reactionaries."[2]

Dangers and Opportunities

The opportunities presented by a Goldwater candidacy harbored at least four dangers for YAF. First, given YAF's history of personal ambition and infighting, it was not unrealistic to believe that a Goldwater campaign might become a vehicle for personal advancement. Success would vault individual YAFers into positions of power, but would not necessarily advance a broad conservative movement. Second, there was the danger that the activities of right-wing extremists would so dominate the Goldwater campaign that the public would indiscriminately lump moderates with extremists and condemn the whole lot. As Leonard Finder warned Dwight Eisenhower, the extremists "are not easy for the public to detect, because many are seemingly honest conservatives; of late, they claim to be 'moderates' . . . ."[3] Third, there was the possibility that the need for unity in the heat of political battle would exert such a centripetal pull on YAF that it would join more extremist elements and resort to the rhetoric of apocalyptic alarm. Should that be the case, YAF would be the architect of its own demise. Finally, there was the fact that Barry Goldwater, not Young Americans for Freedom, would be the focus of the campaign. As such, YAF faced the likelihood that it would be shunted aside either by the Goldwater campaign organization or by the Republican Party organization as both sought victory in November. Since both were electoral machines rather than principled purists, their emphasis would be to promote the candidate and the party rather than to advance the cause per se.

Amid these dangers lurked opportunity. In an extended argument defending Goldwater Republicanism, conservative writer Ralph de Toledano highlighted what he thought might be the real significance of the 1964 election—the disintegration of the Roosevelt coalition. Goldwater appealed to southern Democrats and was the vehicle for a new conservative consensus. The first battle, which YAF had been waging for at least two years, was the struggle by conservatives to control the Republican Party. Once successful, that would quickly lead to a confrontation with the liberalism of Lyndon B. Johnson, and would force a new political alignment along ideological lines. Goldwater, de Toledano insisted, represented a "new mood in American politics. He is the symbol of conservatism on the march" and the "answer to the vast waste-land of American Liberalism."[4]

Goldwater himself acknowledged the importance of this new mood, par-ticularly among the young. He had decided to run, he said, because "these young people are interested in conservatism and I felt that if I didn't make myself avail-able they might become discouraged . . . ." By "young people," Goldwater chiefly meant activists in Young Americans for Freedom. This support gave a Goldwater candidacy a core of dedicated workers, but also masked a weakness. Despite the activism and growth of YAF during the past four years, and despite the proliferation of YAF chapters on campuses across America, student apathy remained a major problem. David Keene, president of the University of Wis-consin chapter and executive secretary of the state organization, typified the problem. Keene, a sophomore, was very active on campus and throughout the state, but the campus chapter had only sixty paid-up members, and he admit-ted that many conservative students were more philosophical than activist.[5]

Despite the fact that YAF was about to witness the fulfillment of a cher-ished goal, the nomination of a conservative Republican presidential candidate, Wisconsin was not an isolated case. A lengthy report on YAF in the western states in early 1964, prepared by western regional chair Jack Cox, documented its organizational deficiencies in that region. Even in California, the most pop-ulous state in the region, the state organization had failed to organize a single chapter since its incorporation. Other state organizations were equally inef-fective. In Washington and Oregon, YAF chapters were "almost non-existent." Only Northern California YAF, which he characterized as "an enthusiastic and hard-working group," had been successful. They had set up a recruiting booth at local fairs, and published their own brochure as well as a Goldwater brochure. In addition, they had picketed the northern California head of the Commu-nist Party, protested against Yugoslovian Premier Tito when he visited San Fran-cisco, and run a special leadership conference for their region. All these activ-ities had generated publicity from local newspapers and television stations. But the state organization had not only failed to help them, it had even attempted to thwart their efforts.[6]

Compounding this problem, in California and elsewhere, was some per-sistent disarray within local and state chapters. Some state YAFers were suing national Young Americans for Freedom. Sparring between YAF and Young Re-publicans continued, even as both tried to rally behind the Goldwater effort, and both groups remained unhappy with the traditional party machinery. Ac-cording to YAF western region treasurer Ted Hicks, the conflict was primarily ideological. William Knowland led the Goldwater efforts in California, but Knowland was not in touch with the new conservatism, seemed oblivious to the John Birch influence, and represented the traditional party machinery. Hicks observed that YAFers and other new conservatives were largely "excluded from the Goldwater committtees—naturally they are mad. The committees are very largely composed of the old timers, many of whom supported Nixon. Nixon among California conservatives is a dirty word." Among Young Republicans, liberals were demoralized and conservatives had captured almost the entire organization. Birchite YAFers like Robert Gaston remained a problem, Hicks warned William Rusher, but he hoped that this would be worked out.[7]

On the other side of the country, in Westchester County, New York, Goldwater volunteers split between two slates of convention delegates. Each group attacked the other. Herman Bates Jr., chair of the Goldwater for President Committee in the county, headed one group, which had Goldwater's support. Bates complained that the other group had done little to promote conservatism. The problems, he insisted, stemmed directly from the condition of Young Americans for Freedom in Westchester County. Under its former chair, Edmund Zanini, YAF was active and capable. But once Zanini was elected to YAF's national board and Mrs. Charles Elms became the county YAF leader, the organization atrophied. Bates asserted that there was now only one active chapter in the county, and that remained active only because its chairman, Anthony Terraforte, "has refused to follow the John Birch oriented policies advocated by the county chairman." YAF's local publication had become nothing more than a mouthpiece for the Birch Society, and Bates argued that "its very name and existence is an embarrassment to the Conservative Party and to the National Young Americans for Freedom organization." In a separate and apparently unrelated letter to national chair Robert Bauman, Terraforte briefly outlined the problem (which was as Bates had described it), and said that he had withdrawn the Yonkers YAF from the Westchester YAF Council to avoid its subversion by the John Birch Society. Not one to surrender without a fight, Mrs. Elms wrote Goldwater directly, charging that Bates was really a Rockefeller supporter. She also wrote Carol Bauman that members of her organization were YAFers but, according to instructions, had kept the name of YAF out of sight. Bauman replied that it "would be a terrific coup if you could elect Goldwater delegates from Rockefeller's home town [Tarrytown]."[8]

Unable or unwilling to exercise self-discipline, the national YAF organization seemed to hope either that these conflicts would evaporate with a Goldwater victory or that the upcoming campaign would define conservatism so as to exclude fringe elements like the John Birch Society. For the meantime YAF participated in the national Goldwater effort as one of several "citizens groups." But its leadership rarely lost sight of the main objective. As YAFer Alfred Regnery noted, a Goldwater candidacy would "push political attitudes in this country at least one step to the right" and help gain control of the GOP, "even if he loses." Goldwater himself believed that conservatism was more attractive to voters than Democrats and liberals were willing to admit. It is "as simple," he told one interviewer, "as the differentiation between good and bad." The youth of America were the key to a conservative future, and New York Congressman William Miller, who later became Goldwater's running mate, insisted that they were the key to electing Goldwater president in November.[9]

YAF and Barry Goldwater

Young Americans for Freedom was attracted to Barry Goldwater in 1964 because his politics were conservative and unflinching. He offered, as his campaign theme later reminded voters, "a choice, not an echo." The choices he offered were significant because they gave voice to views outside the political consensus. An attack on statism, and the federal government in particular, was his central focus. Although largely confined to domestic issues, in 1964 this attack promised to reverse a decade of social change. White southerners found this particularly appealing, and men like Dallas Republican organizer Peter O'-Donnell Jr. and Alabaman John Grenier had thrown their support to him immediately after Nixon's defeat in 1960. For them, and for many conservatives, the chief issue was civil rights. In the words of one North Carolina attorney: "I have always felt that our country would be much better off and our party would have been much further along if we had not pushed the civil rights issue quite so hard. I, of course, understand that our successor will probably push it much harder. I feel quite sure, however, that if he does, there will be a much stronger Republican Party throughout the South."

Although Goldwater personally condemned discrimination, he opposed (and later voted against) the 1964 Civil Rights Act. YAF also opposed the act, particularly the public accommodations section and the grant of additional powers to the federal government. Both Goldwater and YAF argued that individuals, not the government, should take action. Editorializing against passage, *The New Guard* put the issue in words that echoed Goldwater's position: "it might be well for you to examine your own conscience with regard to prejudice and assess how much of the blame for the passage of such civil rights legislation results from your disinterest in your fellow Americans and their problems." Many white southerners, of course, focused exclusively on the issue of race and cared little about the fine points of an antistatist philosophy. Using similar ideological arguments, YAF also opposed the antipoverty program, insisting that it "coddled" citizens, that poverty was not "endemic, and not, most certainly, begging for Federal intervention."[10]

Throughout the winter and spring of 1964 *The New Guard* was unrelenting in its criticism of administration policies, reflecting the conservative ideology articulated by Goldwater. In January, national chair Robert Bauman telegraphed President Johnson to excoriate him for a recent wheat deal with the Soviet Union. The terms of a recent foreign aid bill, he told Johnson, required that the president determine whether such matters were in the national interest. "Young Americans for Freedom," Bauman wrote, "submits to you that in view of the killing of three American flyers by Russian planes in East Germany last Tuesday it cannot under any circumstances be in the national interest to trade further with Communist Russia. The people of America want no part of blood money—especially when it is our blood and our money which we are being asked to pay to the Communists." Renounce the wheat deal, he urged Johnson, in retaliation for "this cold blooded murder of American servicemen and to state a firm resolve on the part of your administration to end appeasement of the Communists which can only lead to such incidents." YAF also pleaded for a commitment to total victory in Vietnam. The United States should not negotiate with the communists in Vietnam or anywhere else, they insisted. To believe that this advanced national security or the cause of peace was a delusion. To promote these ideas, YAF formed another front group, the World Council of Youth for Freedom, and sponsored a "Captive Nations Rally" in Washington, D.C., on May 23.[11]

YAF activists channeled most of their energies into the Goldwater campaign. Youth for Goldwater was basically a YAF-run organization, and Marvin Liebman Associates churned out public relations materials for the campaign. To capitalize on the early sixties' rage for folk music, a preppy group known as "The Goldwaters" toured college campuses throughout the country. They even issued an album: "Folk Songs to Bug the Liberals." The selections were all topical songs on issues of the day, and attacked liberals and liberal policies. They ranged from upbeat ditties like "Win in '64" that warned "Barry's gonna win in '64/ the Frontier will be no more," to "White House Goodbye." Sung to the music of the Kingston Trio's "Tom Dooley," it crowed: "Hang down your head, left-wingers/Hand down your head and cry/Take one last look at the White House/Before you say goodbye."[12] By and large, however, their lyrics appealed chiefly to true believers and lacked the biting edge of criticism evident from the Left in songs like "Love Me, I'm a Liberal" by Phil Ochs.

Barry Goldwater was more than a candidate for the presidency; he was a vehicle for various political groups in their own search for power. Conservative intellectuals argued that a Goldwater candidacy was important to "reintroduce" conservatism into "the mainstream of American life;" even defeat in 1964 would set the stage for another run in 1968. Meanwhile, individuals connected with the John Birch Society at the grass roots ardently believed that

Goldwater would tap hitherto invisible conservative feelings among the public, capture the White House, and eliminate domestic programs while launching an aggressive campaign against communism at home and abroad.

Conflicts between Young Americans for Freedom, the Republican Party leadership, and the Goldwater campaign persisted. California was a particular trouble spot, not only because of its important primary and delegate strength but also because the national convention was scheduled for San Francisco. Even before the June primary various groups attacked and undercut one another as each sought to claim credit for a Goldwater victory. YAF's western region treasurer warned William Rusher that these intramural battles were fierce and dangerous, and he feared that several "may rage out of control and do serious damage to both the cause of conservatism and the cause of Barry Goldwater." The entire leadership of the California Republican Assembly, for instance, had been systematically excluded from the California Goldwater delegation to the convention. He charged that a "junta" was running the Goldwater campaign in the state and was attacking volunteers and party workers.[13]

Despite these conflicting agendas, YAF forged ahead. Fund-raising efforts in California during the spring and early summer were very successful, and YAFers came to believe that Goldwater actually had a chance to win in November. "Our allegiance is to the conservative principles which have made the Republican Party great," a pro-Goldwater letter from YAF to GOP convention delegates emphasized. "Many of us were Democrats or independent of mind. It is undeniable that we are but the spearhead of the great wave of conservatism that has swept the young people of this Nation during the past four years." From the Left, I. F. Stone argued that a Goldwater candidacy might have a therapeutic effect on the country. "The more the public gets a look at these crypto-Fascist screwballs," he wrote, "the worse for them. Rather than leave the Goldwater coalition of Birchites and Rip Van Winkle McKinleyites feel that they had been cheated of their chance by Eastern seaboard influences, we'd rather see them get it."[14]

While the editors at National Review published their vision of "A Program for a Goldwater Administration," many Republican moderates feared the conservative wave. A few, like Dwight D. Eisenhower, lamented the likelihood that Goldwater had the nomination locked up, but others opposed his nomination. The Ripon Society issued "A Declaration of Conscience" on July 4, supporting the Civil Rights Act and warning that the party faced "its greatest internal crisis since its founding." The crisis was a moral one. Republicans should reject exploitation of the white backlash and avoid a "southern strategy." Confidential polls conducted for the party in June revealed the problems inherent in a Goldwater candidacy. Noting that "internecine conflict" had afflicted the party since John F. Kennedy's assassination, the report on "The National

Presidential Picture" evaluated the strength of various Republican candidates, the salience of key national issues, and the influence of a Goldwater candidacy on other Republican candidates. It concluded that President Johnson remained popular, but bleakly argued that "the situation *must not* be considered hopeless." More to the point was the observation that Goldwater was the "weakest possible choice" for Republicans. "The Republican Party will be writing its own dismal defeat," a supplementary report concluded, "should it finally select the Senator as its standard-bearer." Polling data revealed that Governor William Scranton of Pennsylvania had the best chance to unseat President Johnson.[15]

Noting that the Republican Party was "fighting for its soul," and hoping to secure the nomination for himself, William Scranton attacked Goldwater broadside in mid-July. Perhaps more than any other document, Scranton's letter to Goldwater dramatized the chasm between party moderates and conservatives and underscored the revolutionary change promoted by YAF and other pro-Goldwater groups. "Here the issue is extremely clear," Scranton claimed. "It is simply this: Will the convention choose the candidate overwhelmingly favored by the Republican voters, or will it choose you?" As if this were not enough, he complained that Goldwater's campaign managers considered the convention delegates "*little more than a flock of chickens whose necks will be wrung at will.*" And there was more.

> You will be stopped on the first ballot because a sufficient number of your nominal supporters have already indicated to us that they will not vote for you.
>
> They are not breaking commitments to you; you have broken commitments to them.
>
> You have too often casually prescribed nuclear war as a solution to a troubled world.
>
> You have too often allowed the radical extremists to use you.
>
> You have too often stood for irresponsibility in the serious question of radical holocaust [sic].
>
> You have too often read Taft and Eisenhower and Lincoln out of the Republican Party.

Concluding that "*Goldwaterism has come to stand for a whole crazy-quilt collection of absurd and dangerous positions that would be soundly repudiated by the American people in November,*" Scranton asked for equal time to address the convention because these were "*soul-deep differences over what the Republican Party stands for.*" Clare Boothe Luce forwarded the letter to Eisenhower, asking him to disavow Scranton and work for party unity. Goldwater was going to get the nomination, she said, and these sorts of "dirty tricks" were intolerable.[16]

New York Senator Jacob Javits succinctly outlined the problem for moderate Republicans in a book published on the eve of the Republican convention. Attacking many of Goldwater's positions, Javits warned that he "tends to disconnect himself from, and would have other Republicans disconnect themselves from, the traditions of the Republican Party and its historic role in American life." He urged his fellow Republicans, especially conservatives, to disavow the radical right, including the John Birch Society.

> I would fervently hope that all Republicans who call themselves conservatives, would recognize the Radical Right for what it is. I would fervently hope that they would slam the door shut against the Trojan Horse of nihilism which the Radical Right, in the name of conservatism, has been trying to introduce into the inner citadel of the Republican Party. And I would hope that they would do so in unmistakingly clear terms.[17]

The Republican Convention

In mid-July the Cow Palace in San Francisco rocked with the passion of true believers determined to nominate their leader, Senator Barry Goldwater, and to adopt a platform that would place their mark on the Republican Party for years to come. It was almost a tribal gathering, with the members all well dressed, joined by ideological conviction instead of communal experiences. Melvin Laird presented the platform and pleaded for unity, warning delegates not to "retreat into a suicidal fight among ourselves." Differences within the party, he insisted, were of "detail, and not of fundamentals." Laird's plea fell upon deaf ears. When Pennsylvania Senator Hugh Scott presented an amendment to the effect that the Republican Party respected "the contribution of responsible criticism and defends the right of dissent in the democratic process," but repudiated "the efforts of irresponsible extremist groups," he aroused the ire of Goldwater delegates. The amendment, along with others on civil rights and control of nuclear weapons, failed. Cries of "We Want Barry" often drowned out speakers and other convention activity. A chorus of boos overwhelmed scattered applause when Theodore McKeldrin, the mayor of Baltimore, seconded the nomination of Nelson Rockefeller and attacked extremists, particularly the Ku Klux Klan and the John Birch Society.[18]

On July 15 Illinois Senator Everett Dirksen rose to nominate Goldwater. In his rambling, avuncular style, Dirksen focused on the ideological choice a Goldwater candidacy offered the party and the country. For the past twenty years, he reminded delegates, "the controversy on the conservative position has hovered over our Party like a menacing specter." The refusal to embrace conservatism had led Republicans to stay home, or to vote Democratic in the belief that there was little difference between candidates and parties. "The time has come for a certain sound," Dirksen argued. "The time has come and the chance has come to make a choice. . . . the tide is turning." A raucous forty-minute demonstration followed Dirksen's nominating speech, a demonstration that celebrated the triumph of an ideology as much as it heralded the arrival of a new candidate. Even for Republicans Goldwater represented a difference, as he repudiated most of the 1960 party platform.[19]

In his acceptance speech, Goldwater abandoned his earlier rhetoric of party unity and threw down the gauntlet to friends and foes alike. After booming tirades against false prophets, international tyranny, and communism, he called for a "return" to freedom, for private property, for victory in Vietnam and against communism throughout the world, and issued an antistatist call for free enterprise. But the words that most listeners remembered, words that shocked party moderates, came with his clarion call for a conservative crusade.

> Anyone who joins us in all sincerity we welcome. Those, those who do not care for our cause, we don't expect to enter our ranks in any case. And let our Republicanism so focused and so dedicated not be made fuzzy and futile by unthinking and stupid labels.
> I would remind you that extremism in the defense of liberty is no vice!
> And let me remind you also that moderation in the pursuit of justice is no virtue!

Dwight Eisenhower later talked with Goldwater on several occasions to convince him to repudiate or clarify his remarks and restore party unity. He eventually gave up in despair. In response to criticism from Richard Nixon, Goldwater reiterated his views in a less volatile paraphrase: "that whole-hearted devotion to liberty is unassailable and that half-hearted devotion to justice is indefensible." But private clarifications did not allay public concern. Indeed, the candidate repeated his original statements and proclaimed them to be a "'banner of principles' with which the Republican Party has honored me by making me its nominee for the presidency."[20] Later, as candidate Goldwater became entangled in his own rhetoric, much the same message was articulated more clearly by Ronald Reagan, who quickly became the new knight on horseback for Young Americans for Freedom and other conservatives after Goldwater's defeat in November.

In an enormously successful speech late in the campaign, "A Time for Choosing," Reagan knifed to the heart of the message that YAF had trumpeted for almost four years. The choice, Reagan told audiences, was not between Left and Right, but between up and down. "Up to the maximum of individual freedom consistent with law and order, or down to the ant heap of totalitarianism; and regardless of their humanitarian purpose those who would sacrifice freedom for security have, whether they know it or not, chosen this downward path." Voters had a choice, thanks to Barry Goldwater; a choice in foreign as well as in domestic policy. In a few short sentences, Reagan articulated the message frustrated conservatives had been yearning to hear for years.

> The spectre our well-meaning liberal friends refuse to face is that their policy of accommodation is appeasement, and appeasement does not give you a choice between war and peace, only between fight and surrender. We are told that the problem is too complex for a simple answer. They are wrong. There is no easy answer, but there is a simple answer. We must have the courage to do what we know is morally right, and this policy of accommodation asks us to accept the greatest possible immorality.[21]

With his strident rhetoric, Barry Goldwater certainly provided voters with a choice, but were there enough true believers to give Goldwater a chance? Although Goldwater vacillated between optimism and pessimism throughout the campaign, following the convention he was upbeat. "I can't explain the feeling," he wrote Dwight Eisenhower, "but I have had it before in elections—I feel that we are going to win." Traditional liberals, although frightened by the specter of a Goldwater presidency, seemed more worried by the ideology than by the candidate. Calling his delegates "hard as nails," Richard Rovere warned that they sought "total ideological victory and the total destruction of their critics." *Partisan Review* invited leading liberals to comment on Goldwater's nomination, and almost without exception they worried about the "messianic idealism" evident among his followers that crystallized the anguish, frustrations, and romantic utopianism of what Daniel Bell called "a social stratum with its back to the world." Whether one considered Goldwaterites conservatives or reactionaries, most commentators feared that they represented powerful undercurrents in American culture and tapped a growing discontent with national politics. Although the respondents often failed to mention Young Americans for Freedom, the fears they voiced reflected the very policies YAF had been founded to advance.[22]

The Search for Party Unity

Young Americans for Freedom, of course, rejoiced at Goldwater's nomination. *The New Guard* quoted one conservative that Goldwater-Miller was a "dream ticket." But even at the outset of the campaign YAF kept its eye on a larger strategic prize. In August *The New Guard* editorialized that while the odds were long and the campaign difficult, "if we lose the coming battle, the war will not be lost." The 1964 campaign was more than an effort to elect a candidate; it was an opportunity to proselytize. Former YAF national chair Robert Schuchman reported after the convention that traditional Republicans simply did not understand the new young conservative movement. He thought that seemed odd, but reported that conversations with eastern liberals and former Taft supporters revealed that neither had much "comprehension of what has been happening in this country the past few years." Goldwater's appeal to the younger generation, Schuchman noted, was that he represented "the America of the future in which we want to live." He symbolized "a nation and a world in which the individual is free," and the "young conservative takes very seriously the commandment that thou shall not cringe," from either communists or liberals.[23]

Events during and after the convention proved Schuchman correct. Not only had traditional Republicans tried to moderate Goldwater's message at the convention; when that failed many of them shunned his candidacy. As Eisenhower's HEW Secretary, Arthur Flemming, wrote: "I do not believe that Senator Goldwater meets minimum qualifications for the office of President. As a result, I do not see how I could conscientiously vote for him." This was, he wrote Milton Eisenhower, "a moment of truth." In his opinion, support for Goldwater would not advance the best interests of the party or the nation. Flemming was not yet ready to become a Democrat, and he castigated Republicans who were deserting the party. What was needed, he insisted, was for moderates to remain Republicans and work within the party "to do everything we can to correct the situation that has now arisen." Milton Eisenhower agreed, replying that "I'll not vote for Goldwater but I will work within the Party to restore control as soon as possible to intelligent, moderate Republicans." California Senator Thomas Kuchel warned that

> The Republican Party faces one of the gravest dangers in all its long history. In California, all of the odious totalitarian techniques of subversion and intrigue are now being used by a frenetic and well-disciplined few to capture and control our party, and to make it an antiquated implement of embittered obstruction. If the attempt, God forbid, were successful, then the death knell would have been sounded, and the Republican Party would go the way of the Know-Nothings, the Copperheads and the Whigs.

In a letter to Dwight Eisenhower, David Rockefeller expressed similar concerns: "Now it would appear that the Right Wing has firmly established its supremacy over the Party machinery. This is a result which they had sought unsuccessfully for many years. Perhaps it will be useful to determine through the polls whether in fact they represent a significant proportion of even Republican voters. I only hope that in the process we do not see irreparable damage done to the Party and the country."[24]

YAFers, on the other hand, eagerly plunged into the fray. They had been effective at the Republican National Convention, and now they were determined to use the campaign to advance personal and organizational ambitions. Robert Bauman and David Jones represented YAF in the new organizational structure of Young Americans for Goldwater-Miller. This group, publicly separate but actually under the direction of the YRNF and its chair, Donald "Buz" Lukens, was a conglomeration of Young Republicans, Youth for Goldwater, and YAF organizations and membership. Within that group, YAF struggled to dominate. This quickly produced problems, for Lukens was concerned that Clif White and other Republicans did not trust him, and at the same time he feared a possible YAF takeover of the new organization. Other YAFers in key positions included Lee Edwards, who was Director of Public Information, and Carol Bauman, who was his assistant.[25]

In an effort to forge campaign and party unity, to "save" the party and moderate conservative ideologues, key Republicans held a secret "unity conference" in Hershey, Pennsylvania in mid-August. Pennsylvania Governor William Scranton, Dwight Eisenhower, Richard Nixon, Nelson Rockefeller, George Romney, and Dean Burch (the new chairman of the Republican National Committee) attended, along with Barry Goldwater, William Miller, and others. Although all remarks were off-the-record, a transcript eventually leaked to the press, and then to the Democrats after the election. Eisenhower set the tone from the outset, urging delegates to "get our souls bared" so that they could win in November. Richard Nixon most clearly articulated the problem: "if a party is going to be a national party and not a sectional party, not a party devoted only to one wing or one ideological group . . . there has to be room for disagreement, honest disagreement." Nixon warned that without diversity party candidates would go down to defeat in many states. The Goldwater philosophy wasn't "the best position on a particular issue" in some states. Despite Goldwater's assurances that he sought "the support of no extremist," he reiterated his support of all those who backed his candidacy, particularly the John Birch Society. Goldwater's image problem, along with the civil rights issue, dominated the discussions, which were frank and open.[26]

The meeting cleared the air, but no one really budged from their previous statements and no common ground emerged. Conservatives like Stanton Evans were hopeful, arguing that while Goldwater remained firm the moderates "got closer to him." But about the best that could be said was that the divisions might be obscured for the duration of the campaign. Dwight Eisenhower concluded that the conference was perhaps 85 percent successful, but lamented that there "were opportunities without sacrificing an iota of 'principle' to accomplish more." In a letter to his brother Milton, he admitted that Goldwater had stuck by his earlier remarks on extremism, and worried that the candidate lacked self-assurance. This led him to defend stubbornly everything he had ever said in public life. Ike thought that Goldwater actually meant to conciliate, but could not admit it.[27]

One of the major problems with the so-called unity conference, a problem at least briefly noted by participants, was that only the traditional party leaders were present. None of the Goldwater groups were invited. And those groups, ranging from John Birch Society chapters to *ad hoc* Goldwater organizations to Young Americans for Freedom, produced the most politically volatile rhetoric. More important, like YAF, most of them had agendas with little connection to Republican efforts to regain the White House. Theirs was an ideological rather than a partisan commitment. The splits that fractured the party were strategic as well as ideological. Party regulars and leaders focused on the party as an electoral machine, but grass-roots Goldwater groups saw themselves as conservative guerrillas, while Young Americans for Freedom pictured themselves as the intellectual activists who were to shape the new conservatism.

Indeed, "Building for the Future" became the fall membership theme for YAF, and Carol Bauman (who edited daily "Victory Bulletins" for RNC chair Dean Burch) reminded William F. Buckley Jr. that "the nomination (or election) of a conservative to the presidency is but one first step in our efforts to create a new respect for freedom and responsibility." Despite its problems, she noted, YAF had grown steadily during the past two years. Within five years, Bauman argued, it would have twice the budget and staff. In addition, many YAFers had made the transition from Youth for Goldwater to the main campaign. Bauman, George McDonnell, Lee Edwards, and Mary Ann Ford all worked for the RNC; Lammot Copeland Jr. and Fulton Lewis III were members of William Miller's campaign organization.[28]

YAF's fourth annual meeting that September drew fewer delegates than usual because so many YAFers were out on the campaign trail. Delegates passed a series of resolutions, commending Goldwater for his defense of human rights (including his vote against the civil rights bill) and praising the FBI and various congressional internal security committees for their efforts to combat domestic communism. They also opposed the Supreme Court's decision on legislative reapportionment, arguing that it exceeded its jurisdiction and threatened to destroy the concepts of federalism and states' rights. Instead, YAF backed a constitutional amendment explicitly stating that state apportionment and state elections were the exclusive jurisdiction of the states themselves. Delegates also supported the separation of church and state, but insisted that it occur "without hostility between them or any bias on the part of the state in favor of secularism." Other resolutions attacked the National Student Association, supported fraternities and the principle of voluntary association, and commended Herbert Hoover and Douglas MacArthur as epitomizing the ideals of liberty, duty, honor, and country.[29]

Young Americans for Freedom focused primarily on the upcoming election, however. *The New Guard* blasted "turncoat Republicans" who refused to back Goldwater, and argued that the election would "revolutionize American politics" as southern Democrats broke party ranks to vote for Goldwater. Combined with the West and the Midwest, it insisted, this would ensure a Goldwater victory in the fall. South Carolina Senator Strom Thurmond's switch from Democrat to Republican seemed a potent omen for the future. YAF believed that it marked the beginning of the two-party system in the South, and *The New Guard* approvingly quoted Thurmond's charges that the Democratic Party had "abandoned the people" and "turned its back on the spiritual values and political principles which have brought us the blessings of freedom under God and a bountiful prosperity." It also drew attention to the large crowds Goldwater was attracting and the obvious dedication of his supporters as signs of impending change. Perhaps conservative philosopher Willmoore Kendall expressed their hopes best: "What is up for grabs is the status of a whole governing class—of the entire elite upon whom we have depended in recent decades for our political wisdom, our picture of the world, our guidelines in public policy."[30]

By the time the presidential campaign entered its final months, moderate Republicans were increasingly alarmed, not only about the prospect of a major defeat in November, but about the broader implications of Goldwater's candidacy for the future of the party. By late September a Committee to Support Moderate Republicans formed. Chaired by Charles P. Taft, and supported by such stalwart Republicans as Arthur S. Flemming, Henry Cabot Lodge, Malcolm Moos, and several other individuals with close ties to the Eisenhower administration, it warned that "our country is in a state of political crisis." The crisis, they insisted, was "due in large part to the fact that our kind of Republicans are in disarray." Moderate Republicanism was the "most responsible force on the American political scene," they asserted, and was the "fulcrum upon which all constructive accomplishments ultimately depend." More to the point, it was "the only reliable guardian against excesses of any kind." Their task was to elect moderate Republicans to political offices across the country, and they provided a lengthy list of individuals whose election or reelection was essential. They were silent about the contest for the presidency, but their very existence revealed a conviction that either a Goldwater victory (highly unlikely by then) or a Goldwater defeat would be disastrous for the Republican Party. A victory would give him control of the party, unless moderates demonstrated electoral strength around the nation. A defeat, particularly a devastating defeat, would drag other Republican candidates down with him and ruin the party.[31] Moderate Republicans feared that party troubles ran far deeper than simply defeat in November.

Letters from Goldwater supporters revealed that, for many, the candidate remained too moderate in his attempt to capture the White House. Conservatives like Elizabeth Churchill Brown, a personal friend of Goldwater, illustrated the problem. Brown, who had worked with Senator Joseph McCarthy in anti-Stevenson efforts during the 1950s, complained repeatedly that Goldwater failed to understand the significance of the 1964 campaign. "He does not know this is a crusade," she wrote. "He doesn't even understand that this is NOT politics. It is a war against a conspiracy." After January, she warned, "THE revolution will commence in earnest. In other words, his followers know more about the score than he does. They know the government is rotten with soviet agents." In a similar letter to the Republican National Committee, Brown urged Goldwater to take on the communist issue and the question of Vietnam.[32]

Throughout the fall various publications documented the progress of the radical Right. In doing so they demonstrated once again the larger problem for conservatives. The National Council of the Churches of Christ typified the dilemma. Although it singled out the John Birch Society, which embraced a conspiracy theory of American history, the Council nonetheless lumped together organizations ranging from Americans for Constitutional Action and *Human Events* to Young Americans for Freedom and *National Review* as "extreme conservatives." They admitted that this latter group rejected the impeachment of Chief Justice Earl Warren and shied away from a belief in conspiratorial plots, but insisted that they were well outside the pale of conventional conservatism. Their lack of "moderation" made them inherently dangerous. Other watchdogs of the Right, especially Group Research, Inc., also talked about YAF in the same breath with the John Birch Society and other extremist elements. National chair Robert Bauman tried to clarify YAF's position in an appearance on the Manion Forum in mid-October. Although his appearance in itself somewhat compromised his position (since Manion was a vocal John Bircher), Bauman insisted that YAF was not a reactionary organization even though it was militantly conservative. The Sharon Statement and its explication of freedom was what drove YAF, Bauman asserted, and he claimed more than 350 chapters and more than 30,000 members nationwide. YAF backed Goldwater for reasons of principle, not revenge. It was a nonpartisan organization and not an adjunct of the Republican Party. The central issue in 1964, Bauman concluded, was communism. The United States, in Cuba, Vietnam, or anywhere else, should abandon appeasement and pursue a policy of victory. Goldwater's endorsement of that position was what had led YAFers to do voter registration and precinct work, and to organize Goldwater rallies around the country. Young Americans for Freedom, in short, saw 1964 as a crusade for conservatism. Barry Goldwater was the vehicle for rather than the object of that crusade.[33]

Looking Ahead

YAF's return to its earlier emphases was important, for it signaled hope even where despair reigned. Although his most zealous supporters remained outwardly confident, Goldwater was far behind in the polls and even many of his early supporters had given up hope. Drew Pearson noted that the Goldwater camp pushed the panic button in early August. "They see no way to win," he observed, "and have no breakthrough strategy." By mid-October Marvin Liebman had shut down the New York Goldwater-Miller headquarters, unplugging the copy machine and removing most of the telephones. A speech by William F. Buckley Jr. at YAF's annual convention indicated the shape of things to come. Meeting almost two months before the November elections, and ostensibly at least in part to rally YAFers for the final weeks of the fall campaign, the convention heard Buckley's plea to rally around the conservative cause even in the face of impending defeat.[34]

Buckley implied the unthinkable, that Goldwater's chances were essentially nil: "the nomination of Barry Goldwater, when we permit ourselves to peek up over the euphoria, reminds us chillingly of the great work that has remained undone; a great rainfall has deluged a thirsty earth, but before we had time properly to prepare it. *I speak of course about the impending defeat of Barry Goldwater.*" Delegates were stunned; some cried. Buckley tried to rally them, warning that "it is right to reason to the necessity of guarding against the utter disarray that sometimes follows a stunning defeat . . . to take thought . . . about the potential need for regrouping . . . ." The 1964 campaign was merely the first step in a long crusade for conservative principles, not the final chapter. The purpose of the Goldwater candidacy, he observed, was to recruit legions to the conservative cause. What was important was not necessarily a victory in November 1964, but in Novembers to come. YAFers should focus not on "the ashes of defeat, but at the well-planted seeds of hope."[35]

Buckley reminded his audience that where once they had labored in the hopes of nominating a conservative candidate, too many now assumed that with that nomination came the possibility of victory. But "any election of Barry

Goldwater," he argued, "would presuppose a sea-change in American public opinion: presuppose that the fiery little body of dissenters, of which you are a shining meteor, suddenly spun off nothing less than a majority of the American people." This had not happened, and to imagine it was premature. Instead, he insisted, the "Goldwater movement is in the nature of an attempted prison-break." The effort was essential, success unlikely, and demoralization danger-ous to the future of the conservative cause. "I fear," he warned YAFers, "that the morale of an army on the march is the morale that is most easily destroyed in the unanticipated event of defeat." Expectations of victory were unrealistic, and Buckley urged his listeners to look ahead to future Novembers. "We have in mind, do we not, a counter-revolution? Counter-revolutions are not ac-complished by defeating Nelson Rockefeller or William Scranton. The enemy is made of sterner stuff." YAFers should emerge from the November 1964 elec-tions "confident in the knowledge that we weakened those walls, that they will never again stand so firmly against us."[36]

Buckley's pessimism proved well-founded. On election day Lyndon B. Johnson trounced Barry Goldwater, 43,126,218 votes to 27,174,898. Johnson not only received 61 percent of the vote; he carried into office on his coattails a host of Democratic congressmen and senators, creating an almost unprece-dented liberal majority in the Congress. The best that Republicans could sal-vage was a gain of one governor (but they still had only 17), and a breakthrough among white voters in the South. The crusade for conservatism had sputtered at the ballot box.[37]

Chapter 10   Past as Prologue

Barry Goldwater's crushing defeat at the polls in November appeared to demonstrate that American voters embraced a liberal consensus and rejected the new conservatism. But observers focused on the candidate rather than the cause, on the electoral results rather than on the evidence of transformation within the Republican Party. One day prior to the election, Stanton Evans had alerted readers of *National Review* that despite "the doom-laden utterances of pollsters and pundits, this year's elections may well confirm, for years to come, the political maturity of American conservatism." Although two days later a quick look at the election returns made that seem unlikely, this was not merely wishful thinking. To the real perpetrators of the conservative crusade in 1964, the efforts were more important than the results. In the words of one loyal Republican: "I guess this is the end of Barry. . . . But there still is a huge conservative machine, if only somebody can keep it together."[1]

Many conservative activists had begun to prepare for life after defeat even before the election. Bleak as the future looked in 1964, events during the next four years not only eroded the liberal consensus, but triggered a backlash that turned the country increasingly conservative. Little more than a decade later conservatism had apparently moved to the center of American political life. When that happened, conservative political forces were poised to take advantage of their opportunity as they had not been in 1964. Much of their success stemmed from the efforts of activists who formed Young Americans for Freedom.

YAF and the Republican Future

Even before voters entered the polls in November 1964, Young Americans for Freedom planned for future crusades. Following William F. Buckley Jr.'s speech at their annual convention in September, Robert Bauman asked if he had "given any thought to a general meeting of the 'responsible right' after the November elections." Bauman noted that YAF had begun to develop plans to perpetuate the conservative cause in the event that Goldwater met defeat in November. To the extent that a defeat represented a rejection of political extremism, Bauman sought to align YAF publicly with "responsible" conservatism. YAF remained committed to a muscular anticommunism, but the fading popular belief in a monolithic communist conspiracy, and the growing centrality of domestic issues, further distanced YAF from both the conspiratorial rhetoric and the membership of the radical Right. Six weeks after his YAF convention speech Buckley delivered a more optimistic message at the New York Conservative Party's anniversary dinner.

> A conservative is concerned simultaneously with two things, the first
> being the shape of the visionary or paradigmatic society towards
> which we should labor; the second, the speed with which it is think-
> able to advance towards that ideal society and the fore-knowledge
> that any advance upon it is necessarily asymptotic; not, at least, until
> the successful completion of the Society for the Abolition of Original
> Sin. How this movement, considering the contrary tug of history, has
> got as far as it has got, is something that surpasses the understanding
> of natural pessimists like myself.[2]

Despite Buckley's optimism, Goldwater's defeat was too convincing for the average voter to believe that conservative sparks still kindled flames of rebellion. Moderate Republicans, dismayed but not surprised by the dimensions of the defeat, hoped the election results represented the death knell of radical conservatism. Aside from Goldwater, they believed the problem was people who "had infiltrated into the Party through attachment to the Goldwater cause."[3]

A post-election article in *Look* magazine on "A New Conservative Manifesto" highlighted both the problems and the opportunities for Republicans. Although the article criticized extremists, it warned that "Goldwaterism will not evaporate." His candidacy had voiced the fears of many "bewildered Americans," and although Goldwater had lost badly, "the radical conservative is still there." "Radical Conservatism," the author warned, has "become the most significant political movement of the late 20th century." Conservatives controlled the Republican Party, a party now "convulsed as if by demons" because "in the rightwing alphabet agencies, from the JBS to ISI and YAF, many would rather nourish despair than cure it." This "new breed of political activist," the "fanatic volunteer," now set the tone for the party. Moderates' only hope to win the power struggle was to "hear the message of the movement and find a principle on which to respond to it."[4]

In a speech at the Woodrow Wilson School of Public and International Affairs two weeks after the election, Stephen Horn, legislative assistant to California Senator Thomas Kuchel, examined this problem by asking: "Is There a Republican Future?" Hoping that 1964 would be the last year of its kind to confront the party, Horn observed that there had been "more active infighting in the two weeks following the national election and pious statements on the need for leadership by certain Republican politicians than there were in the crucial two months prior to the San Francisco Republican Convention." Richard Nixon, for instance, had repudiated both party liberals and Goldwater conservatives in an effort to position himself as the logical candidate in 1968. Horn criticized that approach, and voiced his own uncertainty about the Republicans' future. Moderates had done rather well in the election, but he warned that the right wing was not about to compromise.

> The problem is that the Goldwater clique has completely misunderstood American politics. They have sought to structure an ideological program—largely a negative program—onto a political party which, like its counterpart, has succeeded by being pragmative and positive— or realistic. . . . The history—and perhaps the success of American politics—has been marked with flexibility of means within certain broad goals.

The right wing did not endorse that pragmatism, and Horn attacked its singleminded fanaticism. "It is beyond belief," he noted, "until you confront them in the precincts and see the gleam in their eyes, the fear in their faces, and often, sadly, the hate in their hearts. Then it becomes very real."[5]

The Ripon Society, reflecting a liberal Republicanism, issued its own postelection analysis: "The mandate of the San Francisco convention, dominated by a militant minority within the party, has been countermanded by the overwhelming decision of the American voters." The 1964 campaign had been "unreal," driven by the Goldwater crowd's "dream of a political world without politics." It demonstrated, the Society believed, that there was no hidden conservative majority. Even the South was disappointing in their view, for Goldwater captured fewer electoral votes in the South than either Eisenhower or Nixon. The Society worried that "historians of the future may well record that the most significant result of the 1964 election was that America's youth turned against the Republican party."[6]

The Ripon Society's full report proved to be more mixed, however. It lamented, but recognized, Republican gains among white Southerners, and that, despite defeat, Goldwater's candidacy had "significantly strengthened" conservative influence within the party. But in many respects, the report concluded, "the basic flaw of the conservative position was the weakness of their candidate." Goldwater's stands on a range of issues, as well as his sharp-edged language, alienated voters. He proposed radical shifts when most voters seemed to want moderate adjustments at best. What was prophecy to some turned out to be anathema for others. Perhaps most disturbing to the Ripon Society was that Goldwater lost six of the biggest states by more than a million votes each—New York, Pennsylvania, Michigan, Ohio, Massachusetts, and California—all but one of which had a Republican governor.[7]

Despite conservatives' claims that 1964 demonstrated a conservative voter base of 27,000,000, the Ripon Society noted that a Louis Harris poll revealed the great majority of them to be moderates. Only about six million really backed Goldwater and a right-wing takeover of the Republican Party. The rest were hard-core Republicans who refused to desert the party's candidate, regardless of his views. But efforts to undercut or explain away Goldwater's vote faltered when one looked closely at party structure in the South. The Goldwater faction *was* in control there, and the campaign greatly strengthened an emergent Republican Party throughout the region, laying the groundwork for what came to be called the southern strategy. This was an appeal, often implicitly racist, that attracted support from white southern Democrats opposed to civil rights and racial change. In addition, the Society warned that moderate and liberal Republicans' loss of "the organizing focus of the presidential nomination" was a hidden cost of enormous significance."[8]

Other party moderates were even sharper in their criticism. George Gilder and Bruce Chapman attacked the notion that the Republicans' future lay in the South and with extreme conservatism. This was a betrayal of "the party's heritage for tactical advantage," they complained. Major reform was "urgent." A conservative minority had ridden roughshod over an "impotent" moderate majority, which had abdicated its responsibility for leadership and thereby opened the door to the "fanaticism and duplicity of a minority." Not only did the election reject Goldwater, they asserted, it also rejected right-wing positions on the issues. The problem, in short, was *not* just the candidate, but the cause itself, which believed not only that most people were really conservatives, but that, "deep in their hearts, they are narrow-minded, selfish, xenophobic, and racially prejudiced." The chief problem for the party in the short run was not only to reconfigure its message, but to change its entire way of thinking. Conservative strategists, they warned, were not stupid. They could and did count. The problem was that they counted delegates rather than voters. This meant that they could control the party but not win elections.[9]

Conservatives rejected most of that advice. In the words of YAF's mentor, William F. Buckley Jr.: "Counterrevolution—and that, really, is what Barry Goldwater is talking about—is a sweaty, brawly business." From their perspective, the problem was clear. Aside from the victories of Dwight D. Eisenhower and his detestable "modern Republicanism" in 1952 and 1956, no Republican (and no conservative) had captured the White House since Herbert Hoover in 1928. Opposed to moderate or progressive politics, and convinced that minimalist alternatives to Democratic positions were insufficient to create an opposition majority, conservatives argued that the South was the most fertile ground for the future. Goldwater's southern support correlated closely with that for Strom Thurmond in 1948. In the Black Belt he received 72.7 percent of the vote. He consistently outpolled Nixon's 1960 vote among both upper- and lower-class whites. Clearly the racial issue was central to Republican fortunes in the South. But like YAF's struggle with moderate Republicans, much of the important activity occurred out of the public's view. In the words of one reporter:

> We could see bits and pieces of the strategy beginning to develop, especially in the battle for control of the Republican precincts and county convention delegates. That was where the real fight was that year. But we still didn't understand its significance. We did not understand, as many of the insiders did, that a great cleansing was at hand, that political fratricide was the order of the day, rather to be proclaimed to the heavens than meekly apologized for.[10]

The fundamental issue, after all, was power—its acquisition and exercise.

In the case of the South, issues of ideology and political advantage joined in a volatile mix. Clearly, many white southerners backed Goldwater because he opposed the 1964 Civil Rights Act and supported states' rights over federal intervention. For them, race was central. Determined to maintain segregation, they believed they had found a vehicle for their prejudices. But for ideological conservatives, including Young Americans for Freedom, opposition to federal intervention in civil rights rested primarily on the constitutional question of federal power rather than on racism per se. Goldwater himself had repeatedly said that he supported civil rights for all Americans but opposed federal intervention. The real question for leaders of the new conservatism, therefore, was whether the 1964 election was a referendum on ideology or on the achievement of particular social objectives. Either way, the voters it attracted to the conservative cause were a mixed blessing. On the one hand, they were essential to forging a conservative majority. On the other hand, they were not committed to change for the same reasons and did not share the ideological convictions that had underpinned the revolt since its beginnings in 1960. Further complicating the problem was the commitment of groups like Young Americans for Freedom to ideology over party amid the continuing transcendence of party as the means to power.[11]

Determined to continue their quest and foment a conservative revolution, YAF insisted that "we are still right, and we intend to organize, publish, and educate until the majority of Americans *know* that we are right." Marvin Liebman's mail brought letters reflecting that attitude. "You, I am sure," wrote one correspondent, "share with me the view that the Goldwater campaign was only the beginning—not the end—of the conservative movement." A newsletter designed to recruit members for a Strom Thurmond chapter of YAF in New York state made the same appeal more directly. Its editor, Edward Wirzulis, argued that

> The great conservative strength in America lays dormant. But this strength must not be allowed to remain dormant. Election campaigns have little or no effect upon the voting public. The elections are won or lost during the interim periods such as now. If this great mass of conservative strength can be channeled in such a way as to work as hard for conservatism now as it did during the campaign, we will have an effective weapon to combat the growing liberal philosophy and a way to win more people to the conservative principles. Then can we have the strength to elect a conservative President. This will be the real test of whether Mr. Goldwater was defeated or not.[12]

From the perspective of national YAF leaders, the problem was that *they* understood the meaning of Goldwater's rhetoric, but most other Americans did not. Carol Bauman went further, arguing that what defeated Goldwater was fear, not ideology. Americans feared death in nuclear disaster more than their loss of liberty, so they would rather appease communism than fight it. "Forty-one million Americans [who voted for LBJ] confirmed that we are a nation of cowards," she argued. "If a 'moderate' party image" was essential to victory, she asked, then "why did the party consistently lose elections during the Eisenhower years?" Bauman insisted that it was imperative for conservatives to retain control of the Republican Party and continue to provide a choice for voters. The 1964 campaign had been the first one financed primarily by the "little people." Goldwater had received contributions from almost two million Americans (only about 40,000 individuals had contributed to the party in 1960), and they constituted a potent fund-raising base for the future. "Those zealots," she argued, were the "major backbone of the GOP." "Under effective leadership, the Republican National Committee, so long a refuge of incompetents and has-beens, can become a vital force for conservatism. The national party," she concluded, "can once again *stand for* something, and we can again argue philosophies and issues, not just candidates and promises."[13]

In many respects the Goldwater campaign had mobilized rather than dispirited conservative activists. The circulation of *National Review* increased more than 50 percent, from 61,000 to 94,000. YAF reported hundreds of new applications for membership, most of them from veterans of the recent campaign who had just completed their first venture into electoral politics and found the experience exhilarating. Robert Bauman, YAF's national chairman, and David Jones, its executive director, called the response "fantastic." The campaign also gave the cause its firmest financial foundation in history. YAF reported 20,000 dues-paying members and an additional 35,000 occasional contributors. In the second half of 1964 it had picked up more than 5,400 new members. Bauman reported that most "of the members do not regard the recent campaign and election as a decisive confrontation of the liberal and conservative philosophies. They regard it as one step in a long chain of events that will eventually restore conservatism to a dominating position in America."[14]

Moderate Republicans who had backed Eisenhower in the 1950s tried to draft the former president to articulate once again his ideas of "modern Republicanism." Led by men like Sacramento publisher Leonard Finder, they hoped that Goldwater's resounding defeat had eliminated the right-wing threat to the party, and worried chiefly about the kind of legislation Lyndon Johnson would push through the Democratic Congress over the next four years. Eisenhower remained reluctant to act. He admitted to his former press secretary, James Hagerty, that "some of us have got to begin to do something effective" to curb the right wing's influence in the party, but he appeared content to let Dean Burch and the party leadership try to solve the problem. Led by Arthur Flemming, other Republican leaders appealed to the Republican governors, warning that while there "is no need for a witch hunt or a purge . . . there is a need to realize that the most dramatic Republican majorities of last November 3rd were compiled by those who disassociated themselves in the public mind from Senator Goldwater." Eisenhower doubted that the party should be rebuilt around the governors, however, favoring instead a "simple statement of Republican convictions and purposes, so worded as to be both meaningful and acceptable to the vast bulk of the Party membership." But that was the path he had followed in 1960, a path that had helped lead to the Goldwater movement at the 1960 Republican National Convention in Chicago. When it came to defining ideology, conservatives were far more effective than party moderates.[15]

The fundamental difference between party moderates and conservatives was not only ideology, but strategy. While Eisenhower was mulling over ways to better define Republican principles, former RNC chair Leonard Hall outlined the practical problem.

> When we look at the elections of 1960 and 1964, we find that from 90 to 98 percent of the colored people, upwards of 75 percent of the Catholics and four out of five Jewish people are voting against us. As a matter of plain simple practical politics and arithmetic, with these groups against us our chances of winning are very slim indeed, unless someone like yourself comes along. The big job ahead is to make these groups feel at home in the Republican Party.[16]

Moderates tried to craft a program to attract a diverse array of voters. By definition this meant a series of political compromises to avoid sharp-edged ideological positions. Party leaders rejected the suggestion of Barry Goldwater that the parties be realigned into "conservative" (Republican) and "liberal" (Democrat). In a twelve-page rebuttal, Michigan Governor George Romney wrote Goldwater that "dogmatic ideological parties tend to splinter the political and social fabric of a nation, lead to governmental crises and deadlocks, and stymie the compromises so often necessary to preserve freedom and achieve progress." A few months later Republican Congressman John Lindsay of New York stated the problem more directly: "the Republicans must recapture the center . . . where the Republicans have been and should return."[17]

Conservatives embraced an entirely different approach, believing that future success rested on a clear exposition of ideology. Their difficulty was the centrifugal pull exerted by elements of that conservative ideology. This became evident when a surging interest in libertarianism swept Young Americans for Freedom following the November elections. Although YAF's national board remained dominated by "traditional" conservatives, libertarians attracted supporters who embraced their opposition to the military draft and their support for the legalization of marijuana. For the next several years YAF conventions featured persistent battles between "libs" (libertarians) and "trads" (traditionalists). They also threatened a breach within YAF between the political conservatives who founded the organization and a new breed of cultural conservatives whose primary issues and objectives were still unformed. Open debate flared once again over the "proper" definition of conservatism.[18]

The debate was often complicated, but two divisions characterized much of it. First, traditionalists, libertarians, and fusionists continued to argue about the nature of conservatism and the proper definition of human nature. The problem was to find a balance between the objective order and individual freedom. In making a "conservative case for freedom," Stanton Evans questioned "whether the imperatives of individual freedom can be reconciled with the Christian conception of the individual as flawed in mind and will, with its demand for individual subordination to an objective, nonsecular order." This argument had bedeviled the new conservatism since its inception, and was not about to be resolved now. The second division, articulated by libertarian Murray Rothbard, was over priorities. Rothbard attacked YAF because it focused on political concerns. "To my knowledge," he wrote, "not one political action drive of YAF has been directed to an increase of individual liberty or of the free market." The right-wing resurgence, Rothbard complained, had largely ignored libertarian ideas because it was too committed to a "hysterical anticommunism." Groups like YAF shifted from antistatism to anticommunism, and in so doing they "failed to see that both the 'external' and 'internal' threats of statism to liberty were essentially domestic."[19] YAF's leadership was now far more interested in political power than in narrow ideological categories. In the fall of 1964, even as intellectual debates over ideology raged among its members, its leadership turned once again to political organizing.

Even before the election Robert Bauman had talked about forming a conservative umbrella organization for YAF "graduates." Indeed, two years earlier Marvin Liebman, Frank Meyer, and Brent Bozell had drawn up plans for such a group. The Saturday after the election Bauman met in Manhattan with William F. Buckley Jr. and a small group of activists to plan a new conservative organization, the American Conservative Union (ACU). Modeled after Americans for Democratic Action, it sought to find "answers to the questions posed by the landslide victory of the candidates of the liberal establishment." Chaired by Indiana Congressman Donald Bruce, its other officers included Ohio Congressman John Ashbrook, Robert Bauman, Frank Meyer, Brent Bozell, Peter O'Donnell, Lammot Copeland Jr., William Rusher, and Buckley. They adopted a statement of principles that began: "The American Conservative Union holds firm the truth that all men are endowed by their Creator with unalienable rights. To a world floundering in philosophical anarchy, we therefore commend a transcendent moral order against which all human institutions, in every commonwealth, may confidently be judged."[20]

The American Conservative Union sought to accomplish four objectives:

> (a) to mobilize and consolidate the intellectual resources of the conservative movement; (b) to provide leadership and material for existing conservative-oriented organizations, periodicals and political leaders; (c) to influence American public opinion toward the acceptance of conservative principles of economics and government; (d) to stimulate and direct responsible citizen action on social and economic problems and matters of legislation, public policy and in behalf of conservative candidates for public office.

The ACU proposed to work "actively within the Republican Party and with Republican members of Congress" to achieve their common objectives. It represented, in short, the next logical extension beyond Young Americans for Freedom. YAF had formed in 1960 as a political action organization outside the established network of political groups. Now the ACU, building on the success of YAF, sought to construct and become the linchpin of a conservative establishment. Its founders believed that ADA had successfully consolidated the leadership of the liberal establishment without "infringing on the rights or authority of any single part of the liberal organizational apparatus." They intended to emulate that model.[21]

At a secret meeting on December 19, 1964 in Washington, D.C., about one hundred conservatives met to formally inaugurate the new political organization. "We believe," said the invitation, "that there is a vital need for such an organization at this particular juncture of American history." At their first meeting, however, the ACU's board of directors found itself preoccupied with an old question: the John Birch Society. After extensive debate and several votes, the directors finally decided on a simple statement to the effect that the ACU and the John Birch Society were separate organizations. Birchers were not to hold office in the ACU, and the ACU rejected the politics of "extremism." Within a year, however, factions developed and bickering much like that which had plagued YAF afflicted the organization.[22]

What did formation of the American Conservative Union mean for Young Americans for Freedom? It certainly siphoned off much of YAF's early leadership. But that leadership was changing regardless of the ACU. YAF had sustained itself from 1960 to 1964 on the hope that the 1964 election would see a conservative candidate advance the principles of the Sharon Statement and lay the foundation for a political resurgence. They had been at least partially successful, securing their candidate if not their victory. But YAF was poorly positioned to take over the hierarchy of the Republican Party itself. It had no real power. Its strength rested on its ability to publicize the conservative cause among young people, and to train a future generation of conservative leaders. For those who had already been through this process, and harbored professional political ambitions, the American Conservative Union provided an outlet for their continuing activities.[23]

The Contributions of YAF

Young Americans for Freedom had been an active voice of campus conservatism in the early 1960s. But after the 1964 election the liberal consensus seemed dominant, symbolized by Lyndon Johnson's plans for a "Great Society." Then came the war in Vietnam. With the introduction of American ground combat troops in 1965, and steady escalation thereafter, campus politics became antiwar politics. Concern about the war, and more pointedly opposition to the war and to the military draft, dominated students' consciousness. YAF found itself in a difficult position. Opposition to the war and to the draft usually went hand-in-hand. But YAF opposed the draft even while it supported the war.[24] This pro-war and anti-draft position, based as it was on traditional YAF beliefs in anticommunism and individual freedom, was insufficient to seize the limelight from SDS or the counterculture. Like other conservatives, Young Americans for Freedom had to regroup during the late 1960s and early 1970s. They eventually found another white knight in the person of California Governor Ronald Reagan, but in the mid-1960s that lay well in the future.

In the short run YAF seemed destined to undergo a major transition. Many of its founding members moved on to further their own political careers, and a new generation of youth entered its ranks. As they did so, new issues like the war in Vietnam and the need to oppose the New Left and Students for a Democratic Society shaped the immediate future of YAF. What was needed, Lee Edwards concluded, was a twenty-five-year plan. Insisting that the 1964 election represented a "humiliating defeat" for the Republican Party but a "national political beachhead" for conservatism, Edwards argued that Barry Goldwater lost the election "because the nation did not understand him." "He was a conservative," Edwards observed, "who sounded and *was* radical in the increasingly liberal atmosphere of America." The crux of Edwards's message was that conservatives needed to decide "whether they are interested in winning a debate or an election . . . in being totally right [more] than in being President, whether they are truly serious about wanting to direct the fortunes of the nation and the world." In 1964, he concluded, conservatives had organization, money, and a strong candidate. But they lacked broad-based issues and failed to communicate their message. The problem, in short, was that conservatism had been overtaken, or at the very least overshadowed, by the radical Right.[25] Despite Edwards's warning, within a year after the election YAF was again providing a platform for Birchites, blurring the ideological distinctiveness many of its leaders believed essential to the success of the conservative cause. The Republican National Committee followed a similar drift; even as many of its leaders called for a return to a moderate centrism it sold its mailing list to the Liberty Lobby, further exposing rank and file Republicans to enticements from the radical Right.[26]

By the close of 1964 Young Americans for Freedom, like the conservative cause it championed, seemed to have made its run at power and failed. But its efforts during the preceding four years had not been wasted. Young conservatives had tasted battle; some had even been elected to Congress. They had developed the basis for a conservative establishment had developed, and constructed a framework of permanent conservative political organizations. As one campus observer noted: "These students felt they had hold of something so dynamic and exciting that all they needed was to open up discussions, launch debates, challenge other students to think for themselves, and that then the students would catch fire in this new spirit." Two years later, at the May 1966 anniversary dinner of Young Americans for Freedom, Barry Goldwater told YAFers: "You are not a political party, not even a second cousin to a political party." Their job, he reminded them (to great applause), was to advance the cause of conservatism without respect to party. In a sense, this brought them full circle. It was where they had started in September 1960. There remained little question that the most likely avenue to power still lay through the Republican Party, but they needed to reach out to conservatives and not just to Republicans.[27]

If Young Americans for Freedom had come full circle, had they accomplished anything in their four years of existence? YAF did not, of course, singlehandedly revitalize conservative politics in the early 1960s. Not only was there Barry Goldwater; there were millions of conservative voters anxious to be mobilized. But YAF did provide leadership for the years that followed, a cadre of young men and women ideologically committed to the cause of conservatism rather than to the Republican Party or to the politics of compromise and conciliation. When Speaker of the House Newt Gingrich told reporters in 1995 that he would cooperate with President Bill Clinton, but not compromise with him, he was speaking a language advanced by YAF in the early 1960s. Unlike other grass-roots conservative or right-wing groups at the time, YAF wanted to do more than stir the masses; it wanted to create a political commonwealth grounded in conservative principles. YAFers believed their articulation of those principles could mobilize a mass of dormant voters and create a conservative majority. In the words of Robert Bauman, "We were young and we didn't want to live the rest of our lives under [liberalism] and we didn't want communism to destroy the world. . . . I remember reading *The True Believer* at the time and saying, 'Yeah, that's us.'"[28]

In his study of conservative leadership in the 1980s, James Roberts concluded that the "founding of YAF was, in retrospect, probably the most important organizational initiative undertaken by conservatives in the last thirty years."[29] While I have not been able to trace the careers of all the founders of YAF, a look at even a few of them indicates the commitment to conservative political action that drew these young men and women to the cause in the first place and guided their lives thereafter. In each case their experience in Young Americans for Freedom became a stepping stone to future political involvement. The leaders who emerged from YAF were people like Carol Dawson,

Robert Bauman, Lee Edwards, Richard Viguerie, and Howard Phillips. Each was instrumental in the formative years of YAF, and each embarked on a lengthy career in conservative politics after moving on from YAF. As Paul Weyrich, a conservative leader in the 1980s, observed, not only did the Goldwater campaign sow the "seeds of the contemporary New Right;" the "organization of Young Americans for Freedom kept in touch with the young people who had been impressed by Goldwater, and kept them politically viable."[30]

YAF's national chairs led the way. Robert Bauman, who served from 1962-1965 and then later as chair of the ACU, won election to the Maryland State Senate and was later elected to the United States Congress from Maryland. He helped found the Conservative Opportunity Society, a pioneering effort by Congressional conservatives to join with ideological soul mates and trumpet the conservative cause. His arrest in 1980 for committing a homosexual act with a young male prostitute led to his subsequent repudiation at the polls.[31] Tom Charles Huston, national chair from 1965 to 1967, was later active in the ACU and served on the White House staff of Richard Nixon as a deputy to Patrick Buchanan. There he authored the infamous Huston plan to deploy an array of "dirty tricks" at the 1972 Democratic national convention. He later returned to law practice in Indianapolis. Alan MacKay, national chair from 1967 to 1969, became a Boston lawyer and then left his practice to take a position with the Office of Economic Opportunity during the Nixon years. There he worked with other YAFers in an effort to dismantle OEO. David Keene, national chair in 1969 and 1970, became a Special Assistant for Political Affairs to Vice President Spiro Agnew and then to New York Senator James Buckley. Keene later became chair of the American Conservative Union, and then an advisor to the Coalition for America at Risk. He also served as southern field director for the Reagan campaign in 1978, and then signed on as political director of the Bush campaign in 1979.

YAF's national chairs were not the only individuals who later worked for conservative causes. Other early YAFers retained their conservative politics but embarked on nonpolitical careers. William Schulz became an assistant to radio broadcaster Fulton Lewis Jr., and is currently a managing editor of *Reader's Digest*. Lee Edwards kept his hand in politics, formed a consulting firm, and authored several political studies. Together with his wife Anne he wrote a political manual for prospective conservative activists, published in 1968. Later he wrote biographies of conservatives Ronald Reagan, Walter Judd, and Barry Goldwater. Robert Croll turned to a career in academia; Diarmuid O'Scannlain, a member of the Reagan transition team, and then of the Republican National Committee from 1983 to 1986, became a U.S. Circuit Court Judge for the Ninth Circuit (Portland, Oregon); Douglas Caddy practiced law (he was the first lawyer to visit E. Howard Hunt after the Watergate break-in) and became president of the Energy Consumer Coalition; and John Kolbe became a newspaper editor in Arizona.

More activist was Howard Phillips, who worked for the Republican Party throughout much of the 1960s and 1970s and was eventually hired in 1970 by Richard Nixon to head the Office of Economic Opportunity and dismantle the War on Poverty. After the Senate refused to confirm him, he resigned and devoted his political energies to forming the New Right. With Phillips's advice, Nixon appointed several former YAFers to eliminate various OEO programs. Among them were two former executive directors of YAF, David Jones and Randall Teague, as well as Daniel F. Joy, a former editor of *The New Guard*. Phillips eventually moved away from the Republican Party and spearheaded efforts to organize a third party more stringently attached to the conservative cause. In the mid-1970s Phillips, together with Paul Weyrich and Richard Viguerie, tried to take over George Wallace's American Independent Party, and in the late 1970s they urged the Reverend Jerry Falwell to start the Moral Majority. Phillips also formed the Conservative Caucus in 1975, which he currently serves as president, and helped organize the Committee for the New Majority.

Other YAFers who joined the Nixon administration included Patrick Buchanan, former editorial writer for the *St. Louis Globe-Democrat*. Buchanan had worked in the Goldwater effort and served as a speechwriter for Nixon and Agnew. He later launched his own conservative candidacy for the presidency. Carol Bauman, who first worked for Youth for Nixon in 1960 before becoming a founding member of YAF and then communications director for the ACU, joined Nixon's White House staff as a researcher and writer. In the Reagan years she served as deputy press secretary for the Department of Energy and later as a commissioner of the Consumer Products Safety Commission. John Weicher served in the Department of Housing and Urban Development. The Nixon administration's employment of so many former YAFers became a bit ironic when, together with leaders of several other conservative groups, Young Americans for Freedom denounced his reconciliation with China in 1971 and tried to finance challenges to his reelection in the Republican primaries. In the early 1970s, in a move reminiscent of earlier YAF factionalism, former YAFer David Nolan (who had served as an organizer for Nixon in 1972) formed the Libertarian Party.

Several early YAFers later joined the Reagan administration. Richard Allen, who had been a Nixon aide and a member of the National Security Council, became national security adviser. He also served as a senior staff member at the Center for Strategic and International Studies at Georgetown University and at the Hoover Institution on War, Revolution and Peace at Stanford University. Donald Devine, an associate professor of governmental politics at the University of Maryland, a director of the ACU, and a conservative activist in Maryland who twice chaired the Reagan campaign in that state, was appointed director of the Office of Personnel Management. Perhaps encouraged by the Reagan victory, in 1984 James Kolbe was elected Republican congressman from the fifth district in Arizona following service in Vietnam, a career in real estate, and six years in the Arizona Senate.

Later, during the Gulf War in the Bush administration, former YAFer and John Birch Society veteran Scott Stanley led a pro-war group. As Sara Diamond has noted, Stanley and others were later indicted for "failing to report millions of dollars they received from Kuwait as part of a propaganda campaign to sway public opinion in favor of war." Other early YAFers who followed through with political careers include former *New Guard* editor Daniel Joy, who became an ACU board member and legislative assistant to Senator James Buckley; and Stephen Winchell, YAF's Michigan director for Youth for Goldwater in 1964, who went to work for the Viguerie Company before starting his own firm in 1975.

By the 1980s a second generation of YAFers had emerged. Perhaps the central figure was Dana Rohrabacher, who served as a speechwriter in the Reagan years and was later elected to Congress from California. A former editorial writer for the *Orange County Register*, Rohrabacher chaired the California state chapter of YAF during the late 1960s. Other YAFers from the second generation who joined the Reagan administration included Michelle Easton as an under secretary in the Department of Education, James Lacy in a similar position in the Department of Commerce, and former YAF executive director Frank Donatelli, who became a field man for the Reagan campaign. Numerous other YAFers dotted the Reagan campaign in state organizations throughout the country. In addition, Ronald Docksai, former YAF chair, became a legislative assistant to Senator Orrin Hatch and chaired the Council for Inter-American Security, a conservative foreign policy think tank. He was joined at the latter organization by former YAF activist L. Francis Bouchey. John Buckley, former chair of YAF, was elected to the Virginia legislature. John Dolan became chair of the National Conservative Political Action Committee, a leading right-wing PAC. Randall Teague, former YAF executive director, became an administrative assistant to Congressman Jack Kemp. Former Indiana YAF chairman R. Emmett Tyrrell Jr. became editor-in-chief of the *American Spectator* and a biting critic of moderates and liberals. The publisher of the magazine, John Von Kannon, was also a former YAFer.

From the late 1960s into the 1990s, arguably the most influential former YAFer was Richard Viguerie. An early and obviously adept student of Marvin Liebman's fund-raising tactics, Viguerie was the individual most responsible for the rise and influence of direct-mail fund-raising in the United States. Because of his philosophical convictions and conservative activism, Viguerie's expertise gave conservative causes a seemingly insurmountable advantage over their liberal opponents. Like Howard Phillips and Paul Weyrich, Viguerie remained somewhat disenchanted with the Republican Party and constantly sought new organizations or coalitions to advance the conservative agenda. He also moved beyond political conservatism to embrace the cultural conservatism of the 1980s. Indeed, he became one of the central figures in the shadows of that effort, an individual whose fund-raising wizardry was responsible for many of its public relations successes. Viguerie formed the Richard Viguerie Company, expanded his computer-based mail efforts, became chief fund-raiser for the National Conservative Political Action Committee (NCPAC), and started the *Conservative Digest* to publicize the efforts of the New Right. In 1980 he wrote *The New Right: We're Ready to Lead* as a clarion call to the New Right.

The emergence of this new conservative leadership was no accident. From its formation in 1960, Young Americans for Freedom had demonstrated that there were two sides to activism in the sixties. YAF provided youthful conservatives with a functioning political action organization not tied completely to the election cycle or to party hierarchies. Since it was neither candidate-dependent nor candidate-specific, YAF was able to maintain a continuing presence in the face of electoral adversity. When the war in Vietnam, riots in American cities, and the steady erosion of traditional institutions and authorities led people to question the need for continued change and doubt their own and their country's ability to accommodate that change, the conservatism advanced by Young Americans for Freedom gained strength. As before, this resurgent conservatism was not unsullied by racism or reaction. And as before, it attracted extreme voices who clamored for radical retrenchment and attacked moderates. Unlike the Left, whose organizational energies and spirit seemed to have died by the end of the sixties, the Right was just beginning to flex its muscles.

Appendix A   The Sharon Statement

Adopted by the Young Americans for Freedom
in conference at Sharon, Conn., September 9–11, 1960

In this time of moral and political crisis, it is the responsibility of the youth of America to affirm certain eternal truths.

We, as young conservatives, believe:

That foremost among the transcendent values is the individual's use of his God-given free will, whence derives his right to be free from the restrictions of arbitrary force;

That liberty is indivisible, and that political freedom cannot long exist without economic freedom;

That the purposes of government are to protect these freedoms through the preservation of internal order, the provision of national defense, and the administration of justice;

That when government ventures beyond these rightful functions, it accumulates power which tends to diminish order and liberty;

That the Constitution of the United States is the best arrangement yet devised for empowering government to fulfill its proper role, while restraining it from the concentration and abuse of power;

That the genius of the Constitution—the division of powers—is summed

Source: Buckley Papers, Box 12, folder: YAF.

up in the clause which reserves primacy to the several states, or to the people, in those spheres not specifically delegated to the Federal Government;

That the market economy, allocating resources by the free play of supply and demand, is the single economic system compatible with the requirements of personal freedom and constitutional government, and that it is at the same time the most productive supplier of human needs;

That when government interferes with the work of the market economy, it tends to reduce the moral and physical strength of the nation; that when it takes from one man to bestow on another, it diminishes the incentive of the first, the integrity of the second, and the moral autonomy of both;

That we will be free only so long as the national sovereignty of the United States is secure: that history shows periods of freedom are rare, and can exist only when free citizens concertedly defend their rights against all enemies;

That the forces of international Communism are, at present, the greatest single threat to these liberties;

That the United States should stress victory over, rather than coexistence with, this menace; and

That American foreign policy must be judged by this criterion: does it serve the just interests of the United States?

	Attendees,
Appendix B	*Sharon Conference*

Sharon, Conn.
(Sept. 10–11, 1960)

James Abstine
Indianapolis, Indiana
INDIANA UNIVERSITY

Robert Caruthers Adams
Westport, Connecticut
UNIVERSITY OF WISCONSIN

John Baxter
Chicago, Illinois

Eliot D. Bernat
Sarasota, Florida
NORTHWESTERN GRADUATE SCHOOL OF BUSINESS
    ADMINISTRATION

Arthur Bingham
Bloomfield, Connecticut
COLUMBIA UNIVERSITY

Source: Buckley Papers, Box 12, folder: YAF.

Marjorie E. Bingham
Bloomfield, Connecticut

Robert O. Boardman
Belmont, Massachusetts
HARVARD BUSINESS SCHOOL

Anne M. Bobson
New York, New York
HUNTER COLLEGE

David Bontrager
Elkhart, Indiana
HANOVER COLLEGE

William S. Bowman
Louisville, Kentucky
N.Y.U. LAW SCHOOL

James George Boylan
Seattle, Washington
UNIVERSITY OF WASHINGTON

R. Dennis Brennen
Bronx, New York
MANHATTAN COLLEGE

Douglas Caddy, Exec. Dir.
McGraw-Edison Committee for Public Affairs
New York, New York

Francis Cassidy, Jr.
New Haven, Connecticut
YALE UNIVERSITY

Annette Y. Courtemanche
Springfield Gardens, New York
MOLLOY COLLEGE

Regis Courtemanche
Springfield Gardens, New York

Richard C. Cowan
Fort Worth, Texas
YALE UNIVERSITY

Robert Croll
Glencoe, Illinois
NORTHWESTERN UNIVERSITY

Carol Dawson
Arlington, Virginia

Carl Decapua
Indianapolis, Indiana
INDIANA CENTRAL COLLEGE

George C. Decas
Wareham, Massachusetts
UNIVERSITY OF PENNSYLVANIA LAW SCHOOL

John DeVault
Springfield, Illinois
MACMURRAY COLLEGE

George M.C. Dole
Merion, Pennsylvania
HARVARD UNIVERSITY

Jeanette Doronzo
New York, New York
HUNTER COLLEGE

Lee Edwards
Washington, D.C.

John H. Eilert
Sterling, Illinois
FORDHAM COLLEGE

Stan Evans
Indianapolis News
Indianapolis, Indiana

Ed Facey
Brooklyn, New York
LONG ISLAND UNIVERSITY

David Franke
New York, New York

George W. Gaines
New Iberia, Louisiana

Ann-Marie Gleeson
New York, New York
MARYMOUNT COLLEGE (NYC)

Robert Goldsborough
House Un-American Activities Committee
Washington, D.C.

Andy Gollan
c/o *National Review*
New York, New York
UNIVERSITY OF MIAMI

Anne L. Goodspeed
Natick, Massachusetts
NORTHWESTERN UNIVERSITY

Frank Christian Gray
New Haven, Connecticut
YALE UNIVERSITY

Frank M. Grazioso
New Haven, Connecticut
YALE UNIVERSITY

John P. Greenagel
Edina, Minnesota
UNIVERSITY OF MINNESOTA

Robert Harley
Georgetown University
Washington, D.C.

G. Daniel Harden
Minneapolis, Minnesota
UNIVERSITY OF MINNESOTA

Katherine Hartter
Boulder, Colorado
UNIVERSITY OF COLORADO

Haywood H. Hillyer, III
New Orleans , Louisiana
TULANE UNIVERSITY

Robert M. Hurt
New Haven, Connecticut
YALE LAW SCHOOL

Michael Jaffe
Jamaica, L.I., New York

Paul Jankiewicz
Highland, New York
FORDHAM UNIVERSITY

Dick Jorandby
Minneapolis, Minnesota
UNIVERSITY OF MINNESOTA

Peter M. Kilcullen
Alexandria, Virginia
UNIVERSITY OF VIRGINIA

James Kolbe
Patagonia, Arizona
NORTHWESTERN UNIVERSITY

John W. Kolbe
Patagonia, Arizona
NORTHWESTERN UNIVERSITY

Herbert V. Kohler, Jr.
Kohler, Wisconsin
KNOX COLLEGE

James J. Lee
New York, New York
NEW YORK UNIVERSITY

Don Lipsett
Indianapolis, Indiana

Bruce A. McAllister
Brooklyn, New York
HARVARD LAW SCHOOL

Carl T. McIntire
Collingswood, New Jersey
SHELTON COLLEGE, RINGWOOD, NEW JERSEY

Eileen S. McIntosh
Winnetka, Illinois
BARAT COLLEGE

Walter V. McLaughlin, Jr.
Philadelphia, Pennsylvania
HARVARD UNIVERSITY

J. Alan MacKay
Rutherford, New Jersey
HARVARD LAW SCHOOL

Mary Ann Krasusky
Grosse Ile, Michigan
UNIVERSITY OF DETROIT

Joseph P. Leo
New Brunswick, New Jersey
RUTGERS UNIVERSITY

Ross D. MacKenzie
Winnetka, Illinois
YALE UNIVERSITY

William J. Madden, Jr.
Washington, D.C.
HOLY CROSS COLLEGE

E. Victor Milione, I.S.I.
Philadelphia, Pennsylvania

Jack E. Molesworth
Boston, Massachusetts

Carol Ann Nevin
Baltimore, Maryland
UNIVERSITY OF MARYLAND

Paul V. Niemeyer
South Bend, Indiana
KENYON COLLEGE

Mr. Gale Pfund
Madison, Wisconsin
UNIVERSITY OF WISCONSIN

Howard Phillips
Brighton, Massachusetts
HARVARD UNIVERSITY

Richard F. Plechner, Esq.
Metuchen, New Jersey

Mrs. Robert W. Preston
Roslyn Heights, New York

Lawrence L. Reif
Lincoln, Illinois

Thomas E. Reilly, Jr.
Indianapolis, Indiana
STANFORD UNIVERSITY

Peter Wheeler Reiss
Sheboygan, Wisconsin
MARQUETTE UNIVERSITY

W. Munro Roberts, III (& Wife)
St. Louis, Missouri
WASHINGTON UNIVERSITY, ST. LOUIS SCHOOL OF LAW

William A. Rusher
New York, New York

Clen Ryan
New York, New York
GEORGETOWN UNIVERSITY

Allan H. Ryskind
Washington, D.C.
GEORGETOWN SCHOOL OF FOREIGN SERVICE

Robert M. Schuchman
New York, New York
YALE UNIVERSITY

Robert Schuettinger
New York, New York
COLUMBIA UNIVERSITY (GRAD. SCHOOL)
AND CHICAGO GRAD.

Bill Schulz
Washington, D.C.
ANTIOCH COLLEGE

D. Bruce Shine
Brookline, Massachusetts
TUSCULUM COLLEGE

Keith E. Simons
Minneapolis, Minnesota
UNIVERSITY OF MINNESOTA

Stephen Marc Slepin
West Miami, Florida
UNIVERSITY OF MIAMI GRADUATE SCHOOL

Deborah C. Steele
West Springfield, Massachusetts
SHELTON COLLEGE, RINGWOOD, NEW JERSEY

David P. Stuhr
Ho-Ho-Kus, New Jersey
R.P.I. GRADUATE SCHOOL

Doris Sukup
Marymount College
New York, New York

(Miss) Lyn Jan-Tausch
Short Hills, New Jersey
SMITH COLLEGE

Clayton H. Thomas, Jr.
Philadelphia, Pennsylvania
UNIVERSITY OF PENNSYLVANIA LAW SCHOOL

Ken Thompson
c/o *Army Times*
Washington, D.C.

Matthew J. Torre
Richmond Hill, New York
ST. JOHN'S UNIVERSITY

John A. Waldron
New York, New York
FORDHAM UNIVERSITY

John Weicher
Chicago, Illinois
UNIVERSITY OF CHICAGO

Brian B. Whalen
Toronto, Canada
LOYOLA UNIVERSITY

Dan Young
Indianapolis, Indiana
INDIANA CENTRAL COLLEGE

Charles Ceroala
National Review
New York, New York

William Cotter
New York, New York
FORDHAM UNIVERSITY

Tom Colvin
Davidson, North Carolina
DAVIDSON COLLEGE

Mike Uhlmann
Yale Daily News
New Haven, Connecticut
YALE UNIVERSITY

Mary Wahlig
National Review
New York, New York

A Note on Manuscript Sources

THE LIFEBLOOD of history lies in archival materials, and a brief note on the manuscript sources for Young Americans for Freedom is needed to explain what went into this study and to point the way for future scholars. Unfortunately, there is no central manuscript archive for either YAF or the right wing. While the Left has some superb collections at the State Historical Society of Wisconsin, and SDS archives are even microfilmed, no core of YAF manuscripts exists in any repository. It seems useful, therefore, to note briefly the various manuscript sources I did uncover apart from major collections at presidential libraries that document mainstream politics and particular administrations.

Without question the most important materials for this study are in the William Rusher Papers at the Library of Congress. These contain materials on conservatism, Republican party politics, and YAF, as well as a great deal of material on *National Review*. Much of the collection for 1960–64 was microfilmed several years ago, but using a peculiar system no longer manufactured and difficult to view on modern equipment. One must come equipped with wrenches and screwdrivers, and the materials on the reels are not paginated or referenced in any way. But the rewards for persistence are great. Also significant, but less so, are the materials in the William F. Buckley Papers at Sterling Library, Yale University. See particularly the inter-office memos for revealing insights. Two other major sources of right-wing manuscript materials were of use in this study. The collections at The Hoover Institution, Stanford University, provide an assortment of materials on the Right. The papers of Marvin Liebman Associates are good, as are those of Walter Judd and scattered other collections (Elizabeth Churchill Brown, Ralph de Toledano, Joseph Dumbacher, Myers Lowman, and Henry Regnery). The other locale with pertinent collections is the University of Oregon Library, which has the Lucille Crain Papers along with several other collections for figures active on the Right. None, however, were directly involved with YAF.

Given that none of the above contain significant writings by YAFers themselves, I canvassed many prominent early members of YAF in search of manuscript materials. Several individuals responded, loaning me items they had retained over the years. These are cited in the notes by a reference to an individual's papers without any designation as to their location. All remain in the hands of their creators. Particularly helpful in this respect were Robert Croll, John Kolbe, George McDonnell, Douglas Caddy, and Diarmuid O'Scannlain. By the time I reached Robert Bauman he had just moved again and had thrown away all his materials from the early years of YAF—materials I believe constituted in effect the YAF archives. Howard Phillips told me that he had nothing to share "at this time." William Schulz said that he had nothing. Richard Viguerie and Lee Edwards did not respond to inquiries. For a few YAF printed materials see the microfilmed Right-Wing Collection of the University of Iowa Libraries, especially reel 154. The national office of Young Americans for Freedom (which still exists) may have additional materials of great importance, but they refused to provide access or help in any way with this project. Perhaps the most important gap in the available materials is at the state and local chapter level. If we are to move beyond a view of YAF from the top leadership cadre, we must uncover sources that reflect concerns at those levels.

Other collections that proved useful include the Americans for Democratic Action Papers (on microfilm). Buried there are the papers for Student ADA along with many key papers for the National Student Association. The Papers of the Democratic National Committee, at the LBJ Library in Austin, Texas, consisted largely of newspaper clippings and were disappointing. Somewhat more useful were the Drew Pearson Papers, deposited at the LBJ Library. Also in Austin, at the Center for American History, the Barry Goldwater Collection provided a few gems. Unfortunately, the Goldwater Papers at the Arizona Historical Foundation seem to contain nothing of political significance. At the Cornell University Library, the F. Clifton White Papers were essential for Goldwater efforts, and both the Republican National Committee Papers and the William Miller Papers also provided some useful materials, although the latter was disappointing with respect to 1964. The Charles F. Norton Collection at Cornell also contains right-wing materials. Republican party views can be found in various collections at the Eisenhower Presidential Library in Abilene, Kansas, as well as in the Richard Nixon Pre-Presidential Papers at the Southwest Region of the National Archives, Laguna Niguel, California. Finally, at the Kennedy Library in Boston, Massachusetts the most useful collection was the Lee White Papers, which contained numerous materials and confidential reports on the right wing.

Notes

Introduction

1. This is from the January 7, 1995 lecture in his course, available on the World Wide Web at http://www.pff.org/renew/trans195.html.
2. Peter Collier and David Horowitz, *Destructive Generation: Second Thoughts About the Sixties* (New York: Holt, Rinehart and Winston, 1989), 14, 15.
3. "The Sixties Are Dead: Long Live the Nineties," *Imprimis* 24 (January 1995): 1.
4. Ibid., 3.
5. Leo Ribuffo, "Why Is There So Much Conservatism in the United States and Why Do So Few Historians Know Anything About It?" *American Historical Review* 99 (April 1994): 445. This essay is part of a three-part forum on American conservatism.
6. For a good discussion of this point, see Alan Brinkley, "The Problem of American Conservatism," *American Historical Review* 99 (April 1994): 409–429.
7. Speech delivered January 1, 1960, in John F. Kennedy, *The Strategy of Peace* (New York: Popular Library, 1960), 28, 241–242.
8. Arthur Schlesinger Jr., "The New Mood in Politics," in Arthur Schlesinger Jr., *The Politics of Hope* (Boston: Houghton Mifflin, 1962), 82, 92–93. The essay was originally published in the January 1960 issue of *Esquire*.
9. Draft of his "The Shape of National Politics to Come: A Memorandum," Gen. Corresp., Box 675, folder: Arthur Schlesinger, Jr., Nixon Pre-Presidential Papers, National Archives, Pacific Southwest Region (hereafter NPP).
10. For Bowles's comments, see Chester Bowles, *The Conscience of a Liberal* (New York: Harper & Row, 1962). "The Moral Gap" was a Commencement Address at Smith College, June 5, 1960; see 346–347. "The Watershed of the Sixties" was an address to the Yale Law Forum, November 21, 1961; see 286–287. Nixon's views are in "Our Resolve is Running Strong," *Life* 49, 29 August 1960, 87–88, 91–93. For Kennedy see "We Must Climb to the Hilltop," *Life* 49, 22 August 1960, 70B, 72, 75–77. An example of other liberals' support for this view is in Edward D. Hollander, National

Director of Americans for Democratic Action, to Thomas K. Finletter, 26 February 1959, reel 25, Americans for Democratic Action Papers (ADA) (microfilm).

11. Lee Edwards, "The Other Sixties: A Flag-Waver's Memoir," *Policy Review* 46 (Fall 1988): 58.

12. Few historians even acknowledge the importance of the right wing in the early 1960s. For one who does see David Farber (ed.), *The Sixties: From Memory to History* (Chapel Hill: University of North Carolina Press, 1994), 4. See also Patrick Allitt, *Catholic Intellectuals and Conservative Politics in America, 1950–1985* (Ithaca, N.Y.: Cornell University Press, 1993), 305–306. Charles Perrow's "The Sixties Observed," in Myer N. Zald and John McCarthy (eds.), *The Dynamics of Social Movements: Resource Mobilization, Social Control, and Tactics* (Cambridge: Winthrop Publishers, 1979), 192–193 is more typical in his focus on civil rights and (Left) student movements. For a discussion and analysis of some early currents of change see two articles by John Andrew: "The Impending Crises of the 1960s: National Goals and National Purpose," *Viet Nam Generation* 6, nos. 1–2 (1994): 30–41, and "Cracks in the Consensus: The Rockefeller Brothers Fund Special Studies Project and Eisenhower's America," *Presidential Studies Quarterly* (forthcoming). See also Joseph Conlin, *The Troubles: A Jaundiced Glance Back At the Movement of the Sixties* (New York: Franklin Watts, 1982), 19–20. The final quotation is from James C. Roberts, *The Conservative Decade: Emerging Leaders of the 1980s* (Westport, Conn.: Arlington House, 1980), 25.

13. A copy of the cartoon, undated, is in the Robert Croll Papers. See also Dan Wakefield, *New York in the Fifties* (Boston: Houghton Mifflin, 1992), 270. Another expression of this sentiment is in Stanton Evans's introduction to the YAF edition of Barry Goldwater's *The Conscience of a Conservative* (1960; Special Reprint, Young Americans for Freedom, 1970). The YAF edition was published in 1970 to celebrate YAF's 10th anniversary; Evans's remarks are an unpaginated introduction.

14. Lee Edwards, quoted in Roberts, *The Conservative Decade*, 26.

15. Throughout the text I have occasionally noted but not elaborated on these parallels. For greater detail on SDS and the Left see Kirkpatrick Sale, *SDS* (New York: Vintage, 1973) and James Miller, *"Democracy Is in the Streets": From Port Huron to the Siege of Chicago* (New York: Simon & Schuster, 1987).

Chapter One   The Origins of the "New Right"

1. The best study of postwar conservative growth is George Nash, *The Conservative Intellectual Movement in America Since 1945* (New York: Basic Books, 1976). Much of the discussion that follows is informed by his work. Nash explores these intellectual currents in much more detail, of course. I am concerned here only with providing an outline of these efforts. See also Paul Gottfried and Thomas Fleming, *The Conservative Movement* (Boston: Twayne, 1988), chapter 1.

2. Ibid., 30–56 passim. William F. Buckley Jr. was the first president of ISI in 1953.

3. A. Louise Sperling, quoted in Mary Brennan, *Turning Right in the Sixties* (Chapel Hill: University of North Carolina Press, 1995), 145 n. 13. For Meyer see his "On What Ball?" *National Review*, 4 January 1958, quoted in Frank Meyer, *The Conservative Mainstream* (New Rochelle, N.Y.: Arlington House, 1969), 85. For Burnham, see Kevin Smant, "Whither Conservatism? James Burnham and *National Review*, 1955–1964," *Continuity* 15 (Fall-Winter 1991): 91.

4. For glimpses of this change see William Rusher, "The New Right," in Robert Whitaker (ed.), *The New Right Papers* (New York: St. Martin's Press, 1982), 6; William Rusher, *The Rise of the New Right* (New York: William Morrow and Co., 1984); James Burnham, *The War We Are In: The Last Decade and the Next* (New

Rochelle, N.Y.: Arlington House, 1967). John Judis, in *William F. Buckley, Jr.* (New York: Simon & Schuster, 1988), argues that the emergence of the New Right caught Buckley and his fellow editors by surprise; see p. 183. A perceptive critique of the New Right's understanding of the twentieth-century revolution in government is in Samuel Francis, *Beautiful Losers: Essays on the Failure of American Conservatism* (Columbia: University of Missouri Press, 1993); see especially pp. 224–227. Francis draws particular attention to the difference between elite and grass-roots conservatism. This is an important distinction, and is reflected in the problems Buckley had with the John Birch Society.

5. Buckley, *Up from Liberalism* (New York: Hillman Books, 1961), 15–16. This is the paperback edition; the book was originally published in 1959.
6. Ibid., 114, 126–127.
7. Ibid., 186, 197.
8. Ibid., 208.
9. Ibid., 210.
10. Ibid., 219.
11. Arthur Aughey, Greta Jones, and W.T.M. Riches, *The Conservative Political Tradition in Britain and the United States* (Rutherford, N.J.: Fairleigh Dickinson University Press, 1992), 17. For a critical interpretation of Buckley's arguments see Charles L. Markmann, *The Buckleys: A Family Examined* (New York: William Morrow & Co., 1973), 157–165. It is important to note that while Buckley became the intellectual godfather for a new generation of conservatives, his was not the guiding hand of political activism. That belonged to William Rusher. Careful readers will note that throughout this study most of the materials on conservative activism come from the Rusher Papers rather than the Buckley Papers, a reflection of that difference.
12. Lee Edwards, "The Other Sixties: A Flag-Waver's Memoir," *Policy Review* 46 (Fall 1988): 58; Barry Goldwater, *With No Apologies: The Personal and Political Memoirs of United States Senator Barry M. Goldwater* (New York: William Morrow & Co., 1979), 99–100.
13. Barry Goldwater, *The Conscience of a Conservative* (New York: Hillman Books, 1960), 10–11. I have used the paperback edition, which was the most widely available edition in 1960. For some comment on Goldwater's effort, see H.W. Brands, *The Devil We Knew: Americans and the Cold War* (New York: Oxford University Press, 1993), 99–100. The best study of postwar conservatism remains Nash, *The Conservative Intellectual Movement in America Since 1945*.
14. Goldwater, *Conscience*, 12–13.
15. Ibid., 17–18, 23.
16. Ibid., 33–38, 58–59.
17. Ibid., 71–72.
18. Ibid., 91–100. Goldwater's fraternity speech is cited in Fred J. Cook, *Barry Goldwater: Extremist of the Right* (New York: Grove Press, 1964), 76. Goldwater concluded that "where fraternities are not allowed, communism flourishes."
19. Cook, *Barry Goldwater*, 100–126. The quotation is on pp. 126–127. See also Theodore Windt Jr., *Presidents and Protesters: Political Rhetoric in the 1960s* (Tuscaloosa: University of Alabama Press, 1990), 241.
20. Arthur Schlesinger Jr., *Kennedy or Nixon: Does It Make Any Difference?* (New York: Macmillan, 1960), 18. For one example of Kennedy's depiction of the decade see "Speech by Senator John F. Kennedy, Washington, January 14, 1960," in Arthur Schlesinger Jr. (ed.), *History of American Presidential Elections, 1798–1968*, 4 vols. (New York: Chelsea House, 1971), 4: 3537. Fairlie's comment is in his *The Kennedy Promise: The Politics of Expectation* (New York: Doubleday, 1973), 87–88. A similar evaluation, first published in the January 1960 issue of *Foreign Affairs*, is in Adlai

Stevenson, "Putting First Things First—A Democratic View," in Adlai Stevenson, *Putting First Things First, A Democratic View: Recent Speeches and Papers by Adlai Stevenson* (New York: Random House, 1960), 3–26. For Nixon's comments, see his speech at the Mid-Island Plaza Shopping Center, Hicksville, New York, 20 September 1960, in *Freedom of Communications. Final Report of the Committee on Commerce, United States Senate, Prepared by its Subcommittee of the Subcommittee on Communications. Part 2*, Senate Report 994, 87th Cong., 1st Sess. (Washington: GPO, 1961), 332.

21. Editors of *Fortune, America in the Sixties: The Economy and the Society* (New York: Harper & Brothers, 1958), passim. The quotations are on pp. xii, xvi, and 89.

22. William Atwood, "How America Feels as We Enter the Soaring Sixties," *Look* 24, 5 January 1960, 12, 15.

23. Daniel Bell, *The End of Ideology: On the Exhaustion of Political Ideas in the Fifties* (New York: Free Press, 1960). I have used the 1962 paperback edition. The quotations are on pp. 16, 120–121, and 404. For a trenchant analysis of Bell's thesis, see Richard Pells, *The Liberal Mind in a Conservative Age: American Intellectuals in the 1940s and 1950s* (New York: Harper & Row, 1985), 133–135.

24. For discussion of these matters see Marian J. Morton, *The Terrors of Ideological Politics: Liberal Historians in a Conservative Mood* (Cleveland: The Press of Case Western Reserve University, 1972), esp. 70–73; Nathan Liebowitz, *Daniel Bell and the Agony of Modern Liberalism* (Westport, Conn.: Greenwood Press, 1985), 23, 156; Seymour Martin Lipset, "The End of Ideology?" in R. Serge Denisoff (ed.), *The Sociology of Dissent* (New York: Harcourt Brace Jovanovich, 1974), 128–138; Lawson H. Bowling, "The New Party of Memory: Intellectual Origins of Neoconservatism, 1945-1960" (Ph.D. diss., Columbia University, 1990), 300–301.

25. Niebuhr's comments are in "America—1960: A Symposium," *The New Republic* 142, 15 February 1960, 15. For Geltman's analysis, see his essay, "Liberalism and Lassitude," *Dissent* 7 (Winter 1960): 25–30; quotations on pp. 26 and 29–30.

26. William F. Buckley Jr., "The Decline of Partisanship," *National Review* 7, 14 February 1959), 523–524, 527; C. Wright Mills, "Letter to the New Left" [1960], in Chaim Waxman (ed.), *The End of Ideology Debate* (New York: Funk & Wagnalls, 1968), 126–140. The quotation is on p. 130.

27. Paul Goodman, *Growing Up Absurd: Problems of Youth in the Organized Society* (1956; New York: Vintage, 1960), 168–169; Kenneth Keniston, *The Uncommitted: Alienated Youth in American Society* (1960; New York: Dell, 1965), 3, 5, 419–420, 428.

28. Richard Flacks, *Youth and Social Change* (Chicago: Markham Publishing Co., 1971), 2.

29. James Wechsler, *Reflections of an Angry Middle-Aged Editor* (New York: Random House, 1960), 67.

30. There are numerous expressions of this shift. For Eddy, see Ed Murray, "The Neatnik," *Dissent* 7 (Spring 1960): 150 and "Tensions beneath Apathy," *The Nation* 188, 16 May 1959, 440–444. Student views are in United States National Student Association, *The Idea of a Student* (Philadelphia: USNSA, 1959), passim; Robert A. Haber, "From Protest to Radicalism: An Appraisal of the Student Movement, 1960," *Venture* 2 (September 1960): 15–18; David Horowitz, *Student* (New York: Ballantine Books, 1962), 7–36, passim; and Alan Haber of SDS to William Rusher (*National Review*), 15 July 1960, reel 8, William A. Rusher Papers (hereafter cited as Rusher Papers).

31. Clarence B. Kelland, "Eisenhower's Fatal Legacy to G.O.P.: The Road Back from the 'New Republicanism,'" *Human Events* 15, 22 December 1958, A2. See also the issues for 10 February 1958: 1 and 14 April 1958: Article II.

For brief overviews see William B. Hixson Jr., *Search for the American Right Wing: An Analysis of the Social Science Record, 1955–1987* (Princeton: Princeton University Press, 1992), and Eckard V. Toy Jr., "Ideology and Conflict in American Ultraconservatism, 1945–1960" (Ph.D. diss., University of Oregon, 1965).

32. "On What Ball?", in Meyer, *The Conservative Mainstream*, 85; William F. Buckley Jr., "The Tranquil World of Dwight D. Eisenhower," *National Review*, 18 January 1958, 59; transcript of "The Open Mind," broadcast on NBC-TV, 6 December 1959, copy in Gen. Corresp., Box 360, folder: Emmett Hughes, NPP. The YR conventions are noted in *Human Events* 14, 29 June 1957, and *Human Events* 16, 1 July 1959, 3.

33. Frank Meyer, "The Politics of 'the Impossible' II: 1960 Dilemma," *National Review*, 19 December 1959; reprinted in Meyer, *Conservative Mainstream*, 237. For Jane B. Smith's warning see Smith to James F. Berti, 29 September 1959, Gen. Corresp., Box 551, folder: *National Review*, NPP. Student efforts for Nixon are noted in Dean Borton to Carol Dawson, 16 November 1959, reel 4, and Robert Bauman to William A. Rusher, 1 December 1959, reel 3, Rusher Papers. These letters also indicate that efforts to mobilize college support for Nixon were not met with complete enthusiasm from the Nixon campaign staff.

34. Russell Kirk, "From the Academy: They Are Stirring in the Colleges," *National Review*, 12 March 1960, 171. The Nixon camp clearly tracked all signs of this conservative upsurge, for copies of these articles can be found in the Gen. Correspondence files, NPP.

35. The administration position is noted in Arthur S. Flemming to James Hagerty, 1 December 1959, Box 21, folder: The President (3), Arthur S. Flemming Papers, DDE. For Caddy's role see Douglas Caddy, "Birth of the Conservative Movement," unpublished manuscript.

36. David Franke, "The Student Loyalty Oath," *The Individualist* 4 (December 1959): 1, 4. See also *Human Events* 17, 14 January 1960, 2.

37. Pollack to Thomas Flinn of Oberlin College, 2 February 1960, reel 139, ADA Papers. Caddy's letter is in the *New York Times*, 5 February 1960. A note on the failure of the repeal is in Flemming to Hagerty, 1 December 1959, Box 21, folder: The President (3), Flemming Papers, DDE. For an overview of the dangers of such loyalty matters see Selma R. Williams, *Red-Listed: Haunted by the Washington Witch Hunt* (Reading, Mass.: Addison-Wesley, 1993), 34. Franke also doubted that the Soviets had actually launched *Sputnik*, believing it an elaborate hoax to scare Americans.

38. Gerald Johnson, "An Outburst of Servility," *The New Republic* 142, 8 February 1960, 11.

39. "By National Student Committee for the Loyalty Oath, Douglas Caddy, Chairman," printed in *The Congressional Digest* 39 (1960): 122, 126. For a list of college presidents in support of the oath, see *Human Events* 17, 10 March 1960, 4.

40. Croll's remarks are in a Youth For Goldwater press pelease, 21 July 1960, in the John Kolbe Papers. For the Midwest Federation meeting, see the Des Moines *Sunday Register*, 10 April 1960, 6L. Progress of the Youth for Goldwater campaign can be followed in the *Washington Post*, 25 May 1960, C2 and *Human Events* 17, 26 May 1960, 3.

41. Rusher to James Wick, 27 April 1960, reel 14, Rusher Papers.

42. A copy of the press release announcing the formation of this group is in Gen. Corresp., Box 293, folder: Barry Goldwater, clippings, 1960 (2 of 3), NPP.

43. Abstine to Nixon, 31 May 1960, Gen. Corresp., Box 18, folder: James Abstine, NPP. See also Abstine to Mid-West Volunteers for Nixon, 21 May 1960, Gen. Corresp.,

Box 18, folder: James Abstine, NPP; and the Des Moines *Sunday Register*, 10 April 1960, 6L.

44. The best study of the committee is Walter Goodman, *The Committee: The Extraordinary Career of the House Committee on Un-American Activities* (New York: Farrar, Straus & Giroux, 1964); see pp. 423–433 for the events leading up to the May protests. The editorial from *The Daily Californian* is cited in the study of the 1960 HUAC riots by Albert T. Anderson and Bernice P. Biggs (eds.), *A Focus on Rebellion: Materials for Analysis* (San Francisco: Chandler Publishing Co., 1962), 5.

45. Both comments are in William F. Buckley Jr. (ed.), *The Committee and Its Critics: A Calm Review of the House Committee on Un-American Activities* (Chicago: Henry Regnery Co., 1963); see pp. 32, 178.

46. Anderson and Biggs, *A Focus on Rebellion*, 101–105; Buckley, *The Committee*, 178–200. The quotation is on p. 178. For an overview of this issue, see Kenneth O'Reilly, *Hoover and the Un-Americans: The FBI, HUAC, and the Red Menace* (Philadelphia: Temple University Press, 1983), especially pp. 259–260 and 379 n. 1.

47. Youth for Goldwater press release, 21 July 1960, John Kolbe Papers. For a critical perspective on "Operation Abolition," see Frank Donner, *The Un-Americans* (New York: Ballantine Books, 1961), esp. 208, 214, 217. Also see Kenneth Rexroth, "The Students Take Over," *The Nation* 191, July 1960, 4–9; and Otto Feinstein, "Is There a Student Movement?" *New University Thought* 1 (Summer 1961): 23–29.

48. Goldwater's remark is quoted in *Time*, 23 June 1961. A clipping is in Box G235, folder: Barry Goldwater (2), Drew Pearson Papers, LBJL. For a brief overview of these events see Caddy, "Birth of the Conservative Movement," 10–14.

Chapter Two   Struggle over "Modern Republicanism"

1. Quoted by Howard Pyle, Deputy Assistant to the President, to Mrs. Jane Reining, 28 February 1957, DDE White House Central Files (WHCF), General File, Box 580, folder 109-A-17 (Modern Republicanism), (1), Dwight D. Eisenhower Presidential Library, Abilene, Kansas (DDE). This is from a 14 November 1956 press conference.

2. Arthur Larson, *A Republican Looks at His Party* (New York: Harper & Brothers, 1956), 11–19. The quotation is on p. 19. See also Jeff Broadwater, *Eisenhower & the Anti-Communist Crusade* (Chapel Hill: University of North Carolina Press, 1992), 19.

3. The dimensions of this effort have drawn only passing attention from historians. For Buckley's criticism see his "The Tranquil World of Dwight D. Eisenhower," *National Review*, 18 January 1958, 59. The best overall analysis is in Nash, *The Conservative Intellectual Movement in America since 1945*; see especially p. 256. Also see John Sloan, *Eisenhower and the Management of Prosperity* (Lawrence: University Press of Kansas, 1991), 63, and Rusher, *The Rise of the Right*, esp. 55.

4. For a synopsis of liberal hopes see Jim Heath, *Decade of Disillusionment: The Kennedy-Johnson Years* (Bloomington: Indiana University Press, 1975), 6–7. Formation of Citizens for Modern Republicanism is noted in Richard Graham (their chair) to Richard Nixon, 27 September 1957, General Correspondence, Box 152, folder: Citizens for Modern Republicanism, NPP.

5. "Principles and Heresies," *National Review* 5, 4 January 1958, 17. For Rockefeller's views see *Prospect for America: The Rockefeller Panel Reports* (New York: Doubleday, 1961). Evidence that Rockefeller kept Nixon informed of the panels' progress is in Rockefeller to Nixon, 3 April 1957, Gen. Corresp., Box 650, folder: Nelson Rockefeller 1955–59, NPP.

6. Confidental memorandum, Alcorn to Dwight Eisenhower, 15 December 1958,

Gen. Corresp., Box 25, folder: Hon. Meade Alcorn, NPP. Alcorn also noted that the G.O.P. did not have the money to implement these proposals fully.

7. Hutcheson to Nixon, 7 November 1958, Gen. Corresp., Box 364, folder: Thad Hutcheson, NPP.

8. Bassett to Nixon, 4 December 1958, Gen. Corresp., Box 66, folder: James Bassett (1), NPP. See also Craig Allen, *Eisenhower and the Mass Media: Peace, Prosperity, & Prime-Time TV* (Chapel Hill: University of North Carolina Press, 1993), 69.

9. L. Brent Bozell, "The 1958 Elections: Coroner's Report," *National Review* 6, 22 November 1958, 333–335.

10. Charles Percy Oral History, The Eisenhower Administration Project, Columbia University, 12. See also News Release, Republican National Committee, 25 February 1959, Box 22, folder: Republican National Committee (1), Arthur S. Flemming Papers, DDE. Demands from party liberals and conservatives are in Charlie McWhorter to Richard Nixon, 17 January 1959, Gen. Corresp., Box 25, folder: Hon. Meade Alcorn, NPP. Background on the committee is in Cornelius Cotter and Bernard Hennessy, *Politics Without Power: The National Party Committees* (New York: Atherton Press, 1964), 195–205. A briefer discussion is in David Murray, *Charles Percy of Illinois* (New York: Harper & Row, 1968), 51–53. Leading Congressional Republicans on the committee were Senator Everett Dirksen and Representative Charles Halleck. Eisenhower later found Henry Wriston of Brown University to chair the nonpartisan Presidential Committee on National Goals.

11. Alcorn's remarks are in a 13 March 1959 press release, Gen. Corresp., Box 25, folder: Hon. Meade Alcorn, NPP.

12. Charles Percy to Interior Secretary Fred Seaton, 24 March 1959, Republican Party Series, 1960 Campaign Subseries, Box 2, folder: G.O.P. National Convention, Miscellaneous (2), Fred Seaton Papers, DDE. Also see Cotter and Hennessy, *Politics Without Power*, 199–200.

13. Stephen Shadegg to Barry Goldwater, 6 April 1959; Barry Goldwater to Charles Percy, 10 April 1959; Stephen Shadegg to Barry Goldwater, 4 May 1959; Box 3H506, Barry Goldwater Collection, 1949–1965, Barker History Center, University of Texas at Austin (hereafter BG).

14. Nixon to Bob Finch, 13 July 1959, Gen. Corresp., Box 630, folder: Republican Committee on Program and Progress (4 of 4); and an undated (1959) memo from Finch to Nixon, Gen. Corresp., Box 588, folder: C.H. (Chuck) Percy (3 of 3), NPP. See also Percy to Arthur Flemming, 6 May 1959, Box 22, folder: Republican National Committee (1), Arthur S. Flemming Papers, DDE. Percy discussed the Harr memo in a 23 July 1959 letter to Nixon, Gen. Corresp., Box 588, folder: C.H. (Chuck) Percy (3 of 3), NPP.

15. Percy to members of the Republican Committee on Program and Progress, 8 September 1959, Box 22, folder: Republican National Committee (2), Arthur S. Flemming Papers, DDE; Percy to Nixon, 11 September 1959, Gen. Corresp., Box 588, folder: C.H. (Chuck) Percy (2 of 3), NPP; Shadegg to Barry Goldwater, 17 September 1959, Box 3H506, BG.

16. Republican Committee on Program and Progress, *Decisons for a Better America* (Garden City, N.Y.: Doubleday, 1960), 18–20, 103–104.

17. Ibid. The quotations are on pp. 30 and 21, respectively.

18. Ibid., 46.

19. Ibid., 89, 97–101. The quotations are on pp. 100 and 101.

20. Ibid., 151, 158, 173–174, 183.

21. Javits to Nixon, 29 January 1960, Gen. Corresp., Box 381, folder: Jacob K. Javits (2 of 3), NPP; George B. Fowler, treasurer of the Valley Paper Company of Holyoke,

Mass., to Spencer T. Olin, 3 November 1959, quoted in Toy, "Ideology and Conflict in American Ultraconservatism," 29.

22. Karl Hess, *In a Cause that Will Triumph: The Goldwater Campaign and the Future of Conservatism* (Garden City, N.Y.: Doubleday, 1967), 59–60.

23. Percy to Eisenhower, 8 February 1960, DDE Central Files, Official Files, Box 710, folder: 138-C-1-F, DDE. Eisenhower's remarks are noted in Javits to Nixon, 29 January 1960, Gen. Corresp., Box 381, folder: Jacob K. Javits (2 of 3), NPP.

24. *Human Events* 16, 4 March 1959, 2. A copy of Byrnes's speech is in the Gen. Corresp., Box 119, folder: The Hon. John W. Byrnes, NPP.

25. Bob Wilson, "The Challenge of Preserving Peace: Part I, The Sino-Soviet Peril," *Congressional Record* 106, Part 1, 86th Cong., 2d Sess. (19 January 1960), 799–802; Gerald Ford, "The Challenge of Preserving Peace: The Seven Dynamic Spearheads of Peace Power," *Congressional Record* 106, Part 1, 86th Cong., 2d Sess. (20 January 1960), 929–932; Robert Griffin, "The Challenge of Labor-Management Relations," *Congressional Record* 106, Part 1, 86th Cong., 2d Sess. (21 January 1960), 1026–1029.

26. John Rhodes, "The Challenge of Enlarging Economic Freedom for Our Children, Part I: The Perils to Economic Freedom," *Congressional Record* 106, Part 1, 86th Cong., 2d Sess. (21 January 1960), 1029–1032; Thomas Curtis, "The Challenge of Enlarging Economic Freedom for Our Children, Part II: The Five Potentials to Roll Back the Economic Peril," *Congressional Record* 106, Part 1, 86th Cong., 2d Sess. (25 January 1960), 1209–1213; Charles Halleck, "The Party Qualified to Meet the Challenges," *Congressional Record* 106, Part 1, 86th Cong., 2d Sess., 1213–1215. Republican Leverett Saltonstall of Massachusetts led a somewhat similar effort in the Senate, which focused on documenting the activities and achievements of the Eisenhower Administration since 1953; see the *Congressional Record* 106, Part 14, 86th Cong., 2d Sess. (1 September 1960), 19033–19089.

27. "Task Force Report: American Strategy and Strength," *Congressional Record* 106, Part 10, 86th Cong., 2d Sess. (20 June 1960), 13418–13502. Quotations are on pp. 13418, 13438, 13460, 13463.

28. Ibid., 13495–13499.

29. "Nineteen Sixty: A Study in Political Change," Box 12, folder: 1960 Campaign and Election, Robert Humphreys Papers, DDE. There were only six copies of the report; and only Eisenhower, Nixon, Leonard Hall, Robert Finch, and William J. Casey received copies. A good summary of public efforts to reexamine the nation's course is in Herbert S. Parmet, *Richard Nixon and His America* (Boston: Little, Brown, 1990), 347–362. Parmet cites Henry Kissinger as another who emphasized the need to encourage a new spirit rather than just manage existing problems; see pp. 361–362.

30. Ibid. For another view of the new decade from a Republican hopeful, see George Romney, "The Challenge of the Sixties," *Modern Age* 4 (Summer 1960): 229–234.

31. Nixon to Robinson, 9 April 1960, Gen. Corresp., Box 647, folder: Claude Robinson 1960 (3 of 3), NPP. See also Robinson to Nixon, 1 April 1960, ibid.; Richard Nixon, *The Challenges We Face* (New York: McGraw-Hill, 1960), 35, 54, 127; and Memoranda for the President, from Jim Hagerty, 21 March 1960, Dwight D. Eisenhower Papers, Ann Whitman Diary Series, Box 11, folder: (ACW) Diary, March 1960 (1), DDE. Robinson was head of Claude Robinson Research, Inc. and a personal friend of Nixon.

32. For a sample of southern feeling, see Mrs. John Britton to Robert Gray, Administrative Assistant to the President, 16 May 1960, WHCF, General File, Box 487, folder: 109-A-2, 1960 (4), DDE. *Human Events* 17, 25 May 1960, 3 warned about the dangers of the Percy appointment.

33. The de Toledano statement is in Gen. Corresp., Box 213, folder: Ralph, Nora, de Toledano (1 of 3), NPP. For correspondence about changes in the party see Robert Wood to Irving Salomon, 7 June 1957 and Morton C. Hull to DDE, 24 June 1957, WHCF, General File, Box 580, folder: 109-A-17 (3) and (4), DDE; Loyd Wright to Nixon, 18 December 1959, Gen. Corresp., Box 834, folder: Loyd Wright, NPP.

34. Meyer, "Principles and Heresies," *National Review* 7, 19 December 1959, 555; M. Stanton Evans, "The Anatomy of a Murder," *National Review* 7, 12 September 1959, 324.

35. Goldwater to Shadegg, 20 January 1960, Box 3H506, BG. For background to *The Conscience of A Conservative*, see Barry Goldwater, *Goldwater* (New York: Doubleday, 1988), 119–120; David Reinhard, *The Republican Right since 1945* (Lexington: The University Press of Kentucky, 1983), 161.

36. Goldwater to Rehnquist, 31 March 1960, Box 3H506, BG. Thad Hutcheson, G.O.P. state chairman for Texas, expressed similar sentiments. See Charlie McWhorter to Nixon, 29 March 1960, Gen. Corresp., Box 364, folder: Thad Hutcheson, NPP. For a brief overview of the Goldwater effort, see Thomas Payne, "A National versus a State Approach to Platform Making: Montana Republicans Go Along," in Paul Tillett (ed.), *Inside Politics: The National Conventions, 1960* (Dobbs Ferry, N.Y.: Oceana Publications, 1962), 96–104.

37. Loyd Wright to Patrick Hillings, 13 April 1960, Box 834, folder: Loyd Wright (a copy was sent to Nixon); Charlie McWhorter to Nixon, 13 April 1960, Box 418, folder: Richard G. Kleindienst; Thad Hutcheson to McWhorter, 5 April 1960, Box 364, folder: Thad Hutcheson; all in Gen. Corresp., NPP.

38. Nixon's reactions are evident in Nixon to Wright, 30 April 1960, Gen. Corresp., Box 834, folder: Loyd Wright, NPP. For the Eisenhower exchange, see Lucy Eisenhower to DDE, 2 May 1960 and DDE to Lucy Eisenhower, 6 July 1960, DDE Papers, Ann Whitman File, Name Series, Box 12, folder: Edgar Eisenhower (1959–60), (2), DDE.

39. The Young Republican endorsement is noted in *National Review* 8, 23 April 1960, 251. Youth for Goldwater efforts are documented in Douglas Caddy to Marvin Liebman, 16 May 1960 and Liebman to Robert Croll, 6 July 1960, Barry Goldwater File, Box 29, Marvin Liebman Associates Collection, Hoover Institution Archives (HIA) and *National Review* 8, 21 May 1960, 316. Bozell's comments are in Bozell, "Goldwater on the First Ballot," *National Review* 8, 18 June 1960, 388. Other efforts are noted in David Franke to Aubrey Barker, 7 June 1960, Barker to Frank Brophy, 21 June 1960, and Barker to Fred Airy, 29 June 1960, all in Box 3H504, and press release, 17 June 1960, Box 3H505, BG. Several of the postcards can be found in DDE White House File, General File, Box 570, folder: 109-A-15, DDE.

40. "Suggested Declaration of Republican Principles," 19 July 1960, DDE Post-Presidential Papers, Secretary's Series, Subject Subseries, Box 3, folder: Politics (PL) Barry Goldwater-1964 (4), DDE. The marijuana quotation is in Reinhard, *The Republican Right*, 154. For assessments of Goldwater's support see *National Review* 9, 30 July 1960, 36; *New York Times*, 23 July 1960, 8; and Richard Rovere, *The Goldwater Caper* (New York: Harcourt, Brace & World, 1965), 3, 115.

41. For some general background on their efforts, see Mary Brennan, "Conservatism in the Sixties: The Development of the American Political Right, 1960–1968" (Ph.D. diss., Miami University, 1988), esp. 73–78; and Toy, "Ideology and Conflict in American Ultraconservatism," 36–37

42. The *Baltimore Sun*, 31 December 1959, reported the Pearson assertion. All delegations to the platform committee received copies of *Decisions for a Better America*;

see Republican National Committee press release, 19 July 1960, Gen. Corresp., Box 588, folder: C.H. (Chuck) Percy (1 of 3), NPP.

43. Rockefeller, "Purpose and Policy," *Foreign Affairs* 38 (April 1960): 370–390; quotation on p. 383. A transcript of his "Meet the Press" interview for 12 June 1960 is in Box 247, folder: '60, Democratic National Committee (DNC) Papers, Lyndon B. Johnson Presidential Library, Austin, Texas (LBJL).

44. Rogers to Nixon, 17 June 1960 and 29 June 1960, Gen. Corresp., Box 653, folder: William P. Rogers 1960 (2 of 2), NPP. Rogers's advice was particularly revealing considering that his name had been put forward as a potential vice-presidential nominee, to the immediate dismay of party conservatives.

45. Transcript of televised interview with Rockefeller from Chicago, 19 July 1960, copy in Box 247, folder: '60, DNC Papers, LBJL. For Rockefeller's proposals and some Republican responses see "Rockefeller's Proposals, Civil Rights," 7 July 1960, Republican Party Series, 1960 Campaign Subseries, Box 3, folder: Republican National Convention (1960 Republican Civil Rights Proposals), Fred Seaton Papers, DDE; *New York Times*, 10 July 1960, clipping in Box 247, folder: '60, DNC Papers, LBJL; John W. Byrnes's remarks before the G.O.P. platform committee, 19 July 1960, Gen. Corresp., Box 119, folder: The Hon. John W. Byrnes, NPP.

46. The story of the platform committee maneuvering can be pieced together from several sources. See Charles Percy Oral History, Columbia University; personal letter, Percy to the author, 28 August 1992; Murray, *Charles Percy*, 47–53; John Kessel, "Political Leadership: The Nixon Version," and Karl Lamb, "Civil Rights and the Republican Platform: Nixon Achieves Control," both in Tillett, *Inside Politics*, 39–54 and 55–84 respectively; Paul David, "The Presidential Nominations," in Paul David (ed.), *The Presidential Election and Transition, 1960–1961* (Washington, D.C.: The Brookings Institution, 1961), 1–30.

47. 1960 Republican Party Platform, in Arthur Schlesinger Jr. (ed.), *History of Presidential Elections, 1789–1968*, 4 vols. (New York: Chelsea House 1971), 4:3510–3535. The quotations are on pp. 3510 and 3532. For an overview of the Nixon-Rockefeller platform fight see Theodore White, *The Making of the President, 1960* (New York: Atheneum, 1962), 183–205, 388–390. For southern maneuvering see a typed memo, 12 June 1964, G281, 3 of 3, folder: Nixon Misc. (as VP), Drew Pearson Papers, LBJL; Chandler Davidson, *Race and Class in Texas Politics* (Princeton: Princeton University Press, 1990), 225; and Tillett, "The National Conventions," 36–40. Nixon aide Charles Lichenstein later recapitulated the scenario for Nixon's use in writing *Six Crises*; see C. Lichenstein memo, 15 September 1961, Series 258, Box 1, folder: 1960 Election Chapter, NPP. In his writings, Nixon took particular care to refute Theodore White's version of events without taking formal notice of White's work.

48. For Royster's comments in the *Wall Street Journal*, see the news summary for 25 July 1960 in Series 69, Box 1, folder: Campaign 1960 (July), Richard Nixon Library, Yorba Linda, California. For the continuing conservative discontent see the *New York Times*, 24 July 1960, 38.

49. Walter Judd, "We Must Develop a Strategy for Victory—To Save Freedom—Freedom Everywhere," 25 July 1960, Box 48, folder: Politics, 1960, Walter Judd Papers, HIA. The most recent biography of Judd is a sympathetic one by former Young American for Freedom Lee Edwards, *Missionary for Freedom: The Life and Times of Walter Judd* (New York: Paragon House, 1990). See pp. 248–251 for convention coverage.

50. *Official Report of the Proceedings of the Twenty-Seventh Republican National Convention* (n.p.: Republican National Committee, 1960), 290–291. For Goldwater's other remarks, see pp. 57–60.

51. Richard Nixon, "It Is Time to Speak Up for America" (28 July 1960), reprinted in Schlesinger, *History of American Presidential Elections*, 4:3550–3555.

52. Rovere's views are in his 1960 "Letter," reprinted in Richard Rovere, *The American Establishment and Other Reports, Opinions, and Speculations* (New York: Harcourt, Brace & World, 1962), 76–78. Goldwater's views were reported in "A Conservative Sets Out His Credo," *New York Times Magazine*, 31 July 1960, 16 and Goldwater, "How to Win in '60: No Mollycoddling," *Newsweek* 56, 1 August 1960, 19. For a report on conservative groups at the Republican convention see a printed "confidential" memorandum from Charles Edison, 5 August 1960, Box 212, folder 6, Clare Boothe Luce Papers, Library of Congress (LC). Buckley's views are in *National Review* 9, 13 August 1960, 69–70.

Chapter Three **The Sharon Conference and the Founding of YAF**

1. Bozell to Goldwater, 15 August 1960, Box 3H506, BG. According to the Republican Party's media consultants, this seemed to work. See National Media Analysis, Weekly Report #22, 27 August–2 September 1960, Box 11, folder: Political Campaign 1960 (1), Robert Merriam Records, 1956–61, DDE.

2. Barker to Fred Airy of Albuquerque, New Mexico, 29 June 1960, Box 3H504, BG.

3. Charles Percy, "New Challenges and New Opportunities," copy in Gen. Corresp., Box 588, folder: C.H. (Chuck) Percy (1 of 3), NPP.

4. This brief overview follows that outlined in Judis, *William F. Buckley, Jr.*, 188–189. Other details are in Marvin Liebman, *Coming Out Conservative: An Autobiography* (San Francisco: Chronicle Books, 1992), 150 and Richard Dudman's column in the *St. Louis Post Dispatch*, 6 December 1964, clipping in Box 55, folder: Republican Party, Conservative Takeover, DNC Papers, LBJL.

5. Douglas Caddy to Robert Croll, 16 August 1960, Robert Croll Papers. Another copy is in Box 12, YAF folder, William F. Buckley Jr. Papers, Sterling Library, Yale University. A list of their home towns is in a memo from Caddy to attendees of the Great Elm Conference, 30 August 1960, Box 12, YAF folder, Buckley Papers. The development of a conservative nucleus is outlined in a letter from Caddy to the author, 9 November 1991, in the author's possession.

6. Caddy to Croll, 16 August 1960, Croll Papers.

7. A copy of this essay is attached to the letter announcing the formation of an Interim Committee in the YAF folder, Box 12, Buckley Papers. This became a recurring theme for YAF. See Douglas Caddy, "How the Businessman Can Directly Support His Local or Alma Mater Campus Conservative Club," *YAF Directory of College Conservative Clubs* (Spring 1961), in Box 17, YAF folder, Buckley Papers.

8. Memo from Caddy to attendees at the Great Elm Conference, 30 August 1960, Box 12, YAF folder, Buckley Papers. For Edison's comments, see Caddy, "Birth of the Conservative Movement," 11.

9. Lee and Anne Edwards, *Rebels with a Cause* (Washington: Young Americans for Freedom, 1969), 2–3; Steven Roberts, "Image on the Right," *The Nation* 194, 19 May 1964, 440–442. According to John Judis, Buckley also made a few changes. See his *William F. Buckley, Jr.*, 188–189.

10. "The Sharon Statement," *National Review* 9, September 1960, 173.

11. Ibid.

12. Ibid.

13. William F. Buckley Jr., "The Ivory Tower," *National Review* 9, September 1960, 172.

14. Cowan's statement is noted in Ross Mackenzie, "Young Conservatives Gather to

Establish National Organization," *Yale News* 82, 22 September 1960, 3. A copy is in the Robert Croll Papers.

15. M. Stanton Evans, "The First Fifteen Years Are the Hardest," *The New Guard* 15 (September 1975): 6.

16. This summary closely follows Nash, *The Conservative Intellectual Movement*, xvi. See also Francis, *Beautiful Losers*, 130–131.

17. Richard Weaver, *Ideas Have Consequences* (Chicago: University of Chicago Press, 1948), 17, 37–38.

18. Ibid., 59, 107, 121–122, 162–163.

19. Richard Weaver, "Up from Liberalism," *Modern Age* 3 (Winter 1958–59): 28–29. For Weaver's influence on the young conservatives see R. Emmett Tyrrell Jr., *The Conservative Crack-Up* (New York: Simon and Schuster, 1992), 32. Ironically, liberals like Reinhold Niebuhr and Arthur Schlesinger Jr. also emphasized human fallibility and worried about the temptations of power. See Robert B. Fowler, *Believing Skeptics: American Political Intellectuals, 1945–1964* (Westport, Conn.: Greenwood Press, 1978), 5, 155–156.

20. The best short overview of Kirk is in Nash, *The Conservative Intellectual Movement*, 68–77. The quotations are from Kirk, *The Conservative Mind, from Burke to Santayana* (Chicago: Henry Regnery Company, 1953), 7–8.

21. Aughey, Jones, and Riches, *The Conservative Political Tradition in Britain and the United States*, 7.

22. Jerome Tuccille, *It Usually Begins with Ayn Rand* (New York: Stein and Day, 1971), 17; Ayn Rand, *For the New Intellectual: The Philosophy of Ayn Rand* (New York: Random House, 1961), 23.

23. Tuccille, *It Usually Begins with Ayn Rand*, 58.

24. Frank Meyer, "Freedom, Tradition, Conservatism," in Meyer, *The Conservative Mainstream*, 16–29. This was first published in *Modern Age* (Fall 1960). For summaries of Meyer see Nash, *The Conservative Intellectual Movement*, 171–180; John Diggins, *Up from Communism: Conservative Odysseys in American Intellectual History* (New York: Harper & Row, 1975), 346–347, 446–447; Judis, *William F. Buckley, Jr.*, 147; and Tyrrell, *The Conservative Crack-Up*, 35. As Tyrrell looked back on this philosophical melange, he noted that it reminded him "of nothing so much as the Austro-Hungarian Empire in its final agonies." In 1960, that was not yet apparent.

25. Frank S. Meyer, quoted in Francis, *Beautiful Losers*, 101.

26. Diggins, *Up from Communism*, 455. Buckley, along with his brother-in-law Brent Bozell, had defended Senator Joseph McCarthy and had also been recruited by Yale Professor Willmoore Kendall for the CIA. There he met both James Burnham and E. Howard Hunt. See Sigmund Diamond, *Compromised Campus: The Collaboration of Universities with the Intelligence Community, 1945–1955* (New York: Oxford University Press, 1992), 176, 328–329. William Rusher had been associate counsel to the Senate Internal Security Subcommittee; see Markmann, *The Buckleys*, 128–129.

27. Patrick J. Buchanan, *Right from the Beginning* (Boston: Little, Brown & Company, 1988), 221. For the Buckley quote see his *God and Man at Yale: The Superstitions of "Academic Freedom"* (Chicago: Henry Regnery Company, 1951), 113.

28. Rusher to Cushing, 12 September 1960, reel 27, Rusher Papers; Rusher, *The Rise of the New Right*, 83. See also Parmet, *Richard Nixon and His America*, 474–475.

29. Rusher has published his own memoir of the conservative upsurge in *The Rise of the Right*, but he often skips quickly over key events. Judis, in *William F. Buckley, Jr.*, has some brief comments on Rusher's role; see pp. 156–157. See also Sidney Blumenthal, *The Rise of the Counter-Establishment: From Conservative Ideology to Political Power* (New York: Times Books, 1986), 30–31. The full influence of Rusher has

yet to be studied. As my discussion of YAF's founders in the next several pages will reveal, the Rusher Papers at the Library of Congress represent an important and untapped resource for Republican politics of the 1960s.

30. The best source of information on Liebman is his autobiography, *Coming Out Conservative*; quotations are on pp. 105 and 111. See also Richard Dudman, *Men of the Far Right* (New York: Pyramid Books, 1962), 144ff; Markmann, *The Buckleys*, 103–104; and Box 29, Group Research File, Marvin Liebman Associates Collection, HIA. For commentary about the tendency of communist zealots to become anticommunist zealots, see Fowler, *Believing Skeptics*, 9. China lobby politics are noted in Stanley D. Bachrack, *The Committee of One Million: "China Lobby" Politics, 1953–1971* (New York: Columbia University Press, 1976).

31. Liebman, *Coming Out Conservative*, 133, 143, 145–146. In his autobiography, Liebman also traced his decision to conceal his homosexuality to his intense belief in the individual's right to privacy.

32. Biographical information on Evans is in the Group Research File, 12 August 1963. Various letters between Buckley and Evans as early as 1958 show their close affiliation; see Box 5, folder: M.S. Evans, Buckley Papers. In 1958 the letterhead of the District of Columbia Young Republican Club indicated that Evans was in charge of publications. See Donald J. Tubridy, President of the D.C. YRs, to league members, 22 September 1958, Box 716, folder: 138-C-9, WHCF, Official File, DDE.

33. Quoted in Melvin Thorne, *American Conservative Thought since World War II: The Core Ideas* (Westport, Conn.: Greenwood Press, 1990), 49.

34. For Evans's writings, see "ADA: The Enemy Within. How the Left Achieves its Political Victories," *Human Events* 15, 30 June 1958, A2–A4; "Some Voices from the Grave," *National Review* 7, 25 April 1959, 23–25; "Moscow Formula for Victory," *National Review* 7, 1 August 1959, 248–249; "What's Real, What's Bluff?" *National Review* 7, 29 August 1959, 308–309; "The Emperor's New Lunik," *National Review* 7, 24 October 1959, 421–424 (where he doubted the Soviets' launch of Lunik III); "Two Standards—or One?" *National Review* 7, 21 November 1959, 491–492; and "Exorcising Conservatism," *National Review* 8, 30 January 1960, 81–82. For Rusher's remarks see Rusher to Evans, 8 July 1960, reel 5, Rusher Papers.

35. The best survey of these studies is in Hixson, *Search For the American Right Wing*, 74-95. The study of the right wing became, for a while during the 1960s and 1970s, almost a cottage industry. Political scientists, psychologists, and sociologists seemed to believe that theories of personality, status anxiety, or some array of dysfunctional disorders that fostered an irrational and conspiratorial world view could best explain the right-wing phenomenon.

36. For Caddy's background see Caddy, "Birth of the Conservative Movement," 1–4; "The New Trend on Campus: Conservatism," *Human Events* 14, 14 September 1957. A copy of his resume is in reel 4, Rusher Papers.

37. "Hugo Black: A Study of Conflict. The Story of the Ku Klux Klan's Favorite 'Liberal,'" *Human Events* 16, 16 December 1959. The essay is in an unpaginated Article section.

38. Caddy, "Birth of the Conservative Movement," 8–11; Douglas Caddy, "What's Really at Stake in Louisiana," *National Review* 7, 15 August 1959, 275–276; "By National Student Committee for the Loyalty Oath, Douglas Caddy, Chairman," *The Congressional Digest* 39 (1960): 122, 124, 126; Robert Bauman to Rusher, 1 December 1959, reel 3, Rusher Papers; Richard Nixon to Caddy, 14 April 1959, Gen. Corresp., Box 121, folder: Douglas Caddy, NPP. For the Caddy-Rusher connection see Caddy to Rusher, 19 March 1960, reel 4; Rusher to John McCarty of General Electric, 23 March 1960, reel 8; and Rusher to White, 23 March 1960, reel 14,

Rusher Papers. Later in his career Caddy served as a liaison between Robert R. Mullen & Company and its client, General Foods. At that time he shared an office with E. Howard Hunt. After the first Watergate arrests, Hunt and the wife of another defendant called Caddy and he showed up at the police station. According to some accounts, the cover-up began at that juncture. See Stanley Kutler, *The Wars of Watergate: The Last Crisis of Richard Nixon* (New York: Alfred A. Knopf, 1990), 188 and Steve Weissman (ed.), *Big Brother and the Holding Company: The World Behind Watergate* (Palo Alto: Ramparts Press, 1974), 170.

39. Margaret Braungart and Richard Braungart, "The Life-Course Development of Left- and Right-Wing Youth Activist Leaders from the 1960s," *Political Psychology* 11 (1990): 258, 265; Franke to William F. Buckley Jr., 7 March 1958, Box 5, Gen. Corresp."F", Buckley Papers; Robert Bauman to Rusher, 1 December 1959, reel 3; Franke to Rusher, 23 June 1958; and Rusher to Franke, 28 June 1958, reel 2, Rusher Papers; *National Review* 8, 23 April 1960, 257; Caddy, "Birth of the Conservative Movement," 9.

40. John Flynn, *The Road Ahead: America's Creeping Revolution* (New York: The Devin-Adair Company, 1961), 7, 9, 59, 76–81, 107, 137–138. This was originally published in 1949.

41. David Franke, "Revolt on the Campus," printed newsletter, McGraw-Edison Company Committee for Public Affairs, August 1960, Robert Croll Papers.

42. *The New Guard* (June 1963): 15; clipping from the Chicago *Daily Tribune*, 1 April 1961, in Gen. Corresp., Box 67, folder: Carol Dawson Bauman, NPP. See also *Who's Who in American Politics*, 1989–90, 1641.

43. Carol Dawson, "What Manner of Man?" *National Review* 7, 12 September 1959, 337–338. See also *The New Guard* (June 1963): 15 for additional information on Dawson's background.

44. For Caddy's comment on Nixon see Dawson to Nixon, 21 March 1959, Gen. Corresp., Box 533, folder: Thruston B. Morton (1 of 5), NPP. Dawson's role in the YRNF is noted in Nixon to Dawson, 26 June 1959, Gen. Corresp., Box 839, folder: Young Republican Groups (3 of 4), NPP, and Rusher to Dawson, 27 August 1959, reel 5, Rusher Papers. For Youth for Nixon see Carol Dawson mimeographed letter, 18 December 1959 and Dawson to Flanigan, 22 April 1960, Box 7, folder: College Youth, F. Clifton White Papers, Division of Rare Books and Manuscript Collections, Cornell University Library. I want to thank Mr. White for giving me permission to examine these papers. The O'Scannlain connection is in Rusher to Dawson, 8 June 1960, reel 27; and Rusher to Ned Cushing, YRNF, 12 August 1959, reel 5, Rusher Papers.

45. Formation of the national Youth for Nixon steering committee is documented in a 12 September 1960 press release, Gen. Corresp., Box 162, folder: College Youth for Nixon, NPP. For background on Dawson and Bauman, see Robert E. Bauman, *The Gentleman from Maryland: The Conscience of a Gay Conservative* (New York: Arbor House, 1986), 86–95. After twenty-one years of marriage and four children, they divorced following revelations that Bauman was gay.

46. For this sequence of events, see Bob Finch to Charlie McWhorter and McWhorter to Finch, 16 August 1960, Gen. Corresp., Box 424, folder: James T. Kolbe, NPP. For a partial list of College Youth for Nixon see Series 57, Box 1, folder: College Youth for Nixon, nationwide, 1960, Richard M. Nixon Library, Yorba Linda, California.

47. Robert M. Schuchman, "Libertarian Reflections on the Failure of Democracy," *Criterion* 4 (February 1960): 16. See also Schuchman to *National Review*, 1 October 1959 and Schuchman to Rusher, 2 November 1959, reel 13, Rusher Papers.

48. Schuchman, "Libertarian Reflections," 17–18. For his views on Kennedy see his

essay "The Hundred Days are Here Again," *National Review* 9, 5 November 1960, 277–278.

49. Niemeyer to William F. Buckley Jr., 22 September 1960, Box 11, Niemeyer folder, Buckley Papers.

50. William Schulz, "The Need for Nuclear Tests: Why Bomb-Banning is More Dangerous than Radiation," *Human Events* 17, 7 April 1960, Article Section I. See also Schulz, "The 'Missile Gap' is the Symington Gap," *Human Events* 17, 23 June 1960, Section IV. "The New Trend on Campus: Conservatism," *Human Events* 14, 14 September 1957, provides background on Schulz. Hopes for unity are noted in Mackenzie, "Young Conservatives Gather," 3. For Rusher's connections to future YAFers see the letters in reel 27, Rusher Papers.

51. Edwards and Edwards, *Rebels with a Cause*, 5. See also Edwards, "The Other Sixties," 58 and *Human Events* 17, 4 August 1960, 324. For Edwards's opposition to organized labor, see his "Labor and the Broadcasting Industry: A Land of Plenty for Unionized Performers and Technicians," *Human Events* 16 (26 August 1959): A4.

52. Edwards and Edwards, *Rebels with a Cause*, 3–4; Buckley, "The Ivory Tower," 172. See also Rusher, *Rise of the Right*, 89 and Roberts, *The Conservative Decade*, 25. A copy of the agenda for the conference is in the Robert Croll Papers, as are copies of a few early financial statements. Charles Edison underwrote many of the initial expenses to launch YAF. A copy of the original press release announcing YAF officers and directors is in Box 108, Marvin Liebman Papers, HIA. For Schuchman's selection, see Douglas Caddy, "Robert Schuchman: As His Friends Remember Him," *The New Guard* 6 (April 1966): 7–9. Schuchman died March 11, 1966 at age 27 of a cerebral hemorrhage.

Chapter Four   **The Thrill of Treason**

1. Quoted in Joseph Keeley, *The China Lobby Man: The Story of Alfred Kohlberg* (New Rochelle, N.Y.: Arlington House, 1969), xii.

2. Harold Taylor, "The New Young are Now Heard," *New York Times Magazine*, 29 January 1961, in Anderson and Biggs (eds.), *A Focus on Rebellion*, 162, 167.

3. "Campus Conservatives," *Time* 77 (10 February 1961), in Anderson and Biggs (eds.), *A Focus on Rebellion*, 171.

4. Tom Hayden, "Who Are the Student Boat-Rockers?" *Mademoiselle* (August 1961), unpaginated.

5. Ibid. For other comments about the surge in conservatism see Frederick Obear, "Student Activism in the Sixties," in Julian Foster and Durward Long (eds.), *Protest! Student Activism in America* (New York: William Morrow, 1970), 11–26; John Sisk, "Conservatism on Campus," *Commonweal* 72, 27 January 1961, 451–454; and Jessica Mitford Treuhaft, "The Indignant Generation," *The Nation* 192, 27 May 1961, 451–456.

6. YAF brochure, no date, Box 12, folder: Young Americans for Freedom, Buckley Papers.

7. For the YAF decision, see the *New York Herald Tribune*, 30 October 1960, 30. Rusher's views are succinctly expressed in Rusher to Buckley, 10 October 1960, reel 4, Rusher Papers. For a contrary argument, see Archibald Graustein to Rusher, 14 October 1960, reel 8, Rusher Papers.

8. Rusher to Dr. William K. Runyeon, 14 November 1960, reel 27, Rusher Papers.

9. Rusher to John Thomson, 16 November 1960, reel 13, Rusher Papers.

10. Frank Meyer, "Only Four Years to 1964," *National Review*, 3 December 1960, in Meyer, *The Conservative Mainstream*, 239–241. See also Frank Meyer, "Freedom,

Tradition, Conservatism," *Modern Age* (Fall 1960), in Meyer, *The Conservative Mainstream*, 16–29.

11. Minutes of the YAF Board of Directors, 1 October 1960, Robert Croll Papers. For Kohler, see Herbert Kohler Sr. to Buckley, 13 October 1960, Box 12, folder: Young Americans for Freedom, Buckley Papers. For NAM support of YAF see William J. P. Cullen's editorial in *NAM News*, 21 October 1960, copy in the Robert Croll Papers.

12. A copy of YAF's "College and Community Organization Manual" is in reel 139, ADA Papers. For Caddy, see *National Review* 9, 8 October 1960, 198; and Buckley to Caddy, 4 October 1960, Box 12, folder: Young Americans for Freedom, Buckley Papers. This letter also reveals problems in communication between Buckley and Caddy about the timely and appropriate handling of those letters from conservatives.

13. For details of the incident see George McDonnell to Buckley, 27 December 1960, and the 28 October 1960 issue of *Varsity News*. Copies of both are in the George McDonnell Papers.

14. Minutes of the YAF Board of Directors, 1 October 1960, Robert Croll Papers. For the bylaws see Box 17, folder: Young Americans for Freedom, Buckley Papers.

15. Minutes of the YAF Board of Directors, New York City, 26 November 1960, Box 173, folder: YAF, 1960–62, Rusher Papers.

16. John Kolbe, "Thunder on the Right," *Insight and Outlook* 3, April 1961, 9-11. See also Rusher to Eugene P. Kenny, 21 December 1960, reel 9, Rusher Papers; and "Young Americans for Freedom in Nebraska," mimeo sheets issued by the Student Affairs & Activities Division, copy in the Robert Croll Papers. Although Seymour Martin Lipset and others have argued that YAF did not get the media attention given SDS because their social behavior was too conformist, in the early 1960s this was not the case. See Virginia Lacy, "The Season of Our Discontent: A Survey Research of Political Knowledge and Attitudes of Three Campus Organizations: Students for a Democratic Society, Young Democrats, and Young Americans for Freedom" (master's thesis, University of Houston, 1969), 42–43.

17. For the political action conference, see *National Review* 10, 21 January 1961, 2. Circulation and financial figures are in Rusher to Willmoore Kendall, 13 January 1961, reel 8, Rusher Papers. A copy of the Directory is in Box 80, YAF file, Henry Regnery Collection, HIA. See also "Campus Conservatives," *Time* 77, 10 February 1961, 34, 37; and "The Highlights of Sen. Goldwater's Manifesto," *The Wall Street Journal*, 11 January 1961, clipping in Box 324, folder: Barry Goldwater, 1960–61, DNC Papers, LBJL. A complete copy of Goldwater's "The Forgotten American" is in *Human Events* 18, 27 January 1961, 57-64.

18. M. Stanton Evans, "Trends," *National Review Bulletin* 10, 4 March 1961, 6; Walter Trohan, "Young Conservatives," *Human Events* 18, 14 April 1961, 235. O'Donnell's offer is noted in Rusher to O'Donnell, 10 February 1961, reel 24, Rusher Papers. The money funded a study of HUAC. For ADA, see Richard Lambert to Howard Wachtel, 8 March 1961, reel 140, ADA Papers.

19. Minutes of the YAF Board of Directors meeting, 12 February 1961, Box 173, folder: YAF, 1960–62, Rusher Papers; M. Stanton Evans, "Trends," *National Review Bulletin* 10, 18 February 1961, 6. For YAF and Judd, see Caddy to Judd, February 1961; Edwards to Judd, no date; and Robert Schuchman to Judd, 6 February 1961, all in Box 256, folder 2, Walter Judd Papers, HIA. Schuchman's letter emphasized that the YAFers were either students or just beginning their professional careers. The recruitment of famous conservatives caused some problems in the relationship between YAF and Buckley; see Buckley to Franke, 13 January 1961, reel 5, Rusher Papers.

20. *The New Guard* 1 (March 1961): 3.

21. David Franke, "Breaking the Liberal Barrier," ibid., 10.

22. Ibid., 4.

23. A text of Goldwater's speech at the March 3, 1961 rally is in the John Kolbe Papers.

24. *New York Times*, 4 March 1961, 1; Murray Kempton, "Freedom's Own," *New York Post*, 5 March 1961, 2, 6.

25. Murray Kempton, "On Growing Up Absurd," *The Progressive* 25 (May 1961): 11–14. For a view of the rally from the Right, see William F. Buckley Jr., "The Ivory Tower," *National Review* 10, 25 March 1961, 187. Also see Raymond Moley, "Youth Turns to the Right," *Newsweek* 57, 13 March 1961, 100.

26. Liebman to YAF Officers and Directors, 23 March 1961, Robert Croll Papers.

27. Minutes of the YAF Board of Directors, 25 March 1961, Box 173, folder: YAF, 1960–62, Rusher Papers.

28. YAF press release, 30 March 1961; press release, Committee for an Effective Peace Corps, 31 March 1961, reel 139, ADA Papers. Howard Phillips, student council president at Harvard, was chair of this group, and Tom Huston, student senator at Indiana University, was executive secretary.

29. John Weicher, "The Next Four Years: An Appraisal," *New Individualist Review* 1 (April 1961): 16–17. Weicher, a founder of YAF and former writer for *Human Events*, was at the time a graduate student in economics at the University of Chicago.

30. Robert Schuettinger, "Modern Education vs. Democracy," *New Individualist Review* 1 (April 1961): 23–27.

31. For Nixon, see Nixon to Lee Edwards, 25 April 1961, Gen. Corresp., Box 837, folder: YAF, NPP. Edwards's attack is in "Which Road for the Peace Corps?" *The New Guard* 1 (April 1961): 2. See also Howard Phillips, "Inside NSA," and Edward Talbot, "To The Rear, March!" in the same issue, 12ff. Rusher's request is in Rusher to Caddy, 6 March 1961, reel 28, Rusher Papers. Early issues of *The New Guard* disguised the fact that one person often authored several articles by the artful use of pseudonyms. See Carol Bauman, "The First Five Years are the Hardest," *The New Guard* 6 (March 1966): 8.

32. Evans's remarks are in *The New Guard* 1 (April 1961): 8. For a summary of Weaver's arguments see ibid.: 11. The arguments of Westby and Braungart are in their "Activists and the History of the Future," in Foster and Long (eds.), *Protest! Student Activism in America*, 158-83.

33. For YAF efforts on campuses, see *The New Guard* 1 (May 1961): 4, 6. The speaker controversy involving Buckley and the University of Detroit is detailed in George McDonnell, State Chairman of Michigan YAF, to John Morad, Editor, *Varsity News*, University of Detroit, 5 May 1961; Britt Lawrence, President of the University of Detroit, to the editor, *Indianapolis News*, 19 June 1961; Stanton Evans to McDonnell, 11 July 1961; and McDonnell to Evans, 1 August 1961; all in the George McDonnell Papers.

34. Patrick Hill, lettter to the editor, 8 April 1961, *America* 105 (6 May 1961): 233.

35. Lee Edwards, "City of Delusions," *The New Guard* 1 (June 1961): 2-7; John Weicher, "The Question of Federal Aid to Education," *New Individualist Review* 1 (Summer 1961): 8-11.

36. Donald Bruce, "Principles are Possible in Politics," Manion Forum interview, 28 May 1961. For the rally, see *The New Guard* 1 (June 1961): 15.

37. Edward Facey, "Conservatives or Individualists: Which are We?" *New Individualist Review* 1 (Summer 1961): 24.

38. Ibid., 25.

39. Ibid.

40. John Weicher, "Mr. Facey's Article: A Comment," ibid., 26–27.
41. Douglas Caddy testimony, 14 June 1961, *Hearings Before the Special Subcommittee on Education of the Committee on Education and Labor, House of Representatives*, 87th Cong., 1st Sess., Part 3 (Washington: GPO, 1961), 786–787.
42. Ibid., 791.
43. Ibid., 793–794. See also Caddy to Walter Judd, 21 June 1961, Box 256, folder 2, Walter Judd Papers, HIA.
44. Caddy to Buckley, 15 May 1961, Box 17, folder: Young Americans for Freedom, Buckley Papers. Caddy probably intended this as a general policy statement, for he sent copies to Robert Schuchman, Carol Dawson, and Lee Edwards.
45. Memorandum from Douglas Caddy, June 1961, Caddy Papers.
46. Stanton Evans is quoted in *National Review* 9, 19 November 1960, 311. See also Alan Elms, "The Conservative Ripple," *The Nation* 192, 27 May 1961, 458–460, 468; and "Current Comment," *America* 105 (24 June 1961): 456.
47. Quoted in the *New York Post*, 22 May 1961, 7.
48. "Confidential Report (preliminary) on the 13th Annual Congress of the NSA," Box 12, folder: Young Americans for Freedom, Buckley Papers. A summary of the NSA's role is in James O'Brien, "The Development of a New Left in the United States, 1960–1965," (Ph.D. diss., University of Wisconsin, 1971), 66–75, passim.
49. Dawson to Peter Flanigan, 10 August 1960, Gen. Corresp., Box 205, folder: Carol Dawson, NPP.
50. Ibid.
51. M. Stanton Evans, "Trends," *National Review Bulletin* 10, 24 June 1961, 6.
52. Walters to Richard Lambert of ADA, 1 July 1961, reel 139, ADA Papers.
53. *The New Guard* 1 (August 1961): 11. See also Edward Cain, *They'd Rather Be Right: Youth and the Conservative Movement* (New York: Macmillan, 1963), 172. Membership statistics are notoriously unreliable, but for one estimate from YAF's opponents see Arnold Forster and Benjamin Epstein, *Danger on the Right* (New York: Random House, 1964), 224.
54. "The Progressive Student League and USNSA" (pamphlet, 1960), reel 139, ADA Papers.
55. Letter to Vi Gunther of Americans for Democratic Action (1960), reel 139, ADA Papers.
56. "Internal Democracy and YAF," reel 139, ADA Papers.
57. Usher Ward, "The Young Americans for Freedom and the New Conservatism," 1–7, reel 39, #4B:409, SDS Papers.
58. Ibid., 9.
59. Ibid., 14.
60. Ibid., 15–16.
61. "ADA Strategy on NSA," reel 139; and David R. Allen, "Campus ADA and the Future" (June 1961), reel 140, ADA Papers. See also Edward Bacciocco Jr., *The New Left in America: Reform to Revolution, 1956 to 1970* (Stanford: Hoover Institution Press, 1974), 112–113.
62. "YAF and the NSA Congress," August 1961, reel 139, ADA Papers. Also see Richard Lambert, ADA field representative, to Prof. Carl Auerbach of Madison, 23 June 1961; memo from Betty Binder, 22 July 1961; Richard Lambert to Page Wilson, 24 July 1961; and the confidential memorandum from Betty Binder to Mike Shagan, Rena Feit, Howie Wachtel, Carl Golanski, Al Haber, Paul Dubrul, Dick Lambert, and Donald Smith, 25 July 1961; all in reel 139, ADA Papers. This last memo also argued that Kay Wonderlic was "more liberal than appearances have given us to believe," and that she had been "wined and dined and conned into the

arms of YAF." This meant that there was still a chance to win her over to the moderates. The ADA decison to aid Campus ADA is in the ADA National Executive Committee Minutes, 21 June 1961, copy in Box 12, folder: Americans for Democratic Action, 1961, Joseph L. Rauh Jr. Papers, LC.

63. "YAF and the NSA Congress," August 1961, reel 139, ADA Papers.

64. Memo Re: the 14th USNSA National Student Congress, from SDS, reel 139, ADA Papers.

65. "Civil Rights in the South," ibid.

66. "Report to the National Executive Committee, 14th National Student Congress, August 1961," ibid.

67. Steven Roberts and Carey McWilliams Jr., "Student Leaders and Campus Apathy," *The Nation* 193, 16 September 1961, 155–156. For YAF's preparations, see O'Brien, "Development of the New Left," 150–151.

68. "Address to the 14th National Student Congress by Wisconsin Governor Gaylord Nelson," reel 139, ADA Papers.

69. The above is pieced together from: a press release announcing a meeting of the "Middle-of-the-Road-Caucus," 27 August 1961, ibid.; George Thayer, *The Farther Shores of Politics: The American Political Fringe Today* (New York: Simon & Schuster, 1967), 170–171; Roberts and Williams, "Student Leaders and Campus Apathy,"156–157; and Robert Schuchman, "Charge of the Right Brigade," *National Review* 1, 9 September 1961, 161.

70. Howard Wachtel, "The Fourteenth National Student Congress," reel 139, ADA Papers. Wachtel was the national chair of Campus ADA.

71. Ibid.; statement by Tom Charles Huston, 23 August 1961, ibid.

72. Roberts and Williams, "Student Leaders and Campus Apathy," 156–157; Wachtel, "The Fourteenth National Student Congress," reel 139, ADA Papers.

73. Ron Dorfman, Paul Levy and Richard Merbaum, "The Right at NSA," *New University Thought* 2 (Autumn 1961): 31-32.

74. Lambert to John McGrath, 26 September 1961, reel 139, ADA Papers. For Lewis's tour, see Edward R. Garvey, President of USNSA, to Richard Lambert, 25 September 1961, ibid.

75. John R. Knaggs, *Two-Party Texas: The John Tower Era, 1961–1984* (Austin: Eakin Press, 1986), 6–7; John Tower, "A New Conservative Leader Addresses the Nation," Manion Forum, 25 June 1961; *The New Guard* 1 (July 1961): 11–12.

76. For commentary on the YRNF convention see Brian Whalen to Nixon, 26 April 1961, Gen. Corresp., Box 650, folder: Nelson A. Rockefeller 1960 (1 of 2), NPP; *New York Times*, 23 June 1961; *Newsweek* 58, 3 July 1961, 20, 25; *London Times* clipping, 21 July 1961, Series 64, Box 2, Richard M. Nixon Library; *The New Guard* 1 (August 1961): 8; William Rusher to John Thomson, 18 July 1961, reel 13, Rusher Papers. For the John Birch Society, see *The Blue Book of the John Birch Society* (Boston: Western Islands Publishers, 1961), 110–111.

77. The prevalent view in the Kennedy administration, for instance, was that intelligence and rational analysis, not ideology, were essential. See David Halberstam, *The Best and the Brightest* (New York: Random House, 1969), 99.

Chapter Five **Divisions in Conservative Ranks**

1. Rusher memo to B. Buckley, B. Bozell, J. Burnham, W. Kendall, F. Meyer, Priscilla Buckley, 3 April 1961, reel 28, Rusher Papers.

2. Ibid.

3. Rusher to Buckley, 6 April 1961, ibid.

4. Rusher to Buckley, 10 April 1961, ibid. *National Review* eventually condemned the John Birch Society. For a mainstream publication that lumped Goldwater and YAF with the John Birch Society, see "The Unhelpful Fringes," *Life* 50, 12 May 1961, 32.

5. David Franke, "Breaking the Liberal Barrier," *The New Guard* 1 (March 1961): 10. See also pp. 11–14 for a profile of Rousselot and uncritical praise for anticommunist testimony before the Senate Internal Security Subcommittee.

6. Rusher, *The Rise of the Right*, 114–115.

7. Carol Bauman, "Mater Si, Magistra Si," *The New Guard* 1 (December 1961): 6–7, 12. The quotation is on p. 12. Judis, in *William F. Buckley, Jr.*, details the battle over the encyclical between *National Review* and the liberal Catholic publication *America*; see pp. 186–188.

8. Edward Gargan, "Radical Catholics of the Right," *Social Order* (November 1961): 409–419. The quotations are on pp. 409 and 415. See also Allitt, *Catholic Intellectuals and Conservative Politics in America*, 31–32, 93–94; Gottfried and Fleming, *The Conservative Movement*, 23–24.

9. Nevin is quoted in Evans, *Revolt on the Campus*, 180. Kolbe's remarks were delivered June 7, 1962. A copy is in the author's possession.

10. Niemeyer is quoted in Evans, *Revolt on the Campus*, 182. See also Holmes Alexander, "Godhead and the Liberals," *The New Guard* 2 (September 1962): 8; Charles F. Barr Jr., "How 'Objective' is Ayn Rand?" *The New Guard* 2 (October 1962): 10; and the "Letters to the Editor" column, *The New Guard* 3 (December 1962–January 1963): 2.

11. "Notes toward an Empirical Definition of Conservatism," in Frank Meyer (ed.), *What Is Conservatism?* (New York: Holt, Rinehart and Winston, 1964), 211–236. The quotations are on pp. 214 and 225. For another critique see Eliza Simmons, "Who's an Objectivist?" *The New Guard* 2 (May 1962): 21–22.

12. L. Brent Bozell, "Freedom or Virtue?" *National Review* 13, 11 September 1962, 181–184.

13. Ibid., 184, 187, 206.

14. Frank Meyer, "Why Freedom," *National Review* 13, 25 September 1962, 223, 225.

15. *The New Guard* 2 (November 1962): 11. Meyer's book was published by conservative Chicago publisher Henry Regnery in 1962. A summary of the fusionist-YAF position, which the Sharon Statement embodied, is in Evans, *Revolt on the Campus*, 184–185.

16. Edstrom to Judd, 14 February 1961, Box 256, folder 2, Walter Judd Papers, HIA.

17. Judd to Charles S. Shuler, 17 July 1961, Box 256, folder 2, Walter Judd Papers, HIA.

18. Caddy, "Birth of the Conservative Movement," 19. See also Caddy to Henry Regnery, 3 January 1961, Box 80, file 15, Henry Regnery Collection, HIA.

19. The telegram, dated 19 May 1961, is in reel 14, Rusher Papers. Also see Rusher, *The Rise of the Right*, 114–115; Judis, *William F. Buckley, Jr.*, 197; Franke to Buckley (1961), and the letter from attorneys Casey, Lane, and Mittendorf to Franke, 18 May 1961, Box 17, YAF folder, Buckley Papers.

20. Memo from Marvin Liebman to Carol Bauman, Douglas Caddy, David Franke, and Robert Schuchman, 24 May 1961, Box 17, YAF folder, Buckley Papers.

21. Memo from Marvin Liebman to Carol Bauman and Robert Schuchman, 26 May 1961, ibid.

22. Liebman to Robert Croll, 8 August 1961, Croll Papers; Confidential Memorandum to the YAF Board of Directors, from Carol Bauman, Robert Croll, Lee Edwards, David Franke, James Kolbe, William Madden, and William Schulz, 12 August 1961, Box 17, YAF folder, Buckley Papers.

23. His resume is attached to the Confidential Memo of 12 August 1961, Box 17, YAF folder, Buckley Papers.
24. See the Confidential Memo of Aug. 12, 1961, in ibid. This copy was also signed by advisors and friends of YAF: Marvin Liebman, William Rusher, M. Stanton Evans. Howard Phillips' name is also included.
25. Rusher to Buckley, Liebman, and Meyer,5 September 1961, reel 3, Rusher Papers. For bylaw changes see Carol Bauman to YAF Directors, 25 August 1961, Box 17, YAF folder, Buckley Papers. The deficit is noted in "Statement of Financial Condition," Robert Croll Papers. Rusher's notes in preparation for the meeting are in reel 14, Rusher Papers. He listed Schuchman, Caddy, Cotter, Gaines, Phillips, Stanley, and McElwaine as "hostile."
26. Rusher to Buckley, Liebman, and Meyer, 5 September 1961, reel 3, Rusher Papers. See also Rusher, *The Rise of the Right*, 116.
27. Rusher to McDonnell, 6 September 1961, reel 9, Rusher Papers. See also Rusher to James Abstine, 8 September 1961, reel 15, ibid. Abstine had backed Caddy.
28. Molesworth to Rusher, 14 September 1961, and Rusher to Molesworth, 15 September 1961, reel 10, Rusher Papers. For Liebman's comments see Liebman to McDonnell, 13 September 1961, George McDonnell Papers.
29. Rusher to Bozell, 28 September 1961, reel 3, Rusher Papers.
30. Ibid. Rusher also informed Goldwater about Rockefeller's overtures to YAF; see Rusher to Goldwater, 2 August 1961, Box 173, Rusher Papers.
31. Rusher to Michael Robbins, 30 October 1961, reel 29, Rusher Papers. For other developments, see Rusher to James Campaigne Jr., 16 October 1961, ibid.; Lynn Bouchey to Rusher, 4 October 1961 and Scott Stanley Jr. to Richard Viguerie (no date), reel 14, Rusher Papers.
32. Rusher to Croll, 10 November 1961, reel 4, Rusher Papers.
33. Ibid. Copies of the letter were sent to James Abstine, Stanton Evans, Marvin Liebman, Richard Noble, Diarmuid O'Scannlain, William Schulz, and Richard Viguerie.
34. Rusher to Peter O'Donnell, 1 December 1961, reel 29, Rusher Papers. O'Donnell had initially funded the position of national organization director, and was a strong Goldwater supporter and Republican State Chairman in Texas.
35. Rusher to Buckley (with copies to Frank Meyer, L. Brent Bozell, and Marvin Liebman), 12 March 1962, reel 4, Rusher Papers. The next several paragraphs are drawn from the same letter.
36. Liebman to the YAF board, 17 January 1962, Box 23, folder: YAF, Buckley Papers. See also the Minutes of the YAF board of directors, 19 November 1961 and Liebman to David Franke, 1961, both in Box 173, folder: YAF 1960–62, Rusher Papers. For the impact of Caddy's remarks at the NAM convention see Rusher to Richard Viguerie, 29 January 1962, reel 14, Rusher Papers. Viguerie's early background is noted in Richard Viguerie, *The New Right: We're Ready to Lead* (Falls Church, Va.: The Viguerie Company, 1980), 19ff.
37. Liebman to the YAF board, 16 February 1962. Copies of the American Nazi pamphlet are in Box 173, folder: YAF 1960–62, Rusher Papers and Box 37, Marvin Liebman Associates Collection, HIA.
38. Rusher to the YAF board, 16 February 1962, Box 23, YAF folder; Rusher to Buckley, 20 February 1962, Box 20, folder: Inter-Office Memos, Buckley Papers.
39. Caddy to Edison, 25 February 1962, Box 21, folder: Marvin Liebman, Buckley Papers. The Andrews letter is noted in Liebman to Rusher, 5 March 1962, Box 99, Marvin Liebman Associates Collection, HIA. See also Rusher to Buckley, 7 March 1962, reel 4, Rusher Papers.
40. Rusher to Buckley et al., 12 March 1962, ibid. Schuchman, Caddy, Gaines, Harley,

McDonnell, McIntire, Molesworth, and Phillips voted against the motion; see the board minutes, 8 March 1962, Box 23, folder: YAF, Buckley Papers.

41. Rusher to Buckley, 12 March 1962, reel 4, Rusher Papers.

42. Croll to Rusher, 27 February 1962, reel 4, Rusher Papers; Rusher to Buckley, 2 March 1962, Box 20, folder: Inter-Office Memos, Buckley Papers.

43. Caddy's letter appeared in the 9 March 1962 *Wall Street Journal.* A copy is in reel 14, Rusher Papers. See also Richard Viguerie's memo to the YAF policy committee, 27 March 1962 in reel 14, Rusher Papers. A copy of Frank Meyer's letter of 26 March 1962 is in reel 8, Rusher Papers. The *Journal's* refusal to print the reply is noted in Rusher to Peter O'Donnell Jr., 28 March 1962, reel 12, Rusher Papers. Rusher's experience with the *Journal* is detailed in Rusher to William F. Buckley Jr., Frank Meyer, and Priscilla Buckley, 3 April 1962, Box 20, folder: Inter-Office Memos, Buckley Papers. For Caddy see Caddy to Buckley, 29 May 1962 and Liebman to Buckley, 5 June 1962, Box 19, folder: Douglas Caddy, Buckley Papers.

44. For Phillips see Tom Stalker to Rusher, 30 March 1962, reel 13, Rusher Papers; and John Fernandes to Dan Carmen, 3 May 1962, Box 173, folder: YAF 1960–62, Rusher Papers. The Viguerie controversy is in Fred J. Weston to Peter O'Donnell, 29 May 1962 and Rusher to O'Donnell, 18 June 1962, reel 12, Rusher Papers.

45. Rusher's side of the Caddy affair is in Rusher to Lynn Bouchey, 10 July 1962, reel 4, Rusher Papers. For Buckley's response, see Buckley to Goldwater, 12 July 1962, Box 23, folder: YAF, Buckley Papers.

46. Madden to William Rusher, 14 July 1962, reel 10, Rusher Papers.

47. Ibid.

48. Rusher to Madden, 17 July 1962, ibid.

49. Madden to Rusher, 23 July 1962, ibid. For Rusher's comments to Viguerie, see Rusher to Viguerie, 19 July 1962, reel 14, Rusher Papers.

50. Buckley to Rusher, 24 August 1962, reel 14, Rusher Papers. Also see Memo to All Concerned from Rusher, 24 September 1962, ibid.

51. Rusher to Bouchey, 4 September 1962, reel 4; Rusher to Bauman, 21 September 1962, reel 3; Viguerie to Bauman, 23 July 1962, reel 14; all in Rusher Papers.

52. A schedule for the convention is in the Robert Croll Papers. For reports on the convention see the *New York Times,* 30 September 1962, 45; *The New Guard* 2 (November 1962): 8–9; and *National Review* 13, 23 October 1962, 297–298. The latter claimed that more than 1,000 people attended, 200 of whom were official delegates. Other details of the convention are in the *Congressional Record,* 87th Cong., 2d Sess. A reprint of this, which represents the extension of remarks by Bruce Alger of Texas, is in reel 14, Rusher Papers.

53. Viguerie to Rusher, 27 September 1962, Box 173, folder: YAF 1960–62, Rusher Papers; Wakefield, *New York in the Fifties,* 267.

54. Rusher to Goldwater, 1 October 1962, Box 173, Rusher Papers. For the convention voting see "Y.A.F. Convention Election Results," Box 173, folder: YAF 1960-62, Rusher Papers.

55. Bauman's remarks are in *National Review* 13, 23 October 1962, 297–298 and the *New York Times,* 30 September 1962, 45. A brief biography and his program are outlined in *The New Guard* 2 (November 1962): 8. Bauman has since published a partial memoir, *The Gentleman from Maryland,* but this focuses chiefly on his later Congressional career and subsequent admission that he was gay. Other tidbits on Bauman are in *The Westchester (N.Y.) Conservative* 1 (September 1962), a copy of which is in Box 8, Elms folder, F. Clifton White Papers. Some of the local YAF chapters also began to adopt more programmatic initiatives. See Toby Behman, Minnesota YAF chairman to Walter Judd, 24 October 1962, Box 256, folder 2, Walter Judd Papers,

HIA for a list of projects to be undertaken by Minnesota YAF. Behman promised a "more mature organization."

56. In his essay "Dreams of the Sixties," *New York Review of Books* 34, 22 October 1987, 10, 12–16, Alan Brinkley notes that much the same problem tormented SDS and the Left during the decade.

Chapter Six *Attacking the New Frontier*

1. Quoted in Marvin Kitman, "The Button-Down Revolution," *Nugget* (October 1961): 71.
2. M. Stanton Evans, "Mold for a Secular Stereotype," *National Review* 11, 9 September 1961, 167–169; M. Stanton Evans, "Revolution, Inside-Out," *National Review* 11, 16 December 1961, 420–421.
3. William F. Buckley Jr., "Conservative Movement Gathers Steam on All Fronts," Manion Forum, 5 November 1961.
4. *Under 30* 1 (July 1962): 4.
5. Lee Edwards, "Taking a Covered Wagon to the New Frontier," *The New Guard* 1 (March 1961): 2.
6. Carol Bauman, "Shall Labor Be King?" *The New Guard* 1 (June 1961): 8–9, 11; Carol Bauman, "Compulsory Unionism: Threat to the Workingman," *The New Guard* 2 (May 1962): 16–17. See also M. Stanton Evans, "Trends," *National Review Bulletin* 1 (14 October 1961): 6.
7. Edwards, "Bread and Circuses," 2; Lee Edwards, "Let Him Begin," *The New Guard* 1 (August 1961): 2; and an editorial in the same issue, p. 4. YAF's highlighting of these issues is noted in *The New Guard* 1 (June 1961): 7.
8. *The New Guard* 1 (July 1961): 2, 3.
9. Phillips's testimony on July 28, 1961 is in volume 2 of *Health Services for the Aged under the Social Security Insurance System. Hearings before the Committee on Ways and Means, House of Representatives*, 87th Cong., 1st Sess. (Washington, D.C.: GPO, 1961), 751–754. The quotations are on p. 752. Also see Evans, "Trends," *National Review Bulletin* 11, 22 July 1961, 6.
10. A copy of Mitchell's speech, delivered August 11, 1961, is in reel 9, Rusher Papers. For Franke's analysis, see his "Newburgh: Just the Beginning?" *National Review* 11, 29 July 1961, 44. Mitchell's program closely resembled that passed by House Republicans more than three decades later, in 1995.
11. For Goldwater see his Manion Forum interview, "New Frontier a Bedlam of Perilous Confusion," 23 July 1961. The anticommunist issue is noted in Daniel Buckley to William Rusher, 25 July 1961, reel 4, Rusher Papers. For the Defense Department directive see the *New York Times*, 21 July 1961, 1.
12. The speeches of this group are in the *Congressional Record* 107, part 14, 87th Cong., 1st Sess. (7 September 1961), 18606–18629. Bruce's remarks are on 18606–18607.
13. Ibid., 18628-18629.
14. Rusher to K. B. Walker, 5 July 1961, reel 14, Rusher Papers.
15. The draft letter is in reel 8, Rusher Papers. Formation of the New York City group is noted in the *New York Times*, 22 July 1961, 22. The ACA effort is in a 14 November 1961 memorandum, reel 8, Rusher Papers. For Nixon, see Molesworth to Nixon, 8 November 1961, Gen. Corresp., Box 837, folder: YAF, NPP. Welch's remarks are in Welch to Liebman, 25 October 1961, G288 (2 of 3), folder: M. Liebman, Drew Pearson Papers, LBJL.
16. For Manion, see "Conservative Clubs—All Over America—Can Save this Nation from Slavery," Manion Forum, 6 August 1961. For early Goldwater efforts see the

interview with F. Clifton White, Box 3J9, folder: S. Shadegg book, Barry Goldwater Collection, Series VIII: Publications, 1949–1965, BG. Ashbrook's remarks are from "Patriotic Groups, Such as Manion Forum Conservative Clubs, Can Preserve Freedom," Manion Forum interview, 17 December 1961.

17. A statement of YAF's financial condition, 31 August 1961, and the minutes of the 5th meeting of the YAF Board of Directors, 2 September 1961 are in reel 14, Rusher Papers. See also the minutes of the YAF Policy Committee, 28 October 1961, Box 173, folder: YAF, 1960–62, Rusher Papers.

18. I have drawn the labels for these three groups from an article on YAF in *Civic Affairs Monthly* 2 (September 1961), a copy of which is in reel 5, Rusher Papers.

19. Lee Edwards, "Bureaucratic Monstrosity," *The New Guard* 2 (March 1962): 25. The resolution against medical care for the aged is in *The New Guard* 2 (May 1962): 13.

20. Ronald Hamoway and William F. Buckley Jr., "*National Review*: Criticism and Reply," *New Individualist Review* 1 (November 1961): 6–7.

21. Lee Edwards, "Which Road for the Peace Corps?" *The New Guard* 1 (April 1961): 2; Lee Edwards, "City of Delusions," *The New Guard* 1 (June 1961): 2.

22. Allan Ryskind, "The Red China Lobby," *The New Guard* 1 (July 1961): 8–9. YAF's resolution against the U.N. bond issue is in *The New Guard* 2 (May 1962): 13. YAF had always supported men like Walter Judd for their anticommunism and support of Nationalist China. For a synopsis of their argument see Lee Edwards, "The U.S. Role in the Post-World War II Struggle between the Nationalists and the Communists," *Tamking Journal of American Studies* 8 (Fall 1991): 49–66.

23. For the demonstrations, see Robert Smith Thompson, *The Missiles of October: The Declassified Story of John F. Kennedy and the Cuban Missile Crisis* (New York: Simon & Schuster, 1992), 333. Evans's comments are in "Trends," *National Review Bulletin* 12, 23 January 1961, 6. See also William Schulz, "Castro's Cuba: Haven for Yankee Turncoats," *Human Events* 19 (26 May 1962): 391.

24. Lee Edwards, "Let Him Begin," *The New Guard* 1 (August 1961): 2.

25. YAF statement on nuclear testing, *The New Guard* 2 (January 1962): 21. See also the editorial "To Test or Not to Test," *The New Guard* 2 (March 1962): 3. Other remarks on foreign policy are in Lee Edwards, "Where the Iron Curtain Begins," *The New Guard* 1 (October 1961): 3; William Schulz, "Trading with the Enemy," *National Review* 11, 26 August 1961, 116; William Schulz, "How Red is Jagan?" *National Review* 11, 9 September 1961, 152; editorial in *The New Guard* 1 (November 1961): 3; Robert G. Harley, "Burma: A Case Study of Neutralism in Asia," *The New Guard* 1 (November 1961): 7–8; Anthony Okotcha, "Moscow Trained Me for Revolution," *The New Guard* 2 (February 1962): 8–9, 15; and R. J. Boxklet, "Red Fox in the Caribbean," *The New Guard* 2 (June 1962): 12–13.

26. Barry Goldwater, *Why Not Victory?* (New York: MacFadden, 1962). I have used the 1963 paperback edition. The quotations are on pp. 9, 16, 35, 61, and 111.

27. A good summary of the issue for the Kennedy administration is in James Giglio, *The Presidency of John F. Kennedy* (Lawrence: University of Kansas Press, 1991), 224–225. The CIA worked steadily if not diligently to get rid of Lumumba through assassination. His death in a plane crash was suspicious, but apparently not the work of the CIA.

28. The YAF resolution on Katanga is in *The New Guard* 2 (May 1962): 13. See also Carol Bauman, "UN Blackmail in the Congo," *The New Guard* 1 (October 1961): 11–12; and the *New York Times*, 17 December 1961, 60. The Yale offer and the Republican comments are reported in *Human Events* 18, 22 December 1961, 862.

29. Confidential Memo #2, 15 December 1961, Box 12, folder: The Radical Right, Lee White Papers, JFKL. See also Box 29, Group Research File, Marvin Liebman As-

sociates Collection, HIA. YAF's position is in *The New Guard* 2 (January 1962): 5. The Aid to Katanga Committee, formed December 9, 1961, included Liebman as a founder. YAF later honored Moise Tshombe at its February 1962 rally in Madison Square Garden, which was organized out of Liebman's New York headquarters.

30. Confidential Memo #4, 23 January 1962, Box 12, folder: The Radical Right, Lee White Papers, JFKL.

31. The paper, "A Conservative Program for the 60's," is in the George McDonnell Papers.

32. Robert Schuchman, "YAF and the New Conservatism," *The New Guard* 2 (March 1962): 3.

33. Robert Novak, "The Contentious Campus Conservative," *The New Guard* 2 (January 1962): 17. This was originally printed in the *Wall Street Journal*.

34. Ibid., 18.

35. Schuchman is quoted in ibid. For Caddy, see his essay "The Conservative Dilemma at the Polls," *The New Guard* 2 (March 1962): 30–31.

36. Brief commentary on the rally is in Rusher, *The Rise of the Right*, 129; a copy of its agenda and schedule is in the Robert Croll Papers. Burnham's observations are in Burnham to William F. Buckley Jr., 11 March 1962, Box 20, folder: Inter-Office Memos, Buckley Papers. See the *New York Times*, 2 January 1962, 19 and 15 February 1962, 10 for commentary on rally preparations.

37. Wakefield, *New York in the Fifties*, 266. For rally coverage see the *New York Times*, 8 March 1962, 1.

38. Michael Beschloss, *The Crisis Years: Kennedy and Khrushchev, 1960–1963* (New York: Edward Burlingame Books, 1991), 487.

39. His speech is reprinted in L. Brent Bozell, "To Magnify the West," *National Review* 12, 24 April 1962, 285–287. The quotations are on p. 285.

40. Ibid., 287. For a study of Bozell's religious transformation, which was underway by the time of this speech, and his subsequent religious conflicts with his brother-in-law, see Roland Gunn, "Ideology and Political Sophistication: Bozell, Buckley, and the Editorial Policy of the *National Review* in the Early 1960s," unpublished ms. kindly loaned to the author by Professor Gunn.

41. Burnham to Buckley, 11 March 1962, Box 20, folder: Inter-Office Memos, Buckley Papers.

42. Eugene Lyons, "Anti-Communism and the 'Radical Right,'" *The New Guard* 2 (January 1962): 8–9. For writings by YAFers that typify these other issues, see M. Stanton Evans, "Trends," *National Review Bulletin* 13, 30 October 1962, 6; Robert Hurt, "Antitrust and Competition," *New Individualist Review* 1 (Winter 1962): 3–12; Robert Schuchman, "J. B. Conant's 'Slums and Suburbs,'" *New Individualist Review* 2 (Spring 1962): 51–52; William Schulz, "Public Power Lobby Gets Tips from Moscow," *Human Events* 19, 3 November 1962, 839; William Schulz, "Reds on College Campuses," *Human Events* 19, 1 September 1962, 667; William Schulz, "The White House: Biggest US Lobby," *Human Events* 19, 22 September 1962, 725.

43. Lee Edwards, "The New Right: Its Face and Future," *The New Guard* 2 (July 1962): 6–7. For other articles see Lee Edwards, "Target: Fraternities," *The New Guard* 2 (August 1962): 6–7; and M. Stanton Evans, "Trends," *National Review Bulletin* 13, 7 August 1962, 6. Barry Goldwater had earlier defended the fraternity system, saying that "where fraternities are not allowed, communism flourishes." See *The Nation*, 17 December 1960, 467.

44. Robert Schuchman, "Civil Liberties in the Welfare State," *New Individualist Review* 2 (Autumn 1962): 24–30. The quotations are on pp. 24, 25, and 30. A similar, less

philosophical attack is in William Schulz, "COPE Wants Control of Your Congress," *Human Events* 19, 19 May 1962, 367.

45. A good summary of some of these efforts is in Edwards and Edwards, *Rebels with a Cause*, 10.

46. Robert Schuchman, "YAF and the New Conservatism," *The New Guard* 2 (March 1962): 5. For an example of YAF's recruitment efforts, see the biographical data sheet for L. Jack Allen of the Nebraska Young Republicans, copy in the Robert Croll Papers.

47. *New York Times*, 14 May 1962, 32; Robert Novak, "The Contentious Campus Conservative," reprinted in *The New Guard* 2 (January 1962): 17–18; Michael Harrington, "Pro-Vest & Anti-Guitar: The Sad Truth about Campus Conservatism," *Nugget* (October 1962): 18, 21, 37; Kenneth Keniston, "American Students and the 'Political Revival,'" *The American Scholar* 32 (Winter 1962–63): 58, 61.

48. *Conservatism on the College Campus*, Research Report of the Public Opinion Index for Industry, 20 (January 1962), 4–41 passim.

49. Robert Martinson, "State of the Campus, 1962," *The Nation* 194, 19 May 1962, 432–437, 456. The quotation is on p. 436. For Harrington, see his essay "The American Campus: 1962," *Dissent* 9 (Spring 1962): 164–168.

50. Allan Brownfield, "America's Angry Young Men," *Modern Age* 6 (Spring 1962): 197–201; Irving Howe, "Notebook: Journey to the End of the Right," *Dissent* 9 (Winter 1962): 79–82. The quotation is on p. 81.

51. The best survey of this literature, which is enormous, is in Hixson, *Search for the American Right Wing*. Also see Jerome Himmelstein, *To the Right: The Transformation of American Conservatism* (Berkeley: University of California Press, 1990) for a close examination of the status anxiety hypothesis of Richard Hofstader and others in Daniel Bell's 1962 collection *The Radical Right*, as well as a perceptive analysis of the rise of the new conservatism.

52. Richard Braungart, *Family Status, Socialization and Student Politics* (Ann Arbor: University Microfilms International, 1979), 56–57, 59, 61–62. See also Lawrence Schiff, "The Obedient Rebels: A Study of College Conversions to Conservatism," *Journal of Social Issues* 20 (October 1964): 74–95; and David Westby, *The Clouded Vision: The Student Movement in the United States in the 1960s* (Lewisburg, Pa.: Bucknell University Press, 1976).

53. Braungart, *Family Status*, 137, 338–339. Braungart presents his data in a series of tables on pp. 142, 144, 147, 149, 153, 158–159, 163, 173, 325–328, 332–333, and 335. Also see Westby, *The Clouded Vision*, 44, 60, 116–117. Apparently, YAF did not accept every conservative who sought to join; see Patrick Buchanan's bitter commentary in his *Right from the Beginning*, 246.

54. These conclusions, and Franke's comments, are drawn from Margaret and Richard Braungart, "The Life-Course Development of Left- and Right-Wing Youth Activist Leaders from the 1960s," *Political Psychology* 11 (1990): 243–282. The quotations are on pp. 261 and 267. Also see the same two authors' "Political Career Patterns of Radical Activists in the 1960s and 1970s: Some Historical Comparisons," *Sociological Focus* 13 (August 1980): 237–254. For a portrait of conservative activists' appeal see Wakefield, *New York in the Fifties*, 267–268. Less laudatory analyses of YAFers are in Steven Roberts, "Image on the Right," *The Nation* 194, 19 May 1962, 440–442 and Cain, *They'd Rather Be Right*.

55. For Bell see "The National Style and the Radical Right," *Partisan Review* 29 (Fall 1962): 519–534. The quotation from Rush and Denisoff is in Westby, *The Clouded Vision*, 29. Higham's complaint is in his "Beyond Consensus: The Historian as Moral Critic," *American Historical Review* 67 (April 1962): 616. For Viguerie, see

The New Right, 54–55. Also see L. J. Davis, "Conservatism in America: A Small Circle of Friends," *Harper's* 261, October 1980, 21–26.

56. M. Stanton Evans, *Revolt on the Campus* (Chicago: Henry Regnery Co., 1961). The quotations come from the Preface and from p. 16.

57. Ibid., 44. For criticism of Evans, see George Gilder and Bruce Chapman, *The Party that Lost Its Head* (New York: Alfred A. Knopf, 1966), 30. Both authors were moderate Republicans who opposed Goldwater.

58. Evans, *Revolt on the Campus*, 180–181.

59. Ibid., 118.

60. Rusher to Evans, 24 May 1961, reel 5, Rusher Papers.

Chapter Seven   JFK and the Right Wing

1. Perhaps ironically, one exception is Arthur Schlesinger Jr.'s insider history *A Thousand Days: John F. Kennedy in the White House* (Boston: Houghton Mifflin, 1965), 749–756. Although he argues that the right-wing activity in the early 1960s was part of a predictable historical cycle of extremism and embodied the "politics of resentment," Schlesinger nonetheless recognizes John F. Kennedy's "deep concern" at its spread and apparent influence, especially as its attacks on his administration multiplied. See especially pp. 751 and 753. Aside from Schlesinger, only Lewis Paper has devoted any sustained attention to the radical Right and Kennedy's concern about its political impact. But Paper traced this concern to 1963, and attributed it to the approaching 1964 election and the increasing likelihood that Kennedy would be facing Barry Goldwater as the Republican nominee. See his *The Promise and the Performance* (New York: Crown Publishers, 1975). Other Kennedy scholars who followed Schlesinger generally avoided the topic of the right wing. Even insiders such as Theodore Sorenson, *Kennedy* (New York: Harper & Row, 1965) and Harris Wofford, *Of Kennedys and Kings: Making Sense of the Sixties* (New York: Farrar, Straus & Giroux, 1980) ignored the topic altogether. Particularly disturbing is the failure by historians of the Kennedy presidency to acknowledge both the growing strength of the right wing during those years and Kennedy's personal concern about its presence. Three premier studies of the Kennedy presidency that fail in this respect are Irving Bernstein, *Promises Kept: John F. Kennedy's New Frontier* (New York: Oxford University Press, 1991), Giglio, *The Presidency of John F. Kennedy*, and Herbert Parmet, *JFK: The Presidency of John F. Kennedy* (New York: Dial Press, 1983). I want to thank Marc Villa, my summer 1994 Hackman Fellow, for research assistance on both the Kennedy literature and the appearance of the radical Right in contemporary periodicals.

2. For a sample of this debate, see the *New York Times*, 9 March 1961, 12; 19 March 1961, 51; 21 March 1961, 8; and 26 March 1961, 60. Ellwood's comments are in his *The Sixties Spiritual Awakening: American Religion Moving from Modern to Postmodern* (New Brunswick, N.J.: Rutgers University Press, 1994), 59. For Nixon, see Nixon to Dwight D. Eisenhower, 5 March 1962, Gen. Corresp., Box 237, folder: Dwight D. Eisenhower (1 of 2), NPP. Nixon sent similar letters to George Romney, Fred Seaton, Mark Hatfield, and Nelson Rockefeller.

3. *New York Times*, 1 April 1961, 1; and 7 April 1961, 15.

4. The literature is enormous. Of direct relevance to material cited are: "Wide-Swinging Bitter-Enders of the Right," *Newsweek* 57, 10 April 1961, 38; "Subversion of the Right" and "Why They Crucify," *The Christian Century* 78, 12 April 1961, 379–380, 443–444; Raymond Moley, "It Is Not Conservatism," *Newsweek* 57, 17 April 1961, 114; Alan C. Elms, "The Conservative Ripple," *The Nation* 192, 27 May

1961, 458–460; Stanley Mosk and Howard Jewel, "The Birch Phenomenon Analyzed," *New York Times Magazine*, 20 August 1961, 12ff; Eugene V. Schneider, "The Radical Right," *The Nation* 193, 30 September 1961, 199–203; William S. White, "The New Irresponsibles," *Harper's* 223, November 1961, 104–108; and "Thunder on the Far Right," *Newsweek* 58, 4 December 1961, 18–30. For General Walker see the *New York Times*, 13 June 1961, 1; 18 June 1961, 1; 7 September 1961, 1; 8 September 1961, 13; 3 November 1961, 1. The Minutemen are noted in the *New York Times*, 22 October 1961, 32; 11 November 1961, 9; and 12 November 1961, 1. For the Kennedys' views see the *New York Times*, 19 November 1961, 1 and "Thunder against the Right," *Time* 78, 24 November 1961, 11–12. In *Radicals or Conservatives? The Contemporary American Right* (Chicago: Rand McNally & Co., 1971), James McEvoy III noted that in 1961 the *New York Times Index* gave thirty-seven and a half column inches of space to the Birch Society, and by 1962 it devoted four and a half inches to Young Americans for Freedom while giving the Birch Society only three inches; see pp. 10-11.

5. "Address in Seattle at the University of Washington's 100th Anniversary Program," November 16, 1961, *Public Papers of the President: John F. Kennedy, 1961* (Washington, D.C.: GPO, 1962), 726.

6. "Address in Los Angeles at a Dinner of the Democratic Party of California," November 18, 1961, ibid., 735.

7. For ADA concerns see "Notes of an Oct. 18, 1961 breakfast meeting" of the ADA Board, reel 120, ADA Papers. Union concerns and their ties to both the Kennedy administration and the New Left are in Peter Levy, *The New Left and Labor in the 1960s* (Urbana: University of Illinois Press, 1994), see especially p. 24; and Victor Reuther, *The Brothers Reuther and the Story of the UAW* (Boston: Houghton Mifflin, 1976), 440.

8. The bitterness and legacy of the Kohler strikes is documented in Walter H. Uphoff, *Kohler on Strike: Thirty Years of Conflict* (Boston: Beacon Press, 1966). Additional material on the role of Reuther and Robert Kennedy is in Robert F. Kennedy, *The Enemy Within* (New York: Harper & Brothers, 1960), 270–281 and Schlesinger, *Robert Kennedy and His Times*, 174–181.

9. The intent of the memorandum is noted in the cover letter, Victor Reuther to Robert Kennedy, 19 December 1961, Box 41, folder: Walter P. Reuther, 1949, 1954–65, 1970, Joseph L. Rauh Jr. Papers, LC. A copy of the memorandum is in Box 377, folder 3, Walter Reuther Papers, Archives of Labor and Urban Affairs, Wayne State University. The quotations are on pp. 1 (emphasis in original), 2, and 6. Hereafter this will simply be referred to as the Reuther Memorandum. By 1963, when the administration had acted on some of the memorandum's recommendations, requests for copies flowed in to the Justice Department. Robert Kennedy's office provided copies until it ran out, but also concocted a cover story that not only denied any connection to the memo but insisted that they had simply filed it without reading its contents. See Andrew F. Oehmann, Executive Assistant to RFK, to RFK, 7 November 1963, and Oehmann to Representative George E. Brown Jr., 10 December 1963, Attorney General, Gen. Corresp., Box 48, folder: Reuther Memorandum 12/19/61, RFK Papers, JFKL. Ironically, Nelson Lichtenstein's splendid recent study of Walter Reuther has no mention of this topic; see *The Most Dangerous Man in Detroit: Walter Reuther and the Fate of American Labor* (New York: Basic Books, 1995).

10. Reuther Memorandum, 6.

11. Ibid., 15–17.

12. Ibid., 18–21. For the Volker Fund see Merrimom Cuninggim, *Private Money and Pub-*

lic Service: The Role of Foundations in American Society (New York: McGraw-Hill, 1972), 108.

13. Reuther Memorandum, 21–24. The quotation is on p. 24.

14. For White's efforts see "Confidential Report #1," 28 November 1961, Box 12, folder: The Radical Right, Lee White Papers, JFKL. It is interesting to note that in his lengthy (386 pp.) oral history interviews for the Kennedy Library, at no time did White mention anything about the right wing or his efforts to monitor it. The interviews were conducted in 1964 and 1970. The other efforts are noted in Athan Theoharis, *Spying on Americans: Political Surveillance from Hoover to the Huston Plan* (Philadelphia: Temple University Press, 1978), 168–169; and *Army Surveillance of Civilians: A Documentary Analysis* (Washington, D.C.: GPO, 1972), 39, 76. The latter was prepared by the staff of the Subcommittee on Constitutional Rights, Committee on the Judiciary, United States Senate, 92d Cong., 2d Sess. Robert Kennedy's remarks are in Edwin O. Guthman and Jeffrey Shulman (eds.), *Robert Kennedy: In His Own Words* (Toronto: Bantam, 1988), 296–297. Two memos from RFK's executive assistant, Andrew Oehmann, try to distance the Attorney General from the report by insisting that he had neither read it nor implemented any of its suggestions. See Oehmann Memo to RFK, 7 November 1963, and Oehmann to Congressman George E. Brown Jr., 10 December 1963, Attorney General Corresp., Box 48, folder: Reuther Memorandum, 12/19/61, RFK Papers, JFKL.

15. David Burnham discusses some of this in *A Law Unto Itself: Power, Politics, and the IRS* (New York: Random House, 1989). In *The American Police State: The Government against the People* (New York: Vintage, 1978), David Wise also makes brief mention of the project. For the question of ideology and taxation, see William J. Lehrfeld, "The Taxation of Ideology," *The Catholic University of America Law Review* 19 (Fall 1969): 50–73. A good summary of the Church Committee, but one that says little about the IRS, is in LeRoy Ashby and Rod Gramer, *Fighting the Odds: The Life of Senator Frank Church* (Pullman: Washington State University Press, 1994), 471 and passim. Even with the Church Committee, however, both the committee and the public focused their attention on Richard Nixon's abuses of the IRS rather than those of John Kennedy.

16. J. F. Worley, Chief, Exempt Organizations Branch, to John W. S. Littleton, Director, Tax Rulings Division, 24 October 1962, RG 56, General Records of the Department of the Treasury, Office Files of Under Secretary Henry Fowler, 1961–1964, Box 17-F, folder: Tax Exemption—Correspondence with Congressman Patman, Archives II (hereafter Fowler Papers). White House agreement is noted in Commissioner Caplin to Treasury Under Secretary Henry Fowler, 9 December 1963 in the same file. For its public "cover," see the background paper issued by the Public Information of the IRS, August 1962, in the same file.

17. Caplin makes note of this project in his oral history Interview with IRS historian Shelley Davis, but tries to brush it off as nothing extraordinary. Indeed, he is careful to argue that both he and Treasury Under Secretary Henry Fowler were aware of IRS interventions under Eisenhower and were determined to be impartial; see pp. 14-15. Also see the testimony of Dr. Laurence N. Woodworth, Chief of Staff, Joint Committee on Internal Revenue Taxation, *Internal Revenue Service Intelligence Operations. Hearings before the Subcommittee on Oversight of the Committee on Ways and Means*, House of Representatives, 94th Cong., 1st Sess. (Washington, D.C.: GPO, 1975), 93.

18. United States Senate, Select Committee to Study Governmental Operations with Respect to Intelligence Activities, *Final Report: Supplementary Detailed Staff Reports on Intelligence Activities and the Rights of Americans*, Book III, 94th Cong., 2d Sess.

(Washington, D.C.: GPO, 1976), 891; hereafter cited as *Final Report*. The footnotes cite the specific memoranda. See also *Investigation of the Special Service Staff of the Internal Revenue Service*, 94th Cong., 1st Sess. (Washington, D.C.: GPO, 1975), 102–103. Despite repeated Freedom of Information Act requests for this material, the IRS has steadfastly refused to release most of it. Although the footnoted references clearly indicate that it is policy-oriented rather than tax-oriented, the IRS continues to claim tax privacy as the reason for withholding the materials. In January 1962 a nineteenth organization was added, the left-wing Fair Play for Cuba Committee; the IRS compiled the original list of 18 chiefly from the December 4 and 8 issues of *Newsweek* and *Time*.

19. See "The Internal Revenue Service: An Intelligence Resource and Collector," in *Final Report*, 837–843. The special access incident is noted in *Political Intelligence in the Internal Revenue Service: The Special Service Staff. A Documentary Analysis Prepared by the Staff of the Subcommittee on Constitutional Rights of the Committee of the Judiciary, United States Senate*, 93d Cong., 2d Sess. (Washington, D.C.: GPO, 1974), 198; for Bellino see Pierre Salinger, *P.S.: A Memoir* (New York: St. Martin's Press, 1995), 52. Bellino had worked with Robert Kennedy on the McClellan Committee, where he had been the chief accountant. The role of Attorney General Robert F. Kennedy in this project has been as neglected as that of his brother. On the one hand, Arthur Schlesinger Jr., in *Robert Kennedy and His Times*, carefully documents Robert Kennedy's use of the IRS in combatting organized crime. But while he notes the existence of the Reuther Memorandum, he argues that the administration moved cautiously on it and omits all reference to the Ideological Organizations Project or any interest in using the Internal Revenue Service against the right wing. See pp. 267 and 283–284 for the IRS and organized crime, and p. 451 for the Reuther Memorandum. For evidence of Schlesinger's ignorance of the project see Acting IRS Commissioner Bertrand Harding to Schlesinger, 27 June 1963, FOIA. (These are materials obtained from the IRS through the Freedom of Information Act, which I have identified as clearly as possible. Because the IRS refuses to indicate citations to particular files, I have to rely on dates and correspondents.)

20. *Final Report*, 892. For Rogovin's analysis see Rogovin to Feldman, 23 March 1964, FOIA.

21. Caplin to Fowler, 14 May 1962, Fowler Papers, Box 11-F, folder: IRS: Tax Exempt Organizations.

22. *Final Report*, 893; *Investigation of the Special Service Staff*, 105; Harding to Patman, 30 October 1964, FOIA. In its first release, the IRS redacted the words "mass media," perhaps an admission of the political nature of this project. Feldman discussed this project very briefly in a letter to the author, 11 August 1994.

23. *Final Report*, 893–894. The *Investigation of the Special Service Staff* claims that eight groups had been audited; see p. 105. It also notes that five of the left-wing groups had undergone audits, including two exempt organizations. A letter from Caplin to Treasury Under Secretary Henry Fowler does not indicate that any action was recommended against the left-wing groups. For the expansion to include tax-paying groups see Audit Division to Assistant Commissioner (Compliance), 9 March 1962, FOIA.

24. *Investigation of the Special Service Staff*, 106; *Final Report*, 894. The two right-wing groups recommended for revocation of tax-exempt status were the Christian Anti-Communist Cruasde and the Life-Line Foundation; see Caplin to Fowler, 23 May 1963, Fowler Papers, Box 11-F, folder: IRS—Tax Exempt Organizations. Rogovin's memorandum to regional commissioners, dated 27 August 1963, is in FOIA.

25. *Investigation of the Special Service Staff*, 106–107. Also see Burnham, *A Law Unto Itself*, 270–272.

26. *Investigation of the Special Service Staff*, 107–108. See also *Internal Revenue Service Intelligence Operations. Hearings before the Subcommittee on Oversight of the Committee on Ways and Means, House of Representatives*, 94th Cong., 1st Sess. (Washington, D.C.: GPO, 1975), 99. The IRS Conference Report for December 4, 1963 on the Political Action Survey reveals another dimension to this project that remains wrapped in mystery. Mitchell Rogovin indicated that not only had the topic come up at a recent Treasury staff meeting, but "an intense interest in this matter existed on the Hill." A copy of this report is in FOIA.

27. *Investigation of the Special Service Staff*, 108–109. The organization later requested and received tax-exempt status as a social welfare rather than a charitable organization. The report of the Congressional investigation is notable for the number of memory lapses on the part of almost all participants. See also *Final Report*, 895 which relies on memoranda of August 21 and 29 from Rogovin. Burnham, *A Law Unto Itself*, 272 cites the two organizations deleted.

28. *Investigation of the Special Service Staff*, 109. For direct commentary on this pressure see the Conference Report for January 4, 1964, FOIA.

29. Ibid., 109–110; *Final Report*, 895–896. In *A Law Unto Itself*, David Burnham concluded that two of the right-wing groups that lost their exempt status were H. L. Hunt's Life-Line Foundation and Dr. Fred Schwarz's Christian Anti-Communist Crusade; see pp. 272–273. Also see *Hearings before the Select Committee to Study Governmental Operations with Respect to Intelligence Activities of the United States Senate, Vol. 3: Internal Revenue Service*, 94th Cong., 1st Sess. (Washington, D.C.: GPO, 1976), 105. Despite the Johnson administration's professed disinterest in the Ideological Organizations Project, evidence indicates that it continued past LBJ's term of office and into the Nixon administration (which soon created its own IRS intelligence/enforcement program). See D. W. Bacon, Assistant Commissioner (Compliance) to Mr. Roger V. Barth, 1 July 1969, FOIA.

30. *Final Report*, 896.

31. Confidential Report #3, 3 January 1962, Box 12, folder: Radical Right, Lee White Papers, JFKL; M. Stanton Evans, "Trends," *National Review Bulletin* 11, 9 December 1961, 6; Marvin Kitman, "New Wave from the Right," *The New Leader*, 18 September 1961, 10–12.

32. Liebman to "All Concerned," 16 January 1962, Box 99, Marvin Liebman Associates Papers, HIA.

33. Ibid. Goldwater's 1961 speech is quoted in Donald Janson and Bernard Eismann, *The Far Right* (New York: McGraw-Hill, 1963), 231, and his *National Review* remarks are noted in Dudman, *Men of the Far Right*, 30. For Judd see Walter Judd to Mrs. Esther Bergquist, 8 February 1962, Box 256, folder 2, Walter Judd Papers, HIA. A general discussion of this problem is in Barbara Green, Kathryn Turner, and Dante Germino, "Responsible and Irresponsible Right-Wing Groups: A Problem in Analysis," *Journal of Social Issues* 19 (April 1963): 3–17.

34. Confidential Memorandum from the ADA Campus Division, January 1962, reel 102, ADA Papers; Richard Lambert, ADA field representative, to Morris Rigar, 31 January 1962, reel 139, ADA Papers; Milton Shapp to Ralph Dungan, 9 January 1962, WHCNF, Box 3092, folder: Young Americans for Freedom, JFKL. Also see Ed Garvey, President of USNSA, to Richard Lambert, 19 February 1962, reel 139, ADA Papers. The SDS position is outlined in Jim Monsonis to Vi Gunther, 19 April 1963, reel 139, ADA Papers.

35. Confidential Memo #6, 19 February 1962, Box 12, folder: The Radical Right, Lee White Papers, JFKL.
36. Confidential Report #4, 23 January 1962, and Memo from Marcus Raskin to Lee White, 23 January 1962, both in Box 12, folder: The Radical Right, Lee White Papers, JFKL. The Gottlieb memo is attached to the Raskin memo.
37. *Final Report*, 457.
38. Memorandum for the President, 15 August 1963, Box 106, folder: Right Wing Movement, Part I, Presidential Papers, President's Office Files, Papers of John F. Kennedy, JFKL.
39. Ibid.
40. Ibid.
41. Ibid.

Chapter Eight **Taking On the G.O.P.**

1. Discussion of the G.O.P. as target is in "The Real Targets," *The Nation* 194, 17 February 1962, 131. See also William Rusher to Buckley, 20 February 1962, reel 4, Rusher Papers; Janson and Eismann, *The Far Right*, 207, 237; and Green, Turner, and Germino, "Responsible and Irresponsible Right-Wing Groups," 3-17, passim. For the Schell quote see Wes Willoughby to Leonard Finder, 12 May 1964, Box 34, folder: Republican, Leonard Finder Papers, 1930–69, DDE.
2. Feldman's report is in Presidential Papers, President's Office Files, Box 106, folder: Right Wing Movement, Part II, Papers of John F. Kennedy, JFKL. For efforts to capture the G.O.P., see T. George Harris, "The Rampant Right Invades the G.O.P.," *Look* 27, 16 July 1963, 19–25.
3. "Introduction to the Liberal Study Group—1963," reel 140, ADA Papers. YAF itself issued *NSA Report*, a critique of the organization, its finances and tax-exempt status, and its "Liberal bias." See M. Stanton Evans, "At Home," *National Review Bulletin* 14, 28 May 1963, 6.
4. Shaul to Lambert, 27 May 1963, reel 139, ADA Papers. Evidence of attacks in 1962, and background for the 1962 conservative-liberal confrontation in NSA, is in Arthur Gorson, National Chairman of Campus ADA, to Richard Lambert, 23 July 1962, ibid.
5. From a 30 September 1963 YAF fund-raising appeal, copy in Box 451, Stanley K. Hornbeck Collection, HIA. For Viguerie's remarks see his fund-raising letter of 18 January 1963, Box 19, folder: Young Americans for Freedom, F. Clifford White Papers, and Viguerie to YAF members, 17 September 1962, Box 3092, folder: Young Americans for Freedom, WHCNF, JFKL.
6. Bauman's remarks, from a letter to YAF members, are reprinted in *The New Guard* 3 (December–January 1963): 10. The same issue discusses the question of Ayn Rand; see p. 2. Comments on the spring board meeting are in Kay Kolbe to Robert Bauman, 26 May 1963 and Bauman to Kolbe, 31 May 1963, reel 20, Rusher Papers. For Youth for Goldwater see *The New Guard* 3 (October 1963): 9. Not only did two YAFers run the organization; the steering committee consisted largely of YAFers. Of the eight members, six (C. Bauman, Harff, R. Bauman, Donald Shafto, Fred Coldren, and William Boerum) were YAFers. The other two (Morton Blackwell and Walter Gebelein) were Young Republicans. See Proposal by Carol Bauman, 16 November 1963, Box 10, folder: Youth for Goldwater, F. C. White Papers. The same file indicates that later other YAFers were added, including Robert Croll, Richard Noble, and Kay Kolbe.
7. *The New Guard* 3 (December–January 1963): 12, 16. YAF eventually had to can-

cel its national conference for conservative youth when it failed to secure a key senator to deliver a keynote address; see Box 28, folder: Young Americans for Freedom, Buckley Papers.

8. *New York Times*, 14 April 1963, 63. The indictment of Kennedy is in *The New Guard* 3 (May 1963): passim.

9. *The New Guard* 3 (August 1963): 6, 10.

10. *National Service Corps. Hearings before the Special Subcommittee on Labor of the Committee on Education and Labor, House of Representatives*, 88th Cong., 1st Sess. (Washington, D.C.: GPO, 1963), part 1, 381–383. The other group was the American Farm Bureau, who also feared the loss of local initiative; see ibid., part 2, 487.

11. Ibid., 384, 394.

12. Reports on YAF can be found in several GRI publications; see vol. 2 (12 February 1963): 11; (29 March 1963): 21; (21 June 1963): 47; (12 November 1963): 83. For YAF's reply see Antoni Gollan, "Semi-Secret Organization on the Left, and It's [sic] Plans to Discredit YAF," *The New Guard* 3 (July 1963): 7–8.

13. A copy of the committee's report is in Box 22, folder: RNC (4), Arthur S. Flemming Papers, DDE. See also Cotter and Hennessy, *Politics without Power*, 209 and Gilder and Chapman, *The Party that Lost Its Head*, 78.

14. Evans's comment is in "Goldwater, Rockefeller, and the Young Republicans," *National Review* 15, 13 August 1963, 97. For Hatfield's remarks see Travis Cross to Stephen Shadegg, Series VIII: Publications, 1949–1965, Box 3J9, folder: Shadegg Book, BG. Miller's remarks are reported in Gilder and Chapman, *The Party that Lost Its Head*, 84. For evidence that much of this maneuvering was designed to set up Goldwater in 1964, see F. Clifton White to Roger Milliken, 9 January 1963, in Box 155, folder: Political Campaigns & Related Materials, National Draft Goldwater Committee, 1963, Rusher Papers; Edward Feilor to Buz Lukens, 12 August 1963, Box 18, folder: Young Republicans, F. Clifton White Papers; Cook, *Barry Goldwater*, 135; and Robert Novak, *The Agony of the G.O.P. 1964* (New York: Macmillan, 1965), 196–201. Miller became the Republican vice-presidential nominee on the Goldwater ticket.

15. The report to Rusher is in reel 18, Rusher Papers. See also Cotter and Hennessy, *Politics without Power*, 155–156; and Evans, "Goldwater, Rockefeller, and the Young Republicans," 98–100. The Maryland report is in Novak, *Agony of the G.O.P.*, 197, as is the Adelstein observation.

16. *Congressional Record*, vol. 109, part 12, 88th Cong., 1st Sess., 23 August 1963, 15691–15692.

17. Ibid., 15693.

18. Reprinted in ibid., 15698.

19. Kuchel to Finder, 8 June 1963, Box 16, folder: Extremist Associations, Leonard Finder Papers, 1930–69, DDE. Also see Finder to Brig. Gen. Robert Schulz, Exec. Ass't to Gen. Eisenhower, 15 July 1963, Box 1, folder: Finder-Eisenhower Staff Correspondence, 1961–69; and Finder to Richard Nixon, 7 November 1963, Box 14, folder: N. Both are in the Leonard Finder Papers, DDE.

20. Conrad Joyner, *The Republican Dilemma: Conservatism or Progressivism* (Tucson: University of Arizona Press, 1963), v, 94–95.

21. Nelson Rockefeller, "Call for a United Republican Party in the 1964 Election," July 14, 1963, in Schlesinger (ed.), *History of U.S. Political Parties*, 4:3095–3099. Also see the *New York Times* clipping, 15 July 1963, in Box 245, folder: Nelson Rockefeller, DNC Papers, LBJL. According to a *Washington Post* clipping, 17 July 1963, in the same file, Rockefeller had earlier turned down a request for $50,000 to help fight a conservative takeover of the Young Republicans.

22. Ihde to Noble, 26 September 1963, and William H. Best III to Rusher, 23 October 1963, reel 18, Rusher Papers; Rusher to Lawrence Cott, 14 January 1963, W. A. Rusher, 1959–63, Rusher Papers; Nancy Merrill, co-chair YRNF, to RNC, 17 September 1963, and Peter O'Donnell to F. Clifton White, 21 September 1963, Box 8, folder: Peter O'Donnell, F. Clifton White Papers. John Birch activities are noted in the *New York Times*, 16 March 1963, 4; 8 April 1963, 31; and 12 May 1963, 68. For the importance of California see William Rusher to Richard Noble, 10 December 1962, reel 30, Rusher Papers. See Rusher to Ned Cushing, 18 February 1963 in the same file for Noble's role in California.

23. Ripon Society, "A Call to Excellence in Leadership," January 1964, 1. A copy is in the DDE Post-Presidential Papers, 1964 Principal File, Box 22, folder: ST-1: Statement-Sent In, DDE. The cover letter is misdated January 1963, but internal evidence clearly indicates that it was prepared after the assassination of John F. Kennedy.

24. Ibid., 3.

25. Ibid., 6, 8.

26. Eisenhower to Sig Larmon, 3 June 1963, DDE Post-Presidential Papers, 1961–69, Secretary's Series, Correspondence Subseries: 1963, Box 10, folder: La., DDE. Numerous letters in the same collection provide evidence of Eisenhower's persistent encouragement of other candidates, particularly Charles Percy and William Scranton.

27. Clif White confidential memos to William Rusher, 29 May 1962 and 9 July 1962, Box 155, folder: Political Campaigns and Related Material, National Draft Goldwater Committee, 1961–62, Rusher Papers. The letter from Mrs. Katharine Kennedy Brown, G.O.P. committeewoman, to William Miller, 12 July 1962, is in the same file. The story of the Goldwater effort has been told well elsewhere. See especially F. Clifton White, *Suite 3505: The Story of the Draft Goldwater Movement* (New Rochelle, N.Y.: Arlington House, 1967).

28. Lee Edwards, "Needed: A Conservative Establishment," *The New Guard* 2 (June 1962): 2. See also John Ashbrook, "We Need a Conservative Congress for Affirmative Conservative Reform," Manion Forum interview, 30 September 1962.

29. Rusher to William F. Buckley Jr., 14 January 1963, Rusher to Goldwater, 23 January 1963, and Rusher to L. Brent Bozell, 29 January 1963, reel 30, Rusher Papers. The analysis is in William Rusher, "Crossroads for the G.O.P.," *National Review* 3, 12 February 1963, 109–112; quotation on p. 112. Frank S. Meyer expressed similar sentiments; see Meyer to Goldwater, 11 February 1963, Box 18, F. Clifton White Papers.

30. McDonnell to Rusher, 4 March 1963, reel 17, Rusher Papers; *The New Guard* 3 (April 1963): 4, 12; Buckley to Hunt, 2 April 1963, Box 26, General Correspondence, Buckley Papers. He apparently failed to get any money from Hunt. See also John Madden, "Young Americans for What?" *America* 108 (19 January 1963): 83–85.

31. For Shafto see Richard Viguerie to F. Clifton White, 11 April 1963 and Donald Shafto to White, 15 April 1963, Box 19, Rally folder, F. Clifton White Papers. Also see George McDonnell to White, 24 April 1963, Box 19, YAF folder, F. Clifton White Papers, and Rusher to White, 11 July 1963, reel 17, Rusher Papers. A copy of the *Human Events* conference program is in Box 59, folder: Human Events PAC, DNC Papers, LBJL. The same folder contains a copy of the keynote address by Admiral Ben Moreel (Ret.), chairman of Americans for Constitutional Action.

32. McGee to Feldman, 14 August 1963, JFK Papers, Presidential Papers, President's Office Files, Box 106, folder: Right-Wing Movement Part I, JFKL.

33. For the Westchester case, see Robert Bauman to Edmund Zanini, 19 August 1963

and Bauman to Herman Bates Jr., 10 October 1963, Box 8, Elms folder, F. Clifton White Papers. The California problem is noted in Best to James Harff, Youth for Goldwater, 4 September 1963, Box 155, folder: Political Campaigns & Related Materials, National Draft Goldwater Committee, 1963, Rusher Papers. Other local chapter problems are noted in Green, Turner, and Germino, "Responsible and Irresponsible Right-Wing Groups," 9.

34. For fund-raising, see Bauman's special YAF appeal letter, 30 September 1963, Box 155, folder: Political Campaigns & Related Materials, National Draft Goldwater Committee, 1963, Rusher Papers. Convention activities are noted in *Group Research Report* 2 (27 November 1963): 87; Buckley to Goldwater, 11 April 1963, Box 25, folder: Barry Goldwater, Buckley Papers; Goldwater to Bauman, n.d., Box 8, F. Clifton White Papers; and Marilyn Manion to F. C. White, 23 October 1963, Box 5, folder: YAF, F. Clifton White Papers. The latter file also contains a September flyer and the program for the convention.

35. Evans to Ferdinand L. Mayer, Bennington, Vt., 27 September 1963, reel 20, Rusher Papers.

36. Convention maneuvering is noted in a "Strictly Confidential" memorandum, "Notes on the 1963 Y.A.F. Convention," by Antoni Gollan, 18 February 1964, Robert Croll Papers. Also see Evans to Bauman, 11 November 1963 and Buckley's telegram of 14 November 1963, Box 25, folder: M. Stanton Evans, Buckley Papers.

37. Thurmond to "Dear Friend," December 1963, copy in WHCF, Name File, Congressional; Thurmond to Robert Bauman, 19 December 1963, WHCF, Box 119, folder: PL6-3 Republican Party; and Harry S. Dent, Admin. Ass't to Thurmond, to Walter Jenkins, Special Ass't to the President, 27 December 1963, WHCF, Name File, General/PL6-3/Barry Goldwater; all in LBJL.

38. Bauman to Peter O'Donnell Jr., 1 December 1963, Box 10, folder: Youth for Goldwater, F. C. White Papers. For the RNC position, see Fred Scribner Jr., RNC's General Counsel, to Fred Seaton, 7 December 1963, Fred Seaton Papers, Post-Eisenhower Administration Series, Box 9, folder: 1964 Presidential Campaign, DDE. Aaron's letter to Robert Bauman is noted in the *New York Times*, 1 December 1963, 50.

39. Allan Brownfield, "America's Angry Young Men," *Modern Age* 6 (Spring 1962): 37. For Gollan see his "YAF: '64 and After," *The New Guard* 3 (November-December 1963): 6. Two contemporary assessments of the conservatives' impact are in Dan Wakefield, "The Campus Conservatives: Where Are They Now?" *Mademoiselle*, August 1963, 292–293, 329–332; and "A Survey of the Political and Religious Attitudes of American College Students," *National Review* 15, 8 October 1963, 279–301.

Chapter Nine   YAF and Conservatism

1. Tyrrell, *The Conservative Crack-Up*, 145.

2. Finder to Nixon, 1 October 1963, Box 14, folder: N, Leonard Finder Papers; Finder to Joseph Ridder, 13 May 1964, Box 15, folder: R, ibid.; and Finder to Eisenhower, 14 May 1964, Box 1, folder: Finder-Eisenhower Correspondence, 1955–69, ibid., DDE. For an overview of this threat see Nicol Rae, *The Decline and Fall of the Liberal Republicans from 1952 to the Present* (New York: Oxford University Press, 1989), especially pp. 48–59.

3. Finder to Eisenhower, 30 May 1964, Box 35, folder: Fi (2), Finder Papers, DDE. This group represents what Richard Hofstadter called the "pseudo-conservatives;" see his *The Paranoid Style in American Politics and Other Essays* (New York: Alfred A. Knopf,

1965), 43–46. A good summary of these groups is in Kessel, *The Goldwater Coalition*, esp. 130. Evidence that the Goldwater campaign did become a springboard to future political careers is the theme of F. Clifton White and William J. Gill, *Why Reagan Won: A Narrative History of the Conservative Movement, 1964–1981* (Chicago: Regnery Gateway, 1981).

4. Ralph de Toledano, *The Winning Side: The Case for Goldwater Republicanism* (New York: G. P. Putnam's Sons, 1964), 120–121; see also pp. 8–9, 15, 73 for arguments that 1964 represented a political watershed.

5. Keene's remarks are noted in a 1964 news clipping in Box 2, folder 2, Judith Faber Papers, State Historical Society of Wisconsin. Goldwater's remarks are in *Human Events* 23, 25 January 1964, copy in Box 91, Marvin Liebman Associates Collection, HIA.

6. A copy of the report, dated 1 February 1964, is in reel 20, Rusher Papers.

7. Hicks to Rusher, 23 February 1964, reel 18, Rusher Papers. For the Knowland problem see Leonard Finder to Knowland, 15 May 1964, Box 14, folder: K, and Finder to Eisenhower, 30 May 1964, Box 35, folder: Fi (2), Finder Papers, DDE.

8. Circular letter from Herman Bates Jr., 26 February 1964, Ruth Elms to Goldwater, 27 February 1964, Terraforte to Bauman, 27 February 1964, and Bauman to Elms, 5 March 1964, all in Box 8, Elms folder, F. Clifton White Papers.

9. For citizens' groups, see Box 7, Citizens' Group folder, F. Clifton White Papers. For Regnery, see *The New Guard* 4 (February 1964): 10. Goldwater's and Miller's comments are in *The New Guard* 4 (March 1964): 5–7.

10. Sim DeLapp to William Rogers, 18 January 1961, Box 61, folder: Letters of Leaving (1), William P. Rogers Papers, DDE. In his *Local People: The Struggle for Civil Rights in Mississippi* (Urbana: University of Illinois Press, 1994), 273–274, John Dittmer describes the actions of white Mississippi Democrats in opposing civil rights and backing Goldwater. See also Davidson, *Race and Class in Texas Politics*, 226 and *The New Guard* 4 (February 1964): 6; *The New Guard* 4 (April 1964): 4. For the views of conservative clergy see James F. Findlay Jr., *Church People in the Struggle: The National Council of Churches and the Black Freedom Movement, 1950–1970* (New York: Oxford University Press, 1993), 63.

11. Bauman telegram to LBJ, 30 January 1964, WHCF, General, TA 4/CO303, Box 7, LBJL; *The New Guard* 4 (January 1964): 7; *Group Research Report* 3 (30 March 1964): 23 and (1 May 1964): 31–32.

12. For Youth for Goldwater see Box 89, Marvin Liebman Associates Collection, HIA. The National Youth for Goldwater steering committee included the following YAFers: Robert Bauman, Fred Coldren, Robert Croll, Mrs. Kay Kolbe, Richard Noble, Donald Shafto, and Brian Whalen. See Roster of Youth for Goldwater National Chairman (June 1964), Box 10, F. Clifton White Papers. I want to thank William Schurk of the Popular Culture Archives at Bowling Green State University for digging up a copy of "Folk Songs to Bug the Liberals" by The Goldwaters.

13. Ted Hicks to Rusher, 5 May 1964 and 11 May 1964, reel 18, Rusher Papers.

14. The double-edged analysis of the Goldwater effort is in an unsigned and undated (1964) letter in Box 88, Marvin Liebman Associates Collection, HIA. For Stone see *I. F. Stone's Weekly* 12, 15 June 1964, 1. An article in the 2 July 1964 *Los Angeles Times* by Richard Bergholz cited secret meetings of a militant right-wing G.O.P. group trying to control the party machinery, clipping in Box 29, folder: Birch Society, California, 1964, DNC Papers, LBJL. For YAF see Hicks to Rusher, 23 June 1964, reel 18, Rusher Papers. The preconvention letter to delegates is in *The New Guard* 4 (July 1964): 5.

15. E. John Bucci, "The National Presidential Picture," June 1964, DDE Post-

Presidential Papers, 1961-69, Secretary's Series, Subject Subseries, Box 5, folder: Polls-Opinions-1964 Election, DDE. See also The Ripon Society, "A Declaration of Conscience," Box 51, folder: Sa (2), and Eisenhower to Freeman Gosden, June 4, 1964, Box 19, folder: ME-3-11 (both in DDE Post-Presidential Papers, 1964 Principal File, DDE); and "A Program for a Goldwater Administration," *National Review* 16, 14 July 1964, 585–599.

16. Scranton to Goldwater, 12 July 1964, attached to Luce to Eisenhower, 13 July 1964, Box 220, folder 11, Clare Boothe Luce Papers, LC (emphasis in original).

17. Jacob Javits, *Order of Battle: A Republican's Call to Reason* (New York: Atheneum, 1964), 302, 309.

18. Cook, *Barry Goldwater*, 7–9; *Official Report of the Proceedings of the Twenty-Eighth Republican National Convention, Held in San Francisco, California, July 13, 14, 15, 16, 1964* (n.p.: Republican National Committee, 1964), 190–191, 216–224, 321. For an insider's view of the platform issue, see Hess, *In a Cause that Will Triumph*, 68–75. The convention story, told from different perspectives, is best outlined in Theodore White, *The Making of the President 1964* (New York: Atheneum, 1965) and Gordon Misner, "Police-Minority Group Relations at the 1964 Republican National Convention," (Ph.D. diss., University of California at Berkeley, 1967). White, however, concentrates on Goldwater and says relatively little about the many groups like YAF that were staffing the barricades. These were the real perpetrators of the new conservatism.

19. *Official Report . . . Republican National Convention*, 304–305. For Goldwater and the 1960 platform see Goldwater for President bulletin, 10 July 1964, Box 306, folder: Sen. Barry Goldwater, G.O.P. Convention, 1964 as well as clippings from the *Chicago Sun-Times*, 6 July 1964, and the *Providence Sunday Journal*, 5 July 1964, Box 3232, folder: Goldwater-G.O.P. Politics, 1964, all in the DNC Papers, LBJL.

20. Goldwater acceptance speech, July 17, 1964, in Schlesinger (ed.), *History of U.S. Political Parties*, 4:3107. Also see Eisenhower to Roemer McPhee, 31 July 1964, and Goldwater to Nixon, 7 August 1964, DDE Post-Presidential Papers, Secretary's Series, Subject Subseries, Box 2, folder: Politics (PL), Barry Goldwater 1964 (1) and (2), DDE.

21. Ronald Reagan, "A Time for Choosing," in *A Time for Choosing: The Speeches of Ronald Reagan, 1961–1982* (Chicago: Regnery Gateway, 1983), 39–57. The quotations are on pp. 42 and 56. Dean Clarence Manion broadcast much the same message in "Goldwater has Given You a Choice; Take It or Leave It," Manion Forum, 2 August 1964.

22. Goldwater's optimism is in Goldwater to Eisenhower, 22 July 1964, DDE Post-Presidential, 1964 Principal File, Box 37, folder: Barry Goldwater (1), DDE. Rovere's comments are quoted in Richard Hofstadter, "Goldwater & His Party: The True Believer and the Radical Right," *Encounter* 23 (October 1964): 12. For the *Partisan Review* forum, "Some Comments on Senator Goldwater," see *Partisan Review* 31 (Fall 1964): 584–608. Other perspectives are in Stephen Shadegg, *What Happened to Goldwater? The Inside Story of the 1964 Republican Campaign* (New York: Holt, Rinehart and Winston, 1965), 7–8; Irving Crespi, "The Structural Basis for Right-Wing Conservatism: The Goldwater Case," *Public Opinion Quarterly* 29 (Winter 1965): 523–543; Hixson, *Search for the American Right Wing*, 107–108.

23. *The New Guard* 4 (August 1964): 4, 6.

24. Flemming to M. Eisenhower, 27 July 1964, and M. Eisenhower to Flemming, 6 August 1964, Box 23, folder: Republican Party (3), Arthur S. Flemming Papers, DDE. Kuchel is quoted in Burton Levy, "Profile of the American Right: A Case Study of

Michigan" (Ph.D. dissertation, University of Massachusetts, 1965), 6; Rockefeller to Eisenhower, 15 July 1964, DDE Post-Presidential Papers, 1964 Principal File, Box 51, folder: Ro (2), DDE.

25. For YAF's work see William Croft to Henry Regnery, 7 August 1964, Box 80, file 15, Henry Regnery Collection, HIA; and Ted Hicks to William Rusher, 9 August 1964, reel 18, Rusher Papers. Karl Hess noted that YAFers were not the only individuals in the Goldwater camp with personal ambitions; see his *In a Cause that Will Triumph*, 137. For campaign organization, see Lukens to John Grenier, 6 August 1964, Box 6, folder: Young Republicans; and the Goldwater Press Information Kit, Box 6, F. C. White Papers. John Kessel asserted that Edwards not only lacked experience, but immediately put many of his YAF friends on the national committee payroll; see *The Goldwater Coalition*, 139.

26. "Confidential Proceedings of Closed Session Meeting of Republican Unity Conference," Hershey, Pennsylvania,12 August 1964, copy in LBJ Papers, WHCF, Box 117, folder: PL6-3, Republican Party, LBJL.

27. M. Stanton Evans, "At Home," *National Review Bulletin* 16, 21 July 1964, 6; Eisenhower to David Kendall, 13 August 1964, DDE Post-Presidential Papers, 1964 Principal File, Box 44, folder: David W. Kendall, DDE; DDE to Milton Eisenhower, 14 August 1964, DDE Post-Presidential Papers, Secretary's Series, Subject Subseries, Box 2, folder: Politics (PL) General 1962-66; Richard Nixon to Leonard Finder, 24 August 1964, Box 14, folder: N, and Finder to Thomas Kuchel, 25 August 1964, Box 14, folder: Thomas Kuchel, Finder Papers, DDE.

28. Bauman to Buckley, 18 August 1964, Box 29, "B" file, Buckley Papers; Dean Burch to all Division Heads, 29 August 1964, Series VI: 1964 Presidential Campaign Files, Box 3H510, folder: Memos on Staff Procedures, BG; *The New Guard* 4 (September 1964): passim; *New York Times*, 12 September1964, 13. For the Miller campaign and its frequent friction with the Goldwater staff see "William Miller Maine Visit," 8–9 September 1964, G235, 1 of 3, folder: B. Goldwater #4, 1964, Drew Pearson Papers, LBJL. Francis, in *Beautiful Losers*, 226 suggests some of these Republican divisions.

29. *The New Guard* 4 (November 1964): 12.

30. *The New Guard* 4 (October 1964): 3, 6, 12; *The New Guard* 4 (November 1964): 4, 6.

31. Charles P. Taft, "Dear Friend" letter, 30 September 1964, Series 127, Box 2, folder: 1964 Campaign, Committee to Support Moderate Republicans, NPP. Another copy is in the C. Langhorne Washburn Papers, Box 17, folder: 1964 Election, DDE.

32. Brown to Edna Fluegel, 25 October 1964, Box 2, file 2.1; Brown to Tony Jurich of the RNC, 25 October 1964, Box 39, folder 16, Elizabeth Church Brown Papers, HIA.

33. *Information Service* 43 (10 October 1964): 6; "Barry Goldwater and the Organized Right Wing," *Group Research Special Report #17* (12 October 1964); Robert Bauman, "Young American Embraces Conservatism the Only Guarantee of Opportunity and Freedom," Manion Forum, 11 October 1964.

34. "Political Notes," G235, 1 of 3, folder: B. Goldwater #4, 1964, Drew Pearson Papers, LBJL; Confidential Memo from Marvin Liebman to New Yorkers for Goldwater & Miller, 20 October 1964, Box 92, Marvin Liebman Associates Collection, HIA.

35. Quoted in Judis, *William F. Buckley, Jr.*, 230–231.

36. William F. Buckley Jr., "We, Too, Will Continue," *The New Guard* 4 (December 1964): 10–11.

37. Election figures are noted in White, *Making of the President 1964*, 380.

Chapter Ten   **Past as Prologue**

1. M. Stanton Evans, "What to Look for on November 4," *National Review* 16, 3 November 1964, 965; Elizabeth Churchill Brown to Daisy and Mark Fluegel, 4 November 1964, Box 2, file 2.1, Elizabeth Churchill Brown Papers, HIA.

2. Bauman to Buckley, 15 September 1964, Box 33, YAF folder, Buckley Papers; Buckley's speech is quoted in Judis, *William F. Buckley, Jr.*, 232.

3. Leonard Finder to Nelson Rockefeller, 22 September 1964, 29 September 1964, Box 15, folder: R, and Finder to Dwight Eisenhower, 3 November 1964, Box 1, folder: Finder-Eisenhower corresp., 1955–69, Leonard Finder Papers, DDE; Dwight Eisenhower to Sinclair Weeks, 6 October 1964, Box 56, folder: We(2) and Finder to Eisenhower, 3 November 1964, Box 35, folder: Fi(1), DDE Post-Presidential Papers, 1964 Principal File, DDE.

4. T. George Harris, " A New Conservative Manifesto," *Look*, 29 December 1964, inserted into the *Congressional Record*, 111, part 4 (15 March 1965): 4958–4961.

5. A copy of the speech is in Box 23, folder: Republican Party (5), Arthur S. Flemming Papers, DDE. For Nixon's remarks, and a sharp reaction, see Dwight Eisenhower to James Hagerty, 9 November 1964, DDE Post-Presidential Papers, 1964 Principal File, Box 38, folder: Ha (1), DDE.

6. Ripon Society, *From Disaster to Distinction: A Republican Rebirth* (New York: Pocket Books, 1966), 22, 24. See also the *New York Herald Tribune*, 24 November 1964, clipping in Box 48, folder: Republican Party, Ripon Society, DNC Papers, LBJL.

7. Ripon Society, *From Disaster to Distinction*, 14, 46, 77.

8. Ibid., 48-49, 82-83.

9. Gilder and Chapman, *The Party that Lost Its Head*, 3, 6–7, 11, 27, 195.

10. Hunter James, *They Didn't Put That on the Huntley-Brinkley!: A Vagabond Reporter Encounters the New South* (Athens: University of Georgia Press, 1993), 164. Buckley's comment is quoted in the *Congressional Record*, 111, part 4 (15 March 1965): 4960. Goldwater's Black Belt vote is noted in Davidson, *Race and Class in Texas Politics*, 228–230. Debbie Louis insisted that Goldwater's candidacy also stimulated young blacks to become involved in politics; see her *And We Are Not Saved: A History of the Movement as People* (New York: Doubleday, 1970), 281. This is the paperback edition.

11. For a discussion of these issues see James McEvoy III, "Conservatism or Extremism: Goldwater Supporters in the 1964 Presidential Election," in Robert Schoenberger (ed.), *The American Right Wing: Readings in Political Behavior* (New York: Holt, Rinehart and Winston, 1969): 241–279; Lloyd Free and Hadley Cantril, *The Political Beliefs of Americans: A Study of Public Opinion* (New Brunswick, N.J.: Rutgers University Press, 1967), 161; and Timothy D. Gilbert, "A Critical Analysis of the Development of the New Right in America with Particular Emphasis from 1964 to 1968" (Ph.D. diss., Southwestern Baptist Theological Seminary, 1987), 109–110.

12. A copy of the newsletter is in Box 96, folder: Young Americans for Freedom, Lucille Cardin Crain Papers, Special Collections, University of Oregon Library. For the views of national YAF leaders see *The New Guard* 4 (December 1964): 3–4.

13. YAF's views are in *The New Guard* 4 (December 1964). In the same issue see Carol Bauman, "Can Conservatives Keep Control of the Republican Party?", 7–9. Also see Vincent Leibell Jr. to Marvin Liebman, 30 November 1964, Box 92, Marvin Liebman Associates Collection, HIA. Leibell was Campaign Director, New Yorkers for Goldwater & Miller.

14. *Chicago Tribune*, 13 December 1964, clipping in Box 105, folder: Young Americans for Freedom, DNC Papers, LBJL. For an overview see Paul Weyrich, "Blue Collar

or Blue Blood? The New Right Compared with the Old Right," in Whitaker, *The New Right Papers*, 48–62.

15. A tabulation of Goldwater's position on the 1960 issues is in Arthur Flemming to Robert Lee, 25 November 1964, Box 15, folder: Lee-Lem, Arthur S. Flemming Papers, DDE. For reorganization issues see Eisenhower to Hagerty, 27 November 1964, Box 38, folder Ha (1); and Eisenhower to Finder, 1 December 1964, Box 35, folder: Fi (1), DDE Post-Presidential Papers, 1964 Principal file, DDE. The letter to Republican governors, 30 November 1964, is in Box 23, folder: Republican Party (3), Arthur S. Flemming Papers, DDE. Eisenhower did make a stab at such a philosophy; see his "Dear Friends" letter, 3 December 1964, DDE Post-Presidential Papers, Secretary's Series, Subject Subseries, Box 4, folder: Politics (PL) Rebuilding the Party (1), DDE.

16. Hall to Eisenhower, 4 December 1964, DDE Post-Presidential Papers, 1964 Principal File, Box 38, folder: Ha (3), DDE.

17. Romney to Goldwater, 21 December 1964, DDE Post-Presidential Papers, Secretary's Series, Subject Subseries, Box 5, folder: Politics (PL) Rebuilding the Party (6), DDE. For Lindsay's views see "The Republican Challenge," *Congressional Record*, vol. 111, part 3 (1 March 1965): 3903.

18. A good summary is in Rusher, *The Rise of the Right*, 183–185. For a discussion of the impact of this political-cultural split within YAF later in the decade see Rebecca Klatch, "The Counterculture, the New Left, and the New Right," in *Cultural Politics and Social Movements*, ed. Marcy Darnovsky, Barbara Epstein, and Richard Flacks (Philadelphia: Temple University Press, 1995), 78.

19. Evans's ideas are in Meyer, *What is Conservatism?*, 68; see also Ralph Raico, "The Fusionists on Liberalism and Tradition," *New Individualist Review* 3 (Autumn 1964): 29–36. For Rothbard, see his "The Transformation of the American Right," *Continuum* 2 (1964): 220–231. The quotations are on pp. 229 and 226 respectively. The third group active earlier in YAF, the objectivists of Ayn Rand, faded at this point. As Rand wrote one fan: "I am opposed to the organization known as Young Americans for Freedom. That organization is controlled by, or shares the policies of, the *National Review* magazine and is my avowed enemy." See Rand to Michael G. Moody, 23 May 1965 in Michael Berliner (ed.), *Letters of Ayn Rand* (New York: Dutton, 1995), 635.

20. A brief summary is in Judis, *William F. Buckley, Jr.*, 233. For a full report see "Confidential Preliminary Report: The American Conservative Union," Box 34, folder: American Conservative Union, Buckley Papers. Prior efforts are noted in Liebman, *Coming Out Conservative*, 158–159.

21. "Confidential Preliminary Report," passim.

22. Telegram, 7 December 1964, American Conservative Union, Gen. Corresp., October-December 1965, and Minutes of Meetings, 1964–65, Boxes 132 and 134, Rusher Papers. Although the press was banned from the meeting, Richard Dudman filed a story with the *St. Louis Post-Dispatch*, 21 December 1964; copy in Box 4, folder: American Conservative Union, Richard Dudman Papers, LC. See also Liebman, *Coming Out Conservative*, 159–161.

23. For recognition of this future influence see White and Gill, *Why Reagan Won*, 76–79.

24. For a study of this position, see my "Pro-War and Anti-Draft: The Young Americans for Freedom and the War in Viet Nam," in Marc Gilbert (ed.), *The Viet Nam War on Campus: Other Voices, More Distant Drums* (forthcoming).

25. Lee Edwards, "Needed: A 25-Year Plan," *The New Guard* (August 1965): 6–7, 18. Edwards, who worked on the 1964 Goldwater campaign, later blamed the campaign

organizers, and to some extent Goldwater himself, for many conservative failures of that year. See his *Goldwater: The Man who Made a Revolution* (Washington, D.C.: Regnery Publishing Co., 1995), 184.

26. A summary of these efforts is in Benjamin Epstein and Arnold Forster, *The Radical Right: Report on the John Birch Society and Its Allies* (New York: Random House, 1966), 52, 63.

27. David Mallery, *Ferment on the Campus: An Encounter with the New College Generation* (New York: Harper & Row, 1966), 64; Stephen Hess and David Broder, *The Republican Establishment: The Present and Future of the G.O.P.* (New York: Harper & Row, 1967), 74.

28. Quoted in Edwards, *Goldwater*, 347.

29. Roberts, *The Conservative Decade*, 25.

30. Paul Weyrich, "Blue Collar or Blue Blood? The New Right Compared with the Old Right," in Whitaker, *The New Right Papers*, 51–52.

31. The material that follows on Bauman and the other YAFers was gathered in bits and pieces from a variety of sources. See *Dialogue on Liberty* 2 (Summer 1972): 7 (copy in Box 96, folder: Young Americans for Freedom, Lucille Cardin Crain Papers); Forster & Epstein, *Danger on the Right*, 204; Sara Diamond, *Roads to Dominion: Right-Wing Movements and Political Power in the United States* (New York: The Guilford Press, 1995), 112, 115, 116, 125, 130, 136, 146, 194, 216, 289, 318, 328, 344, 400; Himmelstein, *To The Right*, 86–87; *Human Events* 41, 28 February 1981, 10–11, and 4 April 1981, 10–11; Edwards, *Goldwater*, 423; Andrew Kopkind, *The Thirty Years' Wars: Dispatches and Diversions of a Radical Journalist, 1965–1994* (London: Verso, 1995), 304–305; and James Roberts, *The Conservative Decade*, passim. Viguerie's book was self-published by his own company in 1980. For Edwards's studies see *YOU Can Make the Difference* (New Rochelle, N.Y.: Arlington House, 1968), written with his wife Anne; *Ronald Reagan: A Political Biography* (Houston: Nordland Publishing International, 1981), *Missionary For Freedom*; and *Goldwater*.

Index

About the Author

John Andrew is a professor of history at Franklin & Marshall College. He is interested in the interaction of ideology, idealism, and activism, and has published several studies on those themes. Among them are *Rebuilding the Christian Commonwealth: New England Congregationalists and Foreign Missions* (Lexington: University Press of Kentucky, 1976) and *From Revivals to Removal: Jeremiah Evarts, the Cherokee Nation, and the Search for the Soul of America* (Athens: University of Georgia Press, 1992). He lives in Lancaster, Pennsylvania.